ETHICS

ETHICS

By
DIETRICH
VON HILDEBRAND

FRANCISCAN HERALD PRESS
1434 WEST 51st STREET ● CHICAGO, 60609

NIHIL OBSTAT:
JOHN M. A. FEARNS, S.T.D.
CENSOR LIBRORUM

IMPRIMATUR:
✠ FRANCIS CARDINAL SPELLMAN
ARCHBISHOP OF NEW YORK

October 31, 1952

*The nihil obstat and imprimatur are official declarations that
a book or pamphlet is free of doctrinal or moral error. No implication is contained therein that those who have granted the
nihil obstat and imprimatur agree with the contents, opinions or
statements expressed.*

NEW EDITION OF ETHICS PUBLISHED WITH PERMISSION OF
THE AUTHOR BY FRANCISCAN HERALD PRESS, 1972, LIBRARY
OF CONGRESS NUMBER: 72-83947; ISBN 8199-0445-7.
MANUFACTURED IN THE UNITED STATES OF AMERICA.

PREFACE

In an allocution to the Fédération Mondiale des Jeunesses Féminines Catholiques, His Holiness Pope Pius XII condemns a new concept of the moral life which he characterizes as follows:

The distinctive mark of this morality is that it is in fact not based on universal moral laws, as, for instance, on the Ten Commandments, but on the real and concrete conditions or circumstances in which one must act, and according to which one must act, and according to which the individual conscience has to judge and choose. This state of things is unique and is valid but once for each human action. This is why the champions of this ethics affirm that the decision of one's conscience cannot be commanded by ideas, principles, and universal laws.[1]

This new form of ethical relativism and subjectivism is specifically vicious. It is a wolf in sheep's clothing because it claims to be typically Christian and to stem as a consequence of man's filial relation to God:

Here there is only the "I" of man and the "I" of the personal God; not of God the lawgiver, but of God, our Father, with whom man must unite himself in filial love.[2]

[1] "Le signe distinctif de cette morale est qu'elle ne se base point en effet sur les lois morales universelles, comme par exemple les Dix Commandements, mais sur les conditions ou circonstances réelles et concrètes dans lesquelles on doit agir, et selon lesquelles on doit agir, et selon lesquelles la conscience individuelle a à juger et à choisir. Cet état de choses est unique et vaut une seule fois pour toute action humaine. C'est pourquoi la décision de la conscience, affirment les tenants de cette éthique, ne peut être commandée par les idées, les principes et les lois universelles." (Acta Apostolicae Sedis, 1952, p. 413.)

[2] "Ici il y a seulement le je de l'homme et le Je du Dieu personnel; non du Dieu de la loi, mais du Dieu Père, avec qui l'homme doit s'unir dans l'amour filial." (Ibid.)

The concept of Christian ethics offered in the present work is radically opposed to this "new morality." One of its main objects is precisely to show the inalterable character of the moral law, the absolute nature of moral values, to oppose to the abuse of the term "hierarchy of values" the true hierarchy of values which is at the basis of St. Augustine's *ordo amoris* and of the whole Christian philosophy, and to elaborate the precedence of moral values over all other personal or impersonal values.

We hope that our philosophical analysis of morality may serve to unmask the dangerous fallacies contained in an ethics which declares that acts undoubtedly sinful are permissible under certain circumstances; we hope that this book will also prove that obedience to the inalterable moral law, far from narrowing, thwarting, or stifling our spontaneous life, is the only way conducive to true freedom, and that the moral law and the true hierarchy of values can never be at variance.

I have believed it suitable to place at the beginning of this work a brief epistemological introduction entitled "Prolegomena"—in order to explain at the start the purpose and methods of this ethical analysis. It must be emphasized, however, that the reading of this prolegomena is not indispensable for an understanding of the contents of this book. The reader who is not a professional philosopher may pass it by and still succeed in understanding our treatise on morality.

I wish to express my great indebtedness to the Rockefeller Foundation for the generous help they have granted me toward the completion of this work. I also wish to thank wholeheartedly Mr. Donald A. Drennen, M.A., Dr. William A. Marra, and Miss Madeleine Froelicher, M.A., who, with great devotion and understanding, have cooperated with me in making stylistic corrections and on other technical details. I wish to thank Mr. Bernard B. Gilligan, M.A., of Fordham University for his intelligent and devoted collaboration and for having drawn my attention to several facets of important ethical problems. My gratitude is also due Mr. Robert Sweeney for his preparation of the index to this volume.

Two other persons have aided me in such a way that it is impossible to express my indebtedness in words. The first is Dr.

Alice M. Jourdain of Hunter College, whose collaboration has extended from the discussion of philosophical problems to research in a wide historical field. For a period of over two years she has dedicated every free moment to the completion of this manuscript. Her thorough understanding of my philosophy has enabled her to help me more than I can tell.

Last but not least, I must mention the immense debt I owe my dear friend and colleague Dr. Robert C. Pollock, the great historian of philosophy at Fordham University, Graduate School. No words can adequately express my heartfelt gratitude for his generous help. His deep scholarship, his keen insight, his profound philosophical understanding, his witty criticism, have been invaluable both as a testimony of his friendship and as an inspiration to me.

May this work, by means of a philosophical analysis appealing to reason, clear the path and be helpful for finding "the True Light which enlighteneth every man that cometh into this world."

DIETRICH VON HILDEBRAND

CONTENTS

PROLEGOMENA

WHEN we read in the Acts of the Apostles of the martyrdom of St. Stephen, we are confronted with a "datum" of striking grandeur. The saint's meekness and strength, his prayer for his murderers, and his forgiveness of them, reveal themselves to us as things which are specifically noble and sublime. They obviously differ from the examples of brilliant gifts and talents which fascinate us in reading about men like Alexander the Great or Napoleon. In the instance of the martyrdom of St. Stephen, we are transported to the specifically *moral* sphere, the sphere of moral goodness.

This sphere holds a unique position in the life of man, since it touches the deepest and most central point of the drama of human life and implies the great realities of conscience and of guilt and merit. In our daily lives we are continually aware of the fundamental difference between the moral sphere and all other spheres of human existence. As soon as a moral problem arises, we are transported into a "world" of its own. We take cognizance of its incomparable gravity, implying, as it does, a unique kind of obligation.

In order to understand this moral sphere, we must immerse ourselves, as it were, in the rich qualitative plenitude of a moral datum and bring ourselves to a full state of "wondering" about it. We must seek to analyze the datum, delve into its nature, explore its relations with other fundamental data of experience, and, finally, inquire into the presuppositions which have to be fulfilled in order that a man may be endowed with moral goodness.

In pursuit of our inquiry, however, let us be on our guard against all constructions and explanations which are incompatible with the nature of moral data as presented in experience or

1

which in any way fail to do full justice to them. Thus we must, time and again, come back to the most explicit and unrestricted experience of moral data, and confront every result of our exploration with the full flavor of the experienced data themselves.

The task of ethics is to attain to a full philosophical *prise de conscience* of moral data (i.e., a philosophical awareness implying an explicit and fully conscious grasping of these data) and to arrive thereby at a precise notion of their specific nature, of their full significance, and of the presuppositions of man's conduct required for the possession of moral goodness. Ethics is further bound to inquire into the difference between the moral sphere and all other spheres and to discover especially the relations existing between the moral sphere and God, and between moral goodness and man's destiny. The indispensable prerequisite for this, however, is faithfulness to moral experience, to the moral data which are given to us in our daily life, through great literature, in the lives of the saints, in the liturgy of Holy Church, and, above all, in the Gospel.

Before we begin the analysis of our topic, some fundamental remarks of an epistemological nature are in order. These will serve to clarify further the few introductory remarks we have made thus far.

This work starts from "the immediately given," that is, from the data of experience. The reader will be able to estimate properly our results only if he is willing to hold in abeyance for a while all theories which are familiar to him, and which provide him with a set of terms which he is accustomed to use in sizing up that which is immediately given. I want to begin *from the beginning,* suspending all theories concerning the moral sphere. I want to start with the *moral experience itself.* In the same way Aristotle, speaking about the soul, says at the beginning of the second book of his *De Anima:*

> Let the foregoing suffice as our account of the views concerning the soul which have been handed on by our predecessors; let us now dismiss them and make as it were a completely fresh start, endeavoring to give a precise answer to the question, What is soul?

The reader is asked to look without any philosophical prejudice at the moral data themselves, to "listen to the voice of being" itself, and to ignore everything which does not bear the credentials of that which is immediately given. We ask the reader to be willing to follow our analysis of the data step by step and to suspend all explanations which have been offered in former theories, reductions, or interpretations, many of which, unfortunately, often leave no room at all for the data in question. When a full understanding of our analysis has been achieved, then it will be time to confront our results with those of other ethical theories.

If we ask the reader to set aside for a while all theories in order thus to be unhampered both in his approach to the object of inquiry and in his grasping of that which is given concerning it, we must here extend a similar plea with respect to the philosophical theses which will be forthcoming in our work.

The attitude toward a philosopher and his theses is often prejudiced by the tendency to classify prematurely. Sometimes such classification has a historical character, as when one automatically approaches every philosophical work with the disposition of characterizing the author as a Thomist, an Augustinian, a Kantian, a Spinozist, a Hegelian and so forth. Instead of giving the author credit for some originality, one assumes quite arbitrarily that, after all, he must be a commentator or at least a formal disciple of some other well-known philosopher. From the start one looks at his ideas and theses from this point of view, under this uncalled-for expectation, and consequently bars oneself from a real understanding of his ideas.

This tendency becomes especially grotesque when the main reason for such a classification is a merely terminological similarity. For example, there are some who appear to believe they have sufficient evidence for calling an author a strict Kantian, simply because they have found in his work the terms "categorical" obligation or *a priori*.

But we are asking much more than the avoidance of these rather careless habits of prejudging a philosopher. We ask the reader to try to free himself, in reading the terms used in this work, from any special connotations which the former use of the same terms may carry. It is but too natural that in finding the term "intuition," one person may understand it in the light of Bergson, another in the light of Fichte, and so on, according to the philosophical literature the person in question has mainly studied. But this tendency cannot fail to lead in most instances to a misunderstanding of the meaning of these terms in our context. Hence we ask the reader to take the terms used here in that sense alone which they bear when introduced in our context.

This is not to say that every term will be introduced by a definition; instead the main stress is laid on the meaning which a term receives in the context by our reference to a definite datum. The terms should be understood by following my expositions and analyses, by looking with me at the object, and by restricting the meaning of the terms to that which the object and our analysis of it dictate.

To introduce every term by a definition would even be absolutely contrary to our aim. The full meaning of a term can be grasped only in the course of our analysis and to the extent that we have gained a more adequate knowledge of the datum which the term covers. To expect us to give in few words a complete definition of the term implies the supposition that the reader can understand what is meant without having explored the object with us. The explanation offered in introducing an important term must thus be accepted with the understanding that it will be completed in the measure that we proceed with our analysis. A stubborn refusal to accept anything which is not completely explained at once by a formal definition would frustrate any full contact with reality and any real philosophical exploration. It would be based on a radical misunderstanding of reality and of philosophy, for it would place a philosophical exploration on the same level as consulting a dictionary.

It will be one of our chief aims to avoid any thesis which is not imposed on us by the data and, above all, to abstain from tacit presuppositions which are neither evident nor proved. We take reality seriously in the way in which it discloses itself; we greatly respect everything which is immediately given, everything which possesses a real, intrinsic meaning and true intelligibility.

There are philosophers who take it for granted that everything which is accessible to our immediate experience is doubtful, subjective, or at best only a secondary aspect of reality which cannot demand or win our full attention and interest. Some of these philosophers will announce as their proud discovery that there is a total discrepancy between reality and the data given in our pre-philosophical experience. They will tell us that in reality a color is nothing but a vibration, beauty nothing but a contraction of the viscera, love nothing but a mere sexual instinct, and so forth.

These men will identify the object either with something related to it by causality, or with something which is in some other way connected with it. Such identification simply confuses the philosophical approach with the approach proper to natural science. Physics, chemistry, or biology not only may discover beings of which we had not the slightest idea in our prescientific knowledge, for instance, certain glands or microbes or cosmic rays, but may also show us that certain things which seem to be quite distinct in our naïve experience are in reality the same.

Legitimate as this method of reduction is for the natural sciences with their own special objects and their own purposes of knowledge, it is impossible concerning the objects of philosophy and of no avail toward the end of philosophical knowledge. Philosophy will never discover anything which is absolutely alien to our pre-philosophical knowledge. It cannot possibly discover that two different things, such as knowledge and will, are in reality one and the same thing, or that justice in reality is nothing but a fruit of a bitter grievance of the weak and mediocre (i.e., what, to be more accurate, we call *ressentiment*). It is quite reasonable to state that a man who pretends to be just is in reality only moved by *ressentiment,* but it is absurd to say that justice is in reality a *ressentiment* of the weak. Granted that it could be maintained that real justice cannot be found anywhere in this world, it is still absurd to say that justice as such is only an invention of the weak in order to overcome the strong. The first thesis can be true or false; the second is simply nonsensical.

We repeat what we said above. We take the immediately given data seriously. It is a fundamental error to believe that we have to approach every datum which is given in experience with the presumption that it is a merely subjective impression or at best a mere appearance which obviously differs from the real objective nature of the being. The mere fact that something is accessible to our immediate experience, that it is given to us, in no way establishes the fact that the datum has *but* a subjective validity.

It is time for us to realize the true character of a merely subjective impression, that is to say, an entity which has no other status in reality than to be an object of my consciousness, a mere percept to which the formula *esse est percipi* truly applies. A mere semblance, for instance, is any object the "being" of which really is nothing *but* its "being perceived." This applies first to contents of our consciousness of corporeal things which prove afterward to be mere semblances and not to exist in the real world surrounding us; for instance, a mirage is a mere semblance. The mountain we dreamed of and the bent appearance of the stick in the water are mere semblances. It applies secondly to every fiction: a centaur, a dragon, a golden mountain; everything which either is believed to exist though it does not exist, or is known to be a mere fiction and is entertained by the mind only as a fiction.

It is obviously impossible that an entity should be a mere appearance if it possesses the character of intrinsic necessity and full intelligibility. Justice, love, time, space, and other entities having the same intrinsic necessity and intelligibility are not and never can be mere appearances. Apart from the question of their concrete existence here and now, they are something completely objective and autonomous, independent of their being objects of our consciousness. If somebody said of time, of space, or of justice that each is a mere illusion, a fiction like the golden mountain, we should immediately grasp the nonsensical character of such an assertion. An entity of ultimate, objective meaningfulness and ontological truth, such as justice, never could be invented. The necessarily contingent character of every "invention" and every product of human imagination is essentially incompatible with the intrinsic consistency and ontological truth of justice.

These intrinsically necessary and highly intelligible data exclude not only every interpretation of them as inventions, illusions, fictions, dreams, etc., but even any distinction within them of an appearance on the one hand, and an ontologically serious essence on the other. As far as the objects of natural science are concerned, we distinguish between the aspect which our naïve experience offers to us and the nature of the objects which the scientific investigation discovers. This appearance is certainly

more than the poor existence of a mere object of our consciousness; it is the *valid* "face" of these real beings, their aesthetical
essence, so to speak, which is quite real although not necessarily
in conformity with their constitutive nature. For our naïve experience the whale looks like a fish; science tells us that it is a
mammal. Chemistry reveals to us an essential affinity between
things which have no similarity whatsoever for our naïve experience. This naïve aspect, which is the starting point of our concepts of beings, is not simply a subjective illusion, but an objective appearance. It does not lose its significance and its deep
contents because it belongs to another stratum of being than the
constitutive essence. But this distinction of appearance and real
nature applies only to corporeal substances in their unintelligible
and contingent character.[1]

It makes ño sense whatsoever to say that what we call justice
is perhaps only an appearance and that the underlying reality
is an invention of the weak in order to protect themselves. Justice, love, truth, space, time, numbers cannot be mere semblances,
nor can they be the objective appearances of something else. Each
of these entities is too intelligible, too necessary, too much something definite in itself, to permit any sane man to interpret it as
a mere aspect of something which in reality is different from the
supposed appearance.

If we stress time and again the necessity of remaining above all
with the data, and especially with the *immediately* given, the
question may arise: What precisely is the "given"; what is meant
by opposing the given in experience to theories, explanations,
and hypotheses? It would certainly be a complete misunderstanding of our exhortation to adhere to the given in philosophy if
this were interpreted to mean that philosophy should consist in
a mere description of our naïve experience.

The data from which we have to start and which we have to
penetrate and analyze in philosophy are not at all identical with
the image of the universe which our naïve experience offers to
us; nor does philosophy consist in a mere description of everything which we experience. In order to explain the nature of data

[1] This epistemological problem has been elaborated in detail in our work *Der
Sinn philosophischen Fragens und Erkennens* (Bonn: Peter Hanstein Verlag,
1950).

in our sense we must first grasp a decisive distinction in the realm of naïve pre-philosophical knowledge.

There exist many different types of pre-philosophical knowledge. They have been analyzed in the work of mine mentioned above. I quote only some decisive points. First, there is the knowledge which man has in his lived contact with being: seeing a landscape or enjoying music, stating that the train in which he wants to travel is coming, or that his room is overheated. In it I include every awareness of an object in unreflecting lived contact with being. Secondly, there are the unphilosophical and unscientific theories, i.e., opinions which are held by a man as soon as he begins to reason and reflect on his naïve experience.

This pre-philosophical and unscientific reasoning and theorizing is very often without any real contact with the first naïve experience. In most people there is a definite gap between their immediate impressions and experiences, and their theoretical opinions about the content of their experience. They are indignant at a crime, but soon afterward they will pretend that there exists no objective good and evil. There may well be an unbridgeable gap between what they grasp in hearing a symphony of Beethoven which impresses them deeply, and the explanations they give of why the symphony is beautiful. These pre-philosophical theoretical views are conceived and nourished mostly by books which have been read without being digested, by popular philosophies in newspapers, by illegitimate generalizations and wrong conclusions, by all sorts of unfortunate influences, by everything except the real content of their naïve experience.

In these pre-philosophical theoretical views we find the homeland of dilettantism and of intellectual prejudice. Here blossoms the *doxa*, the random and confused opinions which Socrates tried to overcome with the so-called Socratic irony. Unfortunately these conceptions and convictions, although they are constructed without genuine reference to naïve experience, are not completely without influence on naïve experience; for they darken and confuse the naïve unreflecting knowledge which results from any lived contact with being.

To reach the given in our sense of the term is to purify the content of naïve experience and to purge from it all the unconscious influences of the *doxa*. And this task only philosophy can accomplish. To become aware of all deformations, additions, and interpretations which function as a curtain or fog between our mind and the voice of being in our lived contact is a great and difficult task; the man who believes that he does not need to purify consciously and cautiously his naïve image of the universe and uproot from it all unconscious illegitimate influences proves by that very illusion how much he is a prey of *doxa*.

The second step leading to the datum, as we understand the term, is a further purification of the knowledge resulting from this lived contact with being. It consists in eliminating those narrowing and accidental reductions which the pragmatic outlook imposes upon our approach to being.

Certainly the pragmatic approach has a positive function as a powerful motor for our knowledge. Nevertheless, from the point of view of the adequacy and completeness of knowledge, the pragmatic approach inevitably has the effect that we grasp, in our contact with being, only a segment, viz., that segment which it is indispensable to know for a practical use of the being in question.

The overcoming of this one-sidedness in our experience of being is one of the great prerequisites for reaching the objective data as well as for truly philosophical exploration. As a matter of fact, the very direction of philosophical questioning as such is already an antithesis to the pragmatic approach.

It is obvious that philosophy has to avoid the error of the unphilosophical opinion, of that which ignores the content of our real experience. In freeing the authentic voice of being from all pragmatic one-sidedness, philosophy reaches the datum from which it has to start. What we have so far said, however, is not enough to indicate what is meant by datum or the immediately given.

Our claim to focus on the "given" would be completely misunderstood if it were confused with the claim of all those who, in the name of empiricism, oppose all metaphysical and *a priori* knowledge. We do not take the given to mean the observation of many accidental, contingent facts; our given is neither the experience of an explorer, nor that of scientists making experiments as a starting point for inductions. It is not the experience championed by such a man as Francis Bacon.

The "given" at which we are aiming, and which we oppose to theories, interpretations, and hypotheses, is always a necessary, intelligible entity, the only true object of philosophy, such as being, truth, knowledge, space, time, man, justice, injustice, numbers, love, will, and many others. It is the object possessing a necessary and highly intelligible essence; it is the object which imposes itself on our intellect, which reveals and validates itself fully when we focus on it in an intellectual intuition.

The "given" in our sense is in no way characterized by the fact that it is easy to apprehend, that we are able to grasp it with a minimum of intellectual effort. This would be the "given" of the positivists or of David Hume. The prejudice involved here arises from the idea that sensations have, in their being given, a superiority over other data, a superiority which precisely is not given, but which is rather the postulate of an arbitrary theory.

Nor can the given be identified with that which is seen and admitted by everyone. For in saying that something is seen and admitted by everyone, we still can refer to very different things. In our naïve experience there are many different types of awareness of a being.

For example, there is one type of awareness exhibited in the fully conscious acquaintance with the color red; and there is another type exhibited in the situation before the *Organon* of Aristotle was written, when men were familiar with the laws of syllogism in using them, though they would never have been able to formulate them. Every child is in some way aware that a being cannot simultaneously exist and not exist, though he does not have the same insight into this most fundamental fact which Aristotle had in formulating the principle.

A child constantly asks "why" and wants to learn the cause of many things which confront it, and often even their final cause. The self-evidence of the principles of efficient and final causality is presupposed and implicitly declared in the very question, but the child does not "know" these principles as he knows the house in which he lives, or his toys, or a cat, or the color red, or his mother.

To confuse the given with the objects which are known and admitted by everybody, in the sense of a knowledge which enables everyone to form a concept of them, would mean to exclude

from the rank of the given all those principles which are constantly presupposed and which are among the foremost typical
examples of the given.

Thus the given cannot be identified with those things which
are inevitably known to all, if the term "known" is understood
in the sense of an awareness which enables us to build up concepts and terms referring to them.

The given also embraces that which is apprehended in an implicit awareness; that is to say, the given embraces everything
which is included in the message of being conveyed to everyone,
be it only in an implicit manner. The full *prise de conscience* of
these data is one of the fundamental tasks of philosophy.

Yet, the realm of the given extends still further. Even things
which are not included in this message of being conveyed to
every man can belong to the realm of the given. The given also
includes things which presuppose special talents in order to be
grasped, such as beauty in nature and art.

We now clearly see that the "given" in our sense is synonymous
neither with experience as such, nor still less with the average,
naïve conception of the world. Furthermore, philosophy is far
from being a mere description of any experience. It is in the first
line the full *prise de conscience* of all the "given" in our sense, the
finding of which already implies a difficult task which is to be
cautiously accomplished.

Hand in hand with this *prise de conscience* goes the distinction
between that which is evident and which indisputably validates
itself in its being, and that which is not evident and which must
therefore be critically discussed and analyzed.

The philosophical exploration of these highly intelligible,
necessary data, far from consisting in a mere description of them,
aims at the insight into necessary facts rooted essentially in the
nature of the given being. It aims at an absolutely certain insight into these necessary facts, an insight which implies a deeper
penetration step by step into the nature of this entity.

Needless to say, our claim to adhere to the "given" in no way
means that we could and should forget those data which the
prise de conscience of great philosophers in the past have made
accessible to us. If this were our conviction. it would mean to
pass sentence on philosophy and this book would be condemned

in advance. It would be completely nonsensical to begin a philo-sophical book with the plea that everyone should ignore all the contributions which philosophy is able to make.

All true discoveries of great philosophers of the past, precisely in their character of a full *prise de conscience* of a datum, have opened our eyes to this datum. Prior to the discovery the datum was given only in our naïve experience; we were not fully aware of it, and *a fortiori* still less did we have a philosophical under-standing of it. It would be difficult to state to what extent we are indebted to Plato, Aristotle, St. Augustine, St. Thomas Aquinas, and others for enlarging our knowledge of the given.

It goes without saying that what should be held in abeyance is not the enrichment of the given by great thinkers, but merely all theories, explanations, and hypotheses which are also to be found in their philosophical thought. We should, above all, refrain from believing that we are unable to enlarge the *prise de conscience* of the "given." A consequence of such belief would be to suppose that we are equipped only to become com-mentators on the thoughts of great philosophers instead of phi-losophers ourselves.

Another observation has to be made. Certain authors consider a work as philosophical only when the topic is brought into a system. We grant that it surely belongs to philosophy to treat its topics in a systematic way. We grant, moreover, that it is not enough to discover several important facts without discussing the relation existing between them, without connecting them with other more general facts. In the systematic analysis of a thing it is indispensable that we proceed step by step. But be-tween systematic analysis and the building up of a system there is a great difference. Certainly an ideal fulfillment of an adequate knowledge of the universe would require a system which com-pletely corresponded to the architecture of the universe. But this could obviously be attained only at the end of all philosophical investigation. Granted that certain fundamental general features of being are the first to disclose themselves to us, and that every further step of investigation of a special topic goes hand in hand with some new general differentiations, we must yet be aware of the great danger of a premature systematization.

In the first place, as soon as we believe that from certain general principles we can deduce the rest of the universe, we are bound to build up a system which is not in conformity with reality. This remains true even if the first principles from which we start are in conformity with reality.

All such mathematical procedures (*more geometrico* in the Spinozan sense) cannot but blind us to the plenitude of being, can not but force us to overlook data which are completely new, even those of a fundamental character. A famous example is Descartes' overlooking of the datum of life. It seems unbelievable that a man who had such a remarkable awareness of the fundamental difference between corporeal and spiritual beings could simply ignore the elementary datum of animal life. Because this datum could be deduced neither from the *res extensa,* nor from the *res cogitans,* Descartes chose to deny it. Despite its palpable reality, he firmly ushered it out of the realm of knowledge and being.

We are not interested here in discussing the failure of an attempt to deduce from certain general principles, or from clear and distinct ideas, everything concerning those innumerable contingent facts about which only experience and an experimental investigation of reality can inform us. We are not concerned with the refutation of a rationalism which is, after all, held by no one today. We are interested rather in the refutation of an attempt to deduce the philosophical knowledge of intelligible, necessary facts from certain general principles. We want to stress that there exist many intelligible essences which are so fundamentally new that they can never be reached by deduction, but only and exclusively by an original intuition. It is clearly impossible for a blind man to know what a color is; it is impossible for us to deduce the essence of color from the notion of a corporeal being and thereby transmit to the blind person the notion of color. But this is not the only case where the deduction of an essence is impossible, where appeal must be made to an original intuition of the essence.

For the same observation applies to many ultimate data of a spiritual order, though the original intuition is here not a sense perception, a seeing with our eyes, but an intellectual intuition which is no less immediate than a perception. It is impossible to deduce from the notion of being, and from what have been called the first principles, the nature of life, of time or space, of the person, of moral virtue, or the notion of consciousness. All those ultimate data must be grasped at least once in an original intuition, and the philosophical *prise de conscience* has to be based on this primary experience.

Thus the first danger of premature systematization lies in the temptation to deduce as much as possible from certain general principles. This leads to overlooking all those realities which necessarily require an original intuition in order to be grasped. And this means a crippling of reality in its most general and basic features from the very start.

To many people philosophical knowledge is equivalent to a reduction of all the different essences to certain general fundamental notions. The necessity of an original intuition seems to them incompatible with a systematic philosophical knowledge. To them the definition seems to be the climax of intellectual conquest. Taking "qualitative" in the largest sense—the sense in which essence is more qualitative than existence—we may say of these people that they consider a definition to be the more intelligible in the degree that it is the less qualitative.

This ideal of philosophical knowledge deems it an advantage and a triumph to deduce more and more so that we are less and less confronted with "arche-data" requiring an original intuition. What we possess in a definition seems to such thinkers superior from the point of view of intelligibility to what we possess in an original intuition.

We want to stress from the very beginning that we do not share this ideal of philosophical knowledge. For us definition is not the climax of knowledge. A definition can never exhaust the plenitude of a necessary, intelligible essence; it can only circumscribe it by mentioning some essential features which suffice to distinguish this essence from another. The definition helps also to give to a concept a univocal precision. Only artificial beings which are deprived of an ontological plenitude, only technical objects and mere instruments, can be exhausted by a definition. But as soon as we are no longer confronted with artificial beings, we are faced more and more with the mysteries of being; and then our definition should not pretend to exhaust the nature of this being, but only the modest aspiration to fix it univocally by a concept. As soon as we believe we have definitely conquered a being intellectually because we have a correct definition of it, we deceive ourselves. Certainly the highest form of philosophical penetration implies the insight into all those necessary facts rooted in the essence, and all the essential marks of this being. However, these insights precisely presuppose an intellectual intuition of the object, a full grasping of its nature; they cannot possibly be discovered by approaching the object as if it were readily accessible to our minds by a deduction from other more general notions of being. The anxiety to attain a definition as quickly as possible may well exclude us forever from any genuine insight into the object.

Further, when we have discovered all the necessary facts and marks rooted in this essence and have elaborated all its essential features, we must nonetheless understand that the composition of all these features does not necessarily exhaust the nature of this being.

Another danger lurks in a *premature* systematization: the tendency we have to be caught by the immanent logic of a system, and to become more anxious to preserve the consistency of this system than to do justice to the nature of a being. The interpretation of a new datum is then determined more by the frames built up in the system than by the nature of the object. Even if a philosopher avoids the error of attempting to deduce this datum from general principles, he will nevertheless be blinded to the understanding of the nature of this new datum if he is more preoccupied by fitting it into a system than by the adequate study of the datum itself.

I am not thinking of evident alternatives and general principles which are constantly at the basis of all knowledge, for instance, the alternative of existence or non-existence: the principle of contradiction. Such general principles must be continuously presupposed in approaching any being; without them everything would become nonsensical. I am thinking of a system which naturally is not composed exclusively of self-evident principles, but which to a large extent consists in explanations, interpretations of the immediately given by means of theories which, whether plausible or not, in any case have only the character of hypotheses, and not the character of absolutely certain insights into an intrinsically necessary fact.

But obviously the ideal way of proceeding would be the constant readiness to revise, modify, or give up any hypothesis which a new datum renders impossible. Instead of adapting, like Procrustes, the people to the bed, we should always be ready to adapt the bed to the people.

Summarizing, we can say: First, the evident, as well as everything which is really given, must have undisputed precedence over any hypothesis, explanation, or interpretation.

Second, we have to approach being with a readiness to grasp the specific nature of every new datum, especially if this datum has the character of a fundamentally new ratio, such as personal being, time, space, moral virtue, knowledge, will, and so on.

Third, we must turn our efforts in the direction which will allow us to do full justice to a datum; we must ever be aware of the danger of violating it by reducing it to something already familiar to us, aware of the temptation of a certain intellectual laziness disguised as an epistemological "economy" which deafens us to the voice of being and prevents us from wondering enough about its nature.

Finally, the task of estimating properly the nature of a datum which is given to us must take precedence over the effort to bring the nature of this being into harmony with formerly discovered, undubitable data.

Our primary concern, therefore, is the knowledge of the immediately given datum; the second is to harmonize this with other formerly conquered data. In saying "secondary" concern, we do not intend to minimize its importance, for obviously this part of knowledge belongs essentially and in a specific way to the nature of philosophy. But the term "secondary" indicates that in the process of philosophical exploration, the question of co-ordination must be posed only after justice is done to the new datum. For example, the problem of the relation between freedom of will and the principle of causality presupposes, in order to be fruitfully analyzed, that we have already grasped in an adequate way the nature of freedom. If we begin the analysis of freedom in being primarily concerned with its relation to causality, if we begin by asking how freedom can coexist with the principle of causality, we frustrate the full understanding of freedom. We are in danger either of seeing freedom in the light of causality or of mistrusting the datum because we believe it to be incompatible with causality. Many materialists are unable to grasp the absolutely different and new character of psychical and spiritual reality because they are too much concerned with the relation between soul and body, and with the consistent unity of the corporeal world.

The precedence of the exploration of the nature of a datum over the exploration of its relation to other beings is necessary, first of all, because the real problem of its relation to other beings cannot even impose itself so long as we have not done full justice to the nature of the being which is under consideration.

Moreover, the exploration of the nature of a datum has definite precedence over the question of its relation to other beings because we do not have the right to make the knowledge of its nature depend upon whether or not we are able to give an answer to the host of problems which spring from the original datum. Our admission that there exist spiritual entities, acts of knowledge or will, for example, cannot depend upon our capacity to solve the problem of body and soul, to answer why the accomplishment of an act of thinking presupposes the integrity of certain parts of the brain. It is a fatal "logicizing" of reality to require a smooth intelligibility, an easy transparence concerning all possible problems which a fundamentally new type of being imposes, and to adapt and mangle the nature of this being until all these problems disappear. Every fundamentally new datum which is immediately given and which discloses univocally its nature must be affirmed, even if this admission opens up innumerable difficulties.

Instead of escaping from these problems by violating or denying the true nature of a being, the problems which arise should inspire a new effort to dig deeper, a readiness to accept the difficult and tiresome task of grappling further with them. We should understand and wholeheartedly acknowledge this invitation to seek the solution of the problem in a deeper stratum.

This brings us to a third, the most important, principle: We are not allowed to give up something which has disclosed itself unequivocally to us simply because we are unable to answer many problems which arise with the admission of this fact. Cardinal Newman stressed this fundamental truth with respect to the

content of our faith, in his famous words: "Ten thousand difficulties do not make a single doubt."

Sometimes the reconciliation of fundamental facts is impossible to attain on the level of our natural knowledge. We cannot
understand for example how freedom and predestination can
coexist nor even how human freedom can be reconciled with
efficacious grace. But this should not shake our absolute certitude
that both exist. Again, the existence of evil in a world created and
ruled by an absolutely wise, absolutely powerful and infinitely
good God will always remain an inscrutable mystery. Should we
therefore deny the existence of evil in order to escape from this
dilemma? Or should we deny the existence of God, because of the
indubitable existence of evil? No, we must have the courage to
say: I see something with absolute certitude, and I also see something else with absolute certitude. I shall adhere to both even if
I know not how they can be reconciled.

Another characteristic feature of the right approach to the
problem of morality must be adverted to. In the spirit of complete openness to all that which is given, we want to exclude no
moral value which is accessible to us in our analysis of morality.
The saint is the most perfect embodiment of morality. The fact
that this morality is a new and incomparably higher one is for us
no reason to exclude it from a philosophical analysis. On the
contrary, it will form the pattern for our analysis since, obviously,
we shall choose the highest manifestations of morality in order
to understand the essence of morality as such.[2]

The Christian morality resplendent in the saints is a fact
which only prejudice can deny. This fact is accessible in its
completely different and new quality to any unprejudiced and
healthy mind, even before it possesses faith. How many people
have been converted by this irresistible and victorious charity,
by this touching humility, by this ultimate inner freedom which

[2] Even the non-Catholic philosopher Henri Bergson realized the impossibility
of ignoring the data of the morality of the mystics. In his work *Les deux sources
de la morale et de la religion* (Paris: F. Alcan, 1932), he clearly shows that this
morality differs from any morality without Christ, and that it is the highest and
most authentic one. Without sharing his views on the source of the morality which
he opposes to that of the mystics, we find in his awareness of the unique character of the morality of the mystics and of the Christian saints, and of its being the
highest and most authentic manifestation of morality, a testimony of his unprejudiced openness to reality and of his capacity to grasp moral data.

are to be found in the saints! Though we know by faith that this morality depends upon grace, our mind can grasp the fact of this morality with the light of reason, and our reason can understand the relation existing between this morality and its object; it can trace the motives of this charity, this humility, this generosity, this patience, and it can prove that this morality is the fulfillment of all moral goodness while simultaneously surpassing it as something completely new.

By including in a philosophical work on morality the morality of the saints, the outstanding embodiment of a true Christian morality, we do not at all mean to confuse ethics with moral theology. The way in which ethics proceeds is based on our natural capacities of knowledge and does not refer to supernatural facts as arguments for our knowledge. In taking into account all moral data which we can know by experience, embracing also the morality which manifests itself in the Christian saints, we do not leave the field of things which are "given" to us. Our aim is to grasp the nature of this morality and of all the factors determining its presence insofar as they are accessible to us by the natural light of our mind. We have thus to inquire into the nature of the goods motivating this morality; we have to analyze the role of knowledge implied in this morality as well as the specific character of the responses given to these goods, and the direction of will underlying this morality.

Certainly a great part of the virtues, and even the most sublime and important one, charity, presuppose among other conditions that the person possessing them has knowledge of the Christian Revelation; they presuppose a conception of the world which a person can reach only through the Christian Revelation. But ethics does not discuss here the truth of this revelation and does not appeal to revealed truths as arguments. Ethics only points to the necessary link between those virtues and the Christian Revelation as their intentional object.

Part One

Part One

I. Value and Motivation

CHAPTER 1

THE NOTION OF IMPORTANCE IN GENERAL

EXPERIENCE reveals that a being which can become an object of our knowledge will not necessarily motivate our will or our affective responses such as joy, sorrow, enthusiasm, indignation, and so forth.

Were we to ask a despairing man the reason for his sorrow, and were he to answer, "Because two and two are four," or, "Because the sum of the angles in a triangle is equal to two right angles," we would obviously reject these facts as explanations of his sorrow. We would suppose either that he is putting us off for some reason, in refusing to tell us the true object of his sorrow, or else that he superstitiously connects these facts with some evil. We might perhaps suspect that he is demented or at least the prey of a neurosis in which the true object of his despair has been repressed into the unconscious. In any case we should refuse to concede that mathematical statements as such could possibly motivate his sorrow or despair. For such statements seem to have a character of neutrality, stripped of anything which would enable them to motivate either negatively or positively any affective response.

Now the notions of good (*bonum*) and of evil (*malum*) indicate precisely this property of a being which enables it to motivate our will or to engender an affective response in us. For the present, we will not raise the question of whether every being *as* being has the character of a *bonum;* that is to say, whether there exists a being which is fully neutral. What matters for the moment is whether there exist beings which are given to us as neutral or indifferent at least insofar as they do not reveal to us that character which enables them to move us, to motivate our will, our joy, our sorrow, our hope, or our fear.

The character which enables an object to become the source of an affective response or to motivate our will shall be termed by us "importance." Fully aware that "importance" is often used in another sense, we shall here use this term technically as connoting that property of a being which gives it the character of a *bonum* or *malum;* in short, "importance" is here used as the antithesis to neutrality or indifference.[1]

There is no doubt that the notion of "indifference" is a meaningful and necessary one, even if in the last analysis there exists nothing which is completely indifferent or neutral. The notion of non-existence is also meaningful and necessary even though there does not exist a "non-existence," and even though there is no real being of which we could say that it does not exist.

But besides the fact that the notion of indifference as opposed to the notion of importance is not at all empty and meaningless, there is no doubt that this distinction between the neutral or indifferent as opposed to a positive or negative importance plays a great role in our life. Many facts and many objects have for us the character of neutrality and indifference; and though this does not hinder them from becoming the object of our knowledge, it definitely does exclude them from becoming the object of our will, our wishing, or of any affective response such as joy, sorrow, enthusiasm, indignation, and so forth.

' An object must be endowed with some kind of importance, it must be thrown into relief against mere neutrality or indifference, in order to motivate the will or any affective response. It does not suffice to say, *nihil volitum nisi cogitatum*—Nothing is willed which is not first known. We must add: Nothing can be willed if it is not given to us as being in some way important. So long as the object stands before us completely indifferent or

---

[1] We abstract for the moment from the fact that an object, neutral from the point of view of our affective responses and of our will, may be the source of joy in a process of intellectual research. The mathematical discoveries of Pythagoras must certainly have been a source of joy to him when he discovered them. Yet this does not contradict the relative neutrality in our sense of the objects considered by Pythagoras.

neutral, it is essentially incapable of motivating our will or of engendering in us an affective response.

Thus, insofar as our experience is concerned, we definitely distinguish between beings which are neutral and those which are important. If metaphysics tells us later on that this indifference is not absolute, or that a deeper analysis may reveal every being as having an importance in our sense, we may then consider this experienced indifference as relative. But this metaphysical insight would never do away with the experienced distinction between the indifferent and the important as such. In the first place, it could not erase the significant distinction between the objects which present themselves to us as indifferent or neutral (and thus as unable to move and affect us), and those which present themselves to us as important (and thus as able to motivate our will or our affective responses). This difference is a real and significant one, even if in a deeper stratum indifferent beings reveal a hidden importance.

Moreover, the paramount interest in the distinction between the notions of indifference and importance would in no way be diminished by the fact that even those beings which seem indifferent are ultimately or metaphysically endowed with importance. It is thus of the utmost interest that we recognize the datum of importance and its full meaning. When metaphysics tells us that every being does actually have importance in our sense, this statement has in no way a tautological character. On the contrary, it would imply a surprising discovery and would constitute a typical *veritas aeterna* (eternal truth) in the Augustinian sense or, in the terms of scholastic philosophy, an analytic judgment of the second mode of perseity.

There is no doubt, however, that the relation between importance and our will or any of our affective responses is so evident that we instinctively presuppose it. Notwithstanding a mechanistic or associative psychology, it is presupposed so soon as we deal with reality, as in this case with the motivation of the individual person.

We can find the awareness of this fact at the root of Freud's great discovery of the phenomenon of repression. Though his theoretical basis certainly did not include philosophical insight into this fact, he nevertheless begins with the fact when he considers certain motivations as abnormal and refuses to accept in these cases the consciously admitted object as being the authentic one.

Now the object possessing a positive importance is what we traditionally call a good; the object endowed with a negative importance is called an evil. It is of the greatest necessity to stress from the very beginning that the antithesis between positive and negative importance, between good and evil, is not a contradictory but a contrary one. Thus negative importance is not simply the absence of *positive* importance, since this would mean precisely that the object is indifferent or neutral. Just as bodily pain forms an antithesis to bodily pleasure (clearly differing from a neutral state where neither pain nor pleasure is experienced), so too the negative importance of a sad event is not just the absence of a gladdening event. It is an antithesis of contrariety. This applies to every negative importance, to every evil.

The statement does not yet touch the problem of whether the source of every negative importance consists in a privation of being. Before discussing the ontological basis of negative importance, we must first elucidate the data by examining the nature of that which is given to us as indisputable reality. It will be possible for us to discover the true ontological basis of the "something" to which we refer when using the term sad, disagreeable, unfortunate, bad, wicked, and so forth, but only *after* we have fully understood what this "something" pretends to be. If instead we have a ready explanation before we approach the datum, if we tacitly believe it superfluous even to understand the nature of the datum, then surely we behave like schoolmasters instead of philosophers, or like blind men speaking about colors.

Without anticipating then the metaphysical problem of the source of evil, we must here employ ourselves in wondering about the nature of importance and the type of antithesis which obtains between positive and negative importance. In stating that our first concern should be the nature of the indubitable datum of positive and negative importance, we in no way restrict ourselves to an analysis of merely subjective impressions, of entities which are relative to the human mind. On the contrary, we actually focus on a topic of ultimate metaphysical and philosophical interest: one with a definite objective meaning. The meaningful, intrinsically necessary character of the two data, positive and negative importance, or good and evil, excludes from the outset any possibility of interpreting them as mere "phenomena." [2]

[2] Cf. our explanation in the Prolegomena concerning the nature of the objectivity of these intelligible data.

CHAPTER 2

IMPORTANCE AND MOTIVATION

IN ORDER to elaborate the different types of importance we must first start with an inquiry concerning those data which are capable of motivating our will, or of engendering an affective response, or of touching our soul.

To begin our study with that character of a being which enables it to motivate our desire is not a new approach. A traditional definition of good reads, *bonum est quod omnes desiderant*— Good is what all things desire. In contradistinction, however, to the traditional starting point, we do not want to enlarge the notion of motivation, or *desiderare,* beyond the personal sphere; we want rather to start from motivation in the genuine sense, that is, as a relation which essentially presupposes a person. We want to start from a *desiderare* in the sense of a personal act as it is given to us in experience. We intend therefore to exclude an enlargement of these terms which would apply them to any relation of finality in the sphere of living as well as non-vital beings, by saying, for example, that every being desires self-perfection.

Since we want to start with the immediately given, with data revealing themselves immediately in experience, we shall abstain from any analogical use of these terms which endangers the understanding of the specific nature of motivation or *desiderare.* The danger of such an enlargement consists in using these terms when examining reality by taking some impersonal relationship as a pattern, thereby overlooking the essential personal character of the meaning of these terms. There are many philosophers who might protest that our way of proceeding excludes the metaphysical sphere and restricts us to the psychological. But this seems to us prejudicial. Should something have more of a metaphysical character merely because it does not presuppose a person, or because it refers to impersonal beings? [1]

This prejudice would appear to be based on a confusion of those things which exist only for a human mind (such as mere semblance or fiction) with acts of the person (such as knowledge, will, love, joy); these latter are obviously not only realities *for* the mind of the person, but also objective realities, actualizations and manifestations *of* a person. They are real, conscious entities, as remote from a merely "psychological" reality as is any movement in the material world, or any physiological process. And not only are they realities as objective as any movement in the material world and as distinct from mere illusion or fiction, but also they rank incomparably higher, for they belong to the spiritual sphere.

It is of the utmost importance from a metaphysical point of view that we free ourselves from any state of mind in which impersonal beings, impersonal relations, and impersonal principles function as a pattern (*causa exemplaris*) of the higher sphere. If we do not overcome this approach, we are in danger of failing to grasp the specific nature of such acts, or of falsifying their nature by reducing them to a mere species of movements or tensions, to be found only in the non-personal world.

There is a danger too of overlooking their plenitude, their ontologically superior character, which is intrinsically related to their character as conscious entities. This is a danger analogous to the Freudian error of seeing love as merely a sublimated sexual instinct. In each case, something metaphysically inferior is made the *causa exemplaris* of something superior. In both cases that which is given to us integrally in a conscious experience is disregarded and is viewed only in a psychological context. The sphere of consciousness as such is treated as if it were suspicious and invalid. As feasible as such an approach may be for that which has existence only as object of consciousness, it is not ad-

---

[1] The same metaphysicians who are so chary of the personal sphere and so enamored of the non-personal will nevertheless admit that the person ranks ontologically higher than any impersonal being, and that God is the absolute Person.

missible when applied to real acts of the person, such as knowledge, will, and love, which are in no way mere objects of our
consciousness but *conscious,* objective realities. By their character as conscious realities, by their ontological superiority to
movements or tensions in the non-personal world, these entities
surrender not a whit of their valid title as objective realities.[2]

If we thus exclude here certain enlargements of the terms "motivation" and *desiderare,* the notion of motivation must be
enlarged in another direction. For *bonum* cannot be restricted
to the object of possible desire. On the contrary we must also
include in our inquiry those objects which are capable of motivating joy, enthusiasm, veneration, or esteem, as well as those
objects capable of touching us deeply. Such experiences and
acts obviously cannot be covered by the term *desiderare* even
in its largest sense.

Now even the term *desiderare* is still not as such univocal.
There is first a literal sense in which desire refers to the possession of a good. We desire to eat a food; to drink a wine; to see a
country; to hear beautiful music; to be united with a beloved
person. In all these cases the *desiderare* is directed toward *bona*
which can be possessed; where a fruition in the strict sense is
possible; where it is a question not only of the existence of a good
but also where a specific appropriation, a "becoming mine" is
involved. We can say that this typical desiring is directed toward
the possession of a good; its formal object is possession of, or
fruition in, a good. As we shall see later on, some goods can be
possessed, while other goods exclude this possibility. It is consequently impossible to reduce the notion of *bonum* to the
object of this one type of *desiderare* wherein we seek to possess a
good and to enjoy it as our own.

Desiderare can also be understood in the larger sense of all
affirmative interest in the existence of a good. It then not only
refers to our aiming at the possession of a good, but also extends
to our aiming at the very existence of a good. Its formal object is
the coming into existence of a good which is not yet real. Such
desiring is involved in every real willing as well as in every wish-

---

[2] This is in no way contradicted by the fact that in the human person there
is a stratum of objective reality which has to be distinguished from the consciously experienced sphere.

ing. In this sense, we desire that our friend may be in good health; we desire that justice may triumph; we desire that a sinner may be converted, and so on. These acts have a direction toward the future: either the becoming of something or its continuing in existence.

Yet even in this larger sense, desire does not fully cover our positive attitudes toward a good. Joy, enthusiasm, veneration cannot be interpreted as *desiderare,* either in the strict sense or in the larger sense of this term. It is obvious, for example, that joy over the conversion of a sinner is not a *desiderare* in the strict sense, for the conversion of the sinner is not a good which can be possessed: it cannot be appropriated. This joy rather refers to the very existence of the fact of conversion and not to any possession of it, which is in this case out of the question.

But this joy is also no desire in the enlarged sense. Its formal object is not the coming into existence of something. It is a response which refers to something already existing, to something which has happened.

Thus we must also include in our inquiry into the different types of importance the question: which sense of *bonum* is implied on the object side when we rejoice about the conversion of a sinner, or when we admire the genius of Plato.

A study of the categories of importance which can motivate our will or an affective response, that is to say, an examination of the points of view under which something assumes the character of importance, is of the utmost philosophical interest. Later on we shall have to go beyond this question. We shall have to ask: Which kinds of importance are to be found as properties of beings, independently of the point of view under which they can be approached? This is obviously a new and different question. Nevertheless, the analysis of the possible points of view under which something can be approached as a good is far from being a problem belonging to the realm of empirical psychology. Empirical psychology is concerned with phenomena such as repression, the process of learning, the laws of association, and so forth. Whereas an inquiry into the different points of view under which an object assumes importance deals with necessary, highly intelligible data, analogous to the Aristotelian categories of predication.

Even as points of view of predication, the categories, because of their intelligibility and ultimately meaningful character, transcend the frame of mere empirical psychology. This also applies to the categories of importance. Considered even as possible points of view of motivation, they prove to be notions which are just as clearly shaped and intelligible as those in the sphere of predication. Their intelligibility and meaningful consistency gives them a high philosophical interest. Here we are not confronted with psychological phenomena open only to empirical observation. It is not our aim to state as a blunt, empirical fact that certain types of importance can be found in our motivation; we wish rather to achieve the *a priori* insight [3] that certain types of importance do exist. This insight may be considered analogous to that in which we term a judgment categorical or hypothetical or alternative, or when we say a judgment may be either positive or negative.

Yet their character of necessity and intelligibility only excludes them from the field of *empirical* psychology, and not necessarily from the field of rational psychology. For rational psychology, i.e., the philosophy of man, also deals with necessary and intelligible entities, and aims at *a priori* insights. For another reason, however, the categories of importance cannot be considered as a topic for the philosophy of man. The philosophy of man is concerned only with entities which are a real part of the human person. It is obvious that the categories of predication, though presupposing a thinking person, are in themselves not a real part of the human mind. They therefore are not the object of rational psychology, but of logic. Analogously, the categories of motivation, i.e., the points of view under which something assumes the character of importance, are not a real part of the human soul, and thus cannot be considered as an object of rational psychology. On the other hand, it is not denied that these phenomena also entail many interesting problems for the philosophy of man.

After examining the categories of importance as basic viewpoints of motivation, we shall proceed to inquire into the kinds

[3] The term *a priori* has to be understood here in the sense of the knowledge of *veritates aeternae,* and not in the Kantian sense. Cf. *Der Sinn philosophischen Fragens und Erkennens,* p. 32ff.

of importance which a being may possess independently of any approach.

It should be stressed that an analysis of the different types of importance is not only indispensable to an inquiry into the metaphysical problem concerning the kind of importance which being and beings possess in themselves, but is in addition of paramount interest for the subject of ethics. In ethics not only is the nature of the object of our will in itself paramount, but also the point of view of a person's approach to the object; for clearly, as in the classic example of a morally evil attitude, the point of view under which we choose something is not at all identical with the objective importance which that object has in itself.

CHAPTER 3

THE CATEGORIES OF IMPORTANCE

LET US begin our analysis of the different categories of importance which can motivate our will and our affective responses, by comparing the two following experiences:

In the first, let us suppose that someone pays us a compliment. We are perhaps aware that we do not fully deserve it, but it is nevertheless an agreeable and pleasurable experience. It is not a matter neutral and indifferent to us as in the case where someone tells us that his name begins with a T. We may have been told many things before this compliment, things which had a neutral and indifferent character, but now in the face of all other statements the compliment is thrown into relief. It presents itself as agreeable and as possessing the character of a *bonum,* in short, as something important.

In the second, let us suppose that we witness a generous action, a man's forgiveness of a grave injury. This again strikes us as distinguishable from the neutral activity of a man dressing himself or lighting a cigarette. Indeed, the act of generous forgiveness shines forth with the mark of importance, with the mark of something noble and precious. It moves us and engenders our admiration. We are not only aware that this act occurs, but that it is *better* that it occurs, *better* that the man acted in this way rather than in another. We are conscious that this act is something which *ought to be,* something *important.*

If we compare these types of importance, we will soon discover the essential difference between them. The first, that is, the compliment, is merely *subjectively* important; while the latter, the act of forgiving, is *important in itself.* We are fully conscious that the compliment possesses a character of importance only insofar as it gives us pleasure. Its importance is solely drawn from its relation to our pleasure—as soon as the compliment is divorced from our pleasure, it sinks back into the anonymity of the neutral and indifferent.

In contrast, the generous act of forgiveness presents itself as something intrinsically important. We are clearly conscious that its importance in no way depends on any effect which it produces in us. Its particular importance is not drawn from any relation to our pleasure and satisfaction. It stands before us intrinsically and autonomously important, in no way dependent on any relation to our reaction.

Our language itself expresses this fundamental distinction. The importance of what is agreeable or satisfying always involves the prepositions "to" or "for": something is agreeable *to* or satisfying *for* someone. The terms "agreeable" and "satisfying" cannot be applied as such to an object, but only insofar as they affect a person or, analogously, an animal. On the other hand, the terms "heroic," "beautiful," "noble," "sublime" do not at all require the prepositions "to" or "for," but in fact obviate them. An act of charity is not sublime *for* someone, nor is the Ninth Symphony of Beethoven, or a glorious sunset, beautiful *for* someone.

The intrinsic importance with which a generous act of forgiveness is endowed is termed "value" as distinguished from the importance of all those goods which motivate our interest merely because they are agreeable or satisfactory to us.

But, although these two types of importance are essentially different, are they not in another respect quite similar? Is it not true that those things which are good, beautiful, noble, or sublime deeply touch us, fill us with joy and delight? Certainly they do not leave us indifferent. Does not the full experience of beauty necessarily bestow delight on us; again, do we not experience delight when the charity or generosity of someone touches our heart? Such delight and joy are indeed essentially different from the pleasure derived from the compliment. Yet does this difference really supersede the fact that in both cases a similar relation to a joyful experience is to be found?

Certainly those things which we term intrinsically important, those things endowed with *value,* do possess a capacity for bestowing delight. Yet an analysis of the specific character of delight will prove still more clearly the essential difference between these two kinds of importance. It will prove that the value possesses its importance independently of its effect on us.

The delight and emotion which we experience in witnessing a noble moral action or in gazing at the beauty of a star-studded sky essentially presupposes the consciousness that the importance of the object is in no way dependent on the delight it may bestow on us. Indeed, this bliss arises from our confrontation with an object having an intrinsic importance; an object standing majestically before us, autonomous in its sublimity and nobility. Our bliss implies in fact that here is an object which depends in no way on our reaction to it, an object whose importance we cannot alter, which we can neither increase nor diminish: for it draws its importance not from its relation to us, but from its own rank; it stands before us, a message, as it were, from on high, elevating us beyond ourselves.

Thus, this difference between the bliss emanating from the sheer existence of a value and the pleasure accruing from the subjectively satisfying is itself not a difference of degree, but a difference of kind: an essential difference. A life which consisted in a continuous stream of pleasures, as derived from what is merely subjectively satisfying, could never grant us one moment of that blissful happiness engendered by those objects possessing a value.

The difference between the self-centered pleasure propounded by Aristippus as the only true good, and the happiness for which Socrates and Plato strived, is therefore not a difference of mere degree but of kind of essence.[1] Self-centered happiness at length wears itself out and ends in boredom and emptiness. The constant enjoyment of the merely subjectively satisfying finally throws us back upon our own limitedness, imprisoning us within ourselves.

In contrast, our engagement with a value elevates us, liberates us from self-centeredness, reposes us in a transcendent order which is independent of us, of our moods, of our dispositions. This blissful experience presupposes a participation in the intrinsically important; it implies a harmony which is given forth

[1] Cf. St. Augustine, *Sermo,* 179, 6.

by the intrinsically good, the essentially noble alone; and it displays to us a brightness which is "consubstantial" (congenial) with the intrinsic beauty and splendor of the value. In this priceless contact with the intrinsically and autonomously important, the important in itself, it is the object which shelters and embraces our spirit.

In the Prologue to Wagner's opera *Tannhauser*, that is, in the Venusberg scene, we see Tannhauser longing to break through the circle of a life which affords one pleasure after another. He would prefer even noble suffering to this self-imprisonment. Here we witness some elements of this longing for something important in itself to which alone we can "abandon" ourselves in the true sense of the word. It is indeed a deep characteristic of man to desire to be confronted with something beyond self-centeredness, which obligates us and affords us the possibility of transcending the limits of our subjective inclinations, tendencies, urges, and drives rooted *exclusively* in our nature.[2]

In effect, then, we can say that both the value and the subjectively satisfying can delight us. But it is precisely the *nature* of this delight which clearly reveals the essential difference between the two kinds of goods. The true, profound happiness which the values effect in us necessarily implies an awareness of the object's intrinsic importance. This happiness is essentially an epiphenomenon, for it is in no way the root of this importance, but flows superabundantly out of it. The consciousness that a generous act of forgiveness possesses its importance independently, whether or not I know of its existence, whether or not I rejoice about it, is at the very root of the happiness we experience when confronted with it. This happiness is thus something secondary, notwithstanding the fact that it is an essential mark of the values to be able to bestow delight on us: we even *should* take delight in them. The value is here the *principium* (the determining) and our happiness, the *principiatum* (the deter-

2 St. Thomas clearly distinguishes the difference between delectability resulting from a value and delectability resulting from the merely subjectively satisfying, although he does not use the concept of value: *Honesta sunt etiam delectabilia . . . dicuntur tamen illa propria delectabilia, quae nullam habent aliam rationem appetibilitatis, nisi delectationem, cum aliquando sunt et noxia, et inhonesta . . . Honesta vero dicuntur, quae in seipsis habent, unde desiderentur. Summa Theologica*, I, Q. V, art. vi, ad. 2.

mined), whereas in the case of the subjectively satisfying good our pleasure is the *principium* and the importance of the agreeable or satisfying of the object, the *principiatum*.

A further distinguishing mark is to be found in the way in which each type of importance addresses itself to us. Every good possessing a value imposes on us, as it were, an obligation to give to it an adequate response. We are not yet referring to the unique obligation which we call moral obligation and which appeals to our conscience. This obligation issues from certain values only. Here we are thinking of the awareness which we have as soon as we are confronted with something intrinsically important, for instance, with beauty in nature or in art, with the majesty of a great truth, with the splendor of moral values. In all these cases we are clearly aware that the object calls for an adequate response. We grasp that it is not left to our arbitrary decision or to our accidental mood whether we respond or not, and how we respond. On the other hand, goods which are merely subjectively satisfying address no such call to us. They attract us or invite us, but we are clearly aware that no response is due to them, that it is up to us whether we heed their invitation or not. When a delectable dish attracts us, we are quite aware that it is completely up to our mood whether or not we yield to this attraction. We all know how ridiculous it would be for someone to say that he submitted to the obligation of playing bridge, and overcame the temptation to assist a sick person.

The call of an authentic value for an adequate response addresses itself to us in a sovereign but non-intrusive, sober way. It appeals to our free spiritual center.[3] The attraction of the subjectively satisfying, on the contrary, lulls us into a state where we yield to instinct; it tends to dethrone our free spiritual center. Its appeal is insistent, ofttimes assuming the character of a temptation, trying to sway and silence our conscience, taking hold of us in an obtrusive manner. Far different is the call of values: it has no obtrusive character; it speaks to us from above, and at a

---

[3] Cf. St. Augustine: "I could see the austere beauty of Continence, serene and indeed joyous but not evilly, honourably soliciting me to come to her." *Confessions of St. Augustine,* VIII, 11, trans. F. J. Sheed (New York: Sheed & Ward, 1943), p. 177.

sober distance; it speaks with an objective vigor, issuing a majestic call which we cannot alter by our wishes.[4]

Finally, the essential difference between these two categories of importance is clearly reflected in the type of response which we give. Consider the enthusiasm with which we respond to a heroic moral action, and compare this response with our interest in something subjectively satisfying, such as the interest in a profitable business speculation. We clearly see that in the first case our response has the character of an abandoning of ourselves, a transcending of the boundaries of our self-centeredness, a submission of some sort.

Interest in the subjectively satisying reveals, on the contrary, a self-confinement, a relating of the object to ourselves, using it for our own self-centered satisfaction. Here we do not conform to the good and to its intrinsic importance, as in the case of admiration of the heroic moral action. Interest in the business speculation rather consists in a conforming of the object to ourselves. Our preoccupation may be very intense; we may invest a great deal of energy in the pursuit, abstain from many pleasures for it. But dynamic absorption in the subjectively satisfying still will have nothing of the character of true abandonment, nothing of the character of surrender to the intrinsically important for its own sake.[5]

Thus we have mentioned four marks which reveal the fundamental differences between the intrinsically important, or the value, and the merely subjectively satisfying.

The difference between the value and the merely subjectively satisfying has sometimes been interpreted as simply a difference in rank. It has been assumed that the difference between the intrinsic importance of justice and the merely subjective importance of something agreeable (for instance, the agreeable quality of a warm bath or a pleasant game of bridge) consists only in the

[4] The neutral necessity to conform our actions for the sake of success to the inner logic of the things with which we deal must not be confounded with the obligation to conform ourselves to the call of the values. This difference will be discussed in detail later on.

[5] The difference between being absorbed by a speculation and being abandoned to a value is obviously not erased by the fact that in both cases the aforementioned conforming to the neutral, immanent logic of a being is to be found.

fact that the former ranks higher than the latter. This indeed was the opinion of Max Scheler.[6] It is most surprising that the fundamental difference between the merely subjectively satisfying and the value had not been grasped by Scheler, to whom we owe so many insights into value and other basic ethical problems.

Now every attempt to reduce the essential difference between the two types of importance to a mere difference in rank is futile. Differences of degree always presuppose a common denominator. But such a common denominator is not to be found in these types of importance; we have here two completely different points of view: importance means something different in each case.

There does of course exist a scale in the realm of the agreeable as well as in the realm of values. If we compare the agreeable quality which is proper to a warm bath to the attractive and satisfying element proper to a powerful position, we certainly admit that these two kinds of subjective importance differ very much with reference to their weight and depth. Or if we compare the satisfaction of drinking water when someone is very thirsty during a great heat wave to the satisfaction of drinking water under normal conditions, there is surely a difference of intensity. We speak of a greater and lesser pleasure; of a more superficial, transitory satisfaction; and of a satisfaction possessing a greater weight and depth.

But even the nature of the scale of degrees in the realm of the subjectively satisfying testifies to the essential difference between the value and the merely subjectively satisfying. We can speak of a greater or a lesser pleasure, but the merely subjectively satisfying does not allow us to apply to it the notion of lower and higher as in the sphere of values. The character of a hierarchy which we find in the realm of values has no place here.

As soon as we apply the predication of lower and higher to a pair of pleasant experiences, we immediately judge them from the point of view of value and no longer from the point of view

6 That Scheler did not make this distinction is especially apparent in the chapter "Higher and Lower Values" (*Höhere und niedrigere Werte*) of his great ethical work *Der Formalismus in der Ethik und die materiale Wertethik* (Halle: M. Niemeyer, 1921), p. 84ff. He expressly speaks of the value "agreeable" and puts it higher than the value "useful"; "the feeling of something agreeable" is called "the feeling of a value," etc. (p. 93).

of the merely subjectively satisfying. So we may say that the delight which we feel in hearing a symphony of Haydn is something higher than the pleasure good food can give us. Higher here means nobler; and it is obviously a judgment concerning two experiences from the point of view of value.

What matters is to understand that the nature of the importance of the value is so thoroughly different from the importance of the subjectively satisfying that the possibility of a comparison of degree is thereby obviated, for comparison would presuppose a common denominator. If somebody asked us whether we find a certain red more intense than the headache we have, our answer would be that from the point of view of intensity we can only compare one color with another color, or one pain with another pain, but not a color with a pain. A common denominator needed for all difference of degree is lacking between colors and pains.

The difference between the two categories of importance is even much greater than the difference between a color and a pain. The meaning of importance is so thoroughly different in both cases that we should search in vain for a common denominator which would enable us to compare them from the point of view of degree.

Thus, in traversing the different degrees of the merely subjectively important, in going from the least intensive and most transitory and superficial to the most intense and weighty, we by no means approach the sphere of values. For Macbeth the attractive character of the crown, the deep satisfaction of pride and ambition which the kingdom conveys to him, is by no means nearer to something important in itself than is the agreeable quality of a warm bath. It is, too, as far removed from the modest value of a witty remark as from the high value of a generous act of forgiveness. Thus the sphere of the merely subjectively important has its scale; but the realm of values has its hierarchy: in both we find differences of degree, although in a totally different sense. But it is precisely the consideration of the two respective differences between degrees which clearly reveals that the difference in the two types of importance as such can by no means be reduced to a difference of degree.[7]

[7] It was very consistent and correct of Aristippus that in admitting exclusively the agreeable as the non-indifferent, he never introduced the concepts of low and

The fact that the difference between the value and the sub-jectively satisfying is an essential difference, corresponding to two different meanings of importance, reveals itself above all in a case of conflict between the *invitation* of something agreeable and the *challenge* of a value. In such a case, we have the clear awareness that two disparate points of view appeal to our de-cision. Someone is in a great moral danger and we can help him. The objective value which is at stake presents itself clearly to our mind; we hear the challenge to help him. But there is an entertaining social affair which we should have to give up if we went to his aid. In this conflict we are fully conscious that these two viewpoints of importance are not comparable; that this conflict is completely different from the cases in which we have to choose between two values; for instance, whether we should finish some important work or whether we should assist a sick friend. In the latter case we compare both values, and decide according to the higher value. Here is to be found a con-flict only between two possibilities which exclude each other because they cannot be simultaneously realized; both present themselves under the same point of view, and both appeal to the same center in us. In the former case, however, there is a struggle between two completely different points of view; there are two worlds which clash, each of which appeals to a completely different center in us. If we decide to help the person in great danger and thereby conform ourselves to the value and its chal-lenge, we turn away from the attraction of the party. We over-come the tendency in us which is directed toward the subjectively satisfying. We are aware that the merely subjectively important as such does not count when weighed against the challenge of a value. If we decide instead to go to the promising social affair, we exclude the point of view of the value. In this struggle the respective victory is the victory of a general type of importance, and not only of a single real possibility.

Thus we see that the difference between the merely subjec-

---

high. The only measure he gave for the preference of one pleasure over another was: first, the intensity of the pleasure; second, its duration; third, the question as to whether a pleasure brings about displeasure or not; fourth, the question as to whether it is easier to obtain than another. All these points of view remain completely in the realm of the merely agreeable. They do not presuppose any other kind of importance.

tively satisfying and the value is an essential one and not one of degree. It may be that one and the same thing interests us from both points of view. It may be that one and the same thing is at once agreeable and important in itself. But this coincidence by no means diminishes the essential difference between the two.

The reason why Scheler overlooked the essential· difference between the value and the subjectively satisfying rests in the fact that he did not clearly separate the question concerning the different points of view of importance in our motivation, from the question concerning the importance which the object possesses independently of any motivation. The fact that no being is completely deprived of all valu̇e may divert us from insight into the essential difference between the two points of view. Yet the category of the subjectively satisfying is not directed toward certain things which in themselves would possess no other importance, but toward the point of view under which we *approach* these things. Thus the argument which says that the amusing social affair also has a value, only a lower one, is pointless. In a case where I have to choose between attending the amusing social affair and assisting a man in great moral danger, the conflict is not between the value of assisting this man and the value of attending this party. The conflict is rather between two heterogeneous points of view. In choosing to go to the amusing party, the point of view under which this decision is made is definitely the merely subjectively satisfying. But in the case of the opposite choice in which I decide to assist a sick person, the point of view of my choice is definitely the value.

A common thief does not consider the fact of his obtaining money as a good possessed of a higher value than the property of his fellow men. He is not even interested in the question of whether something is important in itself or not. His approach is exclusively from the point of view of the subjectively satisfying.

Any attempt to explain the morally wrong attitude as the preference for a good having a lower value to a good possessing a higher one is doomed to fail. In the first place, it is impossible to interpret every action as being rooted in an act of preference. There exist many cases in which an end is chosen by disregarding a value without respect to any preference; for instance, somebody avenges himself in killing his enemy, and in so doing he ignores the high value of the life of a human being. Obviously it would be a completely artificial and wrong interpretation to say that this man prefers the satisfaction of his revenge to the life of his enemy. No conscious comparison, no conscious pondering of two goods, is here in question. Instead there is a simple decision to satisfy his desire for revenge, without in any way bothering about the value of a human life. If someone should claim that in deciding to kill his enemy he implicitly prefers the satisfaction of his revenge to the life of his victim, we must answer that the term "preference" would then be used in an equivocal sense. In the one case it is understood as a conscious act in which we choose between two or more possibilities, pondering them in their importance and giving the preference to one of them because of its superior importance. Of this, the authentic sense of preference, nothing is to be found in our example. In the other case the term "preference" is used in the sense that every decision in fact excludes many other possibilities, whether we know of them or not, whether we have any consciousness of them or not. Preference is here used in the analogous sense in which I could call every judgment an intellectual choice between infinite possibilities, because in affirming that something is a table I thereby exclude the possibility that it is a donkey, a house, a man, and so on.

This use of the term "intellectual choice" or "preference" is obviously incorrect. In restricting ourselves to the authentic meaning of preference, we must admit that it is impossible to interpret every action or decision or response as being rooted in an act of preference such as we have just pointed out. An ordinary theft is not based on a preference for the value of possessing money over the sacred character of property rights, but is based rather on an indifference toward the point of view of value as such, which conditions an indifference toward the value of property coupled with an unhampered pursuit of something subjectively satisfying. In the case of a conflict in which a man wavers between a temptation toward theft and the voice of conscience exhorting respect for the property of his fellow men and warning against the injustice of theft, there can be no weighing of both possibilities from the same point of view, no comparison by a common denominator, but only an outspoken clash of two different points of view: the two directions of life of which St. Augustine speaks in *De Civitate Dei* (XIV, 3).

Moreover, if it were true that in preferring a lower good to a higher good the choice would be based on a common denominator, namely the point of view of their value, it would be impossible to explain why one could choose the lower instead of the higher. So long as one and the same point of view is really at stake, there must be a reason why that which is inferior from this point of view is nevertheless preferred.

Every time someone approaches two possibilities from one and the same point of view (for instance, where one chooses the lower of two salaries offered for the same kind and amount of work), we try to find out what other point of view could explain such a choice. We take it for granted that one could not choose from the same viewpoint and by the same measure that which is less, if there were not the possibility of approaching this lesser one from another viewpoint or, as we can put it, if another point of view were not responsible for turning the scale.

Someone may object that the preference of the lower good is due to an error. This is why Socrates considered error as the root of all moral evil.

It must be said in reply that error can have two different meanings in this context. The first type of error consists in confusing one object with another, or in ignoring its true nature. We confide a pupil to a man, believing him to be a holy man, whereas in reality he is a Tartuffe.[8] We offer a friend poisonous mushrooms, because we do not know that they are poisonous. This type of error is the kind of ignorance which Aristotle rightly quotes in his *Nicomachean Ethics* as one reason for an involuntary action.[9]

But this type of error causes us to do something which is in reality completely different from what we believe we are doing and from what we intend to do. It thus dissolves the responsibility for our action; or, if the error is a result of our thoughtlessness, it alters our responsibility in a decisive way.

[8] The hypocrite in Molière's play by that name.
[9] Bk. III, 1110a, sq.

Such an error can even account for the choice of an evil instead of a good in those cases where we believe the evil to be a higher good; for instance, when we confide a child to an educator whom we believe to be a saint, though he is in reality a Tartuffe, instead of giving the child to a reliable, honest man, though no saint. But it is obvious that this kind of error is not the root of moral evil, because a man doing something objectively evil as a result of such an error would act with moral rectitude as far as his intention is concerned. In other words, with respect to the conception of reality which he has, he would choose in the right way.

The second type of error is of a completely different nature. It is the result of what we would call "value blindness"; for instance, the man who says, "I cannot see why libertinism is morally wrong," or the man who, like Raskolnikov in Dostoevski's *Crime and Punishment*, is blind to the dignity of human life.[10]

This value blindness indeed plays a great role as a root of moral evil, and is in fact at the basis of many preferences of a lower in place of a higher good. Patricius, the father of St. Augustine, in placing his son in an intellectually outstanding but morally dangerous school because a brilliant intellectual education was considered a good higher than moral integrity, typifies this value blindness.

But how can we account for such a value blindness? If it were a blindness like color blindness, the result of a mere natural disposition, no one would be responsible for being value blind and for acting in a morally wrong way because of this blindness. But it is not the kind of ignorance which makes an action involuntary.[11]

Value blindness is in no way the result of mere temperamental disposition, but rather of pride and concupiscence. Because here a point of view other than the value dominates the approach to

10 Cf. *ibid.*, Bk. III, 1110b, 25–35.

11 St. Thomas clearly distinguishes between the two kinds of errors in saying: "For example, if a mistaken reason bids a man sleep with another man's wife, to do this will be evil if based on ignorance of a divine law he ought to know; but if the misjudgement is occasioned by thinking that the woman is really his own wife, and she wants him and he wants her, then his will is free from fault." *Summa Theologica*, 1a–2ae, xix, 6.

reality; the point of view, namely of what satisfies our pride and concupiscence: we are therefore blinded to certain values.

The duality in the points of view of importance is thus in fact necessarily presupposed in order to explain the possibility of an erroneous preference of a lower rather than a higher good. The problem of value blindness will occupy us later in more detail. Here it suffices to mention it in order to prove the impossibility of any theory which admits but one denominator of importance or but one point of view of importance; which interprets the subjectively satisfying simply as a lower value; or which makes of the difference between the value and the merely subjectively satisfying a difference only in degree.

Though we have said that Scheler tried to reduce the difference between the two categories of importance to a difference in rank, we must add that, although he tried to interpret the agreeable as a lower type of value, he at least never tried to reduce the important-in-itself to a more refined type of the subjectively satisfying.[12] Scheler tried to reduce every importance to an importance-in-itself or a value. He overlooked the merely subjectively satisfying as a category of its own, as having its own "ratio," and saw every motivation as rooted in a value of the object. In this regard he represents the exact opposite of Aristippus, who denied any other kind of importance except the subjectively satisfying and declared the important-in-itself to be a mere illusion.

Yet the error of Scheler and that of Aristippus cannot be placed on the same level, even if both tried to reduce to *one* category what in reality are two entirely different categories of importance. A philosopher who admits no kind of importance except the merely subjectively satisfying has an utterly deformed conception of the universe: he desubstantializes the cosmos. The opposite position, that of Scheler, in which only the value is seen,

---

[12] There is still a great difference once the error of an undue identification is committed concerning which level of reality is sacrificed; e.g., if somebody denied the difference between *a priori* and empirical truth, it would still remain a matter of great importance whether he believed every contingent fact to be as necessary and intelligible as a *veritas aeterna*, or whether he declared that every truth is of an empirical order. Between an extreme rationalism and an extreme empiricism there is still a great difference, though both have in common a disregard for the essential disparity between these two types of knowledge.

is not at all a desubstantialization of the cosmos. Scheler remained, despite his error, in basic conformity with that part of being which ultimately matters.

Value embodies the true, the valid, the objectively important. It has a place in the order of fundamental notions other than the subjectively satisfying. It belongs (as we shall see in detail) to those ultimate data and notions such as being, truth, and knowledge, which can neither be defined nor denied without tacitly reintroducing them. This is the reason why Aristippus' attempt to do away with any objective measure and to admit only a subjective importance, is in fact always unsuccessful. After eliminating with a rare consistency (as we have seen above) all other measures except those which apply to the degrees of pleasure, he warns against following our instincts in a brutelike way and advises our examining a thing before we choose it to see whether it really guarantees the most intense and lasting pleasure: here he tacitly opposes the reasonable pursuit of pleasure to an unreasonable surrender to every attraction or temptation. And he claims that the reasonable pursuit is the wiser attitude, the attitude we *should* have.

Why *should* we be wise? If the merely subjectively satisfying is the norm, why should anyone object to a man who pretends that he prefers to yield to every instinct without bothering about whether something else could give him more pleasure? Obviously Aristippus silently presupposes still another norm besides that of pleasure, an objective norm: the value of wisdom, in the sense of a reasonable, systematic pursuit of pleasure as opposed to the brutelike and unreasonable instinctual pursuit of pleasure. This norm is independent of the question of whether it is more or less subjectively satisfying. Thus, in a completely general and formal way, the notion of value is presupposed. Certainly there is no question of moral value. But in recommending the systematic and rational pursuit of pleasure as an ideal, as something we should aim at, he implicitly claims that it is objectively preferable to do so, that it should be so rather than not: thereby the notion of value or the important-in-itself is tacitly presupposed.

It is of the utmost interest for ethics to grasp the essential difference between the two categories of importance; although value embodies what is ultimately of objective importance, the other category, the subjectively satisfying, must also be seen clearly, for even the true nature of value cannot be fully understood without a clear understanding of this other category.

Moreover it must be seen that the category of the subjectively satisfying in fact plays a fundamental role in our motivation. It is not possible to claim that whenever a person is apparently motivated by the subjectively satisfying, it is in reality a value which is motivating him. It is undeniable that in many concrete situations the value point of view does not motivate the person. There exist even certain types of persons who know only that kind of importance which we termed the merely subjectively satisfying. The man who is completely dominated by pride and concupiscence knows no other source of motivation, no point of view under which anything could assume the character of importance other than the merely subjectively satisfying. A Cain as well as an Iago, a Richard III as well as a Don Giovanni, each approaches everything exclusively from the point of view of whether or not it is capable of satisfying his pride or concupiscence. The question of whether something has a value, whether it is important in itself or not, does not in any way interest them. Even the question of whether something is objectively a true good for them, whether it is in conformity with their true interest, does not preoccupy them. Their approach is not even orientated toward the objective measure concerning their own good, but exclusively toward their subjective satisfaction. Their will is never motivated, their interest never stimulated, by any objective norm. It is agreeable to *me;* it satisfies *my* pride or concupiscence; it satisfies *my* urges and appetites whether legitimate or not: this is the only kind of importance which such persons admit.

In stressing the absence of any objective norm for such persons, in saying that they do not even bother about the question of whether something is in conformity with their true interest or not, we touch upon a third fundamental type of *bonum;* and this must be distinguished as well from the value as from the merely subjectively satisfying. The elaboration of the third type of importance, which in itself is of the highest interest, will throw even more light on the question just discussed.

When we reflect on gratitude and its true object, we discover

that the benefit which someone bestowed on us, and for which
we are grateful, pertains neither to the point of view of the
merely subjectively satisfying, nor to that of the important-in-
itself. The benefit presents itself as an objective good for me, as
something which is objectively in my true interest, which has
a beneficent character with respect to my person and which is
in the direction of my good. Gratitude also refers to the morally
noble attitude of my benefactor which manifests itself in his
bestowing the benefit on me. What motivates my admiration or
veneration, as distinguished from gratitude, is exclusively something important in itself: the moral value of the donor's act, its
generosity and goodness. But in the case of gratitude, the moral
value is more a necessary presupposition than the formal object of
gratitude. I can admire the moral goodness of someone who helps
another person as much as if I benefited from his deed; but gratitude implies that the help is given to *me* or to one with whom I
am in such solidarity that I consider what happens to him as my
own affair. In this case a new kind of importance is at stake. We
will use for this third category of importance the term "objective good for the person."

When somebody is saved from a danger threatening his life,
or is released from imprisonment, his joy and his gratitude toward God clearly refer to the kind of importance which we have
termed the objective good for the person. What moves him, what
fills his heart with gratitude, is the gift of his life or of his freedom; and this has the character of an objective good *for* him.
It distinguishes itself clearly on the one hand from the important-
in-itself or the value, and on the other from the merely subjectively satisfying.

The gift which I receive, my freedom, for example, is not seen
in the light of something merely subjectively satisfying, as it
might appear to a criminal who succeeds in escaping. It is seen,
on the contrary, as something objectively precious to me, as
something in its very nature positive for me, as something conducive to my true interest. It has the character of a manifestation of God's bounty and love.

On the other hand, it also clearly differs from the important-
in-itself. Life and freedom are here considered not only in their
intrinsic value, but also insofar as they are great gifts for *me*. If

I adore God's infinite bounty and mercy which bestowed these goods upon me, I clearly respond to something important-in-itself, to an infinite value. Similarly, I am motivated by a value when the moral goodness of a human benefactor moves me. In these cases, I am not directed to the importance which implies a relation to a subject, but to a pure importance in itself. In the importance which my life, freedom, health, etc., have for me there is, on the contrary, an essential relation to my own person: they are objectively important *to* me.

The character of this *bonum mihi* (good for me) as a category of importance differing from the value as well as from the subjectively satisfying also reveals itself when we contemplate its negative counterpart: the objective evil for the person, for example the formal object of human forgiveness.

Someone has wronged me; a friend has betrayed me. In forgiving him I am fully aware that my forgiveness refers only to the wrong he has done me. It refers to the objective evil he has inflicted on me, not to the moral *disvalue* which is embodied in his attitude. The moral disvalue by which he has offended God is never the object of human forgiveness. I can never cancel the disvalue but only the wrong inflicted on myself. I may say, "I forgive you; may God pardon you." The pardon of God refers to the guilt which is rooted in the moral disvalue. My forgiveness, on the contrary, refers to the attitude of the offender insofar as it is an objective evil for me. This manifests itself also in the fact that I can forgive only an evil inflicted on myself either directly or indirectly, as when someone wrongs persons whom I consider in a specific way to be united to me. I cannot forgive the wrong which has been inflicted on any other person. I cannot forgive Judas his betrayal of the Lord or Cain his murder of Abel.

We may become indignant about injustice inflicted on our fellow man as well as over an injustice inflicted on ourselves, because indignation refers to the moral disvalue of the injustice. But our forgiveness is possible only with respect to the injury inflicted on us, because it refers itself to the injustice insofar as it is an objective evil for us.

The object of human forgiveness is the wrong inflicted on us, the objective evil for us; whereas the moral disvalue of injustice can be pardoned only by God or his representatives to whom

Christ has granted the power to bind and to loose. Thus St. Stephen, dying a martyr's death, prays that God may pardon his murderers.

Someone may object that we can forgive another only if he is guilty of doing us a wrong. If he involuntarily inflicts on us an objective evil, we have nothing to forgive. He must be responsible for the objective evil inflicted on us, and thus his attitude must also be morally bad. It is therefore false to say that in forgiving we do not refer ourselves to the moral disvalue, for the moral disvalue is presupposed if the objective evil inflicted on us is to become an object of our forgiveness.

Certainly forgiveness presupposes responsibility on the part of the person who has inflicted an objective evil upon us. It is always a voluntary and conscious attitude of our fellow men which is the object of our forgiveness; this is so whether the wrong inflicted on us consists exclusively in an unfriendly, hostile, or unjust attitude or whether it is an action implying a more tangible objective evil for us.

But this does not do away with the fact that our forgiveness refers to the attitude of the offender insofar as it has the negative importance of an objective evil for us, and not insofar as it has the negative importance of a moral disvalue which God alone can forgive. The cancelling of enmity or disharmony which is the effect of our forgiving obviously refers itself only to the negative importance of an objective evil for us and not to the moral disvalue. Our forgiveness does not affect the disharmony rooted in the moral disvalue. The offense to God which it implies is in no way dissolved by the fact that we forgive the evil doer; whereas his contrition and subsequent pardon by God imply a resolution of this disharmony.

The fact that one and the same attitude possesses objectively both kinds of importance, in the case of a hostile act a disvalue and the character of an objective evil for the person, does not erase the difference between the two dimensions of importance. Nor does it erase the fact that my act of forgiving refers only to one kind of negative importance, i.e., the objective evil for me. The confusion arises because of the necessary interrelation between the two dimensions of importance, an interrelation rooted in the fact that a human act is the object of our forgiveness. The hostile, unfriendly, unjust act which directs itself against the objective good for a fellow man, which neglects his objective good or even seeks to injure or destroy it, is always endowed with a moral disvalue. In grasping its injustice toward us, we necessarily grasp also its moral disvalue. Thus not only is the object of our forgiveness necessarily *endowed* with a moral disvalue, but also we are necessarily aware of this moral disvalue. But this does not do away with the fact that our forgiving reaches the act of injustice only insofar as it is done to us, as it has the importance of an objective evil for us, and not insofar as it has a moral disvalue.

In the light of the foregoing, the essential difference between the two types of importance, the important-in-itself or the value and the objective good for the person, discloses itself. In examining the object of forgiveness, we have clearly seen that this latter kind of importance manifests its difference from the intrinsic importance of value and disvalue, which is in no way altered by the fact that one and the same act is endowed with both kinds of importance, nor by the fact that there is a deep and necessary interrelation between the two kinds of importance.[13]

This coincidence however is not only such that one and the same object happens to be endowed with the two categories of importance. The two categories of importance are not juxtaposed. They are not independent of each other. But this does not at all erase the difference between the two categories of importance; indeed, it does not even lessen its significance.[14]

The traditional concept of *bonum* has most often revolved around that category of importance which we termed "the ob-

[13] The difference between the objective evil for the person and disvalue is clearly stated by St. Augustine in his *Confessions* (V, 12) when he says, "My heart hateth them, and not with righteous hatred: for pretty surely I hated them more because of what I myself had to suffer from them than for the wrong they did to teachers generally. . . . But at that time I disliked them for the harm they did me more than I wished them to become good for Your sake." (F. J. Sheed, *op. cit.*, p. 99.)

[14] In many other instances we find such a close relationship that it must not be taken for identity. The fact, for instance, that every will presupposes knowledge does not erase the essential difference between the two; and this applies still more to the difference between the two types of importance. Existence in all contingent things presupposes essence, but this in no way nullifies the difference between essence and existence. Nor is the difference between act and potency erased by the fact that in all contingent things we find act and potency, and the further fact that every potency presupposes an act which is prior.

jective good for the person," at least insofar as man's motivation is concerned. When Socrates stated that it is better to suffer injustice than to commit injustice,[15] he obviously meant that suffering injustice is better for man. He does not mean only that the one is morally better than the other, for to say this would be a mere truism. It goes without saying that to commit injustice is morally bad, whereas to suffer injustice is in no way morally bad. From the point of view of the moral value, the one is not better: rather the one is bad, the other, in no way bad. The comparative, implying a common denominator which permits us to consider the one as the greater evil, excludes the possibility that the moral value is the common denominator, since doing injustice is an obvious moral evil, whereas suffering injustice is, as such, extraneous to the moral sphere. Suffering injustice can certainly become equally an object of morality when the question is directed to the manner in which we suffer the injustice afflicted on us. But this is not the problem which is at the root of the thesis of Socrates.

The meaning of the Socratic statement refers to the fact that it is a greater evil *for man* to go morally astray than to suffer. The measure on which is based the comparative degree "better" is not the moral value, but the importance which something objectively has for man: that category of importance which we have termed "the objective good for the person." It means that, from the point of view of what is ultimately to man's true interest, to suffer injustice is better than to commit it. After having seen that the statement of Socrates cannot be construed as referring to the value, neither a moral value nor any other type of importance in itself, it can easily be seen that it also does not refer to the merely subjectively satisfying.

Aristippus would certainly not accept the statement of Socrates. The only measure which he admits is subjective satisfaction or pleasure, and he would thus consider the suffering of injustice as an evil, whereas the doing of injustice would not be an evil so long as we could avoid punishment. According to his view, the suffering of injustice is not an evil because of the injustice, but exclusively because of the suffering connected with

[15] This is the thesis which Plato puts in the mouth of Socrates in the Dialogue *Gorgias* (469c), and in the first two books of *The Republic*.

it. To suffer justly, to undergo pain or the privation of pleasures would be just as much an evil. It makes no difference to him whether suffering results from an injustice or whether it is a well-deserved punishment. The objective element in the notion of *bonum* in the thesis of Socrates is completely absent in the hedonist notion of good. For Aristippus, the *bonum* is equivalent to the subjectively agreeable or the subjectively satisfying. The only nod he makes to an objective order occurs when he asks whether this pleasure is sought in a reasonable way or in an unreasonable one. The fool turns to every pleasure in a brute-like instinctive way; the wise man, on the contrary, chooses the subjectively satisfying object according to the above-mentioned principles of intensity, duration, and so on.

Thus the notion of *bonum* in the Socratic conception cannot be equivalent to the merely subjectively satisfying. His thesis would be absurd if Aristippus were right in declaring that there exists no other kind of importance than the agreeable or the subjectively satisfying. The Socratic notion of good implies, notwithstanding its reference to the person, an element of objective orientation which permits it to determine the real rank of an evil independently of the question of whether it causes displeasure or not. Without this objective measure beyond the merely subjectively satisfying, the statement of Socrates would collapse.

The difference between the notion of *bonum* given by Aristippus and that of Socrates must not however be confused with the difference between a real *bonum* and a merely apparent *bonum*. With respect to every being we can distinguish the objective reality and its mere subjective appearance. The term objective means that something is in reality what it appears to be; we oppose this objective reality to a mere illusion, which does not correspond to reality.

This distinction between subjective and objective applies to merely subjectively satisfying goods as well as to objective goods for the person. Someone may believe that a bottle of vinegar is filled with wine and thus may look at it as something subjectively satisfying. Only in drinking it will he discover that it is not subjectively satisfying. There exist things which are really capable of bestowing pleasure on us and also things which only appear to do so since objectively they fail to bestow pleasure on us. This appearance may be conditioned by an error concerning the real being at stake or by an illusion concerning the real nature of a being. A child believes it pleasurable to smoke and in doing so gets sick, experiencing displeasure. The distinction between objective and subjective refers here not to the nature of the importance, but only to the question of whether the object really possesses a specific kind of importance or only appears to do so.

We can distinguish between something which is really an objective good for us, and that which is only apparently so. When we fail to attain what we strive for, we often believe that this failure is a great objective evil for us. Later on we may see that it was in reality a great good for us. A man is separated from a friend who had a great influence on him; he believes that this loss is a great misfortune, an objective evil for him. Later on he realizes that the influence of this friend was a bad one, and that the separation from him was in reality an objective good for him.

Thus the difference between the merely subjectively satisfying and the objective good for the person, since it hinges on the very nature of importance, is not equivalent to the distinction between an object which in reality possesses one or the other kind of importance and that which only apparently possesses it.

Though the kind of importance which we termed "the objective good for the person" prevails historically in the notion of *bonum*, it is in reality secondary with respect to the datum of value. In saying secondary, we do not mean to imply that it can be reduced to the important-in-itself, or deduced from it, but only that it already presupposes the value, and that the important-in-itself has in every respect an absolute primacy. This becomes manifest also in the fact that the type of importance which is the objective good for the person necessarily presupposes the important-in-itself, the value.

In order to state that going morally astray is a greater evil for man than to suffer injustice, the moral value must already be grasped. How could Socrates, if he had not already grasped the intrinsic importance of the moral value, state that to be morally tainted is for man worse than to suffer? If Socrates had argued by saying that to do injustice would bring troubles upon us, would perchance make an enemy of the man on whom we inflict an injustice, or perhaps would bring us into conflict with the laws of

the state, etc., he would not have needed to grasp the moral disvalue of injustice in order to consider it as a great evil for man.

But Socrates does not argue in this manner. It is not the utilitarian type of consideration embodied in the proverb, "Honesty
is the best policy," which is at the basis of the Socratic thesis.[16] It
is not the possible consequence of our doing injustice but the
immorality of the underlying attitude which makes it for him a
greater evil.

Because injustice is as such a moral disvalue, it is also an objective evil for the person; it is not because it is an objective evil
for the person that it is morally bad. In order to understand that
injustice is something negative or bad, we do not have to refer
to the question of whether or not it is an evil for the person. We
can grasp it immediately in understanding the nature of injustice. But in order to understand that it is an objective evil for
the person and an even greater one than the obvious evil of suffering injustice, we must already have grasped the intrinsic disvalue
of injustice.

The great insight and contribution made by Socrates—foreshadowing those words of our Lord: "What doth it profit a man,
if he gain the whole world, but suffer the loss of his soul?" (Matt.
16:26)—is precisely the insight that moral integrity, because of
its value, is a higher objective good for the person than the possession of any other good which bestows pleasure or happiness
on us. Or, to remain in a more immediate contact with the statement of Socrates, to be morally tainted is a greater objective evil
for the person than any suffering.

Socrates is eager to show that injustice, in addition to its intrinsic disvalue, is also the greatest objective evil for man, and
that it is such because of its intrinsic disvalue.[17] When our conscience compels us to abstain from an injustice, it is the negative
importance in itself of injustice which imposes the obligation on
us to abstain from it; it is not the objective evil which doing injustice implies for us. Moreover, injustice is primarily bad in
itself; it is an objective evil for us only because of its disvalue.
The disvalue of injustice is the *principium;* if we are to understand that it is an objective evil for us, we have first to grasp its

16 See especially the argument in *Gorgias,* 306, c. 59.
17 This is the topic of the myth at the end of *Gorgias.*

intrinsic disvalue. The essential link between the intrinsic disvalue of injustice and its being an objective evil for the person
is the true theme of the statement of Socrates and expresses his
real contribution.

Thus we see that the statement of Socrates is centered around
a notion of *bonum* that a more minute analysis shows to be the
type of importance which we have called "the objective good
for the person." [18] It differs, as we have seen, from the notion of
bonum of Aristippus, the merely subjectively satisfying. It differs equally from the basic notion of *bonum* which we have
called the important-in-itself or the value. Because Socrates does
not distinguish these three essentially different notions of importance, he fails to elaborate the specific nature of the notion of
bonum around which he in fact orientates himself, namely the
objective good for the person. [19]

The category of importance which we termed "the objective
good for the person" plays a specific role in our motivation when
the good of another person is at stake. In hearing of the conversion of a sinner, we rejoice in a twofold direction. We rejoice
first over the intrinsic goodness of the conversion, its importance
in itself or its value, which glorifies God; and secondly, we rejoice
for the man, because he did what is in the direction of his true
good, because of the priceless gift he received in his conversion.
We could also express this twofold direction of our joy as follows: in the first place as a response to a value; in the second as a
response to an objective good for him. Hence our joy issues on
the one hand from our love of God and on the other out of our
love of neighbor. In effect, one and the same object possesses the
two kinds of importance, viz., the important-in-itself on the one
hand, and the objective good for the person on the other. [20]

[18] The Aristotelian notion of the good is equally orientated around the objective good for the person. This is clearly revealed in his answer to the question of
what is the chief good. In considering happiness as the chief good, he obviously
is concerned with the viewpoint of the objective good for the person.

[19] In the Prolegomena we pointed out that it often happens in history that a
datum is implicitly presupposed without the philosophical *prise de conscience*
of it.

[20] This relation between the value and the objective good for the person does
not apply, however, in the same way to every type of objective good for the person. There are many objective goods for the person in which the character of an

The role of the objective good for the person is clearly evident in our *intentio benevolentiae* [21] toward persons whom we love. We desire to make the beloved happy, we want to cover him with benefits, to do everything for his best interests. We do not ask what will satisfy him subjectively, but rather what is objectively good for him. If he happens to have an uncontrollable liking for alcoholic beverages, we do not provide him with the occasion and the means to indulge himself even though he may be subjectively satisfied. It would be a pseudo love which favors everything which is subjectively satisfying for the beloved without considering whether or not it is an objective good for him. True love will always concern itself with this objective measure of the true good for the beloved. If the beloved has a tendency to be proud, if he relishes cheap flattery, the true lover will not foster this tendency in satisfying his pride. If the beloved happens to be a drug addict undergoing a curative treatment, the true lover will not clandestinely procure for him the hypodermic needle, despite the fact that it affords him something subjectively satisfying.

The notion of the objective good for the person must therefore be distinguished not only from the notion of value, the important-in-itself, but also from the merely subjectively satisfying. The case of forgiveness which earlier helped us to distinguish the objective good or evil for the person from the value and disvalue, also clearly reveals the difference between this category and the merely subjectively satisfying or dissatisfying.

As long as the attitude of another person has only the character of being disagreeable and subjectively dissatisfying to us, there is neither the need nor the possibility of our forgiving him. A friend makes us a justified reproach which is objectively helpful to us; but our pride resents it as being disagreeable and humiliating. We construe it wrongly and bear a grudge against our friend. If we afterward overcome our self-centered cramp, we are fully aware that, though he did something which was

---

objective good is gained through itself and not through its being endowed with a value, as we shall see later on.

[21] In my book, *In Defense of Purity* (New York: Sheed & Ward, 1935), Pt. I, this term is introduced and discussed.

subjectively disagreeable to us, we have no real occasion for an act of forgiveness. On the contrary, we are rather aware that we ourselves need forgiveness because we reacted in such a wrong way to a reproach. As long as something has exclusively a subjectively negative importance, without being simultaneously an objective evil for us, there is no call for an act of forgiveness. Forgiveness presupposes the awareness that the attitude of someone toward us has the negative importance of something objectively unjust or uncharitable in regard to us.

Certainly many attitudes which are disagreeable to us or actions which inflict injury on us are simultaneously an objective evil for us. The intentional infliction on us of pains or injuries for their own sake always has, besides being disagreeable, the negative importance of an objective evil for us. The two kinds of importance are deeply interrelated, since being an objective evil for us here presupposes that it is something painful and disagreeable. But this does not obviate the fact that the two kinds of importance differ essentially, and that we measure an attitude from one point of view when we state only that it is subjectively disagreeable, and from another when we consider it as an objective evil for us. The same applies to the corresponding positive cases: neither is everything which is subjectively satisfying for us an objective good for us, nor is everything which is an objective good for us subjectively satisfying.

The importance which we termed an "objective good for the person" has an element of objectivity which is completely lacking in the category of importance which we called the subjectively satisfying. From the exclusive point of view of the merely subjectively satisfying, there is no essential difference between beholding the sufferings of an enemy, which the revengeful person experiences as satisfying, and the legitimate satisfaction in earning money; no difference between the sadistic enjoyment of inflicting pain on another person and the pleasure in relishing a good wine; no difference between winning money in a lottery and stealing it.

In summarizing we can say: Three fundamentally different categories of importance are to be found in our motivation. They are not only empirical realities which *de facto* occur in human motivations; they are three possible *rationes* on which the importance of an object can be based, three essential points of view of any possible motivation, whether human or angelic. It is imperative that we understand the fundamental and necessary character of these three categories of importance, as well as their essential difference. As different as their rank may be, it is nevertheless strictly true that all three have their *eidos* (intelligible essence). Hence, to discover them is not at all the result of an empirical observation, psychological or otherwise, but of a philosophical insight analogous to the one which distinguishes the different categories of predication.[22]

We see that we know but little, especially from the ethical point of view, as long as we say only that every will is directed toward a good, because what matters is precisely whether the motivating category of importance is the value, the objective good for the person, or the merely subjectively satisfying.

This insight will prove to be of paramount importance later on, because it also reveals the incorrectness of Aristotle's thesis that our freedom is restricted to means and not to ends. The great and decisive difference in man's moral life lies precisely in whether he approaches the universe from the point of view of value or of the merely subjectively satisfying. It is the famous distinction which St. Augustine formulates in his *De Civitate Dei*, when he says:

. . . yet are there but two sorts of men that do properly make the two cities we speak of; the one is of men that live according to the flesh, and the other of those that live according to the spirit.[23]

But we will discuss this topic later on. Before leaving the sphere of motivation, however, we must mention still another difference in the field of importance. Although it is not a new category of importance it is something which plays a great role, a role which has often been stressed in the course of the history of philosophy. It is the difference between direct and indirect importance, or between primary and secondary importance. Whether an object is sought for its own sake or for the sake of something else does indeed make a decisive difference concerning the importance which the object has in the realm of our

[22] Cf. Prolegomena, p. 4ff.
[23] XIV, 1. *The City of God*, trans. John Healey, Everyman's Library (New York: E. P. Dutton & Co., 1947), Vol. II.

motivation. This difference plays a paramount role in Aristotle's *Nicomachean Ethics;* for him it is even the decisive mark of the chief good.

One good is sought for its own sake whereas everything else is chosen for the sake of this good. This distinction is equivalent to the distinction between means and end. Our interest in some medicine is not directed to it for its own sake, but only insofar as it serves to restore our health or to do away with a pain. A good wine, on the contrary, attracts us for its own sake. The medicine is merely a means; the good wine, or rather the enjoyment of it, is an end. A man is in danger of his life. To save him is our end; it interests us for its own sake. The rope with which we draw him out of the water has an importance only as a means to this end.

This distinction between means and ends pervades our entire life; we constantly make a distinction between the things which are sought for their own sake and those which are sought only for the sake of something else. In the latter instance the things take on the character of mere means, since they are considered apart from any value they may possess in themselves. It is imperative to understand that the importance in itself of the value is not equivalent to direct importance, which characterizes all the things which are sought for their own sake. In other words, to be a value is not the same as to be an end or to be an object of direct importance.

The importance in itself of the value refers to the nature of the importance as such, whereas the fact of something being sought for its own sake, which we want to term "direct importance," refers to the manner in which the importance inheres in a being or is proper to it. That which is sought for its own sake is directly important; its importance does not depend upon a relation of finality to something else. Mere means, on the contrary, are only indirectly important, borrowing their importance, as it were, from the importance of the end which they serve. Their aptitude to serve the attainment of an important end endows them with a secondary or auxiliary importance.

The difference between direct and indirect importance, or primary and secondary importance, is to be found with respect to goods possessing a value, as well as with respect to objective goods for the person and goods which are merely subjectively satisfying. Health is an objective good for the person. Penicillin has an indirect or secondary importance as a means for restoring our health.[24] Because it is a means to an objective good for the person, it partakes of this importance and is thus a secondary objective good for the person. Penicillin is indeed a great objective good for humanity, but obviously an indirect one.

Hence we see that the value, the objective good for the person, and the merely subjectively satisfying represent three essentially different types of importance; whereas the difference between direct and indirect importance concerns exclusively the question of how the importance pertains to a being. It is therefore apparent that the one kind of division cuts across the other.

The distinction between the importance of the end and that of the means has often been made and stressed. But this difference does not lead to any new category of motivation which could be enumerated as a fourth type of importance. On the contrary, it goes in an utterly different direction, cutting across the three fundamental types of importance, as we have said above. Thus it would be a complete error to identify the value with the character of an end, that is to say with the character of being sought for its own sake, on the ground that both the value and the end can be called important in themselves. This term has, as we saw, a completely different meaning in each case.

[24] Plato refers to the nature of indirect importance in saying, "I know of many things which are disadvantageous to men, meats, and drinks, and drugs, and a thousand other things, and of things too which are advantageous. There are things also which to men are neither one nor the other." *Protagoras*, trans. J. Wright, in *Socratic Discourses* (New York: E. P. Dutton & Co., 1925), p. 263.

CHAPTER 4

THE USEFUL

ARISTOTLE, in his *Nicomachean Ethics,* distinguishes three different types of goods: the *bonum honestum,* the *bonum delectabile,* and the *bonum utile.* It may be asked: Is the useful really a new category of importance which should be added to the three above-mentioned categories? Or can it be identified with indirect importance? Without intending to offer here a complete presentation of the classical notion of "useful," a brief analysis of its nature and of its different possible meanings will enable us to answer this question.[1]

We have already seen that a means, since it serves a certain end, thereby shares that kind of importance which the end possesses. But as against this indirect importance, which varies according to the importance of the end, there is also that kind of perfection which a means as such has; that is, its capacity for actually serving an end, its *aptitude* for that end. The perfection in which this aptitude consists is not secondary, but primary to the means. The capacity for cutting is a direct property of the knife. Certainly it is essentially related to the end, and is therefore the presupposition for the fact that the knife shares the importance of the end. But as an aptitude for cutting, it belongs to the knife itself. But beyond the aptitude of the knife there is the importance of the end, which is the motive for which I use the knife. I want, for instance, to free a man gagged and bound; and in this connection the knife assumes a great importance because of the specific end at stake. It is evident that the indirect importance of the

[1] A more minute analysis of this rich and complex notion will be presented in another work to appear later.

64

knife—which in this case is a high value—is not identical with the aptitude of the knife for cutting.

But the question may arise: Is not this aptitude a new type of importance? In answer we must observe that being useful cannot be considered a new category of importance when seen from the viewpoint of the possible motivating power which things may assume. For we should never choose a means if we were not aiming at a particular end, and if that end did not actually motivate our action. Nor does aptitude, considered in itself, constitute an independent category of importance, since it does not give to a being a quality enabling it to motivate us, even though we may choose one thing rather than another as a means for an end (which actually motivates us) because of its greater aptitude for this end.

There exists among the means a scale, therefore, which concerns not only the rank of the end but especially this aptitude toward an end. In this sense we might say that penicillin is more efficacious than sulfa. Different means possess a greater or lesser aptitude with respect to one and the same specific end; and what we call progress consists chiefly in replacing one instrument with a more efficacious one. Many points of view enter into the establishment of such a scale of efficacy of means. Not only do greater certainty, precision, speed, and ease in attaining a given end impart to one means a greater aptitude than to another, but the circumstance of whether the end is served with or without an accompanying negative effect is also involved. A certain medicine, for example, despite its superiority in combatting a given disease, may rank lower than a less powerful one because of the disadvantage of possible side-effects. Finally, the facts that one means can be more easily procured than another, that there is a more plentiful supply of one than of another, may give to it a greater preferability over others which are no less efficacious and are equally free of risk.

Thus we see that there exists a scale concerning the aptitude of means which, within the frame of a given end, causes one means to possess a superiority over another. The term "useful" often refers simply to this aptitude. The greater the aptitude, the more useful do we declare something to be. And we may call something useless if it is lacking in aptitude for a certain end.

But this is not the only possible meaning of "useful." This is not yet the full datum to which we refer when predicating usefulness of something. We may call something more or less useful without referring to one and the same end. We can look at things from the point of view of their potential efficacy; that is to say, their potentiality of serving as means for a great variety of ends. Usefulness then means a potential fecundity [2] whereby no comparison of degrees of aptitude for one and the same end is implied. The fact that a thing in its capacity of serving as an efficacious means is not restricted to one definite end constitutes a perfection which grants to something a specific character of usefulness.

When we say that electricity is very useful or that water is one of the most useful things, we praise them because of their fecundity in potential aptitudes. We mean that they can be used as means for many ends and that they are efficacious and powerful in all these different respects. This ambivalence of their character as means is stressed when we speak of their usefulness as such, without referring to any one particular end. The use*less* as opposed to the use*ful* is here characterized by an inaptitude for serving any end whatsoever.

Perhaps the most striking example of usefulness in this general sense is to be found in money. Here not only does the character of a means overshadow any other viewpoint (for money is essentially nothing but a means), but there is also the striking fact of complete neutrality with respect to the end. We have here a means most useful because it leaves the greatest liberty with respect to the end for which it can be used.

But even this potential efficacy, power, and fecundity, this irradiating usefulness, does not yet exhaust the full meaning of the term "useful." Although we do not necessarily restrict ourselves to the consideration of one given end when we call something useful, we nevertheless refer in general to a specific *sphere* of ends. In its most authentic meaning the term "useful" refers to one particular type of what we have called the "objective

[2] In this sense Cardinal Newman characterizes usefulness: "Of possessions, those rather are useful which bear fruit; those liberal, which tend to enjoyment. By fruitful, I mean, which yield revenue; by enjoyable, where nothing accrues of consequence beyond the using." *The Idea of a University* (New York: Longmans, Green & Co., 1902), p. 109.

goods for the person." We may call these the *"elementary* goods for the person." They comprise the things indispensable to our life, as well as all those things which refer to our bodily and mental welfare and security insofar as we are individuals and members of society. Food, clothing, and shelter; health, freedom, peace, and order are such elementary goods. In this respect we oppose the useful to everything superfluous, to all that which is for mere amusement, luxury, pastime, and thereby claim for it a greater seriousness and a more valid significance. Usefulness in this sense seems to have been the starting point for Aristotle and St. Thomas in distinguishing the *bonum utile* from the *bonum honestum,* and both of these from the *bonum delectabile.* The useful in this sense must be considered as a subdivision of the indirect objective good for the person. Hence it is definitely not a new type of importance which could be added to the three mentioned above.

The concept of "indispensability" is not a univocal one. What can rightly be considered indispensable varies with the organization of society. In a civilization such as ours, for example, the means of transportation, automobiles, airplanes, etc., may assume something like the character of elementary goods. The same is true of an elevator in a many-storied building. Electric lights, paved roads, and the telephone can be considered as useful in the sense that they are integrated parts of a whole frame of life now prevalent and somehow *imposed* upon us under given historical conditions. Often these things may serve only to make life easier and more comfortable, but they also may assume the character of elementary goods upon which this meaning of usefulness is centered. Thus an elevator is not a luxury for the person who lives high up in a building or for the person who, because of illness or old age, is incapable of climbing stairs to his apartment. Thus, too, the telephone by which we call the doctor in an emergency has certainly the character of a means for an elementary good.

But, of course, what is considered indispensable may often arbitrarily be enlarged. A man of modest means may consider two suits of clothes indispensable, and a rich man, twenty. Then again, the question as to what is indispensable for somebody who has a special obligation or task demands a new and different viewpoint regarding the meaning of the term. All this demonstrates that the notion of usefulness, insofar as it is orientated around the indispensability of the ends for which something serves as a means, fluctuates and must be considered relative, since it is determined by circumstances and conditions.

This classical notion of usefulness deserves some consideration from still another perspective. We call all work useful not only in that it immediately serves for the production of elementary goods, for example, constructing a house or sewing clothes, but also in that it is a means of making money, which itself in turn is a means for the elementary goods, though it is not restricted to them. Making money is considered useful even in the case of a millionaire who certainly does not use the money primarily for elementary goods. The "neutral" character of money is here somehow shared by the work which is a means for making money. And this is so, independently of the kind of work which we do; i.e., independently of the question of whether or not the result of that work is itself useful. Though playing bridge is not useful but is rather a typical pastime, the production of bridge cards *is* useful because it is a way of making money.

Apart from the relation to money, however, there is still another reason for this paradox: that even though the end which is finally served is deemed typically superfluous, the means to procure that end or to facilitate it are looked upon as useful. There is here a sober reasonability which is connected with the teleological character of means as such. Smoking cigarettes is not to be considered an elementary or an indispensable good. But a cigarette lighter is nonetheless rightly called useful. The aptitude of the means is here considered in its immanent logic. The means fulfills the task when it achieves the end; this alone gives to an instrument the character of a certain "sobriety" and reasonability in contradistinction to ill-constructed things which do not perform their task well or even fail completely to do so in spite of the character of the end achieved. Thus the paradox that a means seems to have a dignity which the end itself does not possess. Even when the end is not specific enough to be endowed with one definite type of importance, the means partakes of a certain dignity inasmuch as it is then the prime object of our consideration and is looked upon as being fitted to serve whatever is serious and of valid significance. But this is not all: even when the end definitely possesses no serious character, e.g., in cases of mere amusement and pure luxury, the means still owns a dignity, for it is considered a trustworthy and efficient instrument.

In reverting to the basic meaning of usefulness, we see that it refers primarily to the capacity of things to serve as means for elementary objective goods for the person; it also includes the dignity which things acquire by the fact that they have a capacity to fulfill some teleological function. Its antithesis concerns all those things which lack such a capacity to serve efficaciously the elementary goods for the person. Useful things are thus opposed to both the useless and the merely agreeable. Furthermore, although they are not opposed to the high objective goods for the person and to the values, they are sharply distinguished from them.

In this latter sense physics, chemistry, and medicine are useful sciences; philosophy is not a useful science. Technique is useful; art is not. Civilization is useful; "culture" is not. To learn a language is useful; to hear great music is not. Even a monastery which has a school or a hospital would be considered useful; but a contemplative order or the liturgical praise of God would not. So long as we adhere to this distinction as a mere classification, without relating it to any appreciation of the characteristics of useful and useless, there is nothing objectionable in this procedure and nomenclature.

But all too often a disastrous perversion sets in at this point. For the utilitarian mentality the *bonum utile* becomes the one exclusive measure of judging things. What is not useful is declared useless, with no right to existence. It is considered a waste of time, something futile and utterly lacking in seriousness. Goods endowed with a high value, such as the liturgical praise of God, all bonds of love with other persons, all beauty, the whole sphere of art, philosophy, in short, all the things which are not practically indispensable, are classed together with the superfluous and marked as useless. The whole sphere of the genuine *frui*—the enjoyment of high goods endowed with values which bestow a true and noble happiness on us—is put in one category together with luxuries and those things which are considered a waste of time. By force of a wrong exclusive alternative the sphere of the elementary goods (enlarged more or less arbitrarily) and all that serves their attainment are considered serious, dignified, and worthwhile; while everything else is considered worthless and futile, or merely romantic. A gray and neutral reasonability is exalted; a pedestrian attitude prevails wherein the sublimity of values fades and the fruition of great and noble goods is silently ignored.

But there is also an analogical sense of "useful" which is quite genuine and meaningful. Here the useful is opposed in a general way to all things void and futile. The term embraces all things which are worthwhile in themselves, the objective goods for the person as well as the values. On the one side are gossip, spiritual laziness, meaningless chatter, running from one social affair to another, daydreaming, frivolity, etc.; and on the other, the noble, serious, meaningful, and necessary—whether or not things have this character because of their value or because of their indispensability. This is the sense in which we should "redeem" the time with "useful things" and not with vain things. In this Scriptural sense usefulness is opposed to vanity and is obviously no longer the indication of a specific sphere of goods or of a specific type of secondary importance which could be distinguished, as in Aristotelian and Thomistic philosophies, from the *delectabile* and *honestum*. It is completely analogous since it is neither restricted to means nor does it have anything in common with the first notion of *utile,* other than being the antithesis to time-wasting and futility.

In the light of the Gospel or of the supernatural destiny of man there is another notion of "useful" according to which the *bonum utile* is more or less useless. It is the meaning of useful implied in the words of St. Aloysius: *Quid hoc ad aeternitatem?* —"What does it mean for eternity?"—or in the words of our Lord: "What doth it profit a man, if he gain the whole world, but suffer the loss of his own soul?"

The useful in the sense of the *unum necessarium,* "the one thing which is necessary," is time and again opposed in the Gospel to the *bonum utile,* for instance, in the words:—"Be not solicitous therefore, saying, What shall we eat: or what shall we drink, or wherewith shall we be clothed?" (Matt. 6:31).

The antithesis of the *unum necessarium* to the *bonum utile* above all discloses itself in the words of Christ spoken to Martha as she accused Mary of neglecting the useful (in the sense of *bonum utile*): "Martha, Martha, thou art careful, and art troubled about many things: But one thing is necessary. Mary hath chosen the best part, which shall not be taken away from her" (Luke 10:41–42).

CHAPTER 5

THE PRIMACY OF VALUE

BEFORE WE turn to an analysis of the kinds of importance which beings possess independently of the possible points of view of motivation, we must first pose the even more decisive question: What kind of importance is the objectively valid one, the true one, the one which has the final word? When asking this question we deal with a topic clearly distinct from the inquiry into the various points of view of importance.

Once we grasp the meaning of importance we become aware that this ultimate question exists independently of our motivation. In approaching a being the question of its importance presents itself not merely from the point of view of any possible motivation. The question of importance has as much an original and objective meaning as the question of truth and existence. It is clearly absurd to suppose that the question of being and existence presents itself only for our knowledge and from the point of view of satisfying our knowledge. The same applies to the question of importance. The contrast between the gray, insipid emptiness of the indifferent and the colorful, meaningful plenitude of the important discloses to us the ultimate import of this question. We could not sustain for one moment the fiction of an absolutely neutral and indifferent world. Importance is as *fundamental as being.* The supposition that there exists no importance, that everything is in reality neutral, that all importance is a mere relational aspect, would mean a complete collapse of the universe. We realize the fundamental—I would even say, *inevitable*—significance of the question: What is the meaning, the importance, of a being?

72

These are ultimate questions rooted in our very existence: *existential* in the truest sense of the term, but transcending the realm of our own being in referring to something which has its inner necessity independently of ourselves, and which touches the ultimate metaphysical stratum. Such is the question of the meaning and importance of a single being, but above all of the entire universe. If we know only that something *is,* or exists, we have not yet reached the full answer which objectively imposes itself and for which our mind essentially thirsts. The existence of something necessarily calls forth the question of its meaning, its importance. The metaphysical dissatisfaction which we experience, as long as we have no answer to this ultimate question concerning the universe, is a prelude in the realm of nature to the "unrest" which, according to St. Augustine, fills our heart until we find God.

Even in the concept of *raison d'être* the notion of importance is ultimately included. For with respect to any final cause which indicates the *raison d'être* of its means, the same question would arise, and only the importance of the object could give a satisfactory answer. Moreover, for many beings the question of their *raison d'être* leads in no way in the direction of a final cause. We must realize that this question of importance is constantly present for us: indeed, it is so self-evident that it often fails to become an object of our philosophical wonder.

But once we become fully aware of this question and its meaning, we grasp that this importance is synonymous with the important-in-itself, with the value. Any other importance could never give the ultimate answer. In stating that something is subjectively satisfying, or even that something is an objective good for the person, the basic question of its ultimate importance remains unanswered.

The real fulfillment of meaning and importance can only be given in terms of importance in itself. As the ultimate fulfillment of our quest for truth can only be offered by the autonomy of being (i.e., its precedence over consciousness and its independence from our mind), so equally, the inevitable metaphysical question of importance can only be answered by the autonomously important, the important-in-itself, the value.

There are problems in philosophy concerning which it suffices only to *pose* the question in order immediately to grasp the answer. In these cases then the main philosophical achievement is to pose the question, which is so easily overlooked, precisely because the answer is so obvious. Such is the question: Which is the true, valid importance? *It cannot but be the value.*

CHAPTER 6

THE ROLE OF VALUE IN MAN'S LIFE

THE DATUM of value is presupposed everywhere. There is no need to stress how many predications imply the notion of value. Whether we praise a man as just, or as reliable; whether we want to persuade someone that science is important; whether in reading a poem, we find it beautiful; whether we praise a symphony as powerful and sublime; whether we rejoice about the blossoming trees in spring; whether we are moved by the generosity of another person; whether we strive for freedom; whether our conscience forbids us to profit by injuring another—there is always presupposed the notion of something important-in-itself. So soon as we try to abstract from the importance and view everything as completely neutral and merely factual, all these predications, all these responses, lose their meaning. As a matter of fact they become impossible. Whenever we deliberate an action from the moral point of view we presuppose the datum of value, of something important-in-itself. In all indignation at something mean and debased; in every exclamation that some event is a great misfortune; in all assertions that one philosopher ranks higher than another, that one painter is a greater genius than another, we always presuppose the datum of value.

If we try to imagine a world which is completely neutral—an essentially impossible fiction—we realize that everything would lose all significance: our life would be reduced to an absurd and vicious circle; it would even sink below the level of animal life. Even in a world where there existed no importance other than the subjectively satisfying, our life would collapse. Imprisoned in our self-centeredness without the "Archimedean point" of objective importance, true happiness as well as all self-donation would be banished: all love, all enthusiasm, and all admiration. It would be impossible even to say that wisdom was preferable to folly. There would be no objective reason for us to turn in one direction instead of another, save that we were impelled either by our instincts or our desires for the subjectively satisfying, or because the neutral laws of nature forced us to conform to them.[1]

In stressing these facts we in no way introduce value as a *postulate*. So to interpret it would be completely to misunderstand our meaning: we *have* to suppose the notion of value to make our life bearable or meaningful. Our aim consists exclusively in drawing the consequences of a denial of the notion of value and in showing to what extent it is constantly presupposed. We wish to give the reader the opportunity for a *prise de conscience* of that of which in a deeper stratum he is always aware, to which he constantly refers, and on which he continuously counts *because* he is implicitly aware of it. Our aim at present is to remind everyone of what he possesses in a deeper stratum, to draw him to this deeper stratum in which the datum of value is grasped and which even constitutes the pivotal point of existence and life.

We want only to aid the reader to realize that, despite the screen which philosophical theories and explanations have placed between his immediate contact with being and his philosophical awareness, value is not something peculiar; that it is not some strange thing introduced by a new philosophical theory; on the contrary, that it is something of which he is constantly aware. We want to make him realize that value is so self-evident that in every moment we presuppose it. Once we free ourselves from all falsifying interpretations and theories, we see the reality of value in such overwhelming clarity that we can no longer understand

[1] Even the fiction of a world in which the only objective measure would be the objective good for the person would leave man imprisoned in himself. If the only motive—besides the merely subjectively satisfying—would be that which is objectively to his best advantage, he would be cut off from all true self-donation, from all transcendence. But this fiction is itself impossible because the objective good for the person, as we have already seen and shall see later on in more detail, necessarily presupposes the datum of value.

how, even theoretically, it was possible for us to overlook it or
fail fully to admit it.

In every page of the liturgy there lives the awareness of value.
The continual praise in the liturgy would lose all meaning were
we to deny the existence of value. What would be the meaning
of the term *gloria* in the passage: *Gratias agimus tibi propter
magnam gloriam tuam*—"We give thanks to Thee for Thy great
glory"—if no other importance exists than the subjectively satisfying? To try to relate this passage to an objective good for the
person would obviously be wrong, since it is its very characteristic—unlike many others, such as *fortitudo mea* (my strength)
or *"spes mea"* (my hope)—that it be focused on God's own infinite goodness and beauty. But apart from this we must realize
that in introducing the notion of a high-ranking objective good
for the person, we already necessarily presuppose the notion of
value. The infinite intrinsic goodness of God is necessarily implied whenever in the liturgy God is addressed as the Absolute
Good for us. He is our Hope, our Peace, our Joy *because* He is
Absolute Goodness and Sanctity.

The hierarchical principle which is so clearly expressed in the
Confiteor and in many other places, or which is manifested in
the ranking of the feasts, refers unmistakably to value or the
important-in-itself. It is both certain and obvious that this hierarchy would collapse as soon as we were confronted with either
a world of complete neutrality or a world in which the Aristippian outlook would be true. Any attempt to interpret this hierarchy as referring to objective goods for the person is completely
impossible, and we have just mentioned the basic futility of sub-
stituting in place of the value the objective good for the person.
For this necessarily presupposes the value. The rank of a saint
is not orientated around an objective importance for us but
rather around his importance in the eyes of God.

The inner rhythm of glorification which finds its expression
in the conclusion of every psalm, *Gloria Patri et Filio et Spiritui
Sancto*, obviously refers to God's infinite intrinsic Goodness,
Beauty, and Glory. It finds its innermost meaning as a response
to the Being of God and all His sublime perfections. The very
fact that we should praise God implies the notion of value; that

is to say, in the *dignum et justum est* of the Preface—*dignum* and *justum* either refer to values or these words have no meaning whatsoever.

Plainly enough, the implicit presence in the liturgy of the notion of value is to be found in every religion. The very nature of *religio*, of a bond toward God, implies the notion of the important-in-itself. However primitive one's notion of God may be, it always implies the notion of value. The notion of total physical dependence upon an all-powerful being would not yet *directly* refer to value. But every consciousness of being morally bound to God, of owing obedience to Him, of owing reverence to Him, clearly presupposes the notion of value in the very notion of God and in our conduct toward Him.

What in a vague way is to be found in every religion shines forth in univocal clarity in Christian Revelation. If only we think of the two main commandments of Christ, the love of God and the love of neighbor, we cannot but see that such love presupposes the datum of value in the infinite goodness and beauty of God to which the love responds. What is more, the intrinsic goodness of this love is again a reference to value.

There can be nothing more radically opposed than is the Christian Revelation to a neutralism which admits only indifferent beings deprived of all values and stripped of anything important-in-itself. The *Deus caritas est*, as well as the very notion of beatitude, are the precise antitheses to the absence of values. The revelation of God's infinite sanctity in Christ; the notion of sanctification to which we ourselves are called; the continuous exhortation to thank and to rejoice, to praise and to love, all this clearly reveals that the plenitude of values is the true reality. We are taught and we understand that the intrinsic movement of the value with its splendor and *oughtness*, in opposition to any mere neutral being and its immanent logic, is in truth the heart and soul of being. Not the mere neutral factuality, the mere indispensability and necessity flowing out of the inner logic of being, but the intrinsic fire of the value, the everlasting glory and splendor: this is the final word.

II. The Reality of Value against Its Detractors

CHAPTER 7

THE CATEGORIES OF IMPORTANCE
AS PROPERTIES OF BEINGS

HAVING ANALYZED the categories of importance in the field of motivation, we must now ask which of them are properties of being and of beings, independently of their function as objects of motivation. Can we classify beings by saying that, independently of a possible motivation, some are subjectively satisfying; some, objective goods for the person; some, endowed with a value? Are these three categories of importance (or at least one of them) properties of a being, as is extension or weight in the case of corporeal beings?

We are not here concerned with the question of whether an importance refers to a person, or has already its full meaning without reference to a person. Our problem rather refers to the question of whether these three kinds of importance are properties of beings or whether they are only points of view of motivation which lose their meaning, therefore, as soon as we abstract from the sphere of motivation. And so we may ask whether or not there are objects of which we can say that they have one or another kind of importance as a characteristic, in the way we can say that corporeal beings have extension or that joy extends in time.

But we have to go a step farther. In posing the question of whether or not these three categories of importance can be found in beings as their properties, we simultaneously include the question as to which importance the beings possess according to their God-given meaning. In distinguishing the points of view of importance under which we can approach a being from the importance which the being possesses independently of our approach, we mean to ask which is the valid title of that being. The problem here is not just a question *de facto,* but a question *de jure.* As far as value is concerned, such a distinction is superfluous. It is indispensable, however, with respect to the merely subjectively satisfying.

If value is an objective property of a being, it is *a fortiori* the valid title of this being. This should be clear after our previous analysis of the nature of value. In the case of the subjectively satisfying, however, the question of whether or not there are objects which possess the potentiality of bestowing pleasure on us as a property of their own, clearly differs from the question of whether their agreeability is part of their God-given meaning, i.e., what we might call their valid, objective title.

The exact formulation of our question should run as follows: What corresponds in beings as their objective, valid meaning to the three categories of importance which we distinguished in the realm of motivation; namely, the merely subjectively satisfying, the objective good for the person, and the value? We shall first analyze this problem with respect to the subjectively satisfying, then with respect to the objective good for the person, and finally with respect to the value.

If we look at those things of which we predicate the quality of agreeability (for instance, a warm bath or a cool, soft breeze during great heat), we easily see that the qualitative content of the agreeable is rooted in the pleasure which these things cause in our body. Nevertheless the term agreeable as such also implies a characteristic of an object. Although the source of this type of importance is the pleasure which we experience through certain goods, yet this capacity of bestowing pleasure on us is without doubt a real quality of these beings. It is *this* quality which we term "agreeable."

It is a true characteristic of certain things to be agreeable and of others to be disagreeable, a characteristic which of course loses every meaning if we abstract from any being which is able to experience pleasure. But the character of agreeability is not the entire objective reality so far as the importance of things is concerned. Let us recall that our love tends naturally to bestow agreeable things on the beloved, and to avert what is disagreeable from him. It belongs to the display of the *intentio benevolentiae* in every love for a creature that we also want to offer to him a good meal, to make everything comfortable for him, and to protect him from disagreeable things. This clearly shows that legitimately agreeable beings have the character of something beneficent, of a gift for the person. They are objective goods *because* of their being agreeable, and the "pro" embodied in the agreeable is here the basis of their character of an objective good for the person. Although it occupies the lowest rung in the hierarchy of the objective good for the person, this type nonetheless possesses the dignity that belongs to all members of that hierarchy. We should indeed thank God that there exist agreeable things, such as the fresh breeze or the restorative swim on a very hot day, the warmth in a room when it is very cold, an excellent wine, a delicious meal, a bed or a chair if one is tired. These things have, as such, the character of objective goods for the person.

But rarely is this importance of agreeable things seen when they are the object of our *own* desire. We are normally tempted to approach them from the point of view of the merely subjectively satisfying. In this case, the importance which an object has independently of our approach does not coincide with the importance usually motivating this approach.

Abstracting from their possible role in our motivation—though obviously including their relation to man's susceptibility—we can state that there exist agreeable and disagreeable things. Their being agreeable certainly implies that they are subjectively satisfying, but it is also the root of their being an objective good for the person, granted that the things are agreeable with respect to a legitimate center. Insofar as we look at their objective significance, which we see much more clearly when the agreeable good for another person is at stake, their real importance lies in their status as objective goods for the person. Strictly speaking then, there exist no things which in themselves are only subjectively satisfying. So soon as there are at stake things which have the character of agreeability (and we imply hereby that they are so with respect to a legitimate center), they are as such objective goods for the person, even if for higher reasons the person should abstain from them in a concrete situation. Insofar as the significance of a being as such and not the point of view under which we approach it is our concern, every legitimately agreeable being is not only subjectively satisfying, but also an objective good for the person. And this is its valid, objective character. Although to approach the merely agreeable things from the point of view of the merely subjectively satisfying is not a distortion, it is at least an incomplete vision of them. Their being agreeable obviously implies their subjectively satisfying character. But we remain on the first level of appreciation if we do not also grasp their valid, objective type of importance.

We must clearly distinguish the point of view of the merely subjectively satisfying as such from the objective quality of the agreeable. This point of view makes our subjective satisfaction, whether legitimate or not, the only measure of our motivation so that when confronted with each and every good we ask but one question: What possible satisfaction for our pride and concupiscence may we get out of it? Now this can never coincide with the importance which a being as such possesses. If we ask what objectively is a being's importance, what kind of importance does it possess, what is its objective, valid title in this respect, we would find there is no being which would be merely subjectively satisfying.

Thus we find here a split between a category of importance which plays a great role in our motivation and the importance with which the object is endowed in its God-given meaning. Plainly enough, the misfortune of a neighbor which is a source of subjective satisfaction to the envious person is objectively and in itself an evil. Here the point of view is in radical contradiction to the objective character involved: a manifest evil is a source of satisfaction; it is considered as something positive. In other cases, there may not be such a radical contradiction but still a thorough distortion. A position of powerful influence granted to a man and implying great responsibility is as such an objective good for him. But the man who relishes his position because of his ambition and pride and who strives for it because of his lust for power, approaches it as something exclusively subjectively satisfying. With respect to any good possessing a value, the approach from the point of view of the merely subjectively satisfying necessarily implies at least a distortion which can assume very different degrees.

As soon as the *merely* subjectively satisfying becomes a general point of view of our approach to life and being, it is in manifest contrast to the innocent subjectively satisfying character which is immanent in the agreeable. The merely subjectively satisfying as a general point of view of our motivation is an egocentric outgrowth of pride and concupiscence; it implies a blindness to the important-in-itself and to the objective good for the person, a blindness to the significance which beings objectively possess. In a word, it implies a falsification of the universe.

There is, however, a naïve motivation by the subjectively satisfying which must be distinguished from the general approach toward life and being under the exclusive or predominant viewpoint of the merely subjectively satisfying. The naïve approach, for instance, of Sancho Panza, is an incomplete but not a distorted approach toward agreeable things. Confronted by a good which is merely agreeable, we rightly grasp that it imposes no obligation on us to take an interest in it, to respond to it. The response which we give is up to us and our subjective inclination, granted that no disvalue connected with its possession forbids a positive interest in it. Far from calling for a conforming to it, the agreeable is objectively a mere offer; it conforms, as it were, to our mood.

But notwithstanding the fact that the agreeable imposes no obligation on us to conform to it, a response to the "gift" character of the existence of agreeable things as such should be given. We should also recognize the bounty of God manifesting itself in the very existence of agreeable things. This does not at all imply that we must strive for them or even accept them in concrete situations. On the contrary, we may refrain from pursuing them because of the danger which they may imply for our concupiscence and pride. Again, this appreciation of agreeable things, insofar as they are objective goods for the person, does not do away with the fact that we are never obliged to enjoy a certain thing when instead we wish to abstain from its fruition. But the right vision of these goods nevertheless ordains that we understand them as such to be a specific type of objective good for the person; and indeed we always do this whenever in a loving attitude we are confronted with agreeable goods for *another* person.

Our present analysis of the subjectively satisfying has already revealed that the character of an objective good for the person is not only a category of our motivation, but also an objective characteristic of a being. There is no split here between the importance which is an objective property of a being, and the importance which is a point of view of our motivation, such as there is with respect to the merely subjectively satisfying. Certainly in predicating of health, for instance, that it is an objective good for the person, we refer to an importance which essentially implies a relation to the person. But independently of the possible motivation, the "pro" or the friendly character of this good toward the person, we understand that it is a gift in agreement with man's true interest, and that its significance is rooted in the nature of health and likewise in the nature of a human person. Again, in predicating of the fruition of beauty that it has the character of an objective good, we clearly grasp that this character is objectively rooted in the value of beauty and in the noble happiness which it is superabundantly able to bestow on man.

We have to state, however, that different instances must be distinguished and that one and the same thing may be at once an objective evil for the person in a first instance, and an objective good in a second higher instance, or vice versa. An operation or a painful cure are in the first instance objective evils, but insofar as they restore health or perhaps even save life, they are objective goods for the person. An injustice inflicted on us is as such an objective evil for the person, but it may be an objective good for our spiritual life.

With respect to this type of importance there exist, so to speak, different levels, one of which is superior to another. But this hierarchy of levels refers not only to different strata in man, but also to causal consequences. Thus it may happen that a former objective evil has the character of being a causal precondition for an objective good which by far surpasses in its rank the good which we lost before.

This dimension of the objective good for the person is not accessible to philosophical analysis; for we touch here the signifi cance which events have in the light of Providence which is, as it were, the final word on them; and this only the entirety of a life can reveal. Even then, however, we could give little more than a vague interpretation since we should be ignorant of the most important and decisive part of human existence: the judgment of God on man's eternal life.

Two dimensions concerning these different levels must therefore be distinguished: In the first, a thing which as such has the character of an objective evil for a man, e.g., an illness, may in a given situation be an objective good for him; it may awaken him from his indifference and turn his mind to eternity. Or any great trial, undoubtedly in itself an objective evil, may be the instrument for purification and for moral and religious progress, and thus a presupposition for a high objective good for the person. As a matter of fact, in many ascetic practices one chooses as a wholesome means something which in itself would be an objective evil; to inflict this on another person without any pedagogical or other necessity would be against charity and perhaps even justice.

This change of sign, this turning into an objective good something which in itself is an objective evil for the person, is here conditioned by the different strata in man. A thing which as such is an objective evil for the person, inasmuch as it is disagreeable (or as we can say, an objective evil of the sphere wherein the lowest type of goods for the person is to be found), happens to be connected with an objective good for the person which is situated in a higher sphere of objective good. Thus the same thing may be an objective evil with reference to a lower stratum, but an objective good with respect to a higher one. A surgical operation is an evil because of the bodily ordeal which it entails, but it becomes an objective good when it saves a human life.

The final word here rests always with the higher ranking stratum. Nevertheless, such things have in the first instance really the character of an evil. This character is a mere appearance as in the case of a simple error. Taken in itself and isolated from any other context, it has as such the character of an objective evil, but it assumes the character of a benefit and objective good as soon as it is related to other higher ranking objective goods in such a way that it is instrumental for the possession of these higher goods. Therefore, in this concrete case, the valid significance of that which in the first instance appears as an evil is determined by its relation to the higher ranking stratum in the person.

The changing of sign, the turning of something evil for the person into something good for him, has a second dimension. Here more is involved than merely the differing strata in man to which the evil and the good respectively refer, namely, the course of events and their extension in time. A thing which is definitely an objective evil as such (for instance, being forced to flee a country, to give up great material goods, or to relinquish the presence of beloved persons, a beautiful house, and so on) may prove years later to have been the way to an even greater and higher ranking good: for example, it may provide the circumstances which prepare the way for a conversion.

In the sphere of the objective good for the person we are also confronted with the fact that one and the same event may be a good for one person and a misfortune to another. The outcome of a war which is victory for one side is defeat for the other. We could name innumerable examples of great events and also of trifles possessing objectively a different significance for different persons.

This fact may impose many difficult problems on man. It is one of the great ethical dilemmas which result from the divergent legitimate aspirations of different persons and the opposite significances which one and the same event possesses objectively for them. But it can only enter into our ethical consideration if an objective value turns the scale for one or another decision, provided, of course, that the divergence of aspirations and difference of events can be ascertained. Yet the intermingling of all things which are at once objective goods for one person and objective evils for another may definitely surpass the frame of human prevision; especially with respect to the significance which they may assume in the light of unpredictable future circumstances. This intermingling belongs to those things which must be left to Providence and to Providence alone.

This may suffice to explain the discrepancy between the aspects which one and the same thing may offer concerning the type of importance which we termed the objective good for the person. We can easily see that a possible and quite frequent discrepancy in no way contradicts the fact that this kind of importance really inheres in the object, although, to be sure, it implies reference to a human person.

The central problem, however, is the question whether the values are real properties of beings, properties which we can find in beings even after we have abstracted from any possible motivation. In saying of an act of contrition that it is morally good, or in praising a man as intelligent or as a genius, or in speaking of the dignity of a human person, we undoubtedly refer to excellences which are properties of the respective beings; we do not refer merely to points of view of possible motivation. The moral nobility of an act of contrition, its importance in itself, is, if we contemplate the nature of such an act, univocally given to us. In order to perceive the intrinsic goodness and moral beauty of contrition we need not approach it from a certain point of view; it suffices merely that our mind be unhampered by pride and concupiscence, that the eyes of our mind be not blinded by a perversion of our will.

And when we grasp this intrinsic goodness, this moral value, as actually inhering in contrition, it is not merely an apprehension similar to that which allows us to state that blood is red. Rather we understand and grasp that there exists an essential link between the value and the object. It is not only another and deeper relation than the one which exists between substance and accident, the typical inherent relation, but it is moreover a necessary intelligible link, not a mere factual and accidental one. We understand that contrition is morally good and that it must be so.

This does not, however, mean that we could prove the value of contrition by deducing its importance from something else. We saw before that the importance in itself can never be deduced from something neutral. Every value has to be grasped; if a person is blind to a value, all we can do to help him grasp it is to pave the way by removing the obstacles of his will and by trying to draw him under its spell.

But if it is true that the value of contrition cannot be deduced from the neutral sphere, from neutral laws, or from the immanent logic of a neutrally conceived being, it is also a fact that once we have grasped the value we understand that it is essentially rooted in the nature of contrition. The essential link between moral goodness and contrition is nonetheless univocally given.

In other words, the relation between a being and its value, insofar as a direct importance in itself is concerned, is not empirical and contingent but is rather necessary and intelligible. In contemplating charity, we grasp at once that it is necessarily good; we do not just bluntly state it, but we understand that it is so and must always be so. It is plainly nonsensical to say of acts of charity or justice that in speaking of their value we only refer to such a point of view of motivation; for evidently the value discloses itself as a property of these acts. In order to grasp that the moral goodness of justice, the beauty of a star-covered sky, the value of a human person, or his dignity as an *imago Dei* are in the fullest sense properties of these beings, we have only to compare the character of being endowed with an intrinsic value with the mere character of being commanded by a true authority.

In the case where the moral significance of an object results exclusively from the commandment of a true authority, the importance is obviously superimposed on the object. It is an importance which is located in the object, but is not rooted in its essence.

Someone may object: The value is only an ideal, rooted in the essence of something but not a property of a real concrete individual act. This objection is based on an error. If extension essentially belongs to the nature of matter, it is obvious that wherever a concrete corporeal being is to be found, extension will also be found as a concrete real property of it. All those elements, marks and properties which are essentially rooted in the nature of some quiddity become real, concrete, and individual as soon as an object possessing this quiddity becomes real. Thus the question of whether the value is also to be found in a concrete individual act of a certain kind is as such already futile. If the value is necessarily rooted in the nature of an act, it must become real as soon as the act is actually accomplished.

But even apart from this, it is mostly in the awareness of a person's concrete real attitude that we perceive certain values for the first time. It is not only in abstract contemplation of the quiddity of certain acts or attitudes that we discover their value, but also and especially we discover the value in concrete real acts. The real concrete existence of a being endowed with a value is, however, in no way an essential condition for discovering its value; the moral value of a heroic deed may be grasped just as well in the action of the hero of a novel.

We see then that the important-in-itself or the value is objective in every sense of the word. It is objective insofar as it is a real property of the being of which we predicate a value; beings are endowed with values even if we abstract from any possible motivation. Values are so much proper to beings that they form the core of their significance. Values can in no way be interpreted as mere relational aspects of being which it possesses with respect to our desire or will.

Values clearly reveal themselves as belonging to a being independently of any desire or will; for even when we look at them in pure contemplation, they continue to resplend in their intrinsic beauty and importance, in their *axiological* character, in the *oughtness* which surrounds their actual being. But, as we saw before, the goodness of justice, the preciousness of an immortal soul, and the value of intelligence are objective also in the sense that their importance does not imply any relation to the person: they are important in themselves, in contradistinction to the objective good for the person.

Many relations exist between the value and the objective good for the person, that is, between the only two kinds of importance which are properties of being independent of the viewpoint under which we approach them. We have already seen that the Socratic statement: "It is better for man to suffer injustice than to commit injustice" stresses that moral goodness is the greatest among the objective goods for the person. We also saw that in order to understand that moral goodness is such a great objective good for the person one must already have grasped the value of moral goodness. Because moral goodness *is* a value, to be endowed with it is an objective good for the person. Obviously the value is here the *principium*, while its character as an objective good is the *principiatum*.

The same applies analogously to being intelligent, gifted, or whatever the value may be with which a human person is endowed. These are all objective goods for the person, and in each case the value is the *principium* while their importance as an objective good is the *principiatum;* that is to say, because they are values, to be endowed with them is an objective good for the person.

The value is also presupposed in another fundamental type of objective good for the person. It is the objective good which consists in the possession and enjoyment of goods, which bestows true happiness on us; for instance, knowledge of truth, contemplation of beauty in nature and art, friendship, acquaintance with an extraordinary personality, and so on. They all imply that the good in question possesses a value, and that the value itself superabundantly bestows happiness on us. Again, the value is the *principium* and the character of an objective good, the *principiatum.* Because of their value these goods are able to bestow true happiness on us *when* they are possessed: because of their value, their possession is a bliss, a gift, for the person. Evidently this applies above all to the absolute good for man. The eternal communion with God is the absolute good for man solely because God is Infinite Goodness.

In both types of high-ranking objective goods the relation between the two types of importance consists in the fact that the character of an objective good is rooted in the value of the object. Notwithstanding the differences, in both cases a being has to be endowed with a value in order to be able to become an objective good for the person. Yet the element which enables a being to become an objective good for the person is not always the value which it possesses. The elementary goods for the person and the legitimately agreeable things do not draw from a value their character of objective goods for the person. We are not here questioning which value the beings which are elementary objective goods or pleasurable objective goods may as such possess, but only whether their character as objective goods is rooted in a value, as is the case in the above-mentioned high-ranking types of objective goods.

Let us first turn to the elementary goods, such as the integrity of man's body, his health, or the minimum of means for his life, a roof over his head, an indispensable amount of heat, and so on. These certainly have an indirect value either as a means of, or as a presupposition for, a part of man's existence which itself is obviously endowed with a high value. But as these are objective goods for the person not on account of this indirect value but on account of their elementary indispensability, we may disregard here this indirect value. What matters for our problem is that their being an objective good for the person is not rooted in this indirect value or in any other value which these beings may possess. Though their indispensability is the source of their indirect value as of their being an objective good for the person, their being an objective good for the person is not rooted in this indirect value.

The same applies to the lowest type of objective goods for the person: the legitimately agreeable and subjectively satisfying. Whatever value pleasurable things may as such possess, their character as an objective good is not necessarily rooted in this value. They are objective goods because of their being legitimately agreeable, and also because of the objectively beneficent gesture embodied in this quality of being agreeable. Thus we see that the relation between the two kinds of importance, by which the value is the basis for the objective good for the person, is absent in the case of the elementary and the pleasurable goods.

But there exists still a completely different relation between the two types of importance to be found in *every* objective good for the person. Every objective good for the person is not indifferent from the point of view of value. It has a positive value because of its "pro" character for the person. The value which is proper to the human person determines that every being having this friendly character of a gift for the human person thereby acquires an indirect value.[1] What is striking here is that the relation between the two types of importance seems to be reversed. The being an objective good is not rooted in the value which this good as such possesses. But it has an indirect value because it is an objective good for the person. The being an objective

---

[1] In calling this value indirect, we do not mean to say that it is of the same type of secondary importance which is to be found in means as opposed to the primary importance of the end. The relation of dependence between the value which an objective good acquires and the value of the person definitely differs from the one between the indirect value of the means and the direct value of its end.

good is the source of this value; and thus it seems that here the value is the *principiatum* and the being an objective good for the person, the *principium*.

But we say "it seems" because this inversion applies only to the relation between the indirect value of the objective good and its character as an objective good for the person. The ultimate source of this value is obviously the value of the human person.[2] Here also, it is a value which is the ultimate basis of this indirect importance.

But above all, every objective good in its very character as objective good for the person implies the datum of value, insofar as it is a fruit and an embodiment of God's bounty. We saw that the gift character belongs to the essence of this kind of importance. The objective beneficence and congruence with the true interest of the human person is necessarily linked to its character as gift. This gift character already includes the manifestation of the donor's bounty, the objectivated gesture of love which is the very soul of the objective good for the person.[3] We saw before that only in seeing the legitimately agreeable in its character as a gift of God, as a manifestation of His infinite bounty and love, are we able to approach this pleasurable good as an objective good for the person.

Yet the value of God's infinite bounty is not only reflected in its being an objective good, but because it is a manifestation of God's love every objective good for the person is endowed with a value. This does not, however, mean that the notion of an objective good for the person implies the notion of God. A pantheist may look at this gift as being bestowed on us by "Mother Nature." Another may interpret it vaguely as being bestowed on him by some unknown impersonal divinity. Even an atheist can clearly understand that health is an objective good for man. This friendly character can be grasped without any reference to God,

---

[2] It must, however, be stressed that so far as the pleasurable objective goods for the person are concerned, this indirect value is visible to us only insofar as other persons are concerned. Here then is another point of difference between the merely agreeable things and the elementary goods for the person; for the indirect value of the latter can be grasped when we ourselves are concerned. We can, for instance, grasp the duty not to injure our health without a serious reason.

[3] Certainly the way in which this value is presupposed differs from the way in which the value of the human person is presupposed.

with respect to all objective goods so long as other persons are concerned; but, as already mentioned, this is not the case with respect to the pleasurable goods insofar as our own person is concerned.

But if we analyze here the objective goods for the person with respect to their value, we must consider their full meaning apart from the question of whether the notion of objective good implies or presupposes the notion of God. Even if the latter question must be definitely answered in the negative, it remains true that objectively their immanent beneficence is a manifestation of God's bounty, and that this thereby endows them with a value.

Thus we see that even from the point of view of value, no objective good for the person is indifferent. It definitely has a positive value. This extends even to the fact that a person enjoys or is in possession of an objective good. It is important in itself that a person receives an objective good. An objective good bestowed on a person has a value simply because of the value of the human person itself. That a man is happy instead of unhappy obviously possesses as such a positive value. The bearer of the value here is, as one clearly sees, not a thing or quality or activity but a fact; or better, a state of facts. The something which we express in a proposition in saying that a man is happy is important in itself; it has a value.[4]

Although the gradation concerning this value is a very great one, assuming a different character so long as the high-ranking types of objective goods or the elementary goods are in question, nevertheless even the fact of someone coming into possession of so modest a good as the legitimately agreeable is not indifferent from the point of view of value.

The priority of the value with respect to the objective good for the person manifests itself anew in this, our analysis. The

---

[4] This state of facts has been happily termed in German, *Sachverhalt*. It is the immediate object of a proposition; that is to say, the entity in the sphere of being with which the proposition, if it is to be true, has to be in conformity. The state of facts is the object of several acts; for instance, conviction or affirmation. We cannot affirm a table or a person, but only "that something is such" or exists. We are convinced that 2 and 2 are equal to 4, or that the night will follow this day. Equally a state of facts is the object when we rejoice about the coming of our friend, or about the restoration of peace. It is impossible in this context to insist on the nature of state of facts. We may refer to the notion of *Sachverhalte* in Adolf Reinach. Cf. *Der Sinn philosophischen Fragens und Erkennens.*

datum of value is necessarily presupposed for the notion of the objective good for the person. In the case of high-ranking goods the being must have a value in order to be an objective good for the person. But in every objective good for the person, the value of the human person is presupposed. Though both categories of importance definitely differ, the notion of the objective good for the person presupposes the notion of value. The notion of value, however, does not presuppose the notion of the objective good for the person. Value is, as we saw, an ultimate datum.

But our aim has not only been to analyze the different relations between the two types of importance, but also to see what significance being an objective good for the person has from the all-decisive point of view of value. We saw before that the question of value is fundamental and inevitable, one which can never be replaced by anything else. We have seen how being an objective good for the person presents itself from this point of view. Being an objective good for the person always has a value. This holds true notwithstanding the great gradation in the rank of the objective goods. Its immanent friendliness to the person endows it with two different values: first, with an indirect value, depending upon the value of the human person; second, with the sublime value that it possesses as an embodiment and message of God's infinite bounty.

CHAPTER 8

THE IRREDUCIBLE CHARACTER OF VALUE

MANY ATTEMPTS have been made to reduce value to something other than itself. But these attempts are futile and vain because the notion of value refers to an ultimate datum, not only in the sense that it is grasped solely in an original intuition and is undeducible (this would also apply to the color red), but also in the sense that it is a fundamental datum which we necessarily always presuppose. Value is an ultimate datum in the same way as essence, existence, truth, knowledge—these we cannot deny without tacitly reintroducing them. We shall now discuss the main attempts to reduce value to something else; such an analysis will simultaneously further clarify the nature of value.

Many objects assume a character of importance because of their suitability to appease an urge or an appetite in us. Water becomes important for the thirsty person; though he looked with indifference at water so long as he was not thirsty, it suddenly assumes a character of importance because of his thirst.[1]

Our life is pervaded by bodily urges and appetites of our soul, and the objects suitable to appease them thereby assume an importance. To drink becomes an attraction for the thirsty; to rest becomes important for the tired; to move and run about is a delight for the vital energies of a child; to remain silent is for the loquacious person painful, and so on. The object which is able to appease an urge or an appetite, so long as this urge or

[1] In saying that someone looks at water with indifference as long as he is not thirsty, we in no way exclude that it could attract him from many other points of view. Only the importance which it possesses by its suitability to appease the urge of thirst would vanish as soon as someone is no longer thirsty.

appetite is not appeased, presents itself to us either as something merely subjectively satisfying or as an objective good for the person.

Now any attempt to reduce value to mere suitability for appeasing an urge or an appetite is futile. The essential difference between value and the importance rooted in this suitability clearly manifests itself in the following marks: First, the relation between the object and our interest in it differs radically in each case. Urges and appetites are rooted in our nature. In order to arise, they do not presuppose a knowledge of the object or activity which is capable of appeasing them. Their arising in us is due to our nature and hence they may even precede the knowledge of the object. The inner movement which is proper to them is not engendered by the object; thus the urge or appetite has the role of the *principium*, and the importance, rooted in the suitability of an object or an activity to appease an urge or appetite, is the *principiatum*. The importance of the object is clearly something secondary; it is a means of appeasement. Its suitability is important only because the urge and appetite exist; as soon as the urge or appetite disappears, the object loses its importance and falls, so far as our experience is concerned, to the level of the indifferent.

Our admiration of a person's humility, on the contrary, is not something arising spontaneously in our nature without a knowledge of the humility of this person. Rather, such admiration essentially presupposes a knowledge of the object. It is an inner movement which depends entirely on the object, which is motivated by the object, and which essentially implies that we understand the importance in itself of the object. The importance of the object presents itself clearly as independent of my admiration; it is the *principium*, and my admiration is the *principiatum*.

There can be no question of any urge or appetite for which the existence of a moral value as such would be an appeasement. To pretend that there exists within the person an unconscious appetite to admire certain things (as, for instance, that an act of forgiveness is important only because it satisfies such an appetite) would obviously be a mere fiction suggested only to save the theory at any cost. In reality there is nothing which supports this supposition.

But even if there were such an urge to admire, to look up to things greater than ourselves, it would yet be impossible to reduce the value of the act of forgiving to a mere capability for appeasing this appetite. An appetite or urge to find an object which we can admire could be appeased only if an object presented itself as *admirandum;* that is to say, as being worthy of our admiration—but this again means being endowed with a value. Admiration essentially presupposes an awareness of the value of the object; thus to pretend that the value is nothing but a suitability to appease our urge to admire is to revolve in a circle. For in order to engender or motivate our admiration, the object must itself possess more than mere suitability; it must present itself precisely *as* important in itself.[2]

This attempt to make value identical with suitability to appease urges is very much like saying that the evidence of a truth is nothing but the capacity of an object to appease our urge to knowledge. Obviously the suitability to appease an urge for knowing is essentially more than a mere suitability; for only the real objective validity of the truth at stake, which is something independent of any urge, can appease the urge for knowing. Hence, the type of urge which is brought forward to save this theory actually serves to defeat it, since the appeasement of these urges presupposes the value as existing independently of them.

---

[2] There exists also a perverted urge for an equally perverted admiration which makes us revel in the gesture or in pseudo self-abandonment. It is something analogous to the urge for knowledge in which truth is no longer sincerely sought. The well-known words of Lessing express in some way this attitude: "If God held enclosed in His right hand all truth, and in His left hand solely the never resting impulse towards truth but this with the condition that I should always and forever err and He should say to me: choose! With humility I would fall into His left and say: Father give! Pure Truth is indeed for Thee alone!" *Eine Duplik* (Braunschweig, 1778).

Likewise this perverted urge to admire as such no longer seeks an object which deserves admiration, but the object functions exclusively as a means for the experience of admiring. The admiring is sought for its own sake. Obviously the admiration which is sought in this case is itself a crippled admiration, deprived of its innermost meaning. Unnecessary to say that these perversions clearly differ from any sincere and genuine joy, admiration, enthusiasm, which is to be found in the above-mentioned cases.

But obviously there is no question of such an urge in all cases wherein we face a value. When a proud and rebellious man is confronted with the generosity of another person, and is touched by it, who will pretend that the generous action has appeased some urge gnawing at the proud man's heart?

The attempt to reduce the value to a mere suitability for appeasing an appetite or urge directs itself toward those cases in which we desire the possession of some good and not toward those in which we simply respond to a value with joy, enthusiasm, or admiration. We mentioned above that it is the *desiderare* (desire) which is generally considered as typical of our relation to a good. In taking for granted that good and desire are correlative concepts, one is inclined to overlook the cases in which we rejoice at the very existence of something, and to restrict one's attention alone to the cases in which the possession of a good is in question. But even here the reduction of the value to mere suitability for appeasing an appetite or urge is an impossible feat. We have only to consider the cases where it is really a question of an appetite or urge—for instance, the tendency of spiritual energy in us to release itself, as distinguished from the longing to live in a beautiful country or the desire for communion with a beloved person—then we can clearly grasp the difference between the importance rooted in the suitability of the object to appease an urge on the one hand and the value which motivates our desire on the other.

The desire for spiritual union with the beloved is rooted in our love. Love presupposes that the beloved presents himself to our mind as lovable, as beautiful and precious, as important-in-himself. Love (and also the *intentio unionis* which is organically and essentially rooted in love) are clearly engendered by the consciousness of the lovableness and beauty of a person, whereas the appetites and urges are, as we saw, essentially spontaneous; they arise in the person independently of an object. Love and the longing for requital of our love obviously presuppose a knowledge of the person, of his beauty and charm. The need to actuate a talent, an artistic talent or the talent of an orator, for example, does not necessarily presuppose a knowledge of the object. The urge may already exist before such an object is discovered. A chance event may bring to the fore the fact that a person's longing for development and unfolding would be appeased by this or that particular activity.

We experience the fact that our love is engendered by the beauty, goodness, and lovableness of the beloved person; there is here a primacy of the object with respect to our response. In the case of urges and appetites, on the contrary, it is obvious that the primacy is in the movement with respect to the object. In many cases this primacy is consciously experienced when such an urge or appetite arises. In the case of love, the value is undoubtedly the *principium* and our love and desire are the *principiata;* whereas with the appetite or urge, the importance of the object is the *principiatum* and our appetite the *principium.*

Evidently, it sometimes happens that a good having a value is desired because it can at the same time appease an appetite. But this coincidence reveals still more clearly the impossibility of reducing the importance in itself to mere suitability for appeasing an appetite or urge.

If someone is filled with an urge for research, he clearly distinguishes between the importance which research possesses for him, the satisfaction of being able to quench his intellectual thirst, and the importance in itself possessed by the discovery of truth. He is well aware that this urge is directed toward something having an importance over and above the appeasement of his urge. If he takes this case, in which truth plays the dual role of a value as well as an object suitable for the appeasement of his intellectual restlessness, and compares it to another case in which he feels an urge to be talkative, he will see the marked difference between the two. In both cases, there is the suitability for appeasing an urge; but only in the one case is there awareness of value.

Or again, though someone has an urge or appetite for a good which is endowed with a value, the value in question can also be grasped by someone who has no such urge or appetite. The value of knowledge and truth can certainly be grasped and seen by someone who has no urge for research into truth, whereas the suitability of this object for appeasing the urge obviously exists only for the one who has it. The attempt to reduce the value to mere suitability for appeasing an urge thus collapses as soon as we examine more minutely both types of importance.

Sometimes tne attempt is made to reduce the value to the suitability an object has to appease an appetite, not insofar as the *experienced* appeasement or the satisfaction is concerned, but insofar as the object answers to and fulfills an innate teleological trend in our nature. Value is then considered as the suitability of an object to bestow on us that which we objectively need for the full unfolding of our entelechy.

Thus, according to this theory, when we speak of the moral goodness and sublimity of an act of charity or forgiveness, we really mean nothing more than the fact that this act is suitable for the unfolding of the entelechy of the man who is charitable or who forgives his enemies. But obviously we do not have this in mind in speaking of moral values; still less would it make sense to say that another person's act of charity is suitable for the unfolding of our own entelechy. Therefore, reference to entelechy in this case can mean only that in accomplishing this act one actualizes his own entelechy. The relation between an act of charity and the unfolding of one's entelechy is obviously so different from that of any good possessing suitability for it (for instance, as physical training would be for the development of the body), that any analogy to such suitability is lacking. Hence the reduction could only tend to replace the notion of suitability by the notion of conformity with the entelechy, or by that of *secundum naturam*. Such a reduction would have to be based on the pretense that the intrinsic goodness of an act of charity and forgiveness which moves us and engenders our joy and enthusiasm is nothing other than the conformity of this act to man's nature; or, in other words, nothing but the fact that this act is a part of the realization of his entelechy. But why this act should be able to move us, to engender joy, enthusiasm, or veneration in our soul when we witness it in another person would seem quite incomprehensible.

We do not here want to discuss this theory further since we shall deal with the role of the *secundum naturam* more thoroughly in another section.[3]

The impossibility of the position which reduces the value to a suitability becomes especially clear if we think of the value of

[3] See p. 185ff.

the human person as such. How could the value of a human being which reveals itself to our mind in certain situations in a specifically drastic manner (for instance, when someone is tortured and injured, or when his life is in danger) be interpreted as a suitability favoring the unfolding of our entelechy? There is no relation whatsoever to *my* nature which would even allow such a misunderstanding of the value as this reduction to a suitability implies. To say that the value of the human person as such—the dignity of a human being—is a suitability for the man in danger in whom this value obviously appears so dramatically is still more ridiculous.

Neither moral values (such as humility or purity), nor the ontological value of a human person, nor the value of life as such, nor the beauty of a great work of art give us the slightest basis for interpreting them as suitabilities. But even in those cases where we find an objective teleological direction of man's nature toward something which presents itself as having a value, the impossibility of reducing the value to the fulfillment of this objective trend clearly manifests itself. We have an objective direction in our nature toward truth. But who could pretend that the value of truth is nothing but the suitability to fulfill this objective tendency. Obviously it is impossible to deduce the value of truth from a tendency which we find as a mere fact in our nature.

But if we minutely analyze these attempts to reduce the value to a suitability for the unfolding of our entelechy, we find above all that the notion of value is tacitly presupposed.

If it is said that something is good because of its suitability to lead to the fulfillment of our entelechy, what else can this mean but that everything which we call good, everything to which we attribute an importance-in-itself, has in reality only a secondary importance as a means for the one value which matters: the entelechy of our person? Would this attempt really replace the notion of value by suitability; would it dissolve our notion of value into a mere neutral relation between some object and the actualization of our nature? Rather, would it not tacitly presuppose the notion of value in man's entelechy as well as in the fact that the entelechy should be fully unfolded? Is it not obvious that this attempt at reduction is in reality only a postponing of the problem; that is to say, a tacit presupposition of the value in that which is at the basis of this relation?

It is impossible to erase the difference between a mere factuality and the important-in-itself, between the mere neutral tendency which we simply declare to be a fact and the tendency whose fulfillment we consider important, as something which *ought* to be. Any attempt to deduce the important-in-itself from the neutral is either a nonsensical prestidigitation or else a silent introduction of the value into the supposedly neutral thing.

There is no reason for trying to reduce any other values to mere suitability once it is understood that, in all attempts to substitute the notion of suitability for the notion of value, the notion of value really has been silently presupposed with respect both to the entelechy of a being and to the full unfolding of this entelechy.

If one must admit in any case that there exists an importance in itself which cannot be reduced to a mere relation to something else; if one must admit the intrinsic character of the value, excluding in its essence any "for" relation, then there is no possible motive for the artificial interpretation that the value of a human person, or the moral sublimity of charity, or the value of justice, is mere suitability for the unfolding of man's entelechy.

The attempt to reduce value to mere suitability for something else is obviously rooted in the desire to be able to prove *why* something is important, i.e., to make the character of importance more intelligible. The ideal of intelligibility here considered is the same as that which makes many people believe that, in the sphere of knowledge, being intelligible is equivalent to being demonstrable. The possibility is ignored that some fact may reveal itself immediately in its necessity to our mind; as, for instance, the fact that something cannot exist and not exist simultaneously, or that moral values presuppose a person.

Thus the modern concept of an axiom, denoting something arbitrarily presumed or at best a mere hypothesis, has replaced the self-evident as a starting point. Forgotten is the fact that the power which a proof or any argument has in making something intelligible, is ultimately rooted in the possibility of linking a proposition with other propositions either self-evident or firmly established through self-evident principles. If self-evidence were really not the climax of all intelligibility and the ultimate source of all absolute certitude, then all proof would be deprived of its intelligibility; it would be as nonsensical as the concept of efficient causality in a universe without a *causa prima*.

Once we have grasped that the self-evident possesses an intelligibility higher than any explanation *ex causis,* and that the entire intelligibility and guaranteeing power of a proof is based on the intelligibility of the self-evident, that equation collapses which identifies intelligibility with being proved by arguments or by reasons. To continue asking for proofs when faced with something evident, to continue asking why it is so, is not the sign of thirst for a deeper intelligibility but, on the contrary, the sign of incapacity to understand the nature of evidence as well as the nature of intelligibility. It is an intellectual obstinacy which begins by confusing a certain type of intellectual procedure with intelligibility as such, and ends by being blind to the source of all intelligibility.

It seems to us that this same intellectual obstinacy underlies the attempt to give importance a greater intelligibility by interpreting it as an importance *for* something or as a functional power or suitability. One believes that in being able to give a "reason" why something is important, one thereby makes it more intelligible. In reality, one necessarily presupposes an importance in itself in order to explain why something suitable for it is important. Moreover, a value which evidently reveals itself in its intrinsic importance is much more intelligible than any proof could make it, and renders superfluous any question of why it is important. And this applies above all to the general notion of value or the important-in-itself. It is a terrible self-delusion to believe one can understand the value without an original intuition or for the sake of intelligibility to try to reduce it to, or deduce it from, any neutral fact. Instead of reaching a higher intelligibility, one only succeeds in misunderstanding the nature of the value. Though consciously denying it, one nevertheless silently presupposes it, just as analogously in argumentation one always presupposes the evidence.

Once we have understood in a full *prise de conscience* the nature of value, we thereby grasp that the question "why" the looking for a point of reference which would "explain" the importance (or rather reduce it to something not important) is as nonsensical as the "why" in the face of something self-evident, such as a first principle. The important-in-itself reveals itself as an ultimate datum, not only in the general sense in which every necessary intelligible quiddity which can be grasped only by an original intuition is an ultimate datum, but also in the specific sense in which being and truth are ultimate data.

But apart from the impossibility of reducing or "explaining" the general notion of value as such, every concrete value which we face belies the interpretation which makes of it a mere suitability for our entelechy. We have already shown the obvious impossibility of interpreting the dignity of a human person, the dignity which forbids us in conscience to use him as a mere means, as a mere suitability for something else. The same applies to the value of justice or to any other moral value, to the beauty of sublime scenes or of a great work of art, or to the value of a great intelligence.

If we carefully examine what we mean by attributing to an action the predicate of morally good or noble, or to a work of art the predicate beautiful or sublime, we easily see that it clearly differs from any mere suitability to fulfill any teleological trend of our nature. When a thing actually has such suitability (as, for instance, communion with other persons) to which man is directed by his very nature, it clearly differs from the value, since the suitable thing has an intrinsic relation to man's nature, an essential "for" character; whereas the value completely lacks this "for" relation.[4] In saying beautiful or good, we mean an importance-in-itself, something which not only *is* but *ought* to be. And if we examine what is given to us in face of a morally good action, or of the dignity of a person, or of the beauty of nature, we immediately grasp that the datum confirms what we mean by those predications: that what we mean in saying good, beautiful, noble, or sublime is not something to which no reality corresponds, but on the contrary something which has the character of an importance-in-itself, which is univocally manifested in reality, and which reveals itself in the data of our experience.

---

[4] This is in no way contradicted by the fact that a good endowed with a value is simultaneously an objective good for us.

The difference is obvious between the nature of an importance consisting in the suitability of fulfilling a teleological trend in man, and the nature of something important-in-itself. We clearly distinguish them at all times. In saying that a certain position is very good for a man because it gives him the possibility of a full unfolding of his talents, we are fully aware that we mean something other than when we speak of the intrinsic beauty and preciousness of a great intelligence; or when the liturgy says: *Quam pulchra et clara est haec casta generatio*—"How beautiful and resplendent is this chaste generation"—it obviously does not refer to any suitability for something.

The importance which this suitability possesses in reality is rather the one which we termed the objective good for the person. We do not intend to say, however, that every objective good for the person can be reduced to such a suitability, but only that every genuine suitability is really an objective good for the person.

We saw before how the notion of the objective good for the person already presupposes the notion of value; and this again shows us that every attempt to reduce value to mere suitability for fulfilling a teleological trend in man's nature becomes involved in a vicious circle.

We want to conclude by stressing that once we have grasped the nature of value, a notion which is already implied in our notion of God, we also understand that in pointing to the value of something we give a much more intelligible *raison d'être* for its existence than we could possibly give in any neutral final cause. To ask "why" in face of the important-in-itself, or to believe that the value is made more intelligible by being interpreted as a suitability for something else, is plainly absurd, since in reality every final cause calls for a "why" so long as we have not grasped its value.

CHAPTER 9

RELATIVISM

ETHICAL RELATIVISM is widespread. It is, unfortunately, the ruling moral philosophy of our age. The term "value" is generally employed now as something merely subjective. In speaking of values, one usually takes it for granted that there is general admission of their relative and subjective nature.

The preceding analysis concerning the nature of the important-in-itself should suffice to unmask the impossibility of any value relativism. He who has understood our statements and arguments will also understand that every attempt to interpret as an illusion the notion of an importance-in-itself or of an objective value collapses as soon as we examine more minutely the nature of value. Nevertheless, because ethical relativism is so ubiquitous, it seems necessary to discuss it in a separate chapter and to refute it in detail.

The first type of ethical relativism is no more than a subdivision of general relativism or skepticism. As soon as someone denies that we are able to have any objectively valid knowledge, as soon as he argues that there exists no objective truth, he necessarily also denies the existence of any objective value. The nature of a general relativism is such that it affects everything. We must observe, however, that even though this type of ethical relativism is a logical consequence of general relativism, nevertheless the unconscious motive for general relativism is very often the desire to do away with an absolute ethical norm. At least deep unconscious resistance against the objectivity of truth frequently has its source in a type of pride which revolts primarily against objective values.

General relativism or skepticism, however, has been over-whelmingly refuted many times, beginning with Plato's *Gorgias* through St. Augustine's *Contra Academicos* (and most especially in his famous *Si fallor, sum*—"If I am mistaken, I am" [1]), through all the many classical *reductiones ad absurdum,* and last but not least in Edmund Husserl's *Logische Untersuchungen.* [2]

Whatever the formulation of the thesis denying the possibility of any objective knowledge or of attaining any objective truth, it is inevitably self-contradictory, because in one and the same breath it denies that which it necessarily implies. In claiming to make an objectively true statement by declaring that we are unable to attain any objective truth, this position clearly contradicts itself. Or in other words, it claims to attain an objective truth in the statement that we can never attain an objective truth.

If every general relativism is untenable because of its intrinsically self-contradictory character, so too is any ethical relativism, which is merely a subdivision of the former and is supported by no other arguments than those offered by general skepticism. But we are here interested in refuting those arguments of an ethical relativism which are not derived from the arguments of general relativism. And there exist many such arguments which are not necessarily derivations of a general value relativism.

To be sure, the ethical relativists are, for the most part at least, value relativists, since theoretically they will deny any importance-in-itself. But their arguments often refer exclusively to the morally good and evil, to moral norms, to any value which imposes on us a moral obligation. Certain other values, e.g., aesthetic values, they believe to be so obviously relative, or subjective and deprived even of any pretention to objectivity, that they no longer argue against their objectivity; again, other values, such as life, health, and democracy, they tacitly accept as objective, even though they will not theoretically admit them to be so. Thus, the real stress is laid on the denial of an objective good

---

[1] *De Trinitate,* XV, 12–21; also *De Civitate Dei,* XI, 26.

[2] (Halle: M. Niemeyer, 1900), "Critique of specific relativism," Pt. I, chap. 7, § 36, pp. 116ff.

and evil in the moral sense, or at least in the sense which implies a moral obligation.

The first well-known argument for ethical relativism appeals to the diversity of moral judgments which can be found in different peoples, cultural realms, and historical epochs. What is considered as morally good or morally evil, this view contends, differs according to peoples and historical ages. A Mohammedan considers polygamy morally justifiable. It does not occur to him to have any pangs of conscience in this respect. With an entirely good conscience he has different wives simultaneously. To a Christian this would seem immoral and impure. Of such diversity in judgments on what is morally good and what is evil, innumerable examples can be offered. Moreover this diversity of opinion concerning the moral color of something is to be found not only in comparing different peoples and epochs, but also in looking at the same epoch and even at the same individual at different times of his life.

Now this first argument for the relativity of moral values is based on an invalid syllogism. From the diversity of many moral judgments; from the fact that certain people hold a thing to be morally evil while other people believe the same thing to be morally correct, it is inferred that moral values are relative, that there exists no moral good and evil, and that the entire moral question is tantamount to a superstition or a mere illusion.

In truth, a difference of opinion in no way proves that the object to which the opinion refers does not exist; or that it is in reality a mere semblance, changing for each individual or at least for different peoples. The fact that the Ptolemaic system was for centuries considered correct but is now superseded by our present scientific opinion is no justification for denying that the stars exist or even that our present opinion has only a relative validity.

There exist a great many fields in which can be found a diversity of opinion, among different peoples and in different epochs, and also among philosophers. Does this then confute the existence of objective truth? Not at all. The truth of a proposition does not depend upon how many people agree to it, but solely upon whether or not it is in conformity with reality.

Even if all men shared a certain opinion, it could still be wrong, and the fact that very few grasp a truth does not therefore alter or lessen its objective validity. Even the evidence of a truth is not equivalent to the fact that every man grasps and accepts it immediately. In like manner, it is erroneous to conclude that there exists no objective moral norm, that moral good and evil are in reality illusions or fictions or that at least their pretention to objective validity is an illusion, only because we find many different opinions concerning what is considered to be morally good and evil.

What matters is to see that in all these diversities the notion of an objective value, of a moral good and evil, is always presupposed, even if there exist contradictory positions concerning the moral goodness of a certain attitude or action. And just as the meaning of objective truth is not touched by the fact that two persons hold opposite positions and each one claims his proposition to be true, so too the notion of moral good and evil, of something objectively valid which calls for obedience and appeals to our conscience, is always untouched, even if one man says that polygamy is evil and another that polygamy is morally permissible.

The distinction between something merely subjectively satisfying and advantageous for an egotistic interest on the one hand, and the morally good on the other hand, is always in some way implied.

Thus conflicting opinions concerning the moral illicitness of something, instead of dethroning the general notions of moral good and moral evil, clearly attest their objectivity. As the diversity of opinions reveals that objective truth as such is always presupposed and is consequently beyond all possibility of the collapse to which the truth of a single fact may be exposed, so the indispensable presupposition of an objective moral norm reveals itself majestically in all diversities of opinions concerning the moral goodness or badness of a single attitude.

On the other hand, the fact that there have existed many more conflicting opinions concerning moral values, for instance, the moral character of polygamy or of blood revenge, than concerning colors or the size of corporeal things, can easily be understood as soon as we realize the moral requirements for a sound and integral value perception.[3]

Without any doubt the perception of moral values differs in many respects from knowledge in any other field. In order to grasp the real value or disvalue of an attitude, in order to see, for example, the disvalue of revenge or polygamy, more moral presuppositions are required than for any other type of knowledge. Reverence, a sincere thirst for truth, intellectual patience, and a spiritual *souplesse* are required in varying degrees for every adequate knowledge of any kind. But in the case of the moral value-perception much more is required: not only another degree of reverence and of opening our mind to the voice of being, a higher degree of "conspiring" with the object, but also a *readiness of our will* to conform to the call of values, whatever it may be.[4] The influence of the environment, of the milieu, of the traditions of a community, in short the entire interpersonal atmosphere in which man grows up and lives, has a much greater influence on this type of knowledge than on any other. In the ethos of a community, moral convictions are present in another way than are convictions concerning other spheres. They are embodied not only in the laws and customs, but above all in the common ideal which forms an ever-present pattern for judging our fellow men and ourselves. The entire atmosphere is so saturated with this moral pattern that the conscious and unconscious influence on the individual is a tremendous one.

And this influence may cripple the capacity for value-perception. Thus it is not difficult to see how errors in this field are more widespread, expressing themselves in conflicting value-judgments in different tribes, peoples, cultural realms, and epochs.

But this only shows why errors and inadequacies in this field are more widespread. It shows us how the tradition of a com-

[3] The problem of value blindness has been discussed systematically in my former work, *Sittlichkeit und ethische Werterkenntniss* (Halle: M. Niemeyer, 1921), p. 24ff.

[4] In his work on St. Augustine, C. N. Cochrane stresses this fact in saying, "Intellectually, this bad will finds expression in an effort 'to make one's own truth,' i.e., to justify one's conduct by rationalizations which are blindly and stubbornly adhered to for the very reason that they cannot stand the light of day." *Christianity and Classical Culture* (Oxford: Clarendon Press, 1940), p. 449.

munity may in many cases hamper the moral value-perception, and in other cases facilitate an adequate value-perception. But in no way does it show that without any such influence of a community there would exist no moral good and evil, or that the morally good is nothing but a convention or a custom of a certain community.

How, moreover, will the moral relativists explain the fact that we often find great moral personalities piercing through the screen laid over morality by the customs and convictions of the environment and discovering parts at least of the true world of values? How do they account for the moral views of Socrates, of Zoroaster, and many others?

Once we have grasped the roots of moral value blindness, it will no longer be astonishing that there exist such diversities of value-judgments; rather we shall be astonished at how many agreements nevertheless exist among all tribes, epochs, and individuals. We must now cautiously examine the origin of this diversity in moral judgments.

In many cases the fact that one tribe in a certain historical age considered as morally evil the same thing which another tribe considered as morally good is due to a difference of opinion or belief concerning the *nature* of a thing, and not its value. If for a tribe certain animals are considered sacred (as, for example, the Egyptians considered the ox Apis to be holy), then to kill this animal assumes the character of something sacrilegious; whereas for one who is aware of the true nature of this animal, to kill it is not at all sacrilegious. Innumerable examples could be given of such diversities which manifest in no way a contradiction concerning moral values, but only a difference of opinion concerning the nature of certain objects. A sacrilegious action is in both cases considered to be morally evil. Thus there is no diversity concerning the disvalue of a sacrilegious action, but only concerning the fact as to whether something is believed to be sacred or not.

There exist no doubt tremendous differences among peoples and epochs concerning the interpretation of nature and the world surrounding us. The interpretation of the universe by a superstitious primitive tribe naturally differs enormously from the universe as it is understood by science in our age. Thus one and the same action necessarily has a completely different moral significance according to the conception which the agent has of the things that he is dealing with. This difference implies no diversity in the moral judgment *as such*. Precisely because the moral judgment as such is the same, because there is agreement concerning the value, the judgment of this concrete action must differ as soon as one set of factual presuppositions has been replaced by another.

One of the most widespread forms of ethical relativism is the thesis of what is called the French sociological school. According to this theory the notion of moral good and evil is in reality only the objectivation of the beliefs and will of a community. As Anatole France puts it, murder is not punished because it is evil, but we call it evil because it is punished by the state. The "objectivity" of the moral norm, its undeniable difference from our arbitrary mood or our subjective desires, is explained according to this theory by the fact that it is the beliefs of a community that the individual finds as something pre-given, imposed on him by tradition.

Moral good and evil are identified with mere convention, with something which has no other basis than the pseudo objectivity of Bacon's *idola tribus,* the idols of the tribe or collective erroneous beliefs, as opposed to the *idola specus,* the idols of the cave or individual prejudices. We do indeed find such a pseudo objectivity of ideas, as when in a particular epoch certain ideas are, as it were, in the air. The individual experiences ideas as if they were possessed of objective power and reality because instead of arising in his mind they have an interpersonal reality, and are considered as common knowledge. The individual experiences them as things which come from "outside" his mind, and thus confuses their mere interpersonal reality with objective truth. In order to see the confusion and fallacy at its basis, we need only concentrate on the thesis of the ethical relativists whereby moral values are identified with their being commanded by a community.

Even though we contended that all our convictions are fallacious, mere *idola tribus,* due to our confusing the pseudo objectivity of the interpersonal reality of an idea with its truth, the notion of truth as such would still remain untouched. There is a clear and unassailable opposition between objective truth and the relativity of all those concrete convictions which have no other basis than a collective belief. When these beliefs and opinions are denounced and belittled as merely relative, then the notion of objective truth, far from being invalidated and reduced to a mere illusion, reveals itself in its full majesty and undethronable reality. Objective truth forms the tacit presupposition of this thesis, for plainly it is only *because* there exists an objective truth that the propositions which have no other worth than to be *idola tribus* are declared relative. Now if we interpret this position as tacitly presupposing objective truth, it becomes tantamount to the thesis that we are unable to attain truth, a skeptical position which is contradictory in itself, as we saw before. If, on the contrary, we interpret the thesis as considering that truth is in reality constituted by nothing more than the preagreement of a community, we are confronted with one of those nonsensical statements which are so often presented in the formula: "It is in reality nothing but. . . ." We have already spoken of the impossibility of these "discoveries" in philosophy, because as far as true essences or necessary, intelligible unities are concerned the reduction of one to the other is inherently nonsensical. If someone tells us that in reality 3 is 4, or green is red, further discussion would be a waste of time. The same applies to every attempt which declares ultimate, necessary, and intelligible entities to be mere illusions.

Besides the simple impossibility of identifying truth as such with the fact that something is held to be true by a community, the very *nature* of conviction also forbids such identification. For whether a conviction is true or false in its content, it nevertheless attempts to aim at something transcendent. The statement itself claims to be not merely the belief of a community but a truth. Therefore as such it presupposes the possibility of knowing an objective truth.

In much the same way the thesis of the ethical relativist which declares that what we call good is in reality nothing but the result of social convention means that every particular statement in which we say something is morally good or evil is therefore on the same level as mere rules of convention, such as those which fix the manner in which one person is to greet another.

Now this thesis leaves untouched the notion of moral good and evil as such in its objectivity. For it amounts to the thesis: the things which we believe to be morally good and evil are not so in reality, since we are unable to distinguish whether something is objectively so or whether it only appears to be good or evil because of the tradition of a community.

As far reaching and disastrous as is the denial of the objective validity of every value-judgment concerning any type of human attitude, the objective validity of the notion of moral good or evil would still not be touched by this ethical agnosticism. It would mean: though there exists a moral good and evil, every concrete statement (e.g., "Murder is morally bad," or "Faithfulness is morally good") is the mere result of a community convention.

Later on we shall discuss the arbitrary and unfounded character of this ethical agnosticism.

Of course the French sociological school would not accept this interpretation. They want to say that the notion of moral good and evil is nothing but a superstition; and that just as totemism ascribes to certain animals a magical power and significance which they do not have in reality, so mankind in general imagines such a thing as importance-in-itself, and even such things as moral goodness and moral wickedness. As superstition consists not only in ascribing magical power to a being but also in the very notion of magical power, so too not only the predication of moral good or evil to a human act but the very notion of moral good itself is pure illusion.

This statement may assume two different forms: First, moral goodness and evil are mere illusions, and we are therefore on the same level with the notion of magic power. In reality, things are neutral. The second formula would run: What people call morally good and evil is in reality only mere convention, the social perspective of a certain community.

This latter formula does not lead to the same consequences as does the former. The idea of moral good and evil is not declared to be a superstition which should be eliminated as in the former case, but rather it is seen as a normal part of man's communal life. All we have to do is simply to understand its true nature, and this consists precisely in its being the expression of a community belief. Both formulas are equally nonsensical.

The first position which declares the notion of good and evil to be mere superstition, a fiction to be explained by psychoanalysis, tries thereby to deny a necessary, ultimate, intelligible quiddity. This is a nonsensical procedure as we have shown before.[5] Just as it is indeed possible to discover that some contingent idea is a mere illusion or fiction (e.g., that a centaur does not exist, or that the phoenix is a mere illusion), so it is absurd to say of any intelligible, necessary entity (e.g., the number two, or truth, or justice) that it is a mere fiction or illusion.

The very nature of these necessary, intelligible entities is such that they are beyond all invention and fiction, and possess a radical autonomy and independence of the act in which we grasp them. To ignore the essential difference between merely contingent facts and these entities, which have essences so potent as to exclude any possibility of denying them objectivity, and to place them on the same level with any contingent quiddity, thus betrays a degree of philosophical incapacity and superficiality which from the start dooms every theory touched by this blindness.

If we think of all the innumerable attempts in philosophy to reduce one thing to another despite the fact that the two things obviously differ in their very nature—whether it be to explain the meaning of a word by saying that it is nothing but association of an image with the sound of the word, or to explain the respect for a moral value as nothing but a specific form of inhibition, or to describe joy as nothing but the experience of a certain *Organempfindung* associated with a certain representation of an object, or whatever the particular form may be—we are at a loss to understand whence this idle and even nonsensical procedure derives its attractiveness. Not only value in general but, more important, moral value is, as we saw before, such an ultimate datum that in order to grasp the evident datum of value which, in spite of all theoretical denials, a person constantly presupposes, it suffices that he become fully aware of his lived contact with reality.

[5] Cf. Prolegomena, p. 5ff.

Adherents of the French sociological school were full of indignation about Hitler's atrocities and racism, notwithstanding the fact that according to their theory there could be no basis for any indignation. Even if, in order to be consistent with their theories, they should deny that they were indignant, nevertheless at the first occasion in which for a moment they forgot their theory, they would be sincerely indignant. Every day offers many situations in which their immediate responses give the lie to their theory.

But we need only think of the attitude which ordinarily accompanies this theory. The "dogmatism" of the moral objectivists is looked upon with contempt. Whether it is looked upon as superstition or reactionary obscurantism or "mystical" phantasy, it is always fought against as something evil, and never as something merely erroneous, as is the case when one or another scientific theory is attacked. Obviously in attacking objectivism as evil the relativists admit what they theoretically deny.

Sometimes we find that those who are in rage against the notion of any objective norm and any objective value nevertheless strive against them in the name of "freedom," or "democracy"; and thereby they fully admit the character of the value of freedom or democracy. They do not speak of freedom as if it were something merely agreeable or as if they wanted it for personal reasons, but they speak of it as an "ideal" which itself implies the notion of value and even of morally relevant value. The entire ethos of those who fight against any objective norm belies the content of their theory. The pathos with which they condemn the attitude of the "dogmatists" is weighted with the pretention of fighting for the nobler cause. Whatever may be the point in which they tacitly admit an objective value and even a moral significance, whatever may be the "ideal" which they presuppose unawares, somewhere the notion of value and even of moral value must inevitably enter. Would they not look with contempt on a colleague who, eager to prove a theory, paid people for giving false testimony, or lied about the results of his experiments? Would they not blame a medical charlatan who foists fake medicines and cures on his unfortunate patients? Lewis brilliantly points to this inconsistency in saying:

In actual fact Gaius and Titius will be found to hold, with complete uncritical dogmatism, the whole system of values which happened to be in vogue among moderately educated young men of the professional classes during the period between the two wars. Their scepticism about values is on the surface; it is for us on other people's values: about the values current in their own set they are not nearly sceptical enough. And this phenomenon is very usual. A great many of those who "debunk" traditional or (as they would say) "sentimental" values have in the background values of their own which they believe to be immune from the debunking process. They claim to be cutting away the parasitic growth of emotion, religious sanction, and inherited taboos, in order that "real" or "basic" values may emerge.[6]

Why indeed should they write books at all proposing their relativistic theory, if they did not think that it is better to know truth than to err? [7]

There may be people who in their lives ignore their moral obligations and become disinterested in the world of moral values and who, like a certain type of criminal or a complete egotist, aspire only to satisfy their pride or concupiscence. But no one who is a sincere theoretical relativist can completely avoid presupposing the datum of moral value.

We repeat: As soon as one of these relativists should, in abstracting from his theories, become aware of his immediate contact with being, he could not fail to discover the datum of moral value in its undeniable reality. Only the relativist who could sincerely answer "yes," when asked whether he would prefer objective moral values, would be capable of reaching this deeper stratum and of gaining awareness of the value.

But some may object: As soon as a person in his search would rejoice in finding one possibility confirmed by reality rather than another, he is no longer unprejudiced and hence in analyzing reality he may become a prey to wishful thinking.

But this does not apply here. What we mean is simply this: The man who wants to commit suicide because he despairs of

---

[6] C. S. Lewis, *The Abolition of Man* (New York: The Macmillan Co., 1947), pp. 18–19.

[7] "For the whole purpose of their book is so to condition the young reader that he will share their approval, and this would be either a fool's or a villain's undertaking unless they held that their approval was in some way valid or correct." *Ibid.*, p. 18.

objective truth or objective values is sincere in his conviction, even though he errs in his attitude. But the one who denies objective truth and objective values and, far from finding such a world tragic, prefers it, completely reveals the psychological and moral reasons which are at the basis of his denial.

The distinction between the notion of moral good and evil on the one hand and a mere convention or a mere "being forbidden by the state" on the other is obvious. To consider moral good and evil as in reality nothing but the result of a positive commandment springing from the self-defense of society against the individual is a typical example of an attempt to dissolve necessary, intelligible entities into contingent fictions and constructs. We might just as well say that in reality a triangle is a square. Such a consideration has sense only if it means that things are often presented under the title of moral laws, or as having a moral value, even though in actual fact those things are prescribed only because they are in the interest of society. This would amount to a judgment analogous to the one wherein we accuse somebody of being a hypocrite and of speaking of God when he really means money. But what must we think of the intellectual capacity of a man who would conclude from the fact of hypocrisy that in reality moral good and evil are only other names for selfish interest? Such a man would deny the hypocritical character of the person whose hypocrisy was the starting point of his disappointment! In the very premise, namely the hypocrisy of this man, he clearly distinguished between the Tartuffe and the morally good man, between what the man pretends to be and what he really is.

Another form of ethical relativism is one that bases itself on a value-subjectivism, and which is in common vogue as a theory concerning values. This theory contends that whenever we attribute a value to something (e.g., in saying that a quartet of Beethoven is beautiful, a dialogue of Plato deep and luminous, or in praising Joseph's noble forgiveness of his brothers), in reality we mean a certain feeling which we experience in connection with those objects. Though we attribute beauty, goodness, or depth to an object, these are in reality nothing but mere states of soul which we objectify, erroneously attributing them to an object.

The adherents of this theory seek support for their contention in the fact that such erroneous projections are often found in everyday experience. We call some food healthy because it contributes to our health. But in the sense in which we say that we are healthy or in which we say that meat comes from a healthy animal, we cannot attribute health as such to a certain food. According to this theory, the same would apply to value-judgments: for instance, we call music beautiful, or an action morally good because they cause certain feelings in us; or because we associate certain feelings with the thought of certain objects.

Of course, so the theory continues, when we say "beautiful," "sublime," "good," or "noble," we are not speaking of mere illusions or fictions. We indicate by these terms something which is very real; but in fact this something is not a property of objects, acts, or persons, but a "feeling" which for one or another reason we connect with an object. Thus too the moral qualifications which we predicate of human actions or attitudes are in reality only feelings, connected for one reason or another with the object. So too, what we call moral obligation is really a specific type of coercive feeling. The experience of a "must" can be found in various forms in man's inner life, ranging from an *idée fixe* to all kinds of inhibitions. Moral obligation appealing to our conscience is thus nothing but a form of coercive feeling. It can thus easily be explained by psychology. To ascribe to this obligation an objective reality, an existence independent of our consciousness, is again the mere result of a psychological tendency, in this case the tendency for objectivizing.

Since values in general and moral values in particular are mere subjective feelings and not properties of things, and since moral obligation is also just a specific kind of feeling, it is accordingly impossible to ascribe to moral values or to moral obligation an objective validity. They are subjective and thus relative. If certain individuals, tribes, or cultural realms differ in their moral value-judgments, this is quite natural, for we can hardly expect everyone to have the same feelings in the face of certain objects. As one person likes very hot food and another dislikes it; as one prefers salty food and another unsalty; as one and the same thing may cause pleasure in one man and displeasure in another; how much more understandable then is it that we have different "value-feelings" with regard to the same thing, since the connection with the object seems to be even looser here than in these cases of certain bodily effects.

The main thesis of this value-subjectivism is, as we can see, one of those unfortunate discoveries [8] fabricated on the pattern that two obviously different essences are in reality one and the same; for instance, that in reality red is green, and that in reality the number two and the number three are identical. An unprejudiced analysis of the datum of values will inevitably reveal that this theory is not only a pure construction, flat and flimsy and deprived of any basis in the realm of data, but also that it is nonsensical in its confusion of concepts.

First of all, there is no reason whatsoever for declaring that the beauty of a melody, or even the moral sublimity of an act of charity, is in reality a feeling and not a property of the object. Experience tells us just the opposite. The beauty is given as a quality of the melody, and the sublimity as the quality of a moral act. This clearly differs from the way in which a typical feeling (e.g., a state of depression or irritation) is given to us.

The situation is just the opposite in the case of healthy foods. As soon as we try to verify what we mean by "healthy" (in saying, for example, that a certain mineral water is very healthy), we realize that we are using the term "healthy" in an analogous sense, and that the primary sense of health is in question only when we speak of a healthy man or a healthy animal or any other living being. We immediately realize that by healthy, we mean with respect to mineral water that it serves our health, either in overcoming or avoiding an illness. Moreover, we clearly see that the relation expressed by the term "serves," as when we say that medicine serves health, is a causal relation.

If on the contrary we ask ourselves what we mean in saying of a melody "How beautiful!" and in saying of an action "How noble!" "How good!" we find that in no way do we use these terms in an analogous sense and that they refer primarily to something else. There is neither a property of ourselves nor any feeling in our soul to which we could attribute the good or beautiful in its primary sense. Rather, we mean something

[8] Cf. Prolegomena, p. 4.

which precisely by its very nature can only be a predicate of the object.

In order to grasp how entirely superficial and senseless it is to reduce the values to feelings, we must consider for a moment the term "feeling." It is, as we shall see later in detail, an equivocal term.[9] It is sometimes used to denote mere states, such as fatigue, depression, irritation, anxiety: sometimes for experiences, such as bodily pain or bodily pleasure; and sometimes for meaningful affective responses, such as joy, sorrow, fear, enthusiasm. We shall see later [10] the essential difference which exists between a mere state of alteration and a meaningful, intentional response such as joy. Here it may suffice broadly to distinguish them, and to see how the subjective-value thesis looks against the background of this distinction.

If we interpret the thesis as asserting that moral goodness or beauty is in reality a feeling like a bodily pleasure, then the absurdity is immediately evident. There is nothing in experience which would allow such a reduction; rather, experience totally excludes it. A bodily pleasure extends in space and time. We can localize it more or less, and we can strictly measure its duration. To predicate of beauty or of moral goodness that it extends in space and in time is sheer nonsense.

Bodily pleasure presents itself univocally as something which can be experienced only by ourselves and which has no existence outside of its being experienced. Moral goodness and beauty clearly show themselves as things independent of our experience; we clearly realize that the moral goodness of another's act of charity in no way depends on its being witnessed by ourselves. On the contrary, we discover it to be good and we know that it would yet be good whether or not we were aware of it.

Now no one will actually try to reduce moral values or the dignity of a human person to certain bodily feelings, or to a projection of such feelings. This attempt is only to be found with respect to aesthetic values, such as beauty. We shall, however, disregard the specificity of this attempt here, because once one has grasped the impossibility of reducing values in general to feel-

9 By this we do not deny that there are some common features which are at the basis of the different uses of this term.
10 Chapter 17, "Value Response."

ings, the attempt to do so with aesthetic values reveals its futile character.

Insofar as values are concerned, moral values especially, this subjectivism contends that they are projections not of bodily but of psychical feelings. This theory holds that in praising as morally noble the action of a man, we only give *expression* to the fact that we rejoice before the object; that it moves us, or pleases us. And the content of these experiences is projected into the object: we express ourselves in our judgments as if the object were endowed with a certain quality.

According to this theory, value-judgments are merely a confused way of expressing ourselves. The real meaning of a value-judgment would then be: "I feel pleasure or displeasure in connection with this object," or "The object causes a positive or negative feeling in my soul." Yet, if we compare a value-judgment with a proposition dealing with our feelings, we immediately see the obvious difference. In stating that forgiveness is morally good, revenge morally evil, we mean by morally good the character of an attitude, and not of any feeling which I experience in witnessing these attitudes in another person. When, on the contrary, someone says, "I cannot stand angry people; they frighten me to death," he means a feeling which angry people cause in him. When someone says of a landscape that it is sublime, or that a human person has a higher value than an animal, he certainly does not mean by sublime or by value a feeling which he discovers in his soul. Sublimity, moral goodness, the value of a human person are either properties of a being or they are fictions. As we have already seen they can never be feelings, because predications which are meaningful and correct when applied to feelings or psychical entities become senseless when applied to values. The thesis that value-judgments are statements concerning one's feelings (and thus that they *are* feelings) is obviously wrong.

A special version of this value subjectivism is Ayer's emotive theory. He contends that value-judgments are not statements referring to our feeling, but rather a mere *expression* of feeling or a command.[11] Thus, according to him, value-judgments can

[11] A. J. Ayer, *Language, Truth and Logic* (London: Victor Gollancz, Ltd., 1950), pp. 20–22, 102ff.

be neither true nor false. The statement: "Justice is good," or "Injustice is evil" should, according to Ayer, be synonymous either with a mere expression of a feeling or with the command: "Be just," or "Do not be unjust."

The term "expression of feelings" is in many respects vague. In the first place, the term "feeling" is, as we mentioned above, equivocal; in order to give sense to this thesis, the datum which is here meant by feeling would have to be carefully elaborated. Secondly, the term "expression" is equally ambiguous. In its most authentic meaning the term refers to the intuitively given transparence of psychical entities in a person's face or in his voice or movements. In this sense we say that a face expresses joy, a voice expresses fear, a way of walking expresses an affected or sophisticated attitude. In this sense, too, we say that a certain face expresses kindness, purity, intelligence. It is obviously impossible in this primary sense of the term to identify a value-judgment with any expression.

By expression we may also mean any exteriorization of our emotions; e.g., tears may be an expression of sorrow, singing an expression of joy, or jumping in the air an expression of exuberant cheerfulness. In this sense certain words or even sentences may be called expressions of our joy, our sorrow, our fear, our enthusiasm. Such words and sentences obviously have a character completely different from any statement. They differ completely from a proposition in which we state that we rejoice or that we are angry. They have the function rather of an exteriorization, the character of a dynamic manifestation of our inner experience. This type of expression, Ayer contends, constitutes the major part of our value-judgments.

We can disregard in our context the thesis of Ayer that value-judgments are neither true nor false because they are not propositions. We may disregard this part of Ayer's thesis for, even if he admitted that value-judgments can be true or false, the main basis for his relativism would not be overthrown: if value-judgments really do only refer to feelings independently of the more logical question whether they can be true or false, then values would truly be something entirely subjective.

The point of interest here is to see whether Ayer is right in saying that value-judgments are an expression of feelings or a command. Now this theory is equally in blatant contradiction to experience. Great music is given as beautiful to me, the quality of beauty revealing itself univocally as a property of the object; it stands before my mind as distinct from pyschical experiences of my soul, such as joy, serenity, being moved, or sorrow and anxiety. The moral nobility of an act of charity is clearly given as a property of the act, as something on the object's side, definitely distinguished from any psychical happening in the soul.

Our primary contact with values is in no way a judgment; it is not the act of imparting a property to an object but the *perception* of something autonomous. The original experience is the perception of the importance of an object; only after this initial disclosure of the value may we by a judgment attribute it to an object.

In the case of an expression, the primary experience is an emotion, e.g., joy, sorrow, fear; and the words we utter as expression of this experience can in no way be interpreted as the formulation of something we perceived before as the property of an object. These dynamic expressions have an analogous character to the "Ouch" someone utters when he is hurt, or to the famous "Uh" of Mozart's Papageno when he sees Monostratos. They are an exteriorization of something, having no meaning in the strict sense, indicating no object, but having only the character of a projection of a psychical experience. They speak exclusively of the psychical entity whose expression they are; they manifest univocally the nature and presence of joy, sorrow, or fear.

This expression itself shows up only in an active, dynamic process of exteriorization. How could one pretend that the beauty of a great work of art, the value of truth, the moral value of justice, the dignity of the person (all of which are primarily known in a perception) are in reality mere expressions of feelings?

We are moved to tears because of the beauty of a work of art. Our being so affected is clearly distinguished therefore from the beauty of the object. How should the expression of our emotion be identical with beauty? Or how could one pretend that in saying that this work of art is beautiful, we are in reality not stating a fact but merely expressing our reaction?

Moreover, the untenable character of a theory such as Ayer's becomes fully manifest when we analyze the kind of feelings of which value-judgments are supposed to be expressions. It is obvious that mere states, such as fatigue, irritation, depression, which are only *caused* by an object, but not motivated by it, are not at all in question in the theory under inspection. Clearly they have not the dynamic trend of exteriorization, although they are typically "expressed" in the first and literal sense of expression. Obviously what Ayer means by the term "feeling" comes under the heading of intentional experiences, experiences having a meaningful conscious relation to an object. Experiences such as joy, sorrow, enthusiasm, indignation, admiration, contempt, love, hatred, hope, and fear are the feelings which, according to this theory, are the very source of value-judgments.

But the futility of this theory discloses itself as soon as we realize the nature of these acts. The intentional nature of affective responses, their meaningful response character, essentially *presupposes* the knowledge of a datum on the object's side which is the very reason for our joy or enthusiasm. So long as an object presents itself to our knowledge as neutral or indifferent such a response is impossible. This elementary fact, as we have already noted in the first chapter, became the starting point for Freud's discovery of the phenomenon of repression. So far are the affective responses from being the sources of the importance of the object that, on the contrary, they presuppose the knowledge of this importance.[12]

To believe that in stating the moral goodness of justice we only exteriorize our enthusiasm about justice is as absurd as to believe that the statement $2 + 2 = 4$ is nothing but an exteriorization of our conviction. The acts which in both these cases are said to exteriorize themselves in a statement cannot be separated from the object which they essentially presuppose. There is no enthusiasm, no veneration, no esteem *as such,* just as there is no conviction *as such.* Every veneration is essentially a veneration of someone; every enthusiasm, an enthusiasm *about* something;

[12] This importance can naturally also be the merely subjectively satisfying in the case of joy. But in these cases we are aware of the difference, for no man would speak of the financial profit about which he rejoices as morally noble, sublime, and so on. He might perhaps say that it is lucky.

every esteem, the esteem for a person; every conviction is necessarily conviction *of* a fact. The feelings to which, according to this theory, the values must be reduced, themselves presuppose an importance on the object side.

Thus Ayer confuses the *principium* with the *principiatum*. But apart from that it is plainly clear that the content of the quality on the side of the object (which we term "beautiful," "sublime," "heroic," "noble," and so forth) clearly differs from the content of our responses, such as joy, enthusiasm, love, admiration, esteem, and so on. Above all, the radical difference which separates the *consciousness of* something, the awareness of an object and its quality, from our response to it should once and for all make manifest the impossibility of identifying the sublimity of Beethoven's Ninth Symphony, which we grasp, with our experience of being moved by it or enthused about it. C. S. Lewis unmasks in a brilliant way the ridiculous confusion of this interpretation of values:

Even on their own view—on any conceivable view—the man who says *This is sublime* cannot mean *I have sublime feelings*. Even if it were granted that such qualities as sublimity were simply and solely projected into things from our own emotions, yet the emotions which prompt the projection are the correlatives, and therefore almost the opposites, of the qualities projected. The feelings which make a man call an object sublime are not sublime feelings but feelings of veneration.[13]

In summarizing we can say that the attempt to interpret the values as mere projections of feelings into an object, either because the object causes these feelings or because we associate them with the object, collapses and reveals itself as sheer nonsense as soon as we take the trouble first to expose the equivocal character of the term "feeling," and then to examine the real nature of the experiences in which we grasp a value and respond to it.

The attempt to interpret value-judgments as sentences, expressions, or commands also collapses when minutely analyzed. It is obviously impossible to interpret as commands statements such as "The Ninth Symphony of Beethoven is beautiful," or

[13] *Op. cit.,* p. 2.

"The human person has a higher value than an animal," or "Truth is something precious." What kind of command should these value-judgments embody? If one would say it is a command to appreciate this music, or to respect the human person, or to worship truth, the question-begging character of such a view is obvious. Not only does one definitely mean something else, but the very reason for commanding such responses is precisely the *value* of the object. This involves the same confusion as if one would say, "It is true that Caesar was murdered in 43 B.C.," and make this statement synonymous with the command to be convinced of it.

Without doubt, this reduction of values to a mere object of commanding is meant only to be applied to moral values. The transposition of the extra-moral value-judgments into commands is so plainly artificial that we can hardly believe anyone would seriously cling to it.

In the moral sphere, of course, commands and prohibitions play a great role. It is here that the view under consideration attains a certain meaning, in the assertion, for instance, that the sentence "Killing is morally evil" is synonymous with the sentence "Thou shalt not kill," or, again, that "Charity is morally good" is synonymous with "Thou shalt love thy neighbor as thyself."

Now it is not difficult to see that the two sentences are not identical in meaning; they express two different facts, although these facts are interrelated. In stating that killing is *evil*, we clearly refer to a property of the act of killing; but we are not expressing any prohibition. We do not even refer to any prohibition. But we are certainly indicating a fact which necessarily leads to the prohibition. We refer to something which is, on the one hand, the reason and basis for the prohibition, and from which, on the other hand, the prohibition logically follows. The same applies when we state that charity is good. We must realize that the connection between both facts—the goodness and the command to goodness—is evidently such that the goodness is the *principium,* and the command, the *principiatum.* Thus, it is impossible to substitute the command for the value, because the command, as soon as it is a moral command and not a mere positive commandment (such as the commandment in the Decalogue to observe the Sabbath), necessarily presupposes the value of the object to which it refers.

It would be just as nonsensical if one said that truth is nothing but the commandment to be convinced of something. In reality the truth of a sentence is presupposed in its independence in order to require conviction and oblige belief in it.

And what kind of command then should the moral value-judgment involve? Arbitrary commands which an incompetent individual places on someone else? Obviously not. Perhaps the commands of a community? This would amount to the relativism of the French sociological school which we discussed above, or at least to a pure value positivism.

If on the contrary the command in question is conceived as issuing from a true authority (e.g., the father in the family, the state, and above all the Church), the value is presupposed in the very notion of true authority. But even a true authority, implying the notion of value, could only be claimed to be the source of a valid positive law. The difference between a merely positive law and a moral commandment is so obvious and has so often been stressed that we need no longer insist on it.[14]

In our age of psychoanalysis it is high time that we had a psychoanalysis of relativism. If anything calls for a psychoanalytic investigation, it is the artificial and desperate effort to deny the most obvious data and to make of them innumerably different things—anything in fact except what they distinctly reveal themselves to be.

[14] As Husserl convincingly showed in his *Logische Untersuchungen,* Part I, it is incorrect to say, "Logic is a normative discipline," because logic does not deal primarily with commands, but shows the objective validity of the principle of contradiction or of the laws of syllogism. The same applies to ethics. The fact that something is endowed with a value is at the basis of every true moral norm.

III. Fundamental Aspects of the Sphere of Values

CHAPTER 10

ONTOLOGICAL AND QUALITATIVE VALUES

WE REFERRED earlier to the hierarchical structure of values when we discussed the difference between value and the merely subjectively satisfying, and the impossibility of reducing their difference to one of mere degree.[1] We have stressed the fact that there exists not only a scale in the realm of values but also a hierarchical gradation which permits us to speak of a higher and lower value, or a higher and lower good, according to their respective values. We may say that one landscape is still more beautiful than another, or that intellectual depth and richness ranks higher than an inexhaustible vitality or an exuberant temperament. We rightly say that humility ranks higher than self-control. This hierarchical order is so fundamental that to conform to it in the *ordo amoris* is, according to St. Augustine, the source of all morality.[2]

It would, however, be wrong to believe that values differ only in their rank. There is no successive gradation which permits an ascent from the lowest values to the highest. Rather, there exist different value domains or value families which are distinguished not only by their rank but also by their profoundly different themes: moral values, intellectual values, aesthetic values, and others.

It can easily be seen that generosity is more congenial to humility, chastity, and justice than to intelligence or wittiness or a great sense of humor. Generosity, humility, purity, justice, and charity all belong to one and the same family of values, the

---

[1] Cf. Chapter 3, "The Categories of Importance."
[2] *De Civitate Dei,* XV, 22.

moral values which are characterized by the basic value of moral goodness. And intellectual acuteness, wit, intellectual depth and brilliance belong again to one and the same family of values, the intellectual values, which, as a whole, clearly differ from the moral ones. The same applies, *mutatis mutandis*, to the domain of aesthetical values which embrace values such as loveliness, gloriousness or grandeur, and center around the basic value of beauty. Each of these value domains has its own basic theme. Each one embraces several values which differ qualitatively among themselves, as, for instance, in the moral sphere, loyalty, reliability, veracity, justice, purity, humility, and many others. Each one has a hierarchy of its own: humility ranks higher than reliability, and intellectual depth ranks higher than acuteness. But the difference in quality and rank of the value types in one and the same family of values cannot be compared with the difference between the value domains. Here the difference is not only a qualitative one, but a difference of theme and *ratio;* a different genus of values is in question.[3]

Thus we have to distinguish between the hierarchy in the frame of one and the same family of values and the hierarchy of the different value families themselves. This latter hierarchy we have in view when we say that moral values rank higher than intellectual values. We then compare the different domains and the difference in rank of their respective themes. Later on we shall come back to the difference between value families when, in Chapter 15, the specific nature of moral values will be examined. Yet the distinction between different value domains on the one hand, and different values in each of these domains, is not the only one which has to be made in the realm of values.

When we speak of the value of the human person, of the dignity of a human being, endowed with reason and free will, when we face the preciousness of personal being, of an immortal

---

[3] Some of these value domains may themselves have subdivisions, each dominated by a new theme which, however, is a ramification of the theme of the entire value domain. In the realm of intellectual values, for instance, we have to distinguish as subordinated value families the domain on the one hand embracing intelligence in the narrower sense of the word—intellectual acuteness as well as intellectual alertness, *esprit*, wit, intellectual depth and power—and on the other hand, a domain embracing all the values which are to be found in an artistic genius, as well as in the receptive susceptibility for artistic values.

soul, then we are undoubtedly confronted with something important-in-itself. But is this preciousness of a human being, which calls for respect and love, a value in precisely the same sense as the value of generosity or meekness? Does it belong only to another domain of values, or is the difference here a more fundamental one? If it is an analogous difference such as the one we found between moral and intellectual values, we must ask to which domain of values this preciousness belongs or whether perhaps it itself constitutes a family of values of its own.

It seems that the value which a human person possesses as such (or in other words, the *ontological* value of a person) does not fit into any of the value domains mentioned above, and differs in many respects from all those qualitative values which we find in the moral, intellectual, or aesthetic value domains.

We have indeed to distinguish between ontological values (such as the value of a living being, a human being, an angel) and the more qualitative types of values which we find gathered in different value families. In order to examine this difference we shall compare, in a minute analysis, typical representatives of the qualitative values and of the ontological values, that is to say, moral values on the one hand and, on the other, the ontological value of the human person.[4]

The first difference which strikes us is that in the sphere of moral values we find a counterpart to each positive value, which we might call a disvalue. For instance, to justice there is opposed injustice; to humility, pride; to goodness, wickedness; to charity, hateful hardheartedness; to purity, impurity. These disvalues are not the mere absence of positive values. They are opposed to them in a qualitative way; as analogously, sorrow is opposed to

---

4 Even before we begin this analysis someone may object that this difference has already been clearly expressed by the distinction between a moral good and a physical good. The value of the person as such is a physical good which has always been distinguished from the moral good.

Important and classical as is the distinction between moral and physical good, and as true as it is that the difference between the fully qualitative values and the ontological values may in some way be at the basis of this distinction, nevertheless it does not coincide with the one we are here discussing. For in this distinction moral values are contrasted to all other types of values, and thus intellectual values as well as aesthetic values belong to the physical goods, whereas in our case the qualitative values, embracing the intellectual and aesthetic values, are contrasted to the ontological values.

joy. They are both distinct qualities, each antithetical to the other.

But in the case of the preciousness of the human being, of the *dignitas humanae substantiae* (the dignity of human nature),[5] of the nobility proper to a being endowed with an immortal soul, such an antithetical disvalue does not exist. Impersonal beings which are deprived of this preciousness are in no way negative. There exists no antithetical quality to this preciousness, but only an absence of it, and this cannot be considered a disvalue. The same applies analogously to the being of which we predicate value. Whereas there exist real attitudes and actions which are morally evil (for instance, hatred, envy, murder, adultery), there exists no real being possessing a negative value or disvalue which would be antagonistic to the preciousness that a human person as such possesses. Animals do not possess this preciousness; and the mere absence of this preciousness is in no way a disvalue. There is no contrary antithesis to a person, but only a contradictory one, such as the non-existence of a person; and this non-existence *as such* is not yet equivalent to a disvalue.

A second feature distinguishing the two types of value from one another is manifested in the relation between the value and the being embodying the value. Moral values present themselves much more as something of their own, as something more independent of their bearer and of the attitude which incarnates them than does the preciousness of the human person with respect to the human person. The very fact that we are able to form a concept of the different moral values, that we have a name for generosity, veracity, humility, and so forth, testifies to this character of the qualitative values.[6] We have no proper name to characterize the ontological value of the human person as such, but we must instead refer to the being which incarnates this value. The nature of generosity or veracity or humility has a full *eidos* of its own. It is something definite which allows us to substantize these values; whereas the ontological value of the

[5] Offertory of the Holy Mass.

[6] It must be stressed, however, that it would be wrong to believe that every qualitative value of which we are aware has its "name" and is fitted to a concept. There are many qualitative values for which we have as yet no name, and which have not yet been conceptualized.

person resists such a procedure and forces us to refer constantly to the person himself.

This becomes especially clear if we compare the ontological value of the will to the moral value of a *good* will. The moral value which we face when somebody refuses to enrich himself by betraying another person, or when he withstands torture rather than tell a lie, clearly differs from the ontological value of free will as such. The ontological value of the will receives its *forma*, so to speak, from the will, and we have no other possibility than to refer to the will in order to distinguish this ontological value from other ontological values. The moral value of honesty, on the contrary, which shines forth from the will is in itself something clearly shaped, possessing a certain independence, having an essence of its own. And so in distinguishing honesty from veracity, charity, purity, and justice, we are always confronted by a definite outspoken qualitative quiddity. Certainly in order to grasp these values we have to know about attitudes, acts, and actions of the person. We have to look at the direction of this particular will, the end of the person's action, the object of the person's love. But this necessity for looking at a human attitude in which a moral value is embodied, in order to grasp the value, in no way contradicts the character of independence mentioned above which the quiddity of the moral values possesses.

On the other hand, the fact that different types of actions and attitudes can be endowed with one and the same moral value (honesty, for example) clearly testifies to this "independence." Once I know this value, I have something quite definite before my mind, something which possesses a true essence of its own.

Perhaps the difference between qualitative and ontological values explains in some way the difference between the Platonic and the Aristotelian approach to the good. For Plato there exists *the Good*, the "idea" of goodness, which is the source of all goodness. It is by participation in this goodness that something becomes good. Goodness transcends every single being which is good. But for Aristotle there exists no such absolute transcendent goodness, but only an immanent perfection of a being. Insofar as a value in the most typical sense of the word is at stake (i.e., a moral or an aesthetic value), the Platonic view is much more correct; insofar as an ontological value is at stake, the Aristotelian seems to be more correct.

A third distinguishing mark is the different way in which the moral value on the one hand and the ontological value of the person on the other reflect God. Moral values speak of God in a specific way. God is *the* Goodness, *the* Veracity, *the* Justice, *the* Charity, and every moral goodness of a human being contains an element of *similitudo Dei.* This becomes quite clear as soon as we think of the supernatural morality which is implied in holiness. To be sure, this morality of the saints is also something incomparably new in quality with respect to all merely natural morality. Nevertheless, the fact that every morally evil action "offends" God clearly reveals the mysterious and intimate relation between God and the moral sphere, even in a merely natural frame. This will become clearer in other parts of this analysis.[7]

When we grasp the moral value in an act of another person, even one of merely natural morality, we are clearly aware that we are confronted by a world above us. But the ontological value of another person is not in the same sense above ourselves as is his generosity, or his charity and justice which are definitely of a rank higher than we. The moral value has the character of a more direct and specific reflection of God; it is a ray of the sun of infinite goodness, a specific message of God. The ontological value, on the other hand, is so linked to the being of a human person that it reflects God in the way in which this being reflects God; the message goes, so to speak, through the nature of this being, which is an *imago Dei,* and its ontological preciousness mirrors God according to the ontological reflection. It is not a direct message of God and of the world of God such as is conveyed by the moral values, or, in a completely new and incomparable way, by the morality of the saints. In comparing the ontological value of man and the moral perfection to which our Lord calls us, we are confronted with the great difference between the *imago Dei* and the *similitudo Dei.*

The deep difference between qualitative values and ontological value also clearly manifests itself in the different attitudes

---

[7] Chapter 14, "God and Values," and especially Chapter 15, "The Nature of Moral Values."

which a man should have toward his own ontological value and toward the qualitative values with which he is endowed. True humility places a veil on all qualitative values which our own person may possess, whether it is beauty, charm, or brilliant gifts of intelligence, and above all on moral values. But humility in no way requires that we should be unaware of the ontological value of the *imago Dei* which we embody as human persons. To minimize or to overlook the ontological value of one's own person, its dignity as *imago Dei,* would be the pseudo humility of the pantheist who sees man as a speck of dust against the enormous background of the universe. The pantheist accuses the Christian of being pretentious in believing that God could love such a speck of dust. But true Christian humility is fully conscious of the preciousness of an immortal soul, and understands the task and responsibility issuing from this dignity as well as our misery when we fail in that task and that responsibility.

Furthermore, we can say that the ontological value of a person is proper to this being as such. Once this being exists, it has this ontological value, and there is no possibility of its losing it. The moral values, on the contrary, may or may not be embodied in a person or in an act of willing. The moral values are not guaranteed by the existence of a human person but depend on a specific attitude of the person, or on a specific direction of his will.

This difference manifests itself especially in the fact that one human person cannot possess his ontological value in a higher degree than can another human being. There exists no gradation of this specific kind, no "more or less" of a specific ontological value. With respect to the moral values, however, we can speak of a "more or less." We can say, for instance, that one man is more reliable than another, more just or more generous. We mean in this case that of two persons, both of whom are reliable or generous, one possesses this virtue in a still higher degree than the other.

We can also speak of a hierarchy of ontological values. We find a hierarchy in the realm of being and clearly see that the ontological value of a living organism ranks higher than that of dead matter; that of an animal higher than that of a plant; that of a human person higher than that of an animal.

But this hierarchy concerns the relation between one ontological value and other ontological values; it is somewhat like the hierarchy existing between different value domains. The superiority of the ontological value of a person as compared with the ontological value of an animal is analogous to the superiority which the moral sphere of values universally possesses as compared with the value family of intellectual or vital values. The hierarchy within the moral sphere which allows us to say that humility ranks higher than reliability finds no strict analogy in the ontological values; this is because, instead of a value family, here the ontological value of a species or genus represents each time a new type of value, such as the value of animal life, the value of a human being or the value of an angel.

I say "no strict analogy" because there is indeed a hierarchy concerning the ontological value of the different capacities of man. The intellect ranks higher than the senses; the will ranks higher than a mere instinct. Even if we prescind from all qualitative values with which they can and should be endowed, it is obvious that a spiritual act of free, conscious willing is something incomparably more precious than an instinct and possesses an entirely different ontological dignity. Thus we may say that though there is no hierarchical gradation in the frame of the ontological value of man corresponding to the hierarchical scale in a single value domain, something similar can be found when we confront the different capacities or parts of man; hence we speak of the spiritual sphere as ranking much higher than the merely vital, irrational sphere. The same applies analogously to different bodily senses when we say, for instance, that sight is nobler than taste.

It remains true, however, that the gradation to be found in the realm of qualitative values is not present in the same way among ontological values. We cannot say with respect to one and the same type of being that this individual possesses its ontological value in a higher degree than another individual. It is impossible to say that the dignity of human nature and of an immortal soul is more to be found in one man than in another, whereas we constantly refer to the fact that one person is more humble or more intelligent or more beautiful than another.

Another possible misunderstanding must be eliminated. We sometimes say of one person that he embodies, as it were, the *idea* of man to a higher degree than another. We say of a great personality, for instance, "This is truly a man"; he seems in an extraordinary way to embody all fundamental human capacities and to overshadow all other men. It is precisely this which we have in mind in distinguishing a great personality from all others. But in saying "personality" instead of "person" we are no longer concerned with the ontological value as such, but with all the qualitative values to which a human person is called and which he is destined to possess. The ontological value as such cannot be possessed by one person to a higher degree than by another. Even in the case of an idiot it is not possible to say that he possesses an ontological value in a lower degree. Rather, what distinguishes him from a normal person is a factor which goes in a different direction, and is more akin to the difference between potency and act than to the difference of gradation of values.

A further fundamental difference between the ontological value of the person and moral values manifests itself in the manner of their realization. The ontological value, the preciousness of the human person as such, is realized by the existence of a human being. If the human person were annihilated—that is to say, if God ceased to sustain him in existence—this ontological value would no longer be realized. Moral values, on the other hand, become real through a free attitude of the person; for instance, when the person is endowed with a virtue. The moral value ceases to be real if the person loses this virtue. Such loss of virtue is a moral evil. If a humble person should collapse into nothingness through the withdrawal of the *concursus divinus,* the value of this humility would also cease to be realized *hic et nunc,* though in a quite different way. This destruction would be a physical evil, not a moral one. The former is a real dissipation of a moral value; while the latter is only a withdrawal of the ontological basis necessary for the realization of the moral value.

Although the human person can be dissipated only by the withdrawal of the *concursus divinus* (a hypothesis that we have to exclude), it would seem that the ontological value of a human person never ceases to be real once the person is granted existence. Yet man is so much ordered toward moral perfection that a failure here would ultimately frustrate the ontological value.

Finally, the way in which the value is proper to the being in question differs insofar as it is an ontological value or a moral value. Some of the forementioned marks clearly evidence this decisive difference. The ontological value, as we have seen, is so closely connected with the respective being (in our example the human person) that it is impossible to describe the relation as a participation in the value; with moral goodness, however, we have a natural tendency to admit that the act of forgiving *participates* in the moral value of generosity and mercy.[8] The ontological value is immanent to the being; but moral values transcend the being which is endowed with them.

This fact would not reduce the ontological value to the being itself; or, in other words, this would in no way identify the being with its ontological value, an attempt which has already been refuted. It is not by chance that in looking at the ontological value of something we speak of a *good*, whereas in the moral sphere we speak rather of a moral *value*. The ontological value is so much embodied in a being, so much included in it, that we are tempted to form one concept embracing the whole—the specific being as well as its value—while the transcendence of moral values, on the contrary, presses us to form a concept of the objective importance as such.

Thus we see that in the realm of values, apart from the distinction between different value domains, a much more radical distinction must be made: the one between the ontological values on the one hand, and the qualitative values on the other.

This distinction is obviously not restricted merely to the ontological value of the person and the moral values. We chose these two only in order to explain the far-reaching difference of the nature of value in both cases. On the one hand, there exists also an ontological value of matter, its solidity, its dynamism and power, as well as an ontological value of vegetative and sensitive life and others. And on the other hand, the aesthetic values are

---

[8] This should not however be interpreted as if these moral values had a subsisting *reality* of their own. They are an ultimate, substantial reality in God, but in the world of creatures they are a concrete reality insofar as they are embodied in an act of a person. They possess this transcendent character, however, by their very nature, and consequently they stand before us as a unique message from something higher than ourselves—from God.

representative of qualitative values just as typically as moral values are.

Thus we find, on the one hand, several ontological values such as the dignity of matter, the dignity of life, the preciousness of a human being or of an angel; and on the other hand, the different value domains, each of which embraces several values of this fully qualitative type. The difference between these is much deeper than the difference existing among the several value families, and one profound enough to permit us to say that when we face an ontological value as opposed to a qualitative value a completely different type of value is at stake.

Chapter 11

UNITY OF VALUES

IT IS a specific characteristic of the qualitative values, as we have seen before, that to each positive value there corresponds a disvalue which is contrary to it. The nature of the antithesis is neither a contradictory one in the strict sense of the term, nor merely a radical difference implying an element of qualitative contrariety. The way in which injustice is opposed to justice, avarice to generosity, or moral wickedness to moral goodness is neither that of the contradictory opposite (for there is more than a mere absence of the positive value), nor is it an antithesis of such a kind as exists between white and black, green and red, or even pleasure and pain. The disvalue is too qualitative, representing too much a quality of its own, to be considered a mere contradictory negation.

On the other hand, the disvalue is too specifically antithetical, prospering too much on its negation of the positive value, to be considered on the same level of being as the positive value. Green is as much something of its own as is red, and it can be grasped without any reference to red. Even in the case of black and white, in which white seems to be more positive, it is never enough simply to call white the positive part and black the negative counterpart. In the case of pain and pleasure, one may call pain negative and pleasure positive, but not in the sense that pain in its very quiddity implies the negation of pleasure and thus necessarily refers to it. The negative aspect in pain is a mere qualitative characteristic which points to its hostile character, and to the fact that it is an attack upon us which should not exist, which calls, as it were, for a dissolution.

The limits of this book make it impossible for us to go into a detailed analysis of qualitative contrariety as it exists between moral good and evil, beauty and ugliness, intelligence and stupidity, superficiality and depth, and so on. In the sphere of ontological values, as we have seen, there exists no analogy to this contrary antithesis. To the ontological value of man, to the dignity and preciousness of a human person endowed with an immortal soul and capable of accomplishing spiritual acts, there exists an antithesis only in the non-existence of this value, and not in any qualitative disvalue antagonistic to it.

In the realm of values, however, there exists still another and completely different type of antithesis which we shall term "polarity." This polarity is not to be found between the disvalues and the positive values, but found rather in the realm of positive values themselves as well as in the realm of disvalues. One and the same thing cannot be as grand, overpowering, and inspiring as the Himalaya Mountains, and lovely, charming, and delicate as a blossoming cherry tree or a violet. Something cannot be solemn and tragic and at the same time amusing and comical. One and the same person cannot at once be endowed with an overwhelmingly powerful vitality and with an ethereal delicacy. In the same way, one and the same thing cannot be simultaneously boring and menacingly fearful, or one and the same person dully impassive and indifferent and at the same time show tremendous irascibility and nervous irritability.

This kind of exclusivity is opposed to any real contrariety or antagonism. It is a polarity among values (or among disvalues). It is not a hostile antithesis but a complementary (even a friendly) polarity so far as qualitative values are concerned. Their exclusivity is not a result of an antithetical character in their very qualities, but rather of the mere incapacity of one and the same being to be endowed simultaneously with those different values or disvalues. It is an exclusivity which certainly includes a qualitative difference, even a polarity, but not insofar as their character as positive values is concerned.

Such exclusive qualities therefore are both positive values, in most cases belonging even to the same value domain. Majestic grandeur and delicate loveliness are both aesthetic values, each a different dimension of a unitary beauty. Far from being antagonistic to one another in the sense of qualitative incompatibility and hostile contrast, both are, on the contrary, messengers of one and the same absolute beauty, completing instead of combatting each other.

This kind of exclusiveness is thus rooted in the limitation of created beings. This limited capacity of a contingent being to be bearer of polar qualitative values is related to the limitation of its ontological perfections. The higher the rank of a being and the greater its ontological plenitude, the wider is the range of qualitative values and the more different and "distanced" are the values which it is able to embody.

If we think of the limitations of matter, we see that the ontological values are here only of one sphere and of one type; whereas a human person implies ontological values and perfections of different orders, for instance of the order of matter, of organic life, and of spiritual being. But we are not now thinking of values which are distanced in the sense of being discrepant perfections, such as a bodily perfection of strength on the one hand and on the other, a spiritual perfection of knowledge. Rather we are concerned with a distance which applies to qualitative values belonging to one and the same value domain, but which represent, as it were, the most distanced dimensions possible within this domain, so far apart that they appear almost in opposition.

And their exclusiveness means only that one and the same *individual* is not able simultaneously to possess two of these *distanced* values. Whereas certain values cannot be possessed by a specific type of being (for instance, moral values cannot be possessed by an impersonal being), two polar values can be found as properties of the same genus or species, but not in one and the same individual.

In order to clarify further the nature of this friendly polarity among values, we shall distinguish four different types of exclusiveness.

The first and most formal type of exclusiveness is that between existence and non-existence. We could call it contradictory exclusiveness.

The second refers to a more qualitative, yet radical antithesis which exists between true and false, and above all between good and evil. It is distinguished from formal contradictory exclusiveness by the fact that its negative counterpart is not a mere absence of the positive, but is itself something possessing an *essence* of its own. Moral evil is, as we have seen earlier, not merely the absence of moral goodness. It opposes moral goodness still more than does the mere absence of it. It is something qualitatively incompatible with it; indeed, antagonistic to it. In this fact we touch a second mark of this type of exclusiveness: the hostile character, the antagonism, the condemnation of the negative by the positive, the rebellion of the negative against the positive. This characteristic also manifests itself in the fact that we can call the one (namely goodness) positive, and the other (namely evil) negative, even though the negative is definitely not synonymous with the mere absence of the positive. This implies the absolute primacy of the positive with respect to the negative.[1]

Thirdly, there exists an antithesis which also implies a certain hostile character, an inevitable struggle of the one against the other, but in a fertile, complementary manner; it is the antithesis which tends to prepare a higher synthesis. This fertile polarity displays itself in history, especially in the history of thought, in the realm of culture, and in the relations between nations. It is this kind of polarity concerning which the words of Heraclitus: *Polemos pater panton*—"War is the father of all things"—assume a certain validity; on the condition, however, that we replace the *panton* (all), by "many things." Here also the Hegelian thesis, antithesis, synthesis finds justification.

Fourthly, there is the polarity among values, which we have discussed here. It is a thoroughly complementary polarity, not only fertile but friendly and in no way antithetic. It could be compared to the polarity of male and female. This polarity is not only compatible with the inner unity of the values, but even implies it. The two values (e.g., of lovely graciousness and powerful strength, or the meekness and imperturbable strength of the *miles Christi*, the soldier of Christ) are rays of one and the same sun: in their diversity they are manifestations of the infinite range of absolute goodness and beauty, and testify to the words

[1] In this sense of antithesis, it is as obviously impossible to call God a *coincidentia oppositorum*, as it was in the sense of formal contradictory exclusiveness.

of St. James, *Pater omnium luminum*—"God, Father of all lights."

The higher a being ranks, the more it is able to actualize different and distanced values. In the supernatural order we find a participation with God which enables man to effect a far-reaching *coincidentia oppositorum,* a conjunction of opposites. The *coincidentia oppositorum* never refers to the antithesis of positive values and disvalues, nor to an opposition such as being and non-being, but precisely to values and perfections which exclude each other because of the limitedness of a being.[2]

What matters for our context is to distinguish this exclusivity from the antithesis existing between negative and positive values. This exclusivity to be found in the realm of positive and even of negative qualitative values is analogous to the one found among ontological values.

The ontological value of a color differs from that which a sound possesses, and *as* color it cannot simultaneously be a sound; these values exclude each other at one and the same "place" in the universe. Sometimes a higher being possesses the ontological value and perfection of a lower being. This may somehow, for instance, be said of an animal possessing the sensitive dimension of life in addition to the vegetative dimension. But in other respects, plants have perfections and values of their own which animals do not have. The absolute being however possesses all possible ontological and qualitative values *per eminentiam.*

If the exclusivity of qualitative values is only due to the limitation of contingent beings, that is to say, if it is based on the impossibility of being realized in one and the same contingent being, their polarity is clearly rooted in their very quality. Their polarity is not a mere "otherness" as in the case of ontological values, e.g., the ontological value of color and of sound. Yet their antithesis does not concern their character as value, but only their quality. And as we have seen before, it is a friendly and complementary antithesis. This polarity thus in no way affects the ultimate unity of all positive values to which only the disvalues are really opposed.

[2] D. von Hildebrand, *Transformation in Christ* (New York: Longmans, Green and Co., 1948).

CHAPTER 12

VALUE AND BEING

ONE OF the most fundamental problems of metaphysics is the relation between being and value. We do not intend to offer here an exploration of this problem, still less to answer all the questions which may arise in this connection. We want only to state different facts which reveal themselves in an undubitable way, and which indicate the direction for a fuller exploration.

The first decisive fact we have to state is this: *The notion of good and the notion of being are not identical.* Whatever may be the real connection between them, we have not yet formulated the datum of importance so long as we state only that something exists. We have already stressed this fact in our analysis of importance in Chapter 1. Now we must repeat it with respect to the relation between intrinsic importance, or value, and being. Every inquiry into whether or not a being really existing is good, whether or not it has a value, testifies to the truth of this statement. In knowing that it really exists, we do not thereby necessarily know whether it is a good or an evil. We hear of a political party, and examine it thoroughly in order to see whether its aims are good or evil, and whether its existence must thus be considered as a good or an evil. We state that something is; but when we affirm its existence, the question of whether or not it has a value is not yet touched.[1] It certainly is possible to analyze a being, its nature and existence, without referring to its value.

1 St. Augustine clearly states this difference in saying: *Hoc autem interest, quod ad cognoscendum satis est, ut videamus ita esse aliquid vel non ita, ad judicandum vero addimus aliquid, quo significemus posse et aliter; velut cum dicimus: "Ita esse debet," aut: "Ita esse debuit," aut: "Ita esse debebit," ut in suis operibus artifices faciunt. De Vera Religione, 58.*

This approach is even very common in certain types of inquiry, e.g., in the scientific exploration of matter and life, or in the everyday pragmatic approach in which many things interest us only as practical means.

Above all, the words of Genesis: "And God saw that they were good" testify to the difference between the notions of good and being. This obviously means more than "He saw that they have being or that they exist." Whatever may be the value which the word "good" expresses here, it is not synonymous with "existing."

In stating that the notions of value and being are not synonymous we are thinking of ontological as well as of qualitative values. Yet this is even true with respect to the value which every being possesses because it is something real.

With this we come to a second fundamental statement which we want to make here: There exists a general value which is proper to being as such. This does not mean that we want to declare by definition that *value* is a property of being. We mean rather that, through philosophical analysis, we can attain the insight that being *as such* possesses a distinctive value. Only after having acquired the notion of value in those cases wherein the specific nature of value discloses itself in the most evident way (for instance, in the qualitative values) can we take up this inquiry and intuit this fundamental fact. Every being possesses a certain value insofar as it is something, as it is a being. We grasp this value when we contrast the being to mere fictions.

If we consider the emptiness and inanity of something fictitious, its dependence upon our arbitrary imagination, and if we compare this with the autonomous consistency of being as such which imposes itself on us, then this most general and basic value of being as such, its dignity, seriousness, and majesty, discloses itself.

If we focus our attention on the mystery of being as such as opposed to non-being (e.g., the object of an error or an illusion), the unique value which is proper to being as such clearly reveals itself. But this contemplation of being as such is to be found only in philosophy. In our non-philosophical approach we do not look at being as such, but only at concrete beings; and with respect to these the value which is proper to being as such is for the most part not grasped.

In the foregoing chapter we distinguished the qualitative from the ontological values. It is clear that the formal value of being as such is not a qualitative value, such as the moral value of purity or the aesthetical value of beauty. But it also differs from what we have termed ontological values. It could without any doubt equally be called ontological, and even, *a fortiori*, deserves this name. But what matters is that it differs from the type of value termed ontological. It is not the value rooted in the nature of a being, such as the value of a plant as a living being, or as the value of a human person, his dignity and preciousness. It is much more formal than any ontological value embodied in the specific nature of a being.

Whereas the ontological values are embodied in the specific nature of a being, in its particular "such-being," the value of being in general is rooted in being as such, as opposed to non-being. It is the value which "to be something" embodies; the value of having an essence and existence as such, without any reference to the specific character of its nature. This value is so formal that we can only grasp it in a radical abstraction, the third degree of abstraction in the Aristotelian-Thomistic terminology. The difference between this quite general and formal type of value of being as such and the values which we termed "ontological" is thus quite clear.

This value of being as such, however, is so formal and so far remote from the qualitative values that it never in a single created individual being discloses itself in its full depth and grandeur. In all high-ranking beings either the qualitative values or their ontological value are so completely in the foreground and surpass this formal value to such an extent that it is, as it were, absorbed by the qualitative as well as the specific ontological values. The formal value of "being something," as opposed to nothingness, is absorbed by the value of its specific essence; and the formal value of existence is absorbed by the value that *this* object, endowed with ontological and qualitative values, has as existing.

In beings, such as a discarded tool, which are deprived of all qualitative values and of any perceptible ontological value, which thus present themselves as neutral or indifferent, this formal value of being as such does not ordinarily disclose itself. This value is primarily proper to being in general; it discloses itself only when we look at being as such in an abstraction. The discarded tool shares in this value in a manner which cannot be compared with the way in which a horse or a human person embody their ontological values.

We must retreat a moment and think of being as such in order to discover the dignity and preciousness which even the discarded tool possesses insofar as it is something real and existing; or, as we can put it, the mystery of being in general possesses this value, and low-ranking individual beings exemplify it more than they really embody it.

In general, we are not aware of this value, for many beings present themselves to us as indifferent in our normal approach to life. We look on a discarded tool or at a stone lying on the road as something neutral, indifferent, lacking a specific value. The same applies to many facts which we accept as inevitable realities; for instance, that a stone has a certain weight, or that it will fall if we drop it. We have to turn to a special situation in order to find a certain awareness of the general value of being as such.

The value of being as such is thrown into relief, for instance, in the voice of our conscience warning us to abstain from lying. A lie implies a typical disrespect for the dignity and majesty of being. The liar treats reality as something at the disposal of his arbitrary sovereignty. He denies the existence of some fact as soon as this fact does not fit into his aims for one or another reason, or when the admission of it is disagreeable, dangerous, or confusing for him. If we abstract from the deception which is connected with lying, a deception which need not in every case be morally illegitimate, the intrinsic immorality of every lie consists partly in the disrespect for the value of being as such and in not conforming ourselves to reality in our affirmation, although the very nature of affirmation implies the claim to do so. Certainly another decisive factor in the immorality of a lie is the abuse of the privilege granted to us to "copy" reality, as it were, by our statements. But this also is linked to disrespect for the unalterable majesty of reality, of existence. In understanding the obligation to tell the truth and to abstain from lying, we respond in a specific way to the value of being as such. Here this value of being flashes up and imposes on us the obligation to conform to it. In the same way, the value of being as such is reflected in the dignity and beauty of truth.

The basic value of being as such is equally thrown into relief by the fact that man on many occasions prefers to know even a sad reality than to remain under a happy illusion. It reveals itself still more clearly if we realize not only that this may often happen, but that it *should* happen. The dignity and intrinsic majesty of being, of reality as such, calls for an acknowledgment by our mind; it forbids us to ignore reality and to take refuge in illusions, whatever their content may be. The question now imposes itself: If it is true that every being as being possesses this general value, can we still call certain beings neutral in contrasting them to beings endowed with a value?

We have to answer: So long as a being has no qualitative value and no ontological value (or at least only one which is so low that it has the character of a *quantité négligeable*), it really is in a certain way neutral.

This neutrality from the points of view of qualitative and ontological values fully justifies our looking at it as neutral, notwithstanding the fact that it participates in the general value of being as such. This general value as such imposes only in extraordinary cases an obligation on us to respond in a specific way. We understand this better if we take into account, not only the difference between the formal value of being as such as opposed to the ontological and qualitative values, but also the difference between the way in which an individual, concrete being exemplifies the general value of being and the manner in which a being embodies an ontological or qualitative value.

What matters here is to see that the difference between objects presenting themselves as neutral and objects endowed with a value has a full *fundamentum in re*.

In summarizing we may say: There exists a formal value of being as such, which we must clearly distinguish from the ontological values and *a fortiori* from the qualitative values. In its full grandeur and depth, this value discloses itself in the con-

templation of being as such. But every being, whatever its specific
character and nature may be, in some way participates in this
value.

In our naïve approach to life and being this value plays no
prominent role. In certain cases only, it speaks eloquently to us,
and the adequate response to it is even something morally obligatory; e.g., in the obligation to abstain from lying, in the virtue of
reverence, in the unworthiness of taking refuge in a dream-
world.

But there are few attitudes corresponding to this general
value of being. As long as we conform only to the neutral immanent logic of being, we are in no way responding to the *value*
of being. If we want to attain our aim, we have to *conform* to
the immanent logic of being. If we want to construct a machine,
we have to respect the laws of mechanics; if we want to boil
water, we have to proceed in a way prescribed by nature; if we
want to protect our health, we have to conform to the laws of
biology. In all these cases we do not need to grasp the general
value of being in order to conform to the immanent logic of
beings. It imposes itself upon us not from the point of view of
value, but as something inevitable, at least if we want to attain
any aim whatsoever. In no way does it challenge us to conform
to it, but it compels us in a completely neutral manner.

Thus, in order to conform to the immanent logic of being, we
do not need to grasp the value of being, nor do we need to grasp
it normally. It is only the saint who may have in mind, even in
all these neutral conformings to reality, the value of being in
general and who responds to it. But then it will be even more
than this value of being as such. It will be the response to the
more sublime qualitative value which every being assumes as
created by God, the Infinite Goodness. We shall understand the
nature of this value better later on.

This brings us to a third statement. Neither the different
ontological nor the qualitative values can be deduced from the
general value of being as such. In knowing only this general
value of being we would not yet know anything about the
different ontological and qualitative values. So long as we know
only that something—because it is real—has this general value,
we ignore its specific ontological value and above all whether it

is endowed with a qualitative value or not. Furthermore, it is utterly impossible to consider the formal value of being as such as the ultimate value to which every other type of value can be reduced, or as the source of every other value. Though it is true that every other value also implies this value, and true that this value is more abstract than any other, it would be a grave error to believe it therefore superior to all other values. The degree of abstraction which is required in order to grasp something is in no way synonymous with the rank which a being holds in the hierarchy of values. It would be a fatal error to believe that ascending to a higher sphere and finally to the Supreme Being would consist in proceeding to a more radical abstraction. This would inevitably lead to such grave errors as are contained in the Spinozistic thesis that God is *beyond* good and evil, or in the Neoplatonic conception that we can predicate of God neither that He exists nor that He does not exist.

Granted that this value of being as such, because of its general and formal character, is to be found in every being (whatever may be its special ontological or qualitative value), nonetheless the ontological and qualitative values in some way surpass it and absorb it. We have therefore to emphasize that it is impossible to consider the general value of being as the highest value.

Neither can we say on the other hand, that this general value of being is the lowest value. The relation between the general value of being as such and the ontological and qualitative values is not such that we adequately cover it in saying that the general value of being is lower in the hierarchy of values than any other ontological or qualitative value. Insofar as a concrete individual being is concerned, it is true that its ontological value, as soon as it attains a certain rank, surpasses its general value of being. And this applies even more with respect to the qualitative values of a being. The ontological value of a human person surpasses by far the general value of being as such which a human person possesses. And still more do the moral values of a person surpass this general value of a being. But insofar as we consider the general value of being as such, not as a property of a concrete contingent being, but as a property of being as such, we cannot say that it ranks lower than the ontological and qualitative values, but it surpasses it in a direction other than the strictly hierarchical one.

In saying that God is Infinite Charity, we obviously say more than in saying He is Infinite Being. Though the latter is presupposed in the former, nevertheless the sublimity of the former is incomparable with the latter.

In God all the values are one. Once we see every being in the light of God's creation, every being thereby possesses independently of its ontological or qualitative value not only the general value of being, but also the value of being created by God, the Infinite Goodness and Sanctity. If the ontological value reflects God and the qualitative value reflects God still more intimately and directly; if the general value of being is still a reflection of God's infinite being, this new value accrues to the object from the link with God, which is given in the fact of its being created. This link with God, the Infinite Good, the Absolute Holiness, deneutralizes the entire reality in giving to everything an indirect dignity and preciousness which we have seen are present to the minds of the saints.

Finding in every real being a dignity by seeing it in the light of God's creation does not, however, level all the differences concerning the values mentioned above. If everything possesses a dignity as stemming from God, the Infinitely Glorious, this dignity alters neither the hierarchy in the realm of ontological values nor in the realm of qualitative values. This cannot be stressed enough. To overlook the hierarchical order in the sphere of values would be equivalent to misunderstanding the nature of value.

Our next and fourth statement pertinent to the relation of being and value refers to the fact that every value is itself objectively a being. Hence the value of being as such, as well as the ontological value of a specific being and the qualitative values which it embodies are themselves being. The idea of adding to being something which itself is not equally being is obviously nonsensical. On the one hand, we clearly see that the notion of value and the notion of being are not identical; that the ontological values and, above all, the qualitative values cannot be reduced to anything else nor deduced from the notion of being; on the other hand, they are themselves being. Here we touch a typical mystery which we can only state without being able to penetrate it fully with our reason.

Our next and fifth statement is concerned with a relation of an axiological order between qualitative values and existence. Qualitative values *should* be realized; their existence is itself something having a value. Qualitative disvalues should not be realized; their non-existence is itself a good. Our striving for moral perfection embraces the coming into existence of virtues in our person as well as the dissipation of vices. The end of ascetic practice is to do away with a disordered attachment to earthly goods, to destroy the dominion of pride and concupiscence over our soul. This implies that the coming into existence of virtues, as well as the dissipation of moral vices, is itself something good.

In like manner, we deplore the coming into existence of an evil action and would prefer that it had not been accomplished. The concrete coming into existence of an act of murder is itself an evil, and so is the existence of hatred in a concrete personality. This implies that the coming into existence or the actual existence of a morally evil attitude is itself an evil.

In these cases it would have been preferable had this concrete act not come into existence. Not only would we wish that, instead of the evil action, a good one would have taken place, or instead of hatred, an act of charity; but even the absence of any concrete act would have been better.

Certainly the question of a realization of qualitative values and disvalues poses itself only with respect to a concrete individual being, which should be endowed with such qualitative values as it is able and destined to embody. Only with respect to a concrete real being can we say that qualitative disvalues should not come into existence. Yet in many cases, a qualitative value is so connected with the *raison d'être* of a being that its embodying a qualitative disvalue turns the scale with respect to its ontological value, and to its general value of being which this being possesses, i.e., it would be preferable had this individual being not existed, or had it ceased to exist. This applies in the first line to many accidents. Hatred or an impure action should rather not have come into existence. A mean, ugly, vulgar melody should rather not have been composed. A heresy should rather never have come into existence. A philosophical error should rather never have seen the light of day.

St. Augustine's statement [2] that even the realization of moral disvalues can be used by God for something good, and that this more than anything else shows the omnipotence of God in no way contradicts what we have just stated. We are here confronted with two fundamental aspects which must be clearly distinguished.

It is obvious that in itself a moral evil should not take place, that its coming into existence is itself an evil, or that it would be preferable had it not come into existence. Only after having understood this fact can the thesis of St. Augustine assume a meaning. It is precisely the revision of this existing principle by God's providence (i.e., that moral disvalues should not exist) that makes the *felix culpa* so extraordinary. Thus this revision in no way contradicts the validity of the principle involved. It not only presupposes it, but further, it does not in any way cancel it. It rather superimposes on it a new sign in making it a link in a causal chain leading to a high good. The fact that it is preferable that certain individual beings should not exist because of their qualitative disvalues shows us, however, something fundamentally important.

To know the general value of being as such would not yet inform us about the physiognomy of the world. A materialist could in principle also grasp the formal general value of being, for certainly matter also possesses this value. But the materialist's universe would definitely be deprived of the higher ontological values and *a fortiori* of all higher qualitative values.

The general value of being which is realized with the very existence of something in no way guarantees that the ultimate feature of the world would not be negative from the point of view of qualitative value. To expose to a radical pessimist the general formal value of being would not be any argument against pessimism. Not only would it not convince him that his pessimism is wrong; it would also in no way objectively

---

[2] "He did not deprive them of this power (free will), knowing it a more powerful thing to make good use of such as were evil, than to exclude evil altogether." *De Civitate Dei*, XXII, 1. (J. Healey, *op. cit.*, Vol. II, p. 358.)

refute it. As soon as we see that the qualitative disvalues can turn the scale with respect to the ontological value of a being, and that the real existence of a fallen angel instead of being a good is an outspoken evil, we understand that the formal general value of being does not yet answer the question of whether the world is ultimately good or evil.

CHAPTER 13

THE GOOD TIDINGS OF VALUES

IF WE are asked how the world presents itself to our mind, we cannot deny that we are confronted with both light and darkness, good and evil, things to rejoice about and things to mourn about. One of the deepest features of the world, as it presents itself in reality, is that it possesses this mysterious duality: the concrete realization of values and of disvalues, the existence of objective goods and of objective evils for the person, the changing rhythm of gladdening things and of misfortunes.

In the existential order the negative, tragic aspect prevails to such an extent that the Church can speak of the earth as a "valley of tears"; and our Lord says: "In the world you shall have distress: but have confidence, I have overcome the world" (John 16:33). Holy Scripture and the liturgy testify time and again to the undeniable and tremendous reality of evil in the world. The expectation of the chosen people for the Messias which pervaded all the centuries before Christ, and the consciousness in the people of Israel of the need for redemption, clearly testify that disharmony and evil are typical features of the universe as it is known to us.

Can there be imagined any greater acknowledgment of the *reality* of evil than the redemption of man through the death on the cross of the God-man, Christ? How could the Gospel speak of Satan as the incarnate evil, the prince of this world; how could the idea of hell be understood without admitting the *reality* of evil?

The reality of evil of all kinds in the "valley of tears" is undeniable. The *Benedictus* speaks of those who are not yet redeemed by Christ as "sitting in the shadow of death." And even in pagan antiquity we find time and again hints of the tragic situation of man and the presence of evil in this world.

If we want to remain truly in contact with reality, we cannot but admit the real presence in the world of evils of all kinds. This negative aspect has seduced certain philosophers into holding a pessimistic metaphysics, i.e., to see in evil the ultimate and abiding reality.

First among the chief kinds of evil are the qualitative disvalues *in* man, especially moral wickedness, and then superficiality, shallowness, stupidity, and similar intellectual disvalues. Secondly, there is the large scale of objective evils *for* man: all kinds of sufferings, physical and spiritual; all types of bodily and mental illnesses; vulnerability to the brutal forces of nature, the existence of wicked men, the inconstancy of friends, our own insufficiency in so many situations; but above all, death.

These latter evils are primarily objective evils for the person, but by this is implied the further truth that they are also in themselves disvalues. The tragic situation of man is not only an evil *for* him, but is something negative *in itself*. If we prescind from all knowledge by revelation and look at reality as disclosed in natural experience, we are confronted with a universe filled on the one hand with innumerable values, ontological and qualitative, with countless objective goods for man, with many events and situations that invite us to rejoice over man's felicity and to praise his circumstance; and on the other hand, with innumerable qualitative disvalues: the wickedness of man, his errors and his shallowness, all kinds of objective evils for man, the disrupture in his own nature, the rebellion of the inferior part of his being against the superior (which Plato described so eloquently in the *Phaedrus*), filled too with so many hostile and threatening forces that the world seems to proclaim with sorrow and alarm the tragedy of the human situation.

Most of the great philosophers have seen the duality of a positive and negative aspect in the world such as it is known to us in experience. Some, however, have been led to see one of the two aspects to the exclusion of the other, and to become either metaphysical pessimists, like Schopenhauer or Sartre, or metaphysical optimists, like the great Leibniz or, in another sense, Rousseau.

But granted that both aspects are seen and the reality of both admitted, the great question arises: "Which of the two has the final word?" That justice is truly good and injustice evil is no problem. It is not the ultimate absolute validity of the values which is in question. It is rather the relation between value and being, the question as to whether the good metaphysically and ultimately triumphs; whether goodness, truth, and beauty are only valid essences or ultimately full substantial realities; whether, despite the terrifying aspect of this world, the noble and the sublime ultimately triumph over the wicked and the base. This is the first great question.

And the second, the fundamental question of *man*: Is harmony, is happiness, *our* ultimate fate? Does there exist another and higher world in which our noblest aspirations, our thirst for absolute harmony, for absolute goodness, for eternal life, shall be fulfilled and where all the vulnerability of our being shall be overcome?

The two questions are deeply interrelated. The positive answer to the second presupposes the positive answer to the first. But the positive answer to the first does not yet answer the second.

Without Revelation, we should never find an answer to the second question. The answer to the first, however, may be reached within a metaphysical framework. This first question is not concerned with the general value of being. It does not ask whether the value of being as such has the final word, which would be synonymous with the question of whether being as such ultimately triumphs over nothingness. This question must be answered positively even by a materialist. But this positive answer would neither refute the pessimist nor be a source of consolation for ourselves.

We only understand the nature of this question if we focus on qualitative values and the message which they convey with respect to the universe. The beauty of a glorious sunset, the purity of Joseph in refusing to yield to the wife of Potiphar, the intrinsic goodness of an act of deep contrition: these in their character of value all imply a message from above. They even imply as it were a *promise* that all the splendor and intrinsic light shining forth from the values is not simply a qualitative entity, but a triumphant metaphysical *reality*. True though it is that the qualitative values have here on earth neither the character of substances nor the power to bend victoriously all the brutal forces inferior to man, they nonetheless imply essentially the promise of a metaphysical power, of a final word also in the order of actual being. In the world known to us in experience we witness that the higher and more sublime beings are more vulnerable to attack and disease than the lower, and indeed are constantly exposed to destruction by inferior forces. It is of this tragic situation that Pascal speaks when he says:

> Man is but a reed, the most feeble thing in nature, but he is a thinking reed. The entire universe need not arm itself to crush him. A vapour, a drop of water suffices to kill him. But, if the universe were to crush him, man would still be more noble than that which killed him, because he knows that he dies and the advantage which the universe has over him, the universe knows nothing of this.[1]

The qualitative values, and above all the moral values, speak so unmistakably of the intrinsic relation between themselves and ultimate reality that Plato considered the idea of goodness to be the peak of true being. But this priority and supremacy of the idea of goodness does not determine anything about the existential triumph of the nobler and higher beings over the brutal forces of this world nor of the victory of the qualitative values over all evil. If, according to Plato, ideas are the fullest being and the idea of goodness is the peak in the realm of ideas, this supremacy is not connected with might and still less with almightiness.

Once, however, we reach the idea of an absolute, almighty person we can grasp that this person *must* be the infinite wisdom, the infinite beauty, and the infinite goodness. It is indeed possible that in a created good, qualitative disvalues also may be found; it is possible too that in this world the inferior being may destroy the nobler one, and possible also that the forces of evil may often triumph, according to the words of our Lord when He calls Satan the "prince of this world." But it is impossible that the Absolute Being could be the embodiment of qualitative disvalues. We can even understand that the supreme Being can-

---

1 Pascal, *Pensées*, VI, 347.

not but be Absolute Goodness. This is not a tautological statement declaring *e definitione* that value is synonymous with
being. On the contrary, it is an overwhelming insight. It is this
insight which accounts for the gap separating Christian natural
theology from radical metaphysical pessimism.

With the datum of value before us, and we mean especially
the datum of qualitative value, we can grasp with our intellect
that insofar as the Absolute Being is concerned, a necessary relation exists between value and being. It is this essential relation
or connection between being and value which makes it possible
for us to grasp in natural theology that the Absolute Person of
God must be absolute goodness and beauty.

This insight concerning the Absolute Person confirms the
message implicitly contained in every qualitative value in a real
being. It confirms the promise; it justifies the mysterious metaphysical power which, above all, moral values claim to possess.
This relation between the qualitative values and being is such
that if we imagined the Absolute Being were neutral or evil,
the message of the qualitative values would become a *lie*.

It has been stressed many times that the relation between
being and goodness is found in God in a unique manner and in
a completely different manner in creatures. Whereas man is only
good by participation, God is essentially good: He is Goodness
Itself. Thus St. Thomas can say of God: "He is therefore the
very goodness itself of every good thing." [2]

But now we must point to and emphasize a most important
consequence of this fact: the essential goodness of God necessarily
implies the absolute substantial existence of the most sublime
of the qualitative values. In the created world these are never
substances. Plato thought of them as existing in a heaven of ideas,
thereby allowing them only the dignity of arch-patterns of the
concrete "realized" values. But in God they have ultimate, substantial reality. And what in metaphysics we can only dimly
conceive, in Revelation we find expressed in overwhelming,
penetrating, and luminous simplicity: *Deus caritas est*—God *is*
love.

[2] *Est igitur Ipse bonum omnis boni. Sent.*, I, 40.

CHAPTER 14

GOD AND VALUES

WE HAVE already stated that the notion of value is included in our concept of God. Natural theology by speaking of the infinite goodness of God and of His absolute wisdom implies the notion of value. An idea of God which would conceive the infinitely perfect being as absolutely neutral would be as non-sensical and terrible as the idea of an evil God.

In Revelation, the role of value in the notion of God is incomparably greater and more manifest. The entire Old Testament is pervaded with the revelation of the justice and goodness of God; the psalms resound with the praise of God's mercy, God's wisdom, God's glory, God's sweetness: . . . *quoniam in aeternum misericordia ejus*—"For his mercy endureth forever" (Ps. 117:1); *Gustate et videte quam suavis est Dominus*—"O taste, and see that the Lord is sweet" (Ps. 33:9). And our Lord says: "None is good but God alone" (Luke 18:19).

In the very act of adoration there is included a response not only to the *ens a se*, nor only to the absolute lordship and omnipotence of God, but also to the infinite goodness of God. The true fear of God and still more the love of God imply and presuppose the notion of value. The same is true of hope,[1] adoration, praise, and confidence in God: they all have meaning only if God is understood as the infinitely good. Even in a servile fear of God there is implied an element of response to God's infinite justice, insofar as the evil feared is understood as a punishment imposed by the eternal judge.

[1] This does not apply to a "pseudo hope" wnich is nothing but a by-product of certain vitality and lacks all the features of true natural hope, and, *a fortiori*, of supernatural hope.

We have already mentioned several times that the relation between every value embodied in a created being and God has the character of a reflection. Every value of a created being in a specific way reflects God, who is the sum of all values. This reflection naturally shows many differences according to the specific nature of the value concerned. The main difference here is related to the difference between ontological and qualitative values. In the case of ontological values, the reflection we speak of is found in the exemplaristic reflection which shines from every being. Throughout the entire realm of created goods this reflection is present in countless gradations, depending upon the nature of the good. There is yet one fundamental point in the scale of exemplarism which marks off a decisive difference between two ways of reflecting divine goodness. These traditional philosophy admirably expressed by the terms *vestigium* (trace) and *imago* (image).[2]

All impersonal substances are traces; man alone, among the creatures known to us by experience, is an "image" of God. The reflection always reaches its most specific point in the ontological value of the being in question. In looking at something not only as created by God but also as reflecting Him, we cannot but focus on the dignity and intrinsic nobility of the being: that is, on its ontological value.

The value is so much the most intimate part in this reflection, so much the message of God who is the infinite goodness and sum of all values, that the mere neutral analysis of a being which prescinds from its specific ontological value is from the exemplarist point of view impossible.

In general, it is not necessary to start from the notion of God in order to grasp the ontological value of a being. For some values, however, this may be necessary to a certain extent. For example, the formal general value of being as such, of being as opposed to nothingness, is a value which normally is not easily grasped without referring to God. It is not so with the majority of ontological values; for instance, we do not need to start from God in order to grasp the nobility and preciousness of a living being or the dignity of man, at least as a rational being capable

2 St. Bonaventure, *The Ascent of the Soul to God,* I, 2.

of knowledge, free will, and love. In the awareness that murder
is evil, or that imposing suffering without necessity is morally
bad, the ontological value of the human person is clearly implied:
it can be, and in fact has been understood by people without
any reference to God.

But even though such values can be grasped without referring
to God, objectively God is definitely presupposed by them. We
have here a situation analogous to the relation between the
existence of God and the existence of contingent beings. We do
not need to know God in order to grasp the existence and nature
of contingent beings, but in the ontological order the existence
of a contingent being necessarily presupposes the existence of
God. So here too the ontological value can be grasped without
referring to God, but objectively it presupposes God. In terms of
the traditional philosophy we can then say that *quoad se* the
ontological value presupposes God, whereas *quoad nos* it leads
to God.

We do not claim that this ascent has the same character of a
strict demonstration of God's existence as the argument based on
the contingency of all created beings. But it cannot be denied
that it is at least a starting point toward God, an indication, a
hinting at God. It is also the basis of the fourth demonstration
of God's existence, the argument based on perfection which
necessarily implies the notion of value. It is evident that the
relation to God of the ontological value of different beings has
in no way the character of a teleological relation; the ontological
value is actually a reflection of God's infinite ontological goodness.

The relation between the values and God assumes, however,
a new character as soon as we are concerned with qualitative
values. As already mentioned, qualitative values contain a
"message" of God which is more direct and intimate than that
transmitted through the ontological values.

This applies above all to moral and aesthetic values—the
most typical representatives of the qualitative values. Though
this character of a message from above reaches still a new and
higher level in moral values, beauty also throws into relief this
more intimate reflection of God proper to qualitative values.

In several articles previously published,[3] I have discussed the mystery of the beauty of visible and audible things, the beauty of nature, of fine arts and music; I have shown that this beauty is not simply the efflorescence of corporeal beings or of the sequence of sounds in which it manifests itself, but that it definitely surpasses in its quality the ontological rank of these beings. We cannot expound this deep problem here. But it should be stressed that there is a special message of God, a specific reflection of God's infinite beauty, contained in a glorious landscape, such as the one seen from the Parthenon in Athens or from the Giannicolo in Rome; in the sublimity of a church such as San Marco in Venice, and in the transfigured music of Beethoven's Ninth Symphony or in one of his late quartets. This beauty speaks of a world above; it is a ray of the Father of all Lights; it elevates our spirit and fills our heart with a longing for this higher world. The sublime beauty of nature surpasses the ontological value of those beings in which we grasp the beauty: in its quality it reflects God in a more intimate way.

Cardinal Newman expresses this "message" from above with respect to music in an admirable way in one of his *University Sermons:*

"There are seven notes in the scale; make them fourteen; yet what a slender outfit for so vast an enterprise! What science brings so much out of so little? Out of what poor elements does some great master in it create his new world? Shall we say that all this exuberant inventiveness is a mere ingenuity or trick of art, like some game or fashion of the day, without reality, without meaning? . . . [Or] is it possible that that inexhaustible evolution and disposition of notes, so rich yet so simple, so intricate yet so regulated, so various yet so majestic, should be a mere sound, which is gone and perishes? Can it be that those mysterious stirrings of heart, and keen emotion, and strange yearnings after we know not what, and awful impressions from we know not whence, should be wrought in us by what is unsubstantial, and comes and goes, and begins and ends in itself? It is not so; it cannot be. No; they have escaped from some higher

---

[3.] "Beauty and the Christian," *Journal of Arts and Letters,* Summer 1951—Vol. III, no. 2, pp. 100–11; and *Zum Problem der Schönheit des Sichtbaren und Hörbaren, Mélanges Maréchal* (Edition Universelle, Brussels, 1950), Vol. II, pp. 180–91.

sphere; they are the outpourings of eternal harmony.in the medium of created sound; they are echoes of our Home; they are the voice of Angels, or the Magnificat of Saints, or the living laws of Divine Governance, or the Divine Attributes; something are they besides themselves, which we cannot compass, which we cannot utter,—though mortal man, and he perhaps not otherwise distinguished above his fellows, has the gift of eliciting them." [4]

Moral values are embodied in the human person or in an act of man in a completely different way than the beauty of visible and audible things are embodied in their bearer. The beautiful mountain and the graceful inlet of the sea are merely pedestals for their beauty, mouthpieces of this message of God. Humility, generosity, purity, and moral goodness are, on the contrary, fully embodied in certain acts and attitudes of men. Moreover, the surprising discrepancy between the ontological rank of the bearer and the sublimity of the qualitative value in the case of the beauty of visible and audible things is not to be found with respect to moral values. Moral values can only be embodied in a person and the person has a high ontological value.

Moreover, notwithstanding the fact that moral values are fully embodied in the act and attitudes of man, they transcend aesthetic values in still another direction; they have to a higher degree the character of a "message from above." For they reflect God in an incomparable way; indeed they are His most intimate reflection and message in the natural realm.

Moreover, the praise of God here assumes a completely new character. If the qualitative values in general contain a silent praise of God, moral goodness praises Him in a far more eloquent manner. And, on the other hand, moral disvalues are an outspoken offense against God.

We see therefore that qualitative and ontological values reflect God in a very different way. We also see that this difference is not the same as the one between *imago* and *vestigium*.

Yet the reflection of God in the qualitative values remains a mere *reflection* and nothing else. It would be quite nonsensical to interpret our emphasis on the superiority of the qualitative

4 John Henry Newman, *Fifteen Sermons Preached before the University of Oxford* (London: Rivingtons, 1880), XV, pp. 346–7.

values in this respect as meaning that they present us with a kind of natural intuition of God.

A reflection in a completely new sense, however, and of an incomparably more intimate nature, coupled with the full glorification of God, is brought about only by supernatural morality, the morality of the saints, those virtues of the new creature in Christ, which St. Paul calls "the fruits of the Holy Ghost," which are simultaneously, despite their completely new character, the ultimate fulfillment of all morality.

Part Two

I. Value and Morality

CHAPTER 15

THE NATURE OF MORAL VALUES

WE HAVE already seen that, in saying of an action or an attitude that it is morally good, noble, generous, or just, the importance which we predicate is the value (or the importance in itself) and not the merely subjectively satisfying or the objective good for the person. We have seen further that moral values are distinguished in many respects from ontological values; that they belong to the qualitative values which exhibit most typically the quiddity of value as such. We have seen too that in the frame of qualitative values, moral values form a distinct value domain which is by far the most important.

Now we shall explore the specific nature of moral values and seek the marks which distinguish them from other qualitative values. This is one of the most important tasks of ethics. It is not our purpose to analyze the nature of discrete moral values, such as justice, purity, and humility, but rather to analyze the nature of moral value as such. We ask: What are the features of this value domain? What specifically characterizes moral values as opposed to intellectual or aesthetic values?

The first preponderant mark of moral values is that they necessarily presuppose a person. An impersonal being could never be endowed with moral values; or in other words, we can never predicate of an impersonal being moral goodness or moral badness. No material body or plant or animal can ever be morally good or bad. It would be absurd to speak of a just stone or a veracious tree or a pure animal. Such expressions could become meaningful only analogically or in a poetical context.

No impersonal being, strictly speaking, can be morally good.[1] Only real persons, their acts and attitudes, can be morally good or bad. Aesthetic values on the other hand, such as beauty, can really be present in a mountain, a tree, or an animal; and they are especially to be found in works of art. Thus, we must state as the first decisive characteristic of moral values that they presuppose a person, that they are essentially values *of* a person.[2]

In saying "person," however, we in no way restrict ourselves to human beings. Who would deny that in speaking of the angels as being holy we thereby think of them as endowed with purity, goodness, reverence, charity? And is not the incarnation of all moral evil and wickedness, Lucifer, a fallen angel and not a human person?

We shall return to this fundamental point at the end of this chapter. Here it may suffice to stress that in characterizing moral values (such as justice, purity, generosity, charity) as necessarily presupposing a person, we in no way mean by this that they necessarily presuppose a human being. Certainly to explore moral values we must start from human beings, the only persons known to us experientially. Nevertheless, just as we do not limit the quiddity of person to human beings, making it something specifically and even essentially human but rather conceive human "person-ness" only as a reflection of the Absolute Person, God, thereby admitting angels too as essentially personal, so too we cannot restrict moral values to human beings even though natural experience reveals these moral values to us only in human beings.

But in stating that moral values necessarily presuppose a person, we have not yet sufficiently characterized the nature of moral values. There exist different types of values which are exclusively bound to persons, for instance, intellectual values. When we praise the great intelligence of a man, e.g., of a great

[1] Certainly we may also speak of the morality or immorality of communities, principles, theories, and works of art, and thereby apply the moral connotation in a fully legitimate and literal sense. But the way in which moral values or disvalues are here properties of those impersonal beings obviously differs from the full realization of moral values and disvalues in a person.

[2] Cf. St. Anselm, "It is obvious that justice is not in any nature which does not perceive rightness." *De Veritate,* in *Selections from Medieval Philosophers,* edit. and trans. Richard P. McKeon (New York: Charles Scribner's Sons, 1929), Vol. I, p. 174.

philosopher like Plato or Aristotle, or when we admire the great gifts of a genius like Beethoven or Michelangelo, we refer to something which is undoubtedly an authentic value, and a kind of value which can belong only to persons. No material body or plant or animal can actualize intellectual values in the proper sense. The depth and richness of a great intelligence, the brilliance of a mind, the grandeur and power of an artistic genius, the wit and sense of humor of a great writer: all these are undoubtedly personal values. But they form nevertheless a group of values clearly distinguishable from specifically moral values. Thus in characterizing moral values as essentially personal values, we have not yet sufficiently circumscribed their nature. Moral values have a unique character which distinguishes them from all others and which gives them an incomparable primacy.

The first striking mark which distinguishes moral values from all other personal values is the fact that man is held responsible for them. We blame a man for being avaricious, impure, or unjust, whereas we do not blame him for not being intelligent, for being poorly gifted, or for lacking vitality.[3] When someone with the best intention fails to succeed in an effort because he lacks the required intelligence, he is not made responsible for his failure. But when somebody acts with a bad intention, then he is held responsible. Guilt and merit are to be found only in the sphere of moral values. Morally negative values always imply guilt; morally positive values always imply merit.

This relation to responsibility constitutes a fundamental mark of moral values distinguishing them from all other values. In stating, however, that moral values imply responsibility, we thereby touch the fact that freedom of will is an essential presupposition for moral values. Responsibility essentially presupposes freedom. A being, such as an animal, which is deprived of freedom of will cannot be held responsible for anything. Even a personal being such as a small child, though essentially but not actively endowed with freedom of will, is not responsible for his doings, because not yet able to make use of his freedom. Again, we cannot make an adult responsible for anything which, though caused by him, is nevertheless withdrawn from

[3] "Good or evil in human acts alone merits praise or blame." St. Thomas, *Summa Theologica*, 1a–2ae, xxi, 2.

his free influence. In order to prove that a person is not to be held responsible for something, we need only show that it was beyond the sphere of his free influence. Similarly, it is enough to prove his responsibility if we can show that he acted in full possession of his freedom.

This reveals to us that all moral values presuppose the *freedom* of the person. Only because of this freedom is the person capable of moral values. Only through a free decision can a man be morally good or bad. No other personal value, for example, intelligence, or great musical talent, wit, brilliant eloquence, or powerful vitality, can be rooted in freedom. They do not stem from a free decision of man, but have rather the character of gifts. Man cannot bestow these values on himself. They do not presuppose freedom, nor is their possession bound to a free decision of man.

Thus by the fact that moral values alone are rooted in freedom, thereby involving personal responsibility for them, they are clearly distinguished from all other personal values. In abusing free will man becomes guilty; and in rightly exercizing his freedom he acquires merit.

Deeply connected with this fact is the completely different seriousness which is proper to all moral values and which sets them apart from all other personal values. A quality beyond compare shines forth as soon as moral values come into question. When we think of Macbeth and the horrible guilt of his deeds, we immediately realize that we have to do with a completely new seriousness and gravity possessed only by the moral sphere. All his fascinating gifts and talents seem superficial and unimportant compared with the fact of his moral guilt.

This unique character of moral values becomes still more evident when we examine a second distinguishing mark: the awareness of a moral failure affects our conscience. When we know that we have done something morally bad, this mysterious voice in our soul which we call "conscience" is disturbed; this voice which speaks to us implacably destroys the peace of our soul and burdens us with an incomparable weight. Certainly we may fret over our intellectual insufficiency; we may feel inferior because of poor vitality; but such depressive feelings are of a character completely different from the terrible disharmony brought on by a bad conscience. This disharmony, which no distraction can abate and no pleasures can disperse, which from the very depths of our soul seeps into our life, which in vain we try to dissipate, which at last we try to camouflage with other things, has its root solely in the moral sphere. The unique character of a bad conscience, having its genesis only in moral guilt, is in evidence in a specifically drastic manner in the last of the Oresteia. Orestes, after murdering his mother, Clytemnestra, is persecuted by the Erinyes and can find no rest. This personification of bad conscience in the Erinyes reveals how deeply even the pagan Greeks grasped the unique role of the implacable voice which follows moral guilt. With this second distinguishing mark, the relation of moral values to conscience, we again come across the unique importance and seriousness of the moral values which set them apart from all other personal values.

A third mark of moral values is their character of indispensability. It is a pity if someone has poor intelligence or is lacking in the charms of life. But it is far more than a pity if someone is unjust, impure, or untruthful. In being morally bad he fails in his principal task; he does not fulfill what is strictly demanded of him. And so long as a person is morally good we do not consider his lack of intelligence or artistic talent or wittiness as a failing in his basic human vocation. We do not expect everyone to be a genius or to possess a specific vital charm. We are aware that objectively such things could not be demanded of everyone. But moral values are required of everyone. However, the indispensability of moral values goes still further. It seems quite natural that one man should not possess every single intellectual gift; but every man *should* possess *all* moral values. It seems quite reasonable when a man says, "I am a musician, but I have no philosophical talent at all"; or when someone says, "I specialize in science and leave art to other persons who have a gift for it." But it would clearly be both unreasonable and ludicrous if a man said, "I specialize in justice; purity I leave to my colleagues." The partition of values which is quite natural for all other personal values does not apply to the moral sphere. Here all moral values are demanded of everyone insofar as he is a man.

All moral values are indispensable for man. This reveals the deep connection between morality and the basic vocation of man. The moral values belong to the *unum necessarium,* to "the one thing necessary"; they are what is primarily demanded of man as such. To be morally good pertains essentially to the end of human existence and to man's destiny. In considering this fact, the unique importance and seriousness characterizing moral values becomes still more evident. They participate in the ultimate seriousness of the *unum necessarium.*

A fourth mark of moral values is their relation to punishment and reward. That moral guilt demands punishment is an elementary datum. The unique disharmony which is created by moral guilt imperatively demands atonement. We experience this demand in facing the guilt of other persons as well as in being conscious of our own guilt. This experience must by no means be confused with the instinct for revenge. Revenge applies only to an evil inflicted upon ourselves. This evil may be something subjectively disagreeable or painful, or it may be an objective evil for us, an objective violation of our rights or the rights of our family, clan, and the like.

Now the subjective reaction which characterizes all kinds of revenge is not to be found in the consciousness that moral guilt necessarily calls for punishment and expiation, which as such refer exclusively to the disvalue of the morally bad. The indestructible awareness that moral guilt demands punishment reveals the majesty of the realm of morality in a special way, and by reason of its solemn objectivity it plainly enough has nothing to do with the dark passionate stream of revenge.

The fact that we cannot separate the knowledge of our own moral guilt from the consciousness that it deserves punishment, that it demands atonement, clearly reveals that here something is in question other than any feeling of revenge. The relation of guilt to atonement is of such an elementary nature that we find it even in the most primitive tribes. Let us not forget the innumerable attempts of the pagans in their various forms of cult to realize this atonement for their sins through sacrifices of animals. All other disvalues, such as lack of intelligence, talents, gifts, or sparkling vitality, in no way call for punishment and atonement. The disharmony which is created by them is so thoroughly different that it involves no relation whatever to punishment or atonement.

Similarly, in facing moral merits we apprehend that they deserve a reward. Although high intelligence or a great artistic talent deserves appreciation and the opportunity of fulfillment, it does not deserve a reward in the strict sense.[4] But moral merit does. We are fully aware that it is unjust when the morally noble suffers or when the moral values remain without reward. Kant so appreciated this relation of moral merit and reward that he argued to an eternal life beyond earthly existence from the fact that this reward is generally not to be found on earth. He regarded this demand for reward of moral merit so imperative that he declared it impossible for earthly life to be the final fulfillment of human existence.

Another characteristic mark of moral values is that it is a greater good for the person to be endowed with them than with any other values. We have referred to this primacy of moral values in our analysis of the famous statement of Socrates: "It is better for man to suffer injustice than to commit it." The antithesis here is between moral good on the one hand, and on the other, the possession of objective goods for the person, such as wealth, influence, great fame, and so on. But the fact that to go astray morally is considered the greater evil for the person, far worse than any kind of suffering, implicitly testifies to the unique role of moral values compared with any other value, intelligence, for example, or great vitality. Socrates does not say it is better for man to suffer injustice than to have a poor intelligence or poor vitality, but he says that it is better for man to suffer injustice than to commit *injustice*.

[4] The fact that we consider it just and adequate when a man of genius or a victorious general is honored, or when he receives a prize for great achievements, does not constitute an objection to the above-mentioned difference between moral and other values. The relation between moral merit and reward which can be but happiness, and between a token embodying an honor and appreciation and extra-moral values and achievements, is obviously quite different. The reward for moral merits has a much deeper and more elementary character. As soon as we realize that reward in the full sense is the counterpart of punishment, its metaphysical depth and its profound difference from the so-called "reward" for extra-moral merits clearly reveals itself. It is something which only God can dispense, whereas the honor for extra-moral values or achievements has definitely a social, human character. It is a response coming from the nation or humanity.

That moral goodness matters more for man than anything else, Socrates grasped without the help of divine revelation, by contemplating the nature of moral values. Indeed, moral values manifest a character of transcendence; to be endowed with them is decisive for man's eternal fate, for they hint at eternity and the fact that man's existence is not exhausted by his earthly life. Such hints are certainly indistinct and implicit. I am not thinking of the promise which many qualitative values contain, the promise of a world above, of a reality full of harmony about which we spoke in Chapter 13. I am thinking rather of the mysterious impact which the moral question possesses for mankind, the impact of the objective good for us which is constituted by moral goodness. It is the implicit message that moral goodness is for us an objective good, transcending the boundaries of our earthly existence.

Even if a person believed, because of some fallacious rationalistic arguments, that the soul of man is not immortal, he could not deny (granted he is really morally awake and amenable to moral values) that moral values involve a mysteriously intimate relation to eternity and a share in determining our eternal fate. He might believe this character of moral values a delusion, but he could not deny the fact of this character as such, which is proper only to moral values and not to other personal values.

This transcendence of moral value is deeply related to several of the marks mentioned above, especially to the mark of the indispensability of moral values and the mark of their relation to reward and punishment. We have seen that the very nature of moral guilt calls for punishment, or is deserving of punishment. The same applies, contrariwise, to moral merit and reward.

Now punishment and reward necessarily imply the notion of God. The ultimate *valid* response to moral evil, which either dissolves or silences the disharmony created by moral evil, can obviously only be given by the Absolute Judge, by an Absolute Person who is Justice Itself. All relative punishment (though incapable of displacing divine punishment) which is inflicted by a human authority, either by the state or by the parents, can be valid, even in its restricted character, only because such authority implies a partial representation of God.

The same applies *mutatis mutandis* to reward.[5] In grasping the fact that moral guilt deserves punishment, we become aware of the transcendent character of moral matters, of the ultimate seriousness of moral good and evil which in its consequences for us surpasses the world which we know experientially. It is therefore not by accident that the moral sphere is intimately linked to religion. Moral wickedness is always considered as in some way directed against divine power; moral goodness, on the contrary, as constituting a harmony with the divine. The unique nature of moral values is profoundly characterized by the fact that the moral sphere, rather than any other kind of perfection, occupies this privilege of being directly connected with religion. Impure and superstitious as the notion of morality may be in particular instances, the connection between the moral and the religious spheres remains extremely significant.

Finally, we must realize that the moral sphere has a privileged role in the relation between nature and supernature. In the process of beatification the proof of sanctity is the fact that a believer has been virtuous to a heroic degree. The decisive point is not the degree of his intelligence, of his talents and gifts, of his powerful vitality, but the heroic degree of his virtues.

It goes without saying that it is here a question of the plenitude of supernatural virtues and not of merely natural virtues. Nevertheless, the role of heroic virtue in the process of beatification remains of significance in showing the relation existing between morality and the supernatural. For, notwithstanding their incomparably new character, these supernatural virtues are also the crowning fulfillment of all morality.

Likewise, the *advocatus diaboli* does not offer objections to the saintliness of the candidate because of a lack of brilliant intelligence, a lack of special artistic talents, and so on. But a moral failure would form an insurmountable obstacle to canonization. The fact that only sin is considered indicative of spiritual death, as destroying the state of grace in our soul, clearly illustrates the

---

[5] This necessary link between the notion of punishment and the idea of God has been discussed in detail in an article of mine, *"Zum Wesen der Strafe,"* in *Zeitliches im Lichte des Ewigen* (Habbel: Regensburg, 1930).

unique place of the moral sphere as compared to all other personal values.

If we stress the completely new splendor of the virtues of the new creature in Christ, we should nevertheless not forget that all natural morality finds its fulfillment in it. The virtues of the new creature in Christ are the fulfillment foreshadowed by all moral goodness; and simultaneously they surpass this moral goodness by being something not only immeasurably higher, but also unimaginably new. Important as is the distinction between saintliness and mere natural morality, we should not lose sight of their deep interrelation. Our Lord said, "I am not come to destroy (the law), but to fulfil." And of the two main commandments, the love of God and of our neighbor, He said that on *them* the entire law and the prophets depend.

Even the natural moral values are resplendent among all other values, whether ontological, intellectual, or vital, in their ultimate depth and seriousness. We must do full justice to their unique character. The unique quality and the matchless impact with which we are already confronted in natural justice, in an unshakeable faithfulness, in veracity, in reverence, in an act of compassion, must be clearly grasped in order to understand why these values, as opposed to other natural values, belong to the *unum necessarium*.

Whether a man is intelligent or of mediocre intelligence, whether he has great charm or makes a poor appearance, whether he is efficient or not, witty or not, desirable as these values are, their absence is not an obstacle to salvation; they play no role in the measure with which we shall be judged by God. But all natural moral values are implied in sanctity (though therein incomparably surpassed), and all moral disvalues form an obstacle to our eternal end; they offend God and separate us from Him. Only by being transformed into Christ, *cum ipso, per ipsum et in ipso*, can we attain the *similitudo Dei*, which implies yet surpasses all natural morality. Nevertheless, all natural goodness—the attitude of Socrates who not only taught but lived the truth that it is better for man to suffer injustice than to commit it, the sacrifice of Alcestis, the piety and moral strength of Antigone, the faithfulness of Pylades—all in their touching beauty and depth are reflections of the infinite goodness of God.

We should understand that man's transcendence is already manifested in his ability and vocation to realize moral values and to attain moral goodness, which are primarily attributed to God and only analogously to man. We cannot understand the nature of moral values, of the mysterious importance-in-itself of moral goodness, nor can we grasp the nature of its antithesis, moral wickedness, if we look at the moral sphere as a merely human one. That moral wickedness is not restricted to man is clearly revealed by the fact that Satan, the fallen angel, is the very embodiment of moral wickedness. And all human moral goodness is a foreshadowing of the *similitudo Dei*. Christ says, "None is good but God alone." And He also says, "Be you therefore perfect, as also your heavenly Father is perfect." Here our Lord speaks of God revealing Himself not only as the one who is, *ego sum qui sum*, but as the one who is Love Itself. The "Be you perfect" clearly refers to that which is the very core and source of all moral goodness, God's infinite goodness, His bounty and mercy; it refers to God who is Charity. To interpret this being perfect like our Heavenly Father as a sharing in the ontological goodness of God would pervert the words of our Lord into the terrible promise of Satan, *Eritis sicut Dei*—"You shall be as Gods" (i.e., like God Himself).

If absolute ontological perfection is already included in the notion of God which is accessible to human reason, if in the Old Testament we hear the words: *ego sum qui sum*—"I am who am" —then the great overwhelming and beatifying message of the Gospel implies the new revelation of God: that He is *Goodness Itself, Charity Itself, Justice Itself, Veracity Itself, Mercy Itself*.

CHAPTER 16

MORALITY AND REASONABILITY

TWO FUNDAMENTAL questions arise in contemplating moral values. First: Which attitudes or activities of man can be endowed with moral values or moral disvalues? Only that can be morally good or bad which has been termed an *actus humanus,* and not that which is a mere *actus hominis.* Walking or sneezing as such can be neither morally good nor bad. But the question to be examined is: Which attitudes among the *actus humani* can embody a moral value or disvalue?

Everyone agrees that acts of willing and other actions can be morally good or bad. It will also be generally admitted that the cognitive acts as such are not the object of moral predication. But concerning the role in morality of affective responses (such as joy, veneration, enthusiasm, love, contrition) or even of virtues, there exists much disagreement. Yet it seems undeniable that we also speak of a morally noble joy and a malicious joy, or that we blame the moral meanness of envy or hatred, and praise the moral sublimity of charity. This first question seeks to discover those attitudes of man of which moral values or disvalues can be predicated.

But of greater importance is the second question: What is the source of the moral goodness or badness of those attitudes, habits, actions, to which we attribute moral good or evil; upon the fulfillment of what conditions does the moral goodness or badness of a will depend; which elements are responsible for the moral value or disvalue of an action; what conditions have to be fulfilled in an act of will or in an action in order to endow it with moral value?

We restrict ourselves to those attitudes and acts which constitute in themselves something morally good or sublime, excluding thereby everything which is only unobjectionable; and which therefore not only does not alter moral integrity, but in some way even partakes of it. Only those manifestations of a person will be analyzed which entitle us to judge his moral standard, to praise him morally.

If a good man eats or sleeps, we shall consider the eating or sleeping as something which does not alter the moral goodness of this man and which even has an indirect share in it. But we can never praise a man as morally good or sublime *because* he eats or sleeps,[1] whereas we can do so when he generously forgives another person or when he prefers to suffer injustice rather than to commit it.

Without discussing at this moment the question of whether any action or human activity can in concrete reality be fully neutral from the moral point of view, we must in any case definitely distinguish those attitudes which by their very nature are morally good, endowed with an outspoken moral value, and which afford us the opportunity of a real *sapere* (tasting) of moral goodness, as compared with those attitudes which from a moral point of view are merely unobjectionable. We must isolate those acts constituting a moral merit, revealing as they do the very nature of morality, as well as their opposites, those acts endowed with a real moral disvalue and intrinsic wickedness. And we must distinguish these in turn from acts which in themselves are not endowed with any moral value or disvalue but only indirectly acquire a moral significance, either by a superimposed special intention or by their accomplishment against the background of the general moral quality of a person.

We have to restrict ourselves to those attitudes alone in which moral values are fully revealed to us, for the obvious reason that only in this way can we discover which elements in a person's

[1] Cf. Plato, *Gorgias*, "And the things which are neither good nor evil, and which partake sometimes of the nature of good and at other times of evil, or of neither, are such as sitting, walking, running, sailing." Trans. B. Jowett, in *The Dialogues of Plato* (New York: Random House, 1937), Vol. I, p. 526.

"An action may be morally neutral when considered in itself. . . ." St. Thomas, *Summa Theologica*, 1a–2ae, xviii, 9.

attitude are the very source of its moral goodness and moral badness.

It is generally admitted that moral goodness has its source in some sort of "conformity" to a norm. But the nature of this relation and of the norm in question are in need of further elucidation.

Two essentially different types of limitations of man's arbitrary sovereignty can be found. Two different kinds of norms demand that we conform to them.

First, we must conform to the nature of a being and take into account its immanent laws. The very nature of this or that specific being imposes definite limitations on our arbitrary sovereignty. If we want to move from one place to another, we cannot step out of a window and walk through air, but we have to step out of the door and walk on the ground. Whenever we want to achieve something, we have to take into account the nature of things, a nature which is not our invention, but which we discover as something previously given. If we want to construct a machine, we have to conform to the laws of mechanics; if we want to demonstrate something, we have to observe the laws of syllogism. Whether it is something complicated or simple, whether material or spiritual, there are always circumstances to be taken into account, certain means to be used, an immanent logic of the thing to be followed, an activity to be performed according to certain rules to which we must conform ourselves if we want to attain our end. To understand the immanent logic of things and to know which means to use in order to attain an end is an important part of intelligence. We call a person stupid who is unable to understand the immanent logic of things and to find out which means must be used in order to attain an end. The one who ignores the immanent logic of things, who refuses to conform to it in order to choose the right means, is typically unreasonable; he acts like a fool.[2] Bonds of this kind

[2] Undoubtedly this refusal can also be morally objectionable. It can be rooted in pride or in concupiscence manifesting itself in our yielding to our arbitrary moods. But we may disregard in our context these cases with which we shall deal in Part Two, IV, "Roots of Moral Evil." What matters here is the decisive difference between the mere factual limitations of our arbitrariness and the moral obligations. This difference is not altered by the fact that immoral motives may even sometimes be at the basis of our neglect of these factual laws.

which are imposed on us have a purely factual character. There is no "oughtness" connected with them; they simply are.

The second type of norm limiting our arbitrary sovereignty is of a completely different nature. Such norms impose themselves on our conscience. They imply a commandment, a challenge, a call. Such are all moral obligations. If our desire comes into conflict with a moral norm, and we hear in our conscience "Thou shalt not," we are clearly aware of the essential difference between this limitation of our arbitrary sovereignty and the former one.

The man who ignores the moral norm not only acts unreasonably and like a fool, but he acts with moral badness; he is tainted with moral guilt. The radical difference between the two types of limitation manifests itself clearly by the following marks:

First, the immanent logic of the nature of beings has a mere factual and neutral character. The moral norms are rooted in values; instead of neutrality they possess an outspoken importance and relevance.

Second, the immanent logic imposes itself only hypothetically; or in other words, the norms have a hypothetical character. They say as it were, "If you want to attain something, you must conform to these rules and choose these means." But there exists no obligation to choose this end. "If you want your meat to be tender, you must cook it for a certain length of time; if you still want to meet your friend, you had better leave now; if you want to overcome this illness, you must rest," etc.

There is an obvious difference between this hypothetical obligation and the categorical obligation of a "Thou shalt not kill," or "Thou shalt not bear false witness against thy neighbor." Now it may be that certain obligations assume the character of being so necessary that they can scarcely be called hypothetical. Thus, "You must eat if you want to live," proposes an end which is far less subject to our arbitrary choice than, "You must purchase your tickets in advance, if you want to see the stage play." In the first case the end is quite necessary, whereas in the second it is much more a matter of taste or disposition. But this *inevitability* of eating does not in the least endow it as such with the categorical obligation that is found only in matters of morality. For the mere factual inevitability of an end could never endow it with the moral impact, with the "oughtness."

Third, our conforming to neutral factual limitations is certainly something positive, and it is precisely this which we call being reasonable. Our reason prescribes for us those means which have the ability to lead us to an end; in choosing these means, we obey the dictates of reason. But as long as our action manifests only this kind of reasonability, our attitude is not yet endowed with a moral value. These prescriptions of reason are fulfilled if someone repairs an instrument in the proper way, if he uses the right means to learn a language, if he drives a car well, if he accomplishes any activity well and according to its immanent logic. But all these attitudes are in themselves neither morally good nor bad.[3]

What matters is to see that a morally good attitude in the full sense of the word (i.e., one which is such that it bestows a moral value on the person) presupposes more than mere conformity to the immanent logic of a neutral being. It is certainly true that morality is the highest fulfillment of reasonability, if we take reasonability to include the call of values and obedience to this call. But never can we deduce from the notion of reasonability the notion of morality. Once we have grasped the nature of morality, we understand that it also implies a new and higher form of reasonability. This reasonability presupposes morality and not vice versa. I must first grasp the completely new and different obligation to conform which issues from the values before I can grasp why it is also *reasonable* to conform to them. If we tacitly include values and their call in the concept of reasonable, then certainly the conformity to this call is reasonable, although in a new and higher sense of the term. Then, in order to be reasonable in this sense, I have to act morally well. This clearly shows that we cannot discover the nature of morality by trying to deduce it from reasonability; rather, it becomes possible for us to understand that it is reasonable to act in this way only after we have discovered the specific sources of morality. Otherwise we move in a circle, explaining reasonability by the

[3] This remains true notwithstanding the fact that the conformity with the immanent logic of the means assumes an indirect moral value or disvalue as soon as the end is morally relevant. The sources of this indirect moral value or disvalue are, however, always beyond this factual reasonability.

conformity to the call of values, and the call of values by reasonability.

One may object, "It is true, of course, that mere conformity to the immanent logic of a neutral being does not give moral goodness in the specific sense of the term. There is something else we have to consider. We have to take into account the specific nature of the being in question. Conformity with the nature of certain beings only is morally relevant. Moral goodness depends especially upon whether or not an attitude is in conformity with *man's* nature, and, more specifically, with the *spiritual* nature of man." The *actus humanus*, which alone can be morally good, will be so, according to this view, if it is in conformity with man's spiritual nature, with that which makes man a personal spiritual being; in other words, an act is good only when it is *secundum naturam*, in conformity with the *nature* of man. But the concept of *secundum naturam* offers the same problems as the notion of reasonability.

We find here the same ambiguity: *secundum naturam* can first be applied to all those things which we can deduce from the immanent teleological relations in a being. In physiology we study the immanent teleological relations in man's bodily life, and from them we can deduce which bodily activities, which desires, trends, and instincts are *secundum naturam* and which are *contra naturam*. The immanent trends, the finalities which we can discover concerning the single organs and members as well as the entelechy of the entire body, enable us to distinguish between normal and abnormal, healthy and unhealthy, and so on.

Now if we try to apply this meaning of *secundum naturam* to the sphere of morality, we see at once that it is impossible. Among Greek philosophers the tendency to stress the analogy between medicine and ethics was the source of many errors; the situation is thoroughly different in each case. We are able to state the immanent logic of the body as something neutral and exclusively factual, and we can find thereby the *secundum naturam* which is the norm for the healthy. If, however, we analyze the soul of man from the point of view of mere factual tendencies, and of the immanent logic in man's nature, we may indeed reach many valuable results, especially concerning the problems of "mental health," but we could never discover the norm which would enable us to distinguish the morally good from the morally evil.

We could never see, for example, that selfishness is *contra naturam*; as a matter of fact, exactly the opposite is revealed by a study of the immanent tendencies in man's nature: there is a natural trend of self-affirmation and of striving for the subjectively satisfying. Why should it be more *secundum naturam* to be generous or just than to be avaricious or unjust? No analysis of merely factual tendencies, as of the immanent entelechial movements of the soul, could ever disclose to us that polygamy or even debauchery or promiscuity is immoral, nor could it show us that purity or faithfulness is *secundum naturam*. Only if we include in the notion of man's nature its being ordered to the world of values and ultimately to God, only if we liberate ourselves from a merely immanent conception of man and include in the nature of man his being destined to realize moral values, only then can we rightly say that all, at least all natural, morally good actions are *secundum naturam*.

But clearly, we must first know moral goodness in order to know that man in his very meaning and nature is destined to be morally good. Thus our understanding of moral goodness is by no means dependent on the analysis of the nature of man; in order to grasp that an act of justice is good, of injustice evil, or that fidelity is morally noble, infidelity morally base, we do not need to analyze the nature of man. On the contrary, in order to understand the nature of man and its most specific mark, its transcendence, in order to grasp the truth that man is destined to be morally good and that this is not a merely factual trend but also an objective relation of "oughtness," we must first of all know moral values. We know that to be just is *secundum naturam* because we know that it is good; and we do not get our knowledge of the goodness of justice from its being *secundum naturam*. An analysis of man's nature which prescinds from moral goodness could never lead us to understand why justice is *secundum naturam;* but the insight into the goodness of justice reveals to us that man is destined to partake of this goodness.

If, therefore, the term *secundum naturam* is meant to include conformity with moral goodness, then it is based on a conception of nature which includes the relation between man and the world of moral values, as well as the fact that man is ordered to these values and their call. The notion of moral value is for our knowledge the *principium* and the being *secundum naturam*, the *principiatum*.

This relation between the *secundum naturam* and the value not only applies insofar as our knowledge of moral goodness is concerned, but *a fortiori* insofar as the ontological structural situation is concerned. Justice is not morally good because it is in conformity with our nature; rather because it is good, our nature is called to be endowed with it, or, in other words, it is a mark of the dignity of our nature to be called to participate in something so sublime as justice by becoming just and acting justly. We saw before that value is an ultimate datum and that every attempt to substitute anything else in place of its intrinsic importance is futile. So long as we ignore value in our analysis of being, so long as we remain in the frame of a neutral immanent logic, we can never find the sources of man's morality. The basis of man's moral values can be found only in a cosmos pregnant with values; it implies man's response to goods endowed with values, and at least in an implicit, indirect way, man's response to God, the Infinite Goodness.

We have seen the relation which exists between ontological and qualitative values, and especially between the ontological value of man and his moral values; we have likewise seen that the qualitative values can never be explained as mere presuppositions of the entelechial unfolding of a being. The objective basis of man's morality is not to be found in a mere adherence to nature in the sense of mere neutral factualness. But to heed the call of God which is implied in the world of values; to conform to the world above himself; to obey God the Infinite Goodness and to conform to His divine law—this is the objective basis for the fact that man is endowed with moral values.

The impossibility of deducing moral values from a *secundum naturam* remains unchanged even if one includes in the phrase all essential human relations involving the relation to God, as well as the relation to one's neighbor and to the community. In the relation to God, we necessarily presuppose the notion of value. A study of man's nature which ignores all values would not enable us to conclude from the datum of human nature that man should adore and obey God; on the contrary, only by the knowledge of God's infinite goodness and sanctity can we understand that to obey God is morally obligatory and good. A notion of God which prescinded from His eternal goodness and sanctity could justify only absolute dependence upon an almighty person who created us, and therefore only the inevitable necessity to submit to God; but it could not account for the moral obligation to obey and adore Him. Our obedience to God is good, not because it happens to correspond to our nature, but because of the infinite goodness and absolute lordship of God to whom this response is due. The same applies in the case of justice toward our neighbor. That we should be just rather than unjust can never be deduced from a consideration of man's social nature prescinding hereby from all values and merely concentrating on the immanent logic of man's being—a type of consideration with which we are confronted in certain types of psychiatry.

We can state that it is against man's nature to be isolated, for there exists in man a tendency for companionship which is rooted in his social nature. So long as we state this as a mere psychological fact without raising the question of whether communion among men has a value or not, we have not yet reached the basis for morality. We can never reach the insight which the psalmist expresses in the words: *Ecce quam bonum et quam jucundum habitare fratres in unum*—"Behold how good and how pleasant it is for brethren to dwell together in unity" (Ps. 132:1).

In the case of justice such an analysis of man's factual relation to other human beings can never lead even to the discovery of a psychological tendency to be just, and still less to the fact that justice is morally good. In order to understand that man *should* be just, we have to grasp the intrinsic goodness of justice, i.e., its value. And in order to understand that man should be just toward his neighbor, we have to grasp the dignity of a human person; we have to grasp his rights and the inviolability of these rights. But in order to grasp the dignity of a human being and the inviolability of his rights, we must transcend the sphere of the mere neutral statement and admit the presence of values.

Thus we have to repeat what has been said above. So long as we start from a neutral conception of man's nature (even one including all possible relations) and prescind from the notion of values, we can never deduce any moral value by the norm of conformity with this nature. But when in our notion of the relations to other beings, we expressly refer to the values of these other beings, and when in the notion of conformity with our nature, we expressly include the idea that we are called to give the right response to these values, then indeed we may call these responses *secundum naturam*. But, evidently, this is possible only when we have already grasped their moral goodness. The same applies with respect to the ontological foundation of beings. To respond in the right way to God or to our neighbor is good, not because it is in conformity with our nature, but because it is *due* to God's infinite goodness or to the dignity of our neighbor as a human being. And because it is morally good, man is destined to it; we may therefore call it in its most noble sense *secundum naturam*.

The impossibility of deducing morality from a neutral and merely factual understanding of the term *secundum naturam* is again clearly seen when we pose the question: Why should we act in conformity with our nature? In all attempts to deduce moral goodness and moral evil from conformity or non-conformity with our nature, one silently presupposes the evidence that we *should* conform to our nature. But either we presume that man should conform to his nature because to do so is *morally* good, and then the moral goodness is the reason for the oughtness of such a conforming, and not vice versa; or else we presume that even if we prescind from all moral values, the conformity to the mere factual and natural tendencies of our nature is obligatory. But this last proposition is in no way evident. So long as conformity is taken in a merely factual sense, the statement would mean either that man is necessitated to act in conformity with nature, or else that he cannot avoid doing so, if he wants to accomplish something. But such a conformity could never impose on us a moral obligation.

In summarizing, we may say that in any inquiry into the sources of moral goodness and moral evil we cannot begin by asking: What is in conformity with human nature? In man's nature the basic impulses or immanent logic accessible to a neutral analysis, like that of the psychologist or psychiatrist, can never disclose to us the basis of morality. They can never explain the fact that we *should* act, that we *ought* to act, in a specific way; that is, that we are morally obligated to act *this* way rather than another. This does not mean, however, that ethics can dispense with the analysis of the nature of man. On the contrary, to understand the meaningful character of man's spiritual acts, to understand the freedom of man, is to understand what makes possible his moral endowment of values and disvalues. The analysis of man's nature in the light of the universe of values is therefore one of the most essential ethical tasks. But the star guiding us in this research, the compass which points the way, is precisely the datum of moral goodness and moral evil. Thus the inquiry into the sources of moral evil and moral goodness in man must start with those acts which are indubitably endowed with moral values, the analysis of which will aid us in discovering those factors determining their moral goodness. Such an inquiry must start from an analysis, not of man's neutral tendencies, but of the goods to which man is ordered by no mere entelechial need in his nature, but because of the intrinsic value of such goods.

We must therefore begin with an analysis of the kinds of acts by which man directs himself to such goods and their intrinsic values, the acts in which man surpasses the frame of mere urges and manifests his response to God and the universe of values.

CHAPTER 17

VALUE RESPONSE

ONE OF the most decisive distinctions to be made in the sphere of man's conscious life is that between intentional and unintentional experiences. In saying "intentional," we refer to a conscious, rational relation between the person and an object.[1] Not all human experiences imply such a conscious relation to an object. All pure states, such as being tired, being in a bad humor, being irritated, and so forth, have no conscious relation with an object. They do not imply the specific polarity of the person on the one hand, as against the object on the other. They do not possess the character of transcending the realm of our mind.

We are not tired *about* something; tiredness is only a state, an experience of something qualitative related to our body, but it does not have any meaningful reference to an object. Of course the state is *caused by* something. But the objective causal relation must not be confused with an intentional relation. Whereas our feeling tired in no way presupposes a knowledge of the cause, any intentional experience (such as joy) essentially presupposes a knowledge of the cause of our experience: that is to say, of an object which motivates our experience. In the case of joy, this intentional character distinguishes it from a mere state of cheerfulness. Tiredness remains the same whether or not I know its cause. Often we look for the cause of our tiredness, and wonder whether it is due to overwork, disease, or great emotion. The

[1] We do not here use the term "intentional" in the common usage, in which it means something done on purpose. We refer to a terminology introduced by Husserl, in which "intentional" means any conscious, meaningful relationship to an object. Cf. *Logische Untersuchungen.*

experience of tiredness as such is not affected by an ignorance of its cause. It is just as intense when we are not aware of the cause as when we have found it. Mere states exist in us as simple facts; their objective causal determination presupposes no knowledge of it; but even when knowledge is given, these states are not connected with their cause in a conscious meaningful way.

If we compare these states with various experiences of a very different character: for instance, any perception or any response (such as conviction, doubt, joy, sorrow, love, or hatred), we easily see that all these are, despite their thorough differences in other respects, of an intentional nature. Perception by its very essence obviously implies the antithesis of a personal subject as opposed to object. It is by its very essence a transcending experience, *a consciousness of* something on the object side, whereby my intellect truly possesses the being of an object in a spiritual manner. The relation of my intellect to the object is essentially a conscious one, possessing a rational, meaningful character. Perception is necessarily a perception *of something* extraneous to my mind (at least functionally). Every perception necessarily refers to something on the object side, which confronts me. The same applies to every kind of knowledge by which I analyze an object or penetrate into it. This is so even in the case in which the object of my knowledge is in reality part of myself. Thus in any reflective analysis of my joy, or my enthusiasm, these experiences stand (functionally) before me as objects. To my intellect at this moment it is something extraneous and definitely distinguishable from my act of analysis as such. In every "consciousness *of*," an object is present to my mind; in having a consciousness of it, I necessarily touch something which functionally at least is beyond the sphere in which the act of perception—or remembrance or imagination or intellectual intuition—itself is to be found. I partake intentionally (*intentionaliter*) in the being of the perceived object, which is necessarily before me.

The difference between this and a mere state is obvious. In experiencing a mere state, for instance tiredness, there is no object standing in front of myself. I am tired. This quality in my body alone is given. Neither is the tiredness an object *of* which I *have* a consciousness, nor is there any object to which the tiredness refers in my conscious experience.

In comparing any response to a mere state, the intentional character of the former appears even more evident. Our conviction, for instance, is necessarily directed toward something, for there exists no conviction as such; it is always conviction *of* something. It necessarily implies a conscious, meaningful relation to something on the object side, transcending, at least functionally, the act of conviction as such, and reaching an object which as such is not a real part of the conviction itself. The conviction itself is a definite *response* to an object; its content is a "yes" to the existence of something. This character of a response reveals most clearly that conviction has an intentional relation to an object. A response obviously implies the polar duality of person on the one side, and object on the other.

The very essence of conviction is its rational, meaningful relation to an object. In being convinced of something, we direct ourselves with a certain rational content to an object. This content is, as we already mentioned, a "yes" to the existence of the object. The intentional character of conviction clearly distinguishes it from all mere states, for they lack intentionality. The same difference becomes evident in comparing joy with a mere state. Joy is essentially joy about something. It necessarily implies a meaningful relation to an object. It can never arise as in the case of a state by mere causation. It presupposes the *knowledge* of the object that motivates my joy. I am, for instance, full of joy because of the arrival of my friend. So long as I do not know of my friend's arrival, it cannot motivate joy in my soul. The fact as such does not suffice to create joy in my soul; I must have a knowledge of it, a consciousness of it. A state, on the contrary (as was seen before), can arise in my mind simply as an effect of an objective cause and does not presuppose in any way a knowledge of the cause. Moreover, even though I arrive at a knowledge of the cause, it is not from the consequent conscious relation that the state arises, but rather it arises as an effect of the cause (physical or psychical) of which I have a knowledge; there is involved a causality which does not go through my consciousness, but goes, so to speak, over the head of the conscious spiritual center of my person.

Joy is a response to an object. We take a positive attitude toward something, we direct ourselves with a certain positive content toward an object; our position has the character of a response to the positive importance of the object. The difference between joy and all mere states is obvious.

The distinction between what is intentional and what is non-intentional divides our psychical experiences into two different spheres, but it is clear that the intentional is the higher one. In order to understand the nature of "intentionality," we have to distinguish intentional experiences, not only from mere states lacking any direction toward an object, but also from all merely teleological trends in man's nature.[2]

In undergoing an experience such as thirst or a craving for food, we clearly grasp that these are not mere states, for they possess an immanent direction toward something. They are characterized by an inner movement toward an object, a seeking of fulfillment or appeasement. In place of the static character of a mere state they have a dynamic one. By dynamic we do not mean the dramatic rhythm which a mere state such as a great bodily pain also possesses, but a definite tension and direction toward fulfillment, whether this fulfillment consists in appropriating something to us, or in an unloading of vital energies, or in something else.

What matters in our context is the difference between the immanent trend pushing or leading us toward something, and the intentional, meaningful relation to an object. This instinctive trend also has an element of meaningfulness. As something teleological, it has the element of intelligibility proper to a final cause. Now every final cause presupposes intelligence and will; but it is not man's intelligence which is at stake in these experiences. Neither our reason nor our will is involved in instincts. It is the intelligence and will of God,[3] which has placed an immanent and unconscious finality in such experiences, in much the same way as the lungs or kidneys have been given a final direction toward fulfilling a certain task in our body. But we remain, so to speak, outside the meaningfulness and *ratio* of these experi-

---

[2] We are thinking here exclusively of teleological trends insofar as they are consciously experienced, because only then is there a danger of confounding a teleological trend with an intentional act.

[3] We here include only natural instincts and urges and not perverted instincts nor the disorder of isolated urges which our faith ascribes to original sin.

ences; their meaningful direction unfolds itself *in* us, as it were disregarding the authority of our personal center.

The final direction is not a personal relation as is the case with intentionality. We experience the trend in our instincts as a blind push toward something. That objectively there is instead a meaningful coordination is something which we may discover only later on "from without" as we do with respect to the finality in a physiological process; but this finality is in no way consciously accomplished in experiencing the instinct.

Intentional experiences, on the contrary, imply a consciously accomplished and meaningful direction toward an object; this meaningful direction is a manifestation of our rational personal character.[4] Here the meaningfulness is a personal one; here we act as persons; here a relation exists which is possible only if accomplished by a person. There exists nothing in the impersonal world which could be interpreted as intentionality. This relation must therefore be clearly distinguished from the teleological relation.

Intentionality, as we employ the term in our context, is a decisive mark of spirituality. Teleological relations, on the other hand, pervade the entire nonspiritual world. Even the teleological trend in a conscious experience such as an instinct or an urge does not endow the experience with a spiritual character. This is also expressed in the fact that we find analogous instincts and urges in animals.

In the realm of the intentional experiences (that is to say, in the sphere of acts), we must make a further fundamental distinction: between cognitive acts and responses.

To the cognitive acts above all belongs perception, in the largest sense of that term. Every time an object, whatever its

---

[4] The fact that a blind instinct and an intentional act may be closely connected in concrete reality does not erase the essential difference between them. Thirst is such an urge, teleologically but not intentionally directed toward a liquid or rather toward drinking. Because of our thirst we desire water, we look for it, and this desire is endowed with an intentional direction to the object, presupposing its knowledge. This will become still clearer if we think of an act of willing which may be motivated by our thirst. We are thirsty and so we decide to drink. The willing definitely has an intentional character, a conscious, meaningful relation to drinking which thirst as such does not possess. So we see that the fact that intentionality and a teleological trend are such close neighbors in reality in no way alters the essential difference between them.

nature, reveals itself to our mind a cognitive act is in question. Cognitive acts encompass not only the perception of colors,[5] tones, and in effect, all so-called sense perceptions (such as seeing, hearing, touching, etc.), but also the perception of space, of material bodies, of relations, of other persons, of values, as well as the intellectual intuition of essences itself. Imagination and memory belong to cognitive acts despite their decisive difference from perception.

But belief, conviction, doubt, hope, fear, joy, sorrow, enthusiasm, indignation, esteem and contempt, trust and mistrust, love and hatred, all belong to the sphere of responses. Both cognitive acts and responses have an intentional character. Yet they exhibit a fundamental difference which is expressed in the nature of their intentionality.

Cognitive acts are first of all characterized by the fact that they are a *consciousness of* something, that is to say, of the object. We are, as it were, void; the whole content is on the object side. When we see the color red, the content (red) is on the object side; *we* are not red, but we have a consciousness of red.

In feeling joy, on the contrary, the content is on the side of the subject: it is in us; we are not void, but "full" of joy. This content in our soul is directed toward an object. Joy is not a consciousness *of* something, but is itself a conscious entity, a consciously accomplished reality. The qualitative content is in our act, that is to say, on the side of the subject, not of the object.

Secondly, in the cognitive acts the intention goes, so to speak, from the object to ourselves: the object reveals itself to our mind, it speaks and we listen. In responses as such, the intention goes from us to the object. Language expresses this fact in the words "we are full of joy about something," or "we are enthusiastic over something." In responses it is we who speak: the content of our act is addressed to the object; it is our response to the object.

Thirdly, all cognitive acts have a fundamentally receptive character even though they are not merely passive. We might call it an active passivity, or an actively accomplished receptivity. And this receptive element is the very essence of all cognition.

---

[5] The knowledge which is also implied in the perception of a color definitely forbids us to treat this perception as if it were deprived of all rationality and were consequently on the same level as the sight which an animal also possesses.

The response, as such, is on the contrary, unreceptive; rather, it has a definitely spontaneous character.

The fundamental difference between these two intentional experiences is obvious. But if it is necessary to distinguish between them, it is equally necessary to grasp their essential connection. All responses necessarily presuppose a cognitive act. The object must first reveal itself in its nature, before it can become an object of our responses.

In this great dialogue between the person and being, cognitive acts form the basis of all other acts and responses. The primary contact with the object is always given by one or another kind of cognitive act. In these acts we partake of being in a unique way; here a being constitutes itself as an object for our minds. We must first know that our friend will arrive before we can be full of joy about the fact; we must first have a knowledge of a person before we can love or hate him. Perception in the largest sense of the term is the fundamental act in which the dialogical situation between person and being is established. Only after we have directly or indirectly grasped a fact, a thing, a person, can we respond to it; or in other words, only after a thing is known to us, can it motivate a response in our soul.

Thus we can state: All responses necessarily presuppose cognitive acts; they are essentially based on cognitive acts. This fundamental truth has been expressed in the scholastic philosophy thus: *Nihil volitum nisi cogitatum* (Nothing is willed unless it be thought). *Volitum* is here the general term for all responses, *cogitatio* the general term for cognitive acts.[6]

In the realm of responses we are confronted with three different basic types. First, there exist responses such as conviction, doubt, expectation, which we can term "theoretical" responses. Second, there is willing in the strict sense of the word, which we can term the "volitional" response. Third, there are responses such as joy and sorrow, love and hatred, fear and hope, esteem and contempt, enthusiasm and indignation, which we can term "affective" responses.

---

[6] There also exists, however, an inverse relation between knowledge and will. Knowledge also presupposes certain directions of will, as we shall see later on. But the nature of this dependence relation clearly differs in its formal character from the relation expressed in the statement: *Nihil volitum nisi cogitatum*.

Theoretical responses, though still responses, belong in theme so much to the sphere of knowledge that they have very often been considered part of knowledge. Their theme is indeed the same as that which dominates the cognitive acts, such as perception, inference, intellectual intuition, and learning, i.e., the theme of existence or truth. In the theoretical response, for example conviction or belief, we say "yes" as it were, to the "such-being" and existence of an object which reveals itself to our mind. The implicit issues involved in the cognitive sphere, embracing acts of knowledge as well as theoretical responses, are: What is the thing's nature? Does it exist or not? The object in the acts of knowledge answers this question; and it does so by revealing its nature and existence. In theoretical responses, for instance conviction, we add, as it were, the voice of our minds to the object's gesture of self-affirmation; we complete it with the "word" of our mind as the expression of our outspoken embrace of the such-being and existence of the object.

The theoretical character of these acts is obvious. In conviction, we say "yes" to the such-being and existence of a fact; in doubt, we refuse a positive "yes" and tend rather to a "no," while yet suspending the definite "no." In an assumption, we say a limited "yes" for we still withhold our definite intellectual assent. Each of these responses obviously corresponds to a different datum in knowledge. If each is adequate to its datum and is objectively justified, then we may say that the conviction presupposes a univocal result in knowledge, the object's univocal answer, so to speak; doubt presupposes that the object does not univocally reveal its nature and existence to us in knowledge; assumption presupposes that the object reveals something as probable.

We see to what extent conviction, doubt, and assumption belong to the sphere of knowledge, for they center around the same theme as the cognitive acts. But, on the other hand, we should not overlook their definite character as responses; we must see that they differ from the cognitive acts, because in a theoretical response the intention goes from us to the object. It is not the object that speaks, but we ourselves who speak. In these responses we do not acquire knowledge; rather, knowledge is presupposed. In these responses, so long as they are adequate to the data and not blind or unfounded, we repeat from our side, as it were, what the object told us in knowledge.[7]

These responses are not "free" in the full sense of this term. Certainly they are not necessitated by a brute causality, as are mere states or urges and appetites. But they are rather meaningfully engendered by the object which we have grasped in knowledge. Their relation to the object is typically intelligible and therefore radically opposed to all brute causality.

Yet they are not free in the sense that the *will* is free: for it is not in our power to be convinced or unconvinced when facing a datum in our knowledge. On the contrary, knowledge itself prescribes what response we should give. As soon as we have grasped something, our conviction of it arises organically.

But if our knowledge reveals the converse, we cannot arbitrarily be convinced of it. Certainly there exist cases of wishful thinking, wherein our conviction is illegitimately influenced by our wishes. This sometimes even affects our knowledge itself; our wishes may already darken or obscure our view of the object or insert an illusory aspect into our knowledge. But this illegitimate influence on conviction or on knowledge can not be interpreted as a free decision. We are free to abstain from these illegitimate influences; it is in our power to eliminate them, but this does not mean that the act of conviction itself is the offspring of a free choice. Our will has not the same free and dominant power over conviction as it has, for example, in the free choice of one of two possibilities, or in freely saying yes or no to a challenge.

Before analyzing the difference between the volitional and the theoretical responses we should state that the term "will" is not always used in the same sense; sometimes it is used in a larger, sometimes in a narrower sense. When used in a larger sense the term "will" seems to embrace all responses whether volitional or affective. In this sense love, veneration, esteem, are called acts of will. When used in the narrower sense it is restricted to the specific act which is at the basis of all actions. So long as the

[7] This must not be understood as if the "inner word" of the theoretical responses would not be simultaneously something new with respect to the self-revelation of the object. Already the very fact that it is a "word" spoken by a person and that in this word are invested and actualized intelligence, reason, throws into relief the character of its own which it possesses.

difference between the larger and narrower sense of the term is not clearly stressed, the danger of confusion and equivocation is inevitable. We shall thus use in our context the term "will" or "willing" only in the strict sense in which it is synonymous with the volitional response.

In speaking of will in the strict sense, we mean the response which is directed toward something not yet real, but endowed with the possibility of being realized. In willing we turn to this not-yet-real fact with the specific interest of bringing it into existence. Willing in this sense is concerned exclusively with the realization of something not yet real. It is thus the basis of all actions. All human actions can be effected only as a result of the will. The will alone is able to command intentionally our bodily activities, to instigate freely and voluntarily a chain of causality. It commands our movements, our speaking, all kinds of activities, and especially all actions in the strict sense of the word. Only through willing can we change something in the world around us as well as something in our own person. The act of willing dominates the whole sphere which is accessible to our free intervention; it is the basis of all that we are called upon to realize in this world. The word with which the will directs itself to its object could be formulated thus: "Thou shouldst exist and thou wilt exist."

As soon as we transcend the sphere in which we function only as a member in the chain of an objective causality (for instance, the physiological sphere of our body with all its changes), we find the will at the basis of all interventions of our person, from the most modest things, such as eating or dressing, to the most complicated processes, such as the creation of a work of art or deeds of great importance.

The true nature of will has been grasped in an incomparable way by St. Augustine. He touches the very nature of man's freedom by stressing in *De Libero Arbitrio* that the will is such a precious good that it suffices to desire it in order to have it present: "Wherefore nothing is so completely in our power as the will itself. For when we will, immediately, without any interval, the act of will is realized." [8] He thus sees the unique and sublime

---

[8] St. Augustine, *De Libero Arbitrio*, III, 3, trans. Francis E. Tourscher (Philadelphia: Peter Reilly Co., 1937), p. 255.

perfection which the will possesses. The will is in our immediate power. Its unique character is clearly revealed by the fact that its immediate issuance from our spiritual center is the only case of a *fiat* in our human existence.

In comparing willing in the strict sense of the term with theoretical responses, we clearly face the following distinguishing marks. In the first place, the theme of the will is not the same as that of knowledge. It is not dominated by the implicit question inquiring into the nature and existence of something.

It is not truth which is here at stake, but rather the *importance* of the fact which is the object of our will. In order to become an object of the will something has to be important in one or another way. But the specific character of will may be found in its twofold theme: the importance of the object and its coming into existence [9] through our own activity.

Thus willing is further distinguished from theoretical responses by the fact that it refers to something which is not yet real (though in principle realizable—and even realizable through me), while a theoretical response such as conviction presupposes the real or ideal existence of a fact.

Finally, this essential relation between the will and the coming into existence of its object endows the will with a specific practical note as against the theoretical character of conviction or doubt or assumption.[10]

[9] Certainly the will can also be directed to a fact which is connected with the destruction or dissipation of something (a person's death, for example), but as a state of facts this too has to come into existence. This applies also to the cases in which our willing is directed to the preservation or conservation of something.

[10] There exist, however, several other acts which, though not identical with willing, share essential features with willing. I am thinking here of acts such as promising, commanding, obeying, and others, which can not be called responses in the strict sense. They share with the will the fact that they are in our immediate power, that is to say, free in the full sense. Yet they are not identical with the act which is at the basis of all actions—the response to something not yet real but realizable, the "inner word" of which is "thou shouldst be and thou wilt be." Promising is an act *sui generis,* including the utterance of words to another person as an essential part of its accomplishment, and, as A. Reinach showed, can never be interpreted as a mere act of willing exteriorized in words. Yet promising includes essentially one element of willing, or in other words, in promising something I also will to promise it; the "yes" of the person's free spiritual center is implied. But it is in no way an activity commanded by the will, like speaking, walking, eating. The "yes" of the will is *in* the act of promise or obedience, whereas willing is something of its own, commanding and innervating these

We come now to another fundamental type of responses: the affective responses. Though in some respects they are more akin to the volitional responses than to the theoretical responses, nevertheless they also clearly differ from the volitional responses and definitely form a group of their own. The affective responses (e.g., joy and sorrow, esteem and contempt) share with the volitional responses the theme of importance. They equally presuppose the importance of an object and an awareness of this importance, and they are motivated by it.

Like willing, they refer to this importance by the "word" which they bestow on the object. By this they definitely distinguish themselves from theoretical responses. Their theme is not the existence and the knowledge of an object; this theme is already settled, for the adequate knowledge of the importance is taken for granted. The affective response imparts to the object a "word" which is in a much more outspoken way a "response." It is, like conviction, not only a repetition of what the object imparts to my mind, a repetition of the self-affirmation of the object on our part, but a completing word, a new word. The theme is thus not noetic, such as we find in knowledge itself, but affective.

If the will and the affective responses share the theme of importance inasmuch as they both presuppose an importance on the object side, they clearly differ in the following points. First, it is not an essential mark of the affective responses as such to presuppose that their object is not yet real, although certain affective responses, such as wishing, desire, and hope, are directed to something not yet real. This does not apply to many other affective responses such as joy and sorrow, love and hatred, esteem, enthusiasm, contempt or indignation.

But much more decisive is a second mark: the affective plenitude which is characteristic of these responses and which is absent in the will. While affective responses are voices of our heart, while in them our entire person is involved, the will has a one-dimensional, linear character, certainly committing our entire

activities from above. Without being able to discuss this problem in detail in this context, we want to state that there exist several acts which are different ramifications of the actualization of the free center of the person, i.e., the center which finds its main expression in willing in the strict sense. They all imply therefore a main element of willing, but, unlike the above-mentioned activities, they are rather brethren than chldren of willing in the strict sense.

person, but being in itself exclusively a position of our free personal center.

And with this property the third most decisive difference between willing and affective response is closely linked. The will alone is free in the strict sense of being in our immediate power, whereas affective responses are not free in this sense. We never can engender any affective response by a *fiat*, nor can we command it by our will as we can any activity.[11] Love, for instance, is always granted to us as a gift.

The affective responses differ from willing not only in that they are beyond our immediate power, but also (and in this we come to a fourth distinction) in that they have no commanding capacity with respect to our bodily activities or to any action. Certainly our joy has many causal effects on our body. It may even express itself in our face and disclose thereby its presence and quality. But this is an unconscious process; it is an objective causality in us, albeit a very extraordinary one. To the will alone is given the capacity to make a conscious command, to raise our hand on purpose, to say something because we want to say it. As we mentioned before, the will is queen of the action, and by this fact too it distinguishes itself from all affective responses. In thus distinguishing the affective from the volitional response, it must be stressed that the affective response is by no means necessarily less "spiritual" than the other responses.[12] The spiritual, intentional, and meaningful character of the theoretical responses, and, above all, of the volitional response, have in some way always been admitted. But concerning the affective responses

---

[11] Their relation to freedom and responsibility will be analyzed in detail in Chapter 25, "Cooperative Freedom." Here it suffices to see that they are certainly not free in the same sense as the will, in the sense of being completely in our immediate power. That love can nevertheless be a matter of moral obligation and thus accessible in some way to our freedom will be shown in the same chapter.

[12] In the affective sphere there exist many gradations in the spiritual character of the different experiences, and in this matter there is an analogy between the affective sph   and the spheres of knowledge and the theoretical responses. Association, for instance, though belonging to the intellectual sphere, is certainly not spiritual in the same sense as a process of reasoning. Analogously, we find in the affective sphere an enormous variety of thoroughly different experiences. But even in the realm of affective responses, which by their intentionality possess a fundamental mark of spirituality, a great gradation in spirituality can be found. What matters is to see that there exist affective responses which are as spiritual as the highest intellectual and volitional acts.

there has been and there remains even now a widespread tendency to overlook their spiritual, intentional, and meaningful character.

One of our main tasks will be to do justice to the dignity of the affective responses: love, joy, hope, longing, contrition, and the like, all of which play such a paramount role in the Gospel, in the liturgy, in the lives of saints, and in the deep and serious experiences of our own lives.[18]

We have already mentioned the confusion issuing from use of the general terms "emotions" or "feelings"; now we must add the term "passions" which compresses into one class experiences which have definitely to be distinguished. We should see that, in subsuming the affective responses under the genus of passion, we thereby overlook their spiritual and intentional character, a character which the passions in the true sense of the term entirely lack.

When Aristotle opposes the irrational part of man, including appetites, urges, and passions, to the rational part, embracing knowledge and will, he leaves no place for affective responses. In confusing them with passions and appetites, he fails to do justice to the paramount role which they play in ethics, because he regards them only as an object for self-control.[14]

For St. Thomas, what we mean by love is either a passion or an act of will. Following the Aristotelian and Platonic conception of the hierarchy in man's soul, he includes the affective responses such as joy and love in the sphere of passions, the sphere of nonspiritual and irrational emotions. But he stresses that apart from the love which belongs to the irrational part of man, there is also a love (*dilectio*) which is an act of will and

---

[18] "What man doth live without affections? And do you suppose, brethren, that those who fear God, worship God, love God, have no affections? Do you really suppose, and do you dare suppose, that painting, the theatre, hunting, hawking, fishing, engage the affections, and that meditation on God doth not engage certain interior affections of their own, when we contemplate the universe and place before our eyes the spectacle of the nature of things, and therein seek to discover the Creator, and find Him nowhere displeasing but pleasing above all things?" St. Augustine, *In Ps.*, LXXVI, 14.

[14] Sometimes, however, Aristotle seems to grasp the positive role of affective responses; for instance, when he says: ". . . the man who does not rejoice in noble actions is not even good." *Nicomachean Ethics*, Bk. I, 1099a, 17–18, taken from *The Basic Works of Aristotle,* trans. Richard P. McKeon (New York: Random House, 1941), p. 945.

thus belongs to the spiritual part of man. St. Thomas thereby extends the term "will" beyond the strict sense in which we use it here.[15]

In any case, it seems that these rational affective responses are not conceived as endowed with an affective plenitude intimately embracing our heart. Rather, they are seen in the light of an act of will (in the sense used here), and so the enlarged use of the term "will" is not without consequence for the interpretation of these acts.

St. Augustine, however, seems to consider love in its full affective plenitude. He sees it as something meaningful, rational, and spiritual; and yet he does not fail to distinguish it from the will. In his famous words: *Parum est voluntate etiam voluptate traheris* (Little is it to be drawn by the will, also by delight shalt thou be drawn),[16] he definitely stresses the difference between love and will; and, without denying thereby the spiritual and meaningful character of love, he sees as its essential features affective plenitude, bliss, and the being drawn by delight, features which are lacking in willing.

In the course of the following analysis, we shall have ample occasion to grasp in detail the spiritual and rational nature of the affective responses, as well as their difference from mere passions or emotions. For the time being our topic will center around the responses from the ethical point of view, wherein we abstract from the first type, the theoretical responses, and concentrate, because of their paramount role in morality, on the two other groups, willing and the affective response.

The specific nature of the object to which intentional acts are directed has a decisive bearing on the character of those acts. We have already mentioned the correlation in the realm of knowledge between the object and the act. There exist many different kinds of perception, according to the object in question. In the sphere of sense-perception, for instance, we can see only colors and not tones, or hear only tones and not colors. Analogously, space-perception is another type, differing from perception of other persons or value-perception.

The modification of the act determined by the nature of the

---

[15] See *Summa Theologica*, 1a–2ae, xxvi, 3.
[16] St. Augustine, *Tractatus 26 in Joannem.*

correlative object is still more outspoken in the realm of other human acts. Adolf Reinach elaborated the notion of social acts, such as promising, telling, commanding, and others, which are possible only insofar as directed to a personal being.[17] Certainly in these acts there always exists in addition an object—the content of our promise, of our command, or of our communication. But another person is necessarily presupposed as the addressee of these acts. It would be nonsensical to promise something to a dog or to make a command to a tree or to tell something to a work of art. These social acts are such that for their validity they must be received by the addressee. But the presupposition of a person as addressee is in no way restricted to the sphere of social acts (in the terminology of Reinach). Forgiving, for instance, though not a social act, presupposes a person as addressee. It is impossible to forgive a stone, a cat, or an event. Again there are acts which essentially presuppose a person *as their object*, acts such as veneration or esteem. We cannot venerate an event or a tree or a work of art, but only a personal being.[18] The theoretical response of conviction, on the contrary, essentially presupposes a state of facts as its object. We can only be convinced *that* something is such, *that* something exists; but never can we be convinced of a tree, of an animal, or of a person. Similarly, the act of willing always refers to a state of fact or an activity. We will that somebody should be saved, or that a fire should be extinguished; or we will to take a walk or dance, and so on. But we cannot *will* a person. Thus we see that the question of which kind of being an act presupposes as its object or addressee is of decisive importance to the nature of an act. We

[17] *Gesammelte Schriften, Die apriorischen Grundlagen des buergerlichen Rechtes* (Halle: M. Niemeyer, 1921), pp. 166, 351.

[18] The correlation between veneration and person is not contradicted by the fact that there exists veneration of relics of saints or of the Holy Cross in the liturgy of Good Friday. First we must realize that the liturgical act of veneration of relics or of the Holy Cross is not identical with the affective response of veneration in our context. Apart from the difference in the "inner word" spoken in veneration to a person and this liturgical act (which is more a doing than a response), we must not forget that even in the cultic act of veneration, similar to the respectful attitude toward sacramentals, the source of the *venerability* is a *person*—the person of the God-Man Christ and His infinite sanctity. The fact that animals considered as sacred have been the object of veneration does not contradict the correlativity of person and veneration, because obviously these "sacred animals" have been considered as personal beings.

are especially interested here in the difference between acts presupposing a person on the object side, either as an object or addressee. An act of obedience essentially presupposes a personal being, whereas, as we have already seen, willing in the strict sense is always directed to something impersonal.

However there are many responses which can be directed to a personal as well as to an impersonal being. Such is the case with joy, sorrow, enthusiasm, indignation, anger, fear, admiration, liking, dislike, and so on. While we can only venerate and esteem a person, we can rejoice over an event, in a work of art or in a person. But also in those affective responses which can be directed to different kinds of being and above all to personal and impersonal beings, the specific nature of the object is of paramount importance to the character of the acts. Though the same species of affective responses is at stake whether directed to a personal or impersonal object, the character of the response is deeply affected by the difference in its objects.

Finally, there are affective responses which, though not essentially restricted to personal beings, nevertheless when directed to persons, assume not only another character but their most authentic character. Such are love and hatred. We can love animals, we can love a work of art, we can love a country, a home, a people, we can love a virtue, but plainly the love of a *person* is the most authentic love. Here alone can so many essential features of love unfold themselves. Here alone love assumes its fullness. The love for a personal being is the pattern for love; all loves for an impersonal being are more or less analogies, derivations, copies of love in its fullest sense.

We understand this clearly if we think of the love *par excellence* in the human realm: the love of God. The abyss separating the love of a personal God and the "love" for an impersonal divinity (e.g., the love which a pantheist may experience) cannot be overlooked nor can anyone deny it. This hint may suffice to show the deep interrelation between the intentional act and the specific nature of the object to which it is directed. The fact that this equally applies to the affective value responses throws a new light on the meaningful and spiritual character which affective responses can possess.

Yet in the affective sphere we find still another basic type of intentional experience, having a counterpart in neither the theoretical nor the volitional spheres. When we say that another's hostile attitude has wounded our heart, or that his insult has offended us, or that his compassion has consoled us, or that his love has gladdened or touched us—we are constantly referring to an affective experience which clearly differs from any mere state as well as from the affective response. This experience we shall term "being affected." Being affected does not, however, necessarily presuppose as its "cause" the act of another person. Being moved by beautiful music is also a typical example of being affected. Again we are confronted with this type of experience when some news fills our soul with deep unrest. In order to understand the specific nature of being affected we must grasp above all its intentional character.

We must clearly grasp the difference between the consolation engendered in our soul by another's sympathy with our grief, from a mere state, such as tiredness, depression, irritation. Being affected presupposes, first, a knowledge of the object which affects me. So long as I do not *know* of the compassion someone feels for my suffering, I cannot be consoled. So long as another's hostile attitude is neither perceived nor known indirectly, it cannot create a wound in my heart.

We saw before that mere states in no way necessarily suppose a knowledge of their cause. Drinking alcohol, for example, causes a state of gaiety and uncontrolled loquacity. The link between the alcohol and a state of jollity is merely causal. The effect goes through us by means of the inner connection between body and soul. The conscious sphere plays no role in this causal link. Whether or not we know that alcohol has this effect in no way influences the achievement of this state.

But when the beauty of noble music or the nobility of a moral act moves us, a grasp of the object and a perception of its value are presupposed. Moreover there exists a meaningful intelligible relation between the object affecting us and the effect created in our soul (when, for instance, a friend's compassion consoles us, a deep, intelligible affinity is to be found between the qualitative content of his compassion and our consolation), their natures are so akin that the fact that compassion is able to bestow consolation is self-evident. This is a highly intelligible relation radically opposed to brute causality. Similarly, there exists a meaningful, intelligible relation between the beauty of great music or the nobility of a moral action and the quality and nature of our being moved. Apart from the capacity to engender such an experience in our soul, there exists an intrinsic affinity between both object and effect, a correspondence in their nature and meaning. And this intelligible relation of inner correspondence is at the basis of the real engendering, at the basis of the ontological dependence of this affective experience on the object engendering it. Unlike any mere state, which is deprived of intentionality, being affected has a definite intentional character and presupposes the meaningful, conscious center of the person. In being touched by beautiful music we consciously *experience* that the beauty bestows this effect upon us, engenders it in us. And what is more, even the relation between the value and our being touched unfolds itself in the sphere of our consciousness: it necessarily goes through the spiritual, conscious center of our person.

After having seen the intentional character which clearly distinguishes being affected from any mere state, we turn now to note the difference between being affected and the equally intentional affective response. Being affected has, so to speak, a centripetal character, while the response has a centrifugal one. In the one case the object bestows something on me; in the other, I, by my response, impart something to the object. Thus, in being affected, the direction is from the object to me; in the response, from me to the object. It has here a character analogous to perception, where likewise the object speaks to me. Closely linked with this mark is the passive, receptive character of being affected. We receive, we "endure" something when the object affects our soul.

Not so, however, with the response. For it has a spontaneous, active character, even in view of the fact that what we impart to the object presupposes knowledge of the object, and depends upon the nature of this object. The response is our position toward the good. We are, as it were, *speaking* to the object, whereas in being affected we are only receiving the "word" of the object.

The difference between affective response and being affected discloses itself especially in the cases where another's attitude affects our soul. Clearly, to be wounded by the hostile or humiliating attitude of our neighbor is not a response addressed to him. To an enemy or offender the response given may be anger, resentment, fear, or loving forgiveness. The difference between all these responses and being wounded is plainly given. Equally, to be gladdened and touched by someone's love is not yet a requital of that love. We shall come back later to the difference between them.

Yet if being affected differs on the one hand from the affective response and must be considered as a type of experience *sui generis,* on the other hand it is obviously closely related to, and ordinarily precedes, the affective response. The experience of being enchanted by a work of art and our enthusiasm over it are so intimately and organically linked, the quality of the former is so akin to the word of the latter, that we may be induced to confuse them. But this would be a definite mistake. Although there are cases in which it may be difficult to disentangle being affected and an affective response, the many cases in which they clearly differ from each other in their quality and in their lasting and formal structures definitely testify to the essential distinction between them.

Being affected plays a paramount role in the development of a personality. Through this channel come seduction, moral poisoning, blunting, narrowing, and cramping, as well as moral elevation, purification, enrichment, widening and liberation. For the pedagogue, one of the principal means for moral education is to expose the souls of his pupils to being affected by values. In every effort toward moral and religious progress, this opening of the soul also plays an eminent role.

The question what type of importance motivates an affective or volitional response has a decision bearing on this response.[19] We have mentioned earlier, in Chapter 3, the fundamental dif-

---

[19] "Finally our doctrine inquires not so much whether one be angry, but wherefore; why he is sad, not whether he be sad; and so of fear. For anger with an offender to reform him, pity upon one afflicted to succour him; fear for one in danger, to deliver him . . ." St. Augustine, *De Civitate Dei,* IX, 5. (J. Healy, *op. cit.,* pp. 257–8.)

ference between responses which are motivated by values and those which are motivated by the merely subjectively satisfying. We noted this difference as one of the specific marks distinguishing the value from the merely subjectively satisfying.[20]

Here we shall endeavor to make a thorough analysis in order to reach a true understanding of the value response, an understanding which is of the utmost importance for the whole of ethics.

We can say that there exist certain affective responses which are essentially value responses, that is, are motivated only by values. Such for instance are esteem, veneration, and admiration. It belongs to the very nature of the inner "word" with which these responses answer the object or which they impart to the object that this object should present itself as endowed with a value. The same applies in an analogous way to indignation or contempt. These responses necessarily presuppose the consciousness of a disvalue of the object.

There also exist responses which can be motivated only by the subjectively satisfying or dissatisfying. Anger, for instance, responds to something which is subjectively dissatisfying in one way or another. We may be angry for many reasons: because somebody tells us something disagreeable though it be for our own good, or because something lasts longer than our patience can bear, or because another person is more efficient than we. In all these cases our anger obviously arises not because of the disvalue of something but rather because something is in some way subjectively dissatisfying. The angry person approaches the object of his anger under the aspect of the merely subjectively dissatisfying, and independently of whether this object is as such an objective evil for him or something *merely* subjectively dissatisfying.

The self-centered irritation proper to typical anger always presupposes a confrontation with something subjectively dissatisfying, that is, with that which goes against our subjective desires and tendencies. Thus anger, as opposed to wrath, seems to be essentially a response motivated by the subjectively dissatisfying; whereas indignation and contempt necessarily presuppose the consciousness of a disvalue. We say "as opposed to

20 Cf. Chapter 3, "The Categories of Importance."

wrath" because wrath seems to belong to another type of affective response, that which can be motivated either by a value or by the subjectively satisfying.

Certainly there exists a *holy* wrath; that is to say, a wrath which is the pure repulsion of something having a disvalue, of something which deserves and calls for such a repulsion. On the other hand, we are aware that it is impossible to speak of a holy anger: the two notions of *holy* and *anger* seem incompatible.

Envy, jealousy, desire for revenge, and covetousness are all essentially motivated by the kind of importance which we termed the subjectively satisfying or dissatisfying. We may envy the brilliant gifts or good fortune of our neighbor because our pride or concupiscence are hurt by them. We consider his gifts or good fortune as subjectively dissatisfying to us only because of our egoistic perversion. Were our approach determined by the important-in-itself, we would admire his brilliant gifts and rejoice at his good fortune.

The same applies to jealousy or to desire for revenge. Covetous desire also essentially presupposes the attractiveness of the merely subjectively satisfying, a loose impetuosity and unrestrained disinterest in the question of moral legitimacy, and an inner incompatibility with the basic attitude of *religio:* all these elements testify to their being engendered by the merely subjectively satisfying.

Thus we see that certain affective responses are essentially motivated by a value or disvalue; others essentially by what is merely subjectively satisfying or dissatisfying. The greater part of affective responses can be motivated either by values or by the merely subjectively satisfying.

We can rejoice over the triumph of justice and we can rejoice over winning a game, or over having had more success than other persons. We can worry at the moral failure of our neighbor, as well as at earning less than another person, or at not being able to buy an elegant car. The same applies to wishing, being wrathful, and many other responses. Certainly this difference in motivation has a deep influence on the nature of joy or sorrow. We shall see immediately how deeply this affects the character of those affective responses. Nevertheless something in common remains to them whether they are value responses or not. Thus we use the same term for both, whereas veneration and esteem are essentially value responses, and there is nothing similar to them in responses motivated by the subjectively satisfying.

If we lay great emphasis here on the difference between value responses and the responses motivated by the subjectively satisfying, thereby omitting the responses motivated by the third fundamental type of importance, namely the objective good for the person, this is entirely due to the fact that our main purpose is to analyze the nature of the value response because of its paramount role in ethics.

The nature of the value response is thrown into sharper relief by contrasting it with a response to something merely subjectively satisfying than in distinguishing it from responses motivated by the objective good for the person. This is so because the objective good for the person mostly presupposes a value, as we have seen before; and, in any case, the response to it is more akin to the value response. As a matter of fact, it is very rare that such a response occurs without a value response connected with it.[21]

Gratitude, as we saw, is a typical response to an objective good for us; so too is the act of thanking. The acceptance of a cross has reference to an objective evil for us while hope is typically directed toward, though not limited to, an objective good for the person. Here also there exist responses which are related exclusively to an objective good for the person, and others, such as joy, sorrow, or fear, which can be motivated either by this type of importance or by values or by the merely subjectively satisfying.

We have mentioned above that the decisive difference between a value response and responses motivated by the merely subjectively satisfying becomes apparent also in the sphere of volitional responses. There is a fundamental difference between

---

[21] This must not however be interpreted in the sense that there is no definite difference between the value response and a response motivated by an objective good for us. As we saw before, there exist many value responses which are in no way directed to an objective good for us. And there undoubtedly exist responses to an objective good for us which are not connected with a value response. But even when both are closely connected, we have to distinguish, in our attitude toward a high objective good for us, the pure value response from the response motivated by the objective good.

an act of willing having the character of a value response and an act of willing motivated by the merely subjectively satisfying. This difference, however, does not prevent our speaking of each as an act of willing. The inner word "thou shouldst exist" or "thou shalt exist" can function as a response to something important-in-itself as well as to something merely subjectively satisfying. Like the affective responses of joy or sorrow, the volitional response of willing can be motivated by values or by something subjectively satisfying or by an objective good for the person.

It is unnecessary to mention that this difference has a great influence on many features of willing. But in each case it still remains an act of willing.

In summarizing, we can say: There are first of all affective responses which by their nature are motivated exclusively by values; secondly, affective responses which are engendered by something merely subjectively satisfying; thirdly, affective responses which are essentially oriented to the objective good for the person; and fourthly, affective responses, such as joy and sorrow, which can be motivated by values or by the objective good for the person or by the merely subjectively satisfying.

So far as the will is concerned, motivation may stem equally from values, from the subjectively satisfying, or from the objective good for the person. In any case, as we have already said, the value response differs profoundly from the response to something merely subjectively satisfying; and this is true independently of the question of whether a response as such can be motivated by the different types of importance or whether it is bound exclusively to one type of importance.

We have now to elaborate in detail the nature of the value response, including its difference from any affective response which is not a value response. The first decisive mark of the value response is its character of self-abandonment. In enthusiasm, veneration, love, or adoration, we break open our self-centeredness and conform to the important-in-itself. Our interest in the object is completely based on and completely nourished by the intrinsic goodness, beauty and preciousness of the object, and the mysterious rhythm of its intrinsic importance. The value response is, therefore, essentially a conforming of ourselves to the logos of the value. The very nature of the inner movement of the value response consists in partaking in the rhythm of the values. This conforming has not the character of mere reasonability such as is in any activity whereby we conform in our will to the neutral inner logic of the being with which we deal. It is not a conforming to the mere neutral rhythm of factuality, but rather to the unique rhythm of the important-in-itself which calls for self-donation of a completely different kind. The nature of this self-abandonment varies to a great extent according to the type of value which motivates the response. The question of whether it is an ontological or a qualitative value, and if qualitative, to which value domain it belongs, has a decisive influence on the nature of the self-abandonment in the value response.

But in every response motivated by something important-in-itself, there is to be found an element of abandonment, involving reverence and a certain submission. Conforming to the value, conforming in our mind to that which is objectively important, implies an antagonism to pride and concupiscence, to any kind of egoism or self-centeredness.[22]

In a response motivated by the merely subjectively satisfying, however (in my coveting a certain good food, for example), these factors are completely lacking. In desiring the merely subjectively satisfying, there is no transcending of the frame of self-centeredness, no conforming to that which is objectively important, no self-abandonment, no reverent submission to something greater than ourselves; on the contrary, there is only imprisonment in the frame of our self-centeredness. The responses motivated by the agreeable must, however, still be clearly distinguished from mere urges and appetites.[23]

[22] In Chapter 30, "The Problem of Moral Evil," we shall discuss in detail the antithesis between the value-response attitude and pride and concupiscence.

[23] Interwoven as urges and responses motivated by the merely subjectively satisfying may often be, there nonetheless exists a definite formal difference between them. This difference is obvious insofar as the sphere of volitional responses is concerned. Nobody will confuse an act of willing, motivated by the subjectively satisfying character of a good wine, with an urge such as thirst. The very fact that the will is free suffices to reveal the difference clearly. But even the joy someone may feel because of an invitation to a good dinner clearly differs from an urge of thirst or the urge of the loquacious for speaking. Urges arise

Every response motivated by the merely subjectively satisfying implies a gesture toward the good in question directed toward its appropriation. The object thus appropriated is considered as something which will be sacrificed to us. This gesture is proper to all affective responses motivated by the merely subjectively satisfying, even when there is involved a good which is not destroyed by serving my satisfaction. The value response, on the other hand, is characterized by an element of respect for the good, an interest in its integrity and existence as such, a giving of ourselves to it instead of a consuming of it. Even in cases where a value response aims at the fruition of a good endowed with a value, the element of self-donation and interest in preserving its ontological dignity and integrity dominate the entire situation.

Compared with any affective response motivated by the merely subjectively satisfying, such as envy, covetousness, jealousy, anger, etc., the value response possesses a completely new, intelligible meaningfulness; and especially as transcendence in

---

spontaneously in our nature and are not engendered by an object and its importance. They do not necessarily presuppose knowledge of the object—whereas the response necessarily does. The urge does not possess true intentionality, whereas the response motivated by something agreeable does. We know that we rejoice about the invitation to a good dinner and in responding we are no longer in a purely formal sense prisoners of our immanence, as in the blind urge. This formal difference is not erased by the manifold relations existing between them. An urge or appetite may exist in a person and may create a favorable disposition for the motivation of a desire by something agreeable; or in the case of many acquired urges, such as the urge to smoke or the urge of a drunkard to drink, a desire has developed by habit into an urge. Again very often an object is simultaneously attractive for us, because of the pleasure it may bestow on us and because it satisfies an urge. Intimate as the relation between them may be in this case, indistinct as may be the transition from one to the other, the response which is motivated by the agreeable and the spontaneous urge tending in a blind finality to an appeasement must definitely be distinguished. Three points must be stressed here. First, pleasure is not identical with a mere appeasement of an urge. There exist urges whose appeasement is not pleasurable and may even be painful, for instance the urge to cough. Though the appeasement of an urge is in itself certainly a relief, the pleasure which is in many cases connected with the appeasement of urges is something of its own and cannot be reduced to the appeasement alone. Second, there exist many cases in which a response (for instance, our willing, our joy, our desire) is motivated by something agreeable, without being connected with an urge. Third, though urges and desires may be deeply interconnected and cooperate in our attitude to a good, this does not in any case erase the essential difference between the blind immanence of a mere urge and the intentional character of every motivated response.

an entirely new sense. Conforming to the important-in-itself has an intelligibility and rationality similar to the conforming of our intellect in knowledge to the nature of a being. It consists not only in motivation and intentionality, but in a meaningful "concerting" with the value and its intrinsic, luminous importance: with its objectivity. It involves a transcendence in a completely new sense, opposed not only to an immanent, blind teleology, but also to a self-imprisonment. The capacity to conform ourselves to the important-in-itself is one of the deepest and most fundamental features of the person; it lights up his character as an image of God, a subject, one called to partake as a partner in the dialogue with God.

We saw before that intentionality is a mark of the higher, spiritual part of man, distinguishing it from the lower irrational part. Yet even in the frame of intentional experiences, a great gradation in spirituality is still to be found; for, although all affective responses are intentional, affective value responses rank incomparably higher, from the point of view of their formal, spiritual, and intentional structure, than responses motivated by something subjectively satisfying.

This does not apply to the same extent to the sphere of volitional responses. The will has *a fortiori* a character of spirituality and rationality, manifesting itself in its very freedom independently of the category of importance of its object. Thus, even when motivated by the importance which we termed the merely subjectively satisfying, an act of willing possesses a higher degree of rationality and intentionality than does an affective response motivated by something subjectively satisfying, such as envy, jealousy, covetousness, or desire.

But great as this formal difference may be, it is nevertheless true that the difference which concerns us here (viz., whether a response is a value response or a response to something subjectively satisfying) manifests itself not only in the sphere of affective responses, but similarly in the sphere of willing. Only the act of willing which is a value response may be endowed with the specific transcendence and spirituality mentioned above; but this is not identical with the formal spiritual and rational character belonging to the will as such.

The fundamental difference between the value response and

the response to something merely subjectively satisfying, whether this latter is of the affective or of the volitional type, becomes further manifest in the following: Only in the value response do we find that such a response is objectively *due* the object.

In love, we have the consciousness that the beloved is objectively lovable; in admiration, that the admired object is objectively admirable; and so on. The consciousness that we fulfill by our response something objectively demanded invests the response with an element of objectivity and a dignity in no way to be found in the response to the merely agreeable. No matter how intense this response to the agreeable may be, it never acquires the unique note of dignity and objective validity. It never reaches a point where it is sustained by a world above us; it can never join in the majestic rhythm of the important-in-itself. In the value responses, we emerge from our self-centeredness and grow beyond the limitations of self.

The capacity to transcend himself is one of man's deepest characteristics. So long as we consider his activities as the mere unfolding of his entelechy, determined by his nature, or as immanent manifestations of principles proper to his nature, we fail to grasp the most decisive feature of his character as a person. Man cannot be understood if we interpret all his activities as manifestations of an automatic striving for self-perfection. So long as we are confined to this pattern, so long as we see man differing from other beings only by the fact that their objective teleological tendency assumes in him a character of consciousness, we overlook the real nature of man as a person. It is not an immanent movement, unconscious or conscious, which is man's typical mark. Certainly this also is to be found in man's nature, in the physiological sphere as well as in the psychical. But the specifically personal character of man as a subject manifests itself in his capacity to transcend himself. This transcendence displays itself above all in participation in the objective logos of being which takes place in knowledge insofar as our intellect conforms itself to the nature of the object, and which again takes place in every value response wherein we conform either with our will or with our heart to the important-in-itself. This kind of participation is absolutely impossible for any impersonal being. Yet in stressing that the value response is motivated solely by the value of the good and in distinguishing it as such from any mere striving for our own good, we in no way intend to oppose interest in the important-in-itself to interest in our own objective good. The nature of the value response in no way requires indifference toward our own objective good. On the contrary, such indifference is not only impossible, but it would be in no way more sublime. Later on we shall see that the value response and our deep, legitimate desire for true happiness, far from being antithetic are organically linked. The all-important question is to understand the true nature of their connection.[24]

Someone may object: It may be true that, insofar as conscious experience is concerned, man is able to be motivated by values and to interest himself in a being because of its importance in itself. But he is able to do so precisely because by his very nature he is ordered toward truth and the good. He has to have a sensitivity for values; thus it is incorrect to say that in the value response he is not unfolding an immanent trend of his nature. His nature simply differs from the nature of other beings on this point, and this gives the impression of transcendence. But in reality this transcendence is an immanent movement of the specific entelechy of man.

It must be said in answer: Man certainly has a sensitivity to values just as man's intellect has a receptivity for the nature of other beings. The possibility of transcendence must certainly be rooted in man's nature. But to infer from this fact that the value response is only an unfolding of man's entelechy would be as erroneous as to believe that, because freedom of will is rooted in man's nature, his free decision must be considered an immanent unfolding of his nature, or as caused by his nature.

The capacity of transcending himself, of conforming to something greater for its own sake, does not become something *immanent* merely because this capacity is rooted in man's nature. An obvious equivocation of the phrase "being rooted in nature" is to be found in this conception of the value response. One

[24] St. Augustine clearly expresses this true connection in saying: "Therefore He Who made me is good and He is my Good." *Confessions*, I, 20 (F. J. Sheed, *op. cit.*, p. 23); and again, "That among all the things which give delight, justice itself should give thee more delight. . . . Let justice in such wise delight as to overcome even lawful delights; and prefer justice to that delight wherewith thou art lawfully delighted." *Sermo*, CLIX, ii, 2.

meaning of the phrase is that there is an *immanent* unfolding of energies and forces of this nature, another that it is merely an essential capacity of man.

The difference between an appetite or urge (the tendency, for example, to develop a talent, to release spiritual energies) and a value response clearly reveals the essential immanence of the first and the transcendence of the second. There is an essential and decisive difference between a priest for whom preaching is the realization of oratorical talent, an occasion to unfold this gift, and a priest for whom preaching is motivated by the desire to spread the word of God and to serve the eternal welfare of his brethren. We constantly make this distinction either for others or for ourselves. There is a yawning abyss between the nurse who ministers to us with care because she wants to appease her motherly instincts and the nurse who surrounds us with all possible attention and care because of her love of neighbor and her real sympathy for our suffering and needs.[25]

With regard to ourselves we clearly distinguish whether we undertake the risk of helping someone whose life is in danger merely as a fulfillment of our physical capacities, a vital tendency to cope with a dangerous and difficult task, to master a dangerous situation, or whether we are motivated by the value of a human life, by the call of God to intervene in this situation.

In all immanent trends to unfold our nature, our attitude has the character of self-affirmation; whereas in every value response our attitude has the basic feature of self-donation.[26]

---

[25] Cf. St. Augustine: "For although he that grieves with the grief-stricken is to be commended for his work of charity, yet the man who is fraternally compassionate would prefer to find nothing in others to need his compassion." *Confessions*, III, 2. (*Ibid.*, p. 43.)

[26] What matters in these cases is not whether there exists such an urge or not, but what underlies our action, the motivation for it. The character of value response in our helping a person in a dangerous situation is not disturbed by the fact that we have an urge for unfolding our energies in this direction. The presence of such an urge does not, as such, frustrate our transcendent value response if only our intervention is *motivated* by a *value* and not by a striving to fulfill or appease our urge or appetite.

It is unnecessary to say that the fulfillment of an urge, as such, is nothing morally evil, so long as the urge is legitimate. It is even something ontologically good. It becomes morally doubtful only if in facing a value, instead of responding to the value, we merely satisfy our urge. To follow the trend of an urge or appetite which as such does not result from pride or concupiscence is in no way

Man's sensitivity to values is precisely the capacity to grasp things important in themselves, to be able to be affected by them, and to be motivated by them in his responses. It is precisely the capacity to *transcend* the frame of mere immanent trends. To interpret it as merely immanent because it belongs to man's nature is an error based on the equivocation of the term "rooted in man's nature"; and this leads to a contradiction which could be formulated: the *transcendence* of man is something *immanent* to man's nature.

But beyond this, man is not only sensitive to values. He is definitely ordered and destined to grasp and to respond to the important-in-itself. The words of St. Augustine, *Fecisti nos ad te, Domine,*—"Thou hast made us for Thyself," do not alter the transcendence of man by a substitution of a teleological trend toward God for the value response to God. On the contrary, they stress the fact that we are created for a knowledge and love of God, to transcend the realm of a mere immanent unfolding of our nature. They stress the fact that we are ordered to a participation in the absolute, a consciously experienced "dialogue with" God.

It would, however, be a misunderstanding if we viewed as opposites the value response and our being ordered and destined for a good. The value response, with its character of self-donation, its transcendence of the immanent unfolding of our nature, its being engendered by the value, in contradistinction to a teleological drive for the appeasement of urges, in no way implies an antithesis between the value response on the one hand, and man's ordination to the being to which he responds on the other.

This kind of "being ordered to," first of all has not the character of a strictly teleological relation. There is no question of a means-end relation. Only by enlarging the term *finis* (end) so that it embraces every meaningful direction can this "being ordered to" be termed final. But such an extension does not dispense with a distinction between the "being ordered to" and a teleological relation of means-end.

---

morally negative and still less is the presence of the urge. Only the absence of a value response as the real motive for which the object calls is morally unsatisfactory.

But above all our ordination to something does not imply that we look at it from the point of view of our self-protection; that we look upon the *raison d'être* of this relation of "being ordered to" as if it were to be found in the nature of a being as a mere neutral need. On the contrary, we have to understand that goodness itself is precisely the *raison d'être* of this being ordered to the good, and ultimately to God, the Infinite Goodness.

Man in his nature has been endowed with the capacity to transcend himself. Thus, being ordered to God is the precise and typical *expression* of man's transcendence: it evidences man's essential difference from any nature having a mere immanent, unconscious striving for self-perfection. It points to the capacity for self-donation, for a value response that is completely engendered by the infinite goodness and sanctity of God.

Thus we see that ordination to God, the fact that our entire being is made and destined for God and ordered to Him, is no antithesis to the pure value response to God. On the contrary, the ordination to God includes being ordered to know and love God; and love of God means precisely the pure value response to Him. Being ordered to God implies the capacity for a pure value response; indeed it culminates in this response. Man as subject and person is ordered and destined to this personal relation with God; his nature is ordained to transcend itself and to be capable of a real self-donation. The fact that this self-donation is the exclusive way for man to attain his perfection, that is, to actualize all the values which he is able and destined to realize, in no way implies that the self-donation is a mere means for self-perfection. We shall see later on that the self-donation or the response to values has its meaning in itself, and that the moral perfection which accrues to the person from the value response has rather the character of a reward. Thus we must say: The transcendent character of the value response, the fact that it is exclusively motivated by the value of the object, is not at all opposed to the fact that we are ordered in our entire being to this good.

Sometimes we even experience the interpenetration of "the being destined to" and the value response. In the case of a great love, we experience the lovability of the beloved as the only reason of our love; his beauty and goodness come as a complete surprise. But at the same time we experience that the beloved is the fulfillment of everything for which in an indistinct way and with our entire being we always longed. And we understand that our finding of the beloved is not something accidental, but providential.

For this reason, to interpret the lovability of the beloved as mere capacity to appease our longing would not correspond to the real situation. I love him because he is lovable, because of the beauty and goodness which he possesses independently of myself; but this beauty and goodness simultaneously fulfill a longing which also by its very nature has a transcendent character: it cannot be interpreted merely as an urge for something that we need.

In our relation to God, we experience on an infinitely higher level this interpenetration of value response with the "being ordered to." When someone is converted to God and His Church, he experiences on the one hand the absolutely new, the absolutely surprising glory and infinite sanctity of Christ; he realizes that the sacred humanity of Christ is absolutely beyond all possible ideals which could be constructed by a human mind. On the other hand he experiences that Christ is the fulfillment of all his innermost desires. In this sense St. Augustine says: *Iniquietum est cor nostrum, donec requiescat in te*—"Restless are our hearts till they rest in Thee" (*Confessions*, I, 1).

Yet still another point has to be stressed. Some value responses, such as love, hope, longing, can assume a character of elementary dynamism which could be misinterpreted as urge or appetite. In the psalms we find time and again expressions of love of God and longing for God which manifest this elementary dynamism: *Concupiscit et deficit anima mea in atria Domini. Cor meum et caro mea exsultaverunt in Deum vivum*—"My soul longeth and fainteth for the courts of the Lord. My heart and my flesh have rejoiced in the living God" (Ps. 83:3); or *Sicut cervus desiderat ad fontes aquarum. . . .* —"As the hart panteth after the fountains of water. . . . (Ps. 41:2). Yet this seemingly common feature is one of those analogies which we so often find between two things which in reality are radically opposed. For example, the blunt indifference of the coarse, phlegmatic type of man is completely opposed to the unshakeable and transfigured serenity of the saint, who has an ultimate abandonment to God's will. Yet the opposition which both form to a man who alternates between *himmelhoch jauchzend zu Tode betrübt* [27] may for the superficial observer seem to constitute a real similarity. In reality the saint is farther removed from the blunt indifference of the coarse man than from the unrest of the man who is torn by contradictory emotions.[28]

To use a comparison from the corporeal world, the saint is *above* the restless man; the blunt, indifferent man is *below* the restless man; hence both are still farther removed from each other than from the medial to which they are both antithetical. Similarly we must realize that the elementary character of certain value responses, though seemingly similar to those of urges and passions, differs radically from urges. In speaking of that love which manifests itself in the fact that every fibre of our person longs for the beloved, or that his presence is as indispensable as the air we breathe, we still speak of a value response which is clearly distinguished from any urge. Here, as in any real love, the intrinsic beauty and nobility of the beloved is the creative source of our love, the principle of its engendering; while in every urge this movement has its source in our own nature and its needs. The urge is an unfolding of an immanent dynamism. At the basis of this elementary character is a specific victory for the value response; a result of its intensity and power and its penetration of our entire being. If a value response "possesses" us to such an extent that it assumes the features of an elementary urge, it remains still something essentially different from the urge. Here the urge-like character is a symptom of the power of self-abandonment and of the intensity of our love and our longing. It is thus as opposed as possible to an urge; instead of a self-affirmation and unfolding of our immanent needs,

---

[27] Goethe, *Egmont:* "Now shouting in triumph,
            Now sunk in despair."

[28] St. Augustine says: "Soundness hath no sickness, but nevertheless when it is touched and molested, it feeleth pain. But torpor hath no pain, hath lost the sense of pain, and the more insensible it is, the worse it is. Again, immortality hath no pain; for all corruption is swallowed up, and this corruptible hath put on incorruption and this mortal hath put on immortality. . . . Hence there is no pain in an immortal body, and no pain in a torpid body. Let not a man without feeling think himself already immortal; the soundness of a man in pain is nearer immortality than the torpor of a man who feeleth not." *In Ps.,* LV, 6.

there is a self-abandonment in the value response which so completely takes hold on us, so victoriously dominates our entire nature, that it assumes the same elementary character as an urge.

It is similar to the love of Blessed Jordan of Saxony who wrote to the Blessed Diana: "In thy foot, which I understand thou injured, I suffer." [29] To feel one's own pain would be in no way an extraordinary victory of love. Similarly, we may say that the overwhelming dynamism which elementary urges may normally possess is, in the case of the value response, a manifestation of a glorious victory of the value response. Thus the presence of this elementary dynamism does not erase the difference between responses and mere urges; in fact, it reveals the difference still more clearly.

There is in the one case a blind force *a tergo;* in the other, a spiritual attitude, rooted in a clear awareness of the value of the object. In one case there is an unfolding of our immanence; in the other, a specific manifestation of transcendence: in the one case, a certain massiveness; in the other, something in which "wings grow to our soul." [30]

We must emphasize the fact that the intentional and spiritual character of the value response in no way excludes the mysterious cooperation of our entire nature, the concomitance of all depths inaccessible to the command of our will. It in no way excludes the fact that we experience this value response as something greater and stronger than we, or the fact that the object of our love assumes a character indispensable as a basis of our life: there is no incompatibility between ecstasy and value response.

We see the clear difference between urge and response if we think of someone who, because of the need for being sheltered, cannot live without another person who supplies him with protection and courage to live. This type of indispensability clearly differs from that which comes purely as a result of love. In the first case, someone needs another in order to appease a personal urge; in the second, one's love is so great and fundamental that

[29] Norbert Georges, O.P., *Blessed Diana and Blessed Jordan of the Order of Preachers.* The Story of a Holy Friendship and a Successful Spiritual Direction (Somerset, Ohio: Rosary Press, 1933).

[30] Plato, *Phaedrus,* in *The Dialogues of Plato,* trans. B. Jowett (New York: Random House, 1937), Vol. I, p. 255.

it *creates* an indispensability; the beloved becomes indispensable *because* of the degree of our love for him. The already-quoted famous words of St. Augustine which speak of the way in which we are drawn by God to Christ: *Parum voluntate etiam voluptate trahimur,* emphasize the elementary character of a love and longing for Christ which in no way contradicts the character of the value response. The love of Christ typified by St. Teresa of Avila in her ecstasies is certainly a great manifestation of transcendence and abandonment in a value response.

In summarizing we can say: Neither being objectively destined for or ordered to a good endowed with values, nor the conscious experience of this being ordered to a fulfillment, is incompatible with a value response. Similarly, the elementary character of our response, which gives the object of our love a character of indispensability, is in no way incompatible with the pure value response. It may even be said that in the case of the most fundamental and most sublime value responses we find all these elements combined in one in the measure that they have fully penetrated the person. Such is the love that a saint has for Christ:

Late have I loved Thee, O Beauty so ancient and so new; late have I loved Thee! . . . . Thou wert with me and I was not with Thee. I was kept from Thee by those things, yet had they not been in Thee, they would not have been at all. Thou didst call and cry to me and break open my deafness: and Thou didst send forth Thy beams and shine upon me and chase away my blindness: Thou didst breathe fragrance upon me, and I drew in my breath and do now pant for Thee: Thou didst touch me, and I have burned for Thy peace.[31]

The decisive difference which exists in the realm of responses between a value response and a response which is not motivated by a value exists analogously in the realm of being affected. If it is purely a value which affects us, our entire experience is thoroughly different from that involved when something merely subjectively satisfying affects us, and *a fortiori* different if it is something which satisfies illegitimate centers, that is to say, pride and concupiscence. There are even certain types of being affected which can be engendered only by values. For instance, in the realm of being affected by something merely subjectively satisfy-

[31] St. Augustine, *Confessions,* X, 27. (F. J. Sheed, *op. cit.,* p. 236.)

ing, there is no counterpart of "being moved." Only something presenting itself to us as endowed with a value can move us.[32] This applies to the two basic types of being moved in the specific sense of the term: the one in which we are moved by something purely because of its sublimity, goodness, or beauty; the second, in which we are moved by something sad possessing the specific quality which we call "touching."

In the first case, the intrinsic relation to the value which acts as an engendering principle is obvious. It is not difficult to grasp that the quality of the experience in which we are moved by someone's purity or charity or by the beauty of sublime music is only possible as an "effect" of values. But even the second type of being moved, which can be engendered only by something sad, necessarily presupposes the presence of a value on the object side. Already the objective sadness of an event implies a disvalue; moreover, in order to make a sad event "touching" there must still be a value at stake. The sadness of an event which is seen against the background of a specific—most often personal— value, either moral or ontological, has a touching character. In order to be touching the sadness must be connected with a specific value, just as a specific value is always involved when an event is not merely sad but tragic.

What matters for us is to see that nothing which presents itself as merely subjectively satisfying can ever move or touch us in the specific sense. The man who approaches everything exclusively from the point of view of the merely subjectively satisfying is *unable* to be moved or touched. Neither Iago nor Trinculo is touched by anything. But even in the life of a Leporello (who may be touched), it is never the merely agreeable or disagreeable which can touch him.[33] On the other hand, being flattered, being unnecessarily offended, being tempted, and so forth, necessarily presuppose something merely subjectively sat-

[32] We prescind here from the perversion of being moved, in those cases in which someone is "touched" by sentimental trash. This self-centered relishing of one's own feelings differs so radically in every respect from the genuine being moved that it can hardly be confused with it.

[33] The fact that something agreeable can also touch us if it is seen as an objective good bestowed on us by the bounty of God or by the generosity of our neighbor does not contradict what we have said above, because it is obviously the value of God's bounty or the human donor's generosity which engenders this experience.

isfying and can never be effected by a value. Thus the difference between being affected by a value or by something subjectively satisfying is clearly manifested in the fact that certain types of being affected can only be engendered by a value and others again only by the subjectively satisfying.

Yet even in the case of a type of being affected which can be engendered as well by the subjectively satisfying as by values, a radical difference between the two experiences is still to be found. The difference between the two types of being affected manifests itself in the following three directions: First, the very quality of the content in our soul differs in each case; a second difference is to be found in the kind of center in us which is affected by the value and the subjectively satisfying. So long as it is a value which affects us, the appeal is directed to a center which we could call the loving, reverent center. A specific realm of receptivity is affected by the values, a qualitatively different center, the one from which charity issues.[34]

If something subjectively satisfying appeals to pride and concupiscence, the difference in the center affected is clear. But even in the case of something legitimately subjectively satisfying, the realm of receptivity clearly differs from the one to which the values appeal. If the values affect us, another depth of our soul is actualized than in the case in which the merely subjectively satisfying is at stake. Thirdly, the formal structure of both experiences clearly differs. In being affected by a value, we are broadened and elevated above ourselves; in being affected by the merely subjectively satisfying, we are rather made narrow and in no way elevated above ourselves. In being affected by values we also experience the unifying power of the values: we become internally more unified, more recollected.[35]

We thus see that the question of whether the engendering principle is a value or something merely subjectively satisfying is as decisive in the realm of being affected as in the realm of the affective and the volitional response.

---

[34] In Part Two, IV, "Roots of Moral Evil," we shall analyze the different "centers" in man.

[35] Cf. *Transformation in Christ*, chap. 5; and D. von Hildebrand, *Metaphysik der Gemeinschaft* (Augsburg: Grabherr, 1930), pp. 140ff.

We have seen before that all responses presuppose as their basis a cognitive act. But the value response presupposes not only knowledge of the object to which it is directed, but also an awareness of its value. The value responses presuppose a grasp of the positive or negative importance in itself of the respective objects: an understanding of its value or its disvalue. The question now arises: In what kind of perception do we grasp the value of something? Or to put it another way: What is the nature of value perception? We referred several times before to this kind of perception.[36] Now we have to examine in more detail value perception and its role in morality.

Someone makes a proposal which is highly advantageous to us, but which involves the injury of another person; for instance, the unjustified dismissal of a factory employee which deprives him of all means of financial support. We grasp the injustice of this situation and therefore reject it. The consciousness of this injustice has the full character of a cognitive act. It may be that we grasp this negative value immediately or it may be that we grasp it only after considering different arguments. But in any case, the injustice is given to us as involved in this particular way of acting. The injustice as well as the proposed act is given to us on the object side. Our grasping of the injustice is, as much as any other cognitive act—such as the perception of space or of a similarity—an awareness of an object. All the marks proper to a true perception are to be found here. But since the perception always varies according to the type of being which is the object of perception, this value perception therefore becomes a specific kind of perception. As the perception of colors is different from that of tones, and both again differ from a perception of relations or of persons, so too the perception of values has its specific and unique character. But it is still authentic perception possessing all the marks of its general type.[37]

36 Cf. Chapter 3, "The Categories of Importance," Chapter 7, "The Categories of Importance as Properties of Beings," and Chapter 9, "Relativism."

37 The three decisive marks of perception in general distinguishing it from all other cognitive acts such as inferring, remembering, and others are: first, the real presence of the object; secondly, the fecundating contact with the object in which the object discloses itself to my mind, informs me, and imposes itself on my mind in its autonomous being; thirdly, the intuitive character of the contact. The ob-

The perception of values certainly belongs to a higher kind of perception, and presupposes spiritual powers higher than those involved in seeing or hearing. But this difference applies equally to the perception of persons and of many other beings.

We already mentioned in dealing with moral relativism that a partial blindness for values is often to be found. The habitual thief, for instance, is no longer aware of the value of property or of the rights of the person. The *débauché* may be so blunted toward the value of purity that he no longer perceives the immorality and intrinsic baseness of impurity. In this sense St. Augustine says: ". . . that he who knowingly does wrong loses the clear knowledge of what is right. And he who would not do right when he could, loses the unimpeded power of doing what he has the will to do, when he does will it." [38]

It has often been stated that an adequate knowledge presupposes not only the integrity of the intellect, but also the rectitude of our will.[39] Now values, more than anything else, are a scandal to our pride and concupiscence. Thus, the right disposition of our will plays a much greater role here for the perception of values than for any other knowledge.

Moreover, the subsumption of any single concrete case under a general principle is hindered by the interference of our interests. We may grasp in general the moral badness of betrayal. And we may honestly become indignant when one person betrays another. Nevertheless because our selfish interests unconsciously darken our conscience or our faculty to grasp a concrete situation in its true nature, we may not realize that our own acts may really constitute a betrayal of another. This type of moral

---

ject deploys its "such being" before my mind, as opposed to all discursive contact through concepts.

[38] *De Libero Arbitrio*. (F. E. Tourscher, *op. cit.*, p. 363.)

[39] "While it (truth) is neither more true when it is seen by us, nor less true when we see it not: but entire and inviolate, it delights those who are turned to it by its lights, and those who are turned away it punishes by blindness." *Ibid.*, pp. 183-5.

Adequate knowledge presupposes not only the absence of a perversion of our will, but also many positive attitudes such as reverence, a readiness to conform our intellect to the object. In an article of mine, "The Idea of a Catholic University," I have dealt more in detail with this fundamental problem of the relation between knowledge and basic moral attitudes of the person. Published in *The University in a Changing World* (Oxford: Clarendon Press).

blindness is illustrated in the words of our Lord in the Gospel: "And seest thou the mote in thy brother's eye: but the beam that is in thy own eye thou considerest not" (Luke 6:41).

The more a value implies consequences in conflict with our pride and concupiscence, the more do we find a human tendency to bar even the knowledge of these values. Our perception of moral values therefore is hindered more than any other value perception by the wrong direction of our will.[40]

But the possibility that our value perception may be darkened in no way proves that value perception is not an authentic cognitive act. Rather, we must understand that it is an original perception *sui generis*.

The scope of the present work does not allow us to insist on the specific nature of value perception and on the epistemological problems connected with it. The question of whether an ontological or a qualitative value is at stake plays a great role also as regards the problem of how the value is given to me, and how I can attain to a knowledge of it, and so on.

Here it suffices to say that there exists a specific type of "consciousness of" by which we grasp values; it is here that we find all the essential marks of an authentic perception. We shall term this: value perception. It is not difficult to see that this type of perception involves a deeper understanding and possesses a much higher intelligibility than color or space perception. In grasping the existence of something, we do not necessarily grasp its value, although it is true that value perception normally goes hand in hand with a grasp of the object. Furthermore, it is not always necessary that the object itself of which we predicate a value be perceived; that is, be itself present in immediate contact. In reading or hearing of an action or an attitude we may grasp its moral goodness. Though we may not witness the attitude in an immediate contact; though we may not be in the presence of the person accomplishing this action, we nevertheless grasp its moral value in an immediate contact and in a fully intuitive manner.

[40] In his work on St. Augustine, C. N. Cochrane refers to this problem: "Intellectually, this bad will finds expression in an effort 'to make one's own truth,' i.e., to justify one's conduct by rationalizations which are blindly and stubbornly adhered to for the very reason that they cannot stand the light of day." *Op. cit.*, p. 449.

To grasp a value, to have a consciousness of it; to understand its importance in itself is already a unique and decisive participation of the person in the world of values. We have mentioned elsewhere [41] that a personality is as rich and deep as is its capacity to grasp values, and that the actualized spiritual wealth and stature of a personality greatly depends upon the participation in the world of values embodied in the value perception.

The knowledge of values, the understanding of them as values, already presupposes a basically reverent attitude and the rectitude of our will. If all objective and unprejudiced knowledge requires not only intellectual capacities but also the absence from our soul of predominant pride and concupiscence, then value perception requires this to a far greater extent.[42] Hence to have an adequate knowledge of values, especially of moral values and all those values implying a moral obligation, a morally right basic attitude is already presupposed.

Yet however great and decisive the participation in values granted us by knowledge, however significant the grasp and understanding of the world of values for the range and plenitude of a personality, these are not yet a participation which bestows moral values on the person. Yet it is true we must not fail to stress the paramount importance which the knowledge of values possesses, inasmuch as it is a fundamental and indispensable basis of all morality. Without a knowledge of values there can be no morality. This is as self-evident as the statement: Without freedom of the person there can be no morality. Even if someone should happen to act according to the moral norm, yet merely accidentally and without any knowledge of values, his action would lack moral value.

It is one of the many great merits of Socrates that he fully grasped the paramount importance, the absolutely indispensable role of value perception in morality. Unfortunately he overstressed this role by claiming that real knowledge of the good already guarantees a man's morality. But he did not claim that the knowledge of moral values as such bestows moral values on man. Rather, he believed only that *certain* or irrefutable knowl-

[41] *Liturgy and Personality* (New York: Longmans, Green & Co., 1944), p. 57.
[42] Cf. *Sittlichkeit und ethische Werterkenntniss*, p. 40ff.

edge (*episteme*) could exclude any aberration of our will, and that it would inevitably motivate our will in the right direction. This opinion was modified and amended by Plato; it was criticized by Aristotle, and contradicted in the famous words of Ovid: *Video meliora proboque: deteriora sequor* (I see and approve what is better, but I follow the worse).[43] But most of all it was refuted in St. Paul's words: "For the good which I will, I do not; but the evil which I will not, that I do" (Rom. 7:19).

Although Socrates erred by overstressing the role of true knowledge in morality, he made an invaluable contribution to philosophy by discovering the paramount importance of knowledge in morality. He clearly saw that knowledge is the *indispensable basis* for any real participation in values on the object side, as well as the indispensable basis of the morally good will.

But in order to find the source of moral values of the person, we must transcend the sphere of value perception and of the knowledge of values and examine the further possible participations in an object endowed with values. Great indeed is that participation in a being which knowledge allows. St. Thomas considered it as a partaking in the being, a becoming it *intentionaliter modo;* St. Augustine considered it a *habere quoddam*. Yet St. Augustine saw in love a partaking of the object, surpassing by far the participation by knowledge even though love presupposes and includes knowledge.

There is indeed a participation in a value-endowed object which goes beyond that union achieved in the value perception, and there are two forms of this higher participation. First, there is the union with values as achieved in being affected by them and, secondly, the union achieved in the value response. Let us first examine that union established by being affected.

Being affected by a value first presupposes the occurrence of value perception; it even implies it. Thus, whenever the fact of being affected by a value is at stake, the union with the value achieved in the value perception is at once given. But from the point of view of the union with the good and its value something new has taken place. A new stage of union already including and surpassing the one proper to knowledge is established by the

[43] *Metam.*, Bk. VII, vs. 20.

fact of being affected. This is evident from an examination of the difference between value perception and being affected by values.

First, it is quite possible that we may perceive the value without being affected by it. We may wonder why a piece of music, which had once moved us deeply does not move us at all at another time, though we really *perceive* its beauty and do not merely recall having perceived it before. For one reason or another, the music does not penetrate the deeper stratum of our soul wherein we are actually affected.

Secondly, in the value perception as such, I am, so to speak, void; and the content is exclusively on the object side, i.e., in the value of the object. In being affected, however, there is a content *in my soul* (e.g., the specific experience of *being moved* which another's generosity or purity effects in my soul, or the consolation I experience in my soul in confronting an object or an event endowed with a high value). The fact that the value acts on my heart in a deep, meaningful manner, in melting it, in piercing through the crust of my indifference and bluntness, is evidently a new and more intimate contact with the value.

In many cases, it is only in being affected by values that the value itself can bestow bliss on my soul, and that the delectability of those values can be experienced. Such is the case with beauty, or with a person's charm and lovableness. Thus we rightly desire to be affected by beautiful music or by the beauty of a landscape; we desire to be affected by the value of a spiritual gift bestowed on us, such as another's kindness; and we are regretful when we are not able to go beyond the mere perception of the value.

The very fact that, in perceiving those values without yet being affected by them, we desire to be affected testifies to the new and higher level of union which being affected represents. Similarly, we pray that we may be touched by the divine beauty and sanctity of Christ: that our hearts may be melted so that the irradiation of His infinite sanctity may transform our nature. Again the fact that we expect still another and deeper influence on our personality from a being affected by the values than from a value perception alone reveals the intimacy of the union in being affected.

Yet, in the value response, our union with the good possessing a value can be still further increased and elevated to an even higher level. This is most manifest in those cases where being affected precedes the affective response. We hear beautiful music; we clearly perceive its beauty. Yet we not only perceive it, but are deeply moved by it. Finally, we respond with enthusiasm. The value response of enthusiasm and the imparting thereby of this specific inner word to the object implies a still greater union and intimacy. It is *our* position in relation to the object, our inner movement toward it, our spiritual embracing of it. There is undoubtedly then a new element which is added to the union effected in being moved: a completion *sui generis*.

This fact becomes still more apparent in the case of love. The beauty of a soul touches my heart, and affects me deeply. I respond with love. While the response of love appears in this case as similar to being affected, nevertheless the spiritual movement of love toward another person, the self-donation to him, the supreme inner word spoken to him—all constitute a new stage in the spiritual union with this person, as compared to the enchantment of my heart which is typical of being affected.

In those cases, however, where a value response is not preceded by, nor rooted in, being affected (as may be the case with esteem and especially in a value-responding act of will), we cannot say that the union established in the value response is in every respect greater than that involved in being affected. But the specific perfection which the value response represents is clearly thrown into relief. It is only in the value response that *our* word is spoken to the object; that we impart something to it, which is in a specific way complementary to it; that we fully cooperate with it. But even within the sphere of value responses there are still distinctions to be made as regards the kind of union afforded with the object and its value.

As regards this wedding with the good and its value, the will, for instance, has one perfection in that it freely commits our person to it, in implying a free decision which a value response, such as joy or love, does not necessarily have as such. But on the other hand joy and love (in their regard) have a perfection of their own which the will does not possess. Joy and love are the voices of our heart; in them we adhere to the good with our heart and therefore with our innermost core. Love again has, in this respect, an incomparable priority.

After having examined the three degrees of union with value which are to be found first in value perception, secondly in being affected by values, and thirdly in the value response, we have to analyze still further the meaningful correspondence between the "inner word" of the value response and the specific nature of the value of the object. This correspondence simultaneously reveals the intimate character of participation with the good endowed with a value and the spiritual, intelligible character of the value responses. The inner word of the value response closely corresponds in quality to the value of its object and forms a meaningful complement to it. As soon as we actually conform to the value, as soon as we are exclusively motivated by it and are sustained in our inner movement by its rhythm, the content of our response necessarily corresponds to the motivating value. This fact manifests itself in the following ways:

First, the content will necessarily be positive when the value by which the response is motivated is positive, and the content will necessarily be negative when a disvalue occasions the response given. It is impossible to be indignant about an attitude which is clearly grasped as morally sublime. It is equally impossible to respond enthusiastically to a person's action which is clearly grasped as of a mean and base character. So long as our response is motivated by nothing other than that category of importance called the value, a positive response to a base action should not only not be given, it *cannot* be given. In other words, the positive or negative character of a response depends completely and necessarily upon the value or disvalue grasped on the object side. This is so, however, only so long as our response is really a value response, i.e., is motivated by nothing *but* the value, so long as it is nourished and determined exclusively by the important-in-itself. The moment our attitude is motivated by other kinds of importance (for example, by something subjectively satisfying or dissatisfying which the object may accidentally have for us in addition to, but independently of, its value), then the positive or negative character of the content of our response need no longer agree with the positive or negative character of the importance in itself which the object possesses.

The proud man who considers all things from the point of view of self-glorification will respond with envy or even hatred to another's nobility and generosity. He thus responds with a negative content to a positive value. But his attitude is in fact opposed to a value response; it is motivated by the importance which something has from the point of view of his pride.

Secondly, the qualitative content of the value response necessarily corresponds to the nature of the value domain to which the value belongs. The content of a response motivated by a moral value differs from one motivated by an intellectual value. Our admiration for the brilliance of a genius is qualitatively different from our admiration for the charity or humility of a saint. Similarly, our response to aesthetic values has necessarily a content qualitatively different from our response motivated by moral values. Our enthusiasm when confronted by a great work of art is qualitatively different from the enthusiasm with which we respond to an outstanding moral action. The specific nature of the motivating value determines the quality of the content of our response.

Some value responses furthermore are possible only as responses to certain types of value. Esteem and veneration, for instance, necessarily presuppose moral values in their object; whereas admiration and enthusiasm can be motivated by different types of values. Again, indignation necessarily presupposes moral disvalues. Silliness, an intellectual disvalue, cannot motivate indignation; neither can a poor work of art. Thus the content of the value response necessarily varies in its quality according to the nature of the value domains to which the motivating value belongs.

Thirdly, the content of the value response does not simply correspond to the general nature of a value domain, but it is necessarily differentiated according to the specific quality and rank of the value involved. This correspondence is expressed in a twofold manner: in the qualitative differentiation of the response according to the qualitative difference which the higher rank implies and in the degree of abandonment to, and affirmation of, the object.

From the moment that a pure value response is at stake and the value of the object has been fully grasped in its objective reality, the rank of the value will be reflected in the "word" with which one responds to the good. Admiration for the martyrdom of St. Ignatius of Antioch has necessarily another and a higher quality than admiration for the attitude of Socrates in the face of death.

The enthusiasm motivated by a sublime work of art such as the "Dying Slave" of Michelangelo has necessarily another quality than the enthusiasm motivated by a minor although authentic work of art, for instance, a painting by Guardi or Canaletto. Sometimes we term this difference "depth," which of course implies but one of many possible meanings of the term.[44] We might call our definition qualitative depth, to distinguish it from the many other types of depth. The higher the value and the more sublime its rank, the deeper the level to which it appeals in our soul.

But even more important than this is a second type of reflection of the value rank in the content of the value response. It is the degree of abandonment to, and affirmation of, the value response, which we express in saying that we admire this work of art still more than another, or that we have still more veneration or esteem for one person than for another.

It would be completely erroneous to interpret this degree of our value response as a degree of intensity, taking "intensity" in the same sense as it is found in mere states, for instance, tiredness, physical pain, or in a sensation of heat. According to the intentional, meaningful character of the value responses, this "more" refers to the object and not simply to a degree of intensity, as is to be found in mere states. But even when we think of intensity in the realm of responses, for instance, an intense joy or an intense love (already differing from the more quantitative intensity of states), this is not adequate to the whole datum which we express in saying: "I love someone *more*," or "I rejoice *more* about this event than about that one." Intensity is only a secondary and subordinate element of the comparative framework, and in no way constitutes its core.

[44] There are many different meanings of the term "depth," referring to different important data in the life of our soul. But it is impossible in this context to enter into this problem. In a former work, however, I have dealt with this problem and distinguished several notions of depth. Cf. *Sittlichkeit und ethische Werterkenntniss.*

The degree here in question refers, on the contrary, to the affirmation of the *object* of our response. The inner word we impart to the object contains a plus factor of affirmation, and in its content corresponds to a higher value. The fact that the "more" or "less" differs even from the intensity we find in value responses, clearly reveals itself once we realize that in many responses where this more or less is present, it would be nonsensical to speak of intensity. This is quite the case in volitional responses. In preferring in an act of will (which is at the same time a value response) one possibility to another, we clearly *will* the one *more* than the other; whereas it is absurd to call one act of will more "intense" than another. The same applies to certain affective responses, like esteem. It would be nonsense to speak of an "intense" esteem, but we may undoubtedly esteem one man "more" than another.

The degree of our response which is expressed in this more or less (which may also be expressed in saying, "I have a greater admiration for one artist than for another," or in saying, "My joy over one good is much greater than over another") refers to the very core of the intentional, meaningful inner word of the value response. It must be sharply distinguished from any merely dynamic qualification of response.

It is not difficult to see that *here*, above all, the necessary relation between value and the inner word of the value response manifests itself. To prefer a higher to a lesser good constitutes the most essential correspondence between the value and the response, and one which from the moral point of view plays the greatest role. The pure value response will always be imparted in a degree corresponding to the rank of the value. It is clear that in the case of a pure value response of joy, the higher the value of the good in question the more we will rejoice; again in a pure value response we admire or venerate the more that whose values rank higher. It must be stressed however that all these necessary relations between the value on the object side and the inner word of the value response exist only insofar as the value has been grasped and understood, and not necessarily with respect to the value which the object possesses in reality.

There are many degrees of depth and completeness in the value perception. A saint has a unique intuition and understanding of the value of humility or of purity which an ordinary man, however highly moral, can never possess. This gradation in the depth and plenitude of a value perception is especially manifest in the realm of aesthetic values. The beauty of a morning in spring may be grasped by many persons. But what a difference in the understanding and awareness of this beauty as it affects Keats, Goethe, Shakespeare, and a John Doe! The role of the subjective factor (referred to as *secundum modum recipientis*—according to the recipient's capacity) which is relative to the depth and richness of a personality obviously plays a great role in the nature of the value perception. Thus we see that the content of the value response necessarily reflects the specific nature of the value insofar as it has disclosed itself to a person or in the measure in which the person has grasped and understood it, provided of course that it is a pure value response, that is to say, that in the motivation of our response there is not the slightest intrusion of another point of view.

This does not apply if we turn from the necessary factual reflection of the value in the inner word of the response to the axiological relation existing between the value and our response. When we turn to the axiological sphere, the deep, meaningful relation between the inner word of the value response and the value-endowed object to which this word is imparted manifests itself in a more specific way. To every good endowed with an authentic value, an adequate response should be given. The rationally complementary character of the inner word of the value response, joy or admiration for example, with respect to the value of the good to which this response is imparted discloses itself clearly in the fact that to a good endowed with a value a positive response ought to be given; whereas to something tainted by a disvalue a negative response ought to be given. Just as an evident fact not only necessarily motivates conviction if it has been grasped in its evidence but also *calls for* conviction since conviction is the due and adequate response to it, so also we find that between the inner word of a value response and the value on the object side, there exists an axiological relation which we could express in saying, "To every good endowed with a value, as well as to every thing tainted by a disvalue, an adequate *response* is due."

The adequacy implies, however, not only such agreement between the value and its response as concerns the positive or negative character of the value or the nature of the value domain in question, but many other affinities. It embraces above all the correspondence between the rank of the value and the depth of the response in all senses of this term, and between the rank of the value and the degree of our affirmation.

Here again, in the axiological order, we have to stress that this correspondence between the degree of affirmation and the rank of the value is of paramount importance from the moral point of view. It is to this conformity to the hierarchy of values that the *ordo amoris* of St. Augustine refers, the *ordo amoris* which he rightly considers to be the backbone of all morality.[45]

There is a *logique du cœur* [46] displayed in the value response: the meaningful spiritual character of the value response and its rational structure. This is clearly revealed by the differentiated correspondence between value response and the value of its object, and especially also by the differentiation with respect to the adequacy of the response which the *good calls for*. We clearly see what an abyss separates these highly spiritual acts, notwithstanding their affective character, from the sphere of mere states and even from affective responses motivated by the merely subjectively satisfying.

A further important structural difference in the sphere of responses in general has to be mentioned. If we approach the inner life of man without prejudice, we easily see that in addition to the difference between conscious, unconscious, subconscious, there exists a fundamental difference between those responses which are essentially restricted in their existence to being consciously experienced, and those responses which essentially have an existence beyond being actually and consciously experienced. Love for a person obviously does not cease to exist whenever we are forced to focus our attention on other objects. There is a definite difference between the moments in which we

[45] "And therefore I think that the best and briefest definition of virtue is this. It is an order of love." *De Civitate Dei*, XV, 22. (J. Healey, *op. cit.* Vol. II, p. 89.)

[46] *Le cœur a ses raisons, que la raison ne connait point* (The heart has its reasons that reason does not know). Pascal, *Pensées*, 277.

are able to actualize our love fully, perhaps when we speak to the beloved person, or perhaps when we think of him in his absence, and the moments in which we must concentrate on some work or in which a deep sorrow about something else fills our heart. But whereas a pain in my finger is by its very nature restricted in its existence to being actually and consciously experienced, whereas it is situated by its very nature in the stratum of actual experience, the love for another person continues to exist even if it is not actualized. If a headache disappears after we have taken aspirin, then the pain really has ceased to exist, even if the physiological causes continue. If after some hours we feel the pain again, then from the point of view of the psychical reality, pain is a new individual entity, even though it happens to result from the same cause. But the love which is actualized in many different moments is one and the same individual entity. The relation between love for a certain person and its different actualizations completely differs however from the relation which we find between an ability and its concrete actualization: for instance, the ability to play the piano and the actual playing of the piano, or even between the will and the concrete act of willing. Love for another person subsists as a full factor in my soul, coloring every other situation, deeply forming my life. It subsists not as any vague subconscious element, but as a meaningful response to the beloved person. It tends indeed to be actualized, but in its character of a meaningful response to the beloved it does not live only on its full actualizations.

This subsistence of certain responses in a stratum deeper than the one in which the full actualization of our experiences takes place, shall be termed "superactual existence." [47] There exist several responses which, by their very nature, are not restricted to a mere actual experience, but must subsist in a superactual way if they are at all real and not mere sham acts. The love for a person which is dissipated as soon as we lose sight of the beloved can not really be love. It is above all love which has such a superactual character; other responses like wrath, a fit of anger, laughing about someone who is comical, cannot subsist superactually but, analogously to certain states or sensations, are

---

[47] In my book *Sittlichkeit und ethische Werterkenntniss*, I have minutely discussed the nature of superactuality in this sense.

restricted in their existence to the mere actual experience. The role of superactual responses is plainly enormous in our life. The most important and fundamental responses are all capable of subsisting in a superactual way, whether it is deep sorrow over the loss of a beloved person, or love or veneration for someone, or our gratitude toward another, or above all our faith in and our love of God. What would be the life of a man if it consisted merely in experiences which live only so long as they occupy more or less the center of our momentary consciousness, if the inevitable rhythm of one replacing another were to extend to all our experiences, that is to say, to our entire inner life, excepting the memory of our experiences and mere capacities, abilities or active potentialities? There would be no place for any continuity, no room for all the plenitude and depth of man.

We shall see later on the decisive role which superactual attitudes and responses play in morality, the evil superactual attitudes as well as the superactual value responses. It is impossible to do justice to the nature of man and to the sphere of morality without understanding that there exist such superactual attitudes, which in no way lose their character of meaningful responses because of their superactuality.

CHAPTER 18

DUE RELATION

WE HAVE already examined the meaningful and deep relation
between the value response and its object. We have seen how
the word imparted to the object corresponds to the value of the
object, at least insofar as the value has been grasped. We have
mentioned too the axiological relation which exists between
a being endowed with value and the adequate response to that
being: It is the fundamental fact that every being endowed
with a value calls for a due and adequate response. Now we have
to concentrate on this axiological relation and examine its nature
in detail.

An adequate response ought to be given to every value; that is
to say, a distinct and ultimate metaphysical value is realized in
the fact that an adequate response is given. Indifference toward a
value, an inadequate response, but still more a contrary response,
constitute an objective disharmony which embodies a disvalue
sui generis. We are aware of this disharmony when we hear a
judgment about a work of art or a man of genius which does not
do justice to the value involved; or still more when we observe
somebody responding contemptuously to a personality deserving
of veneration or responding with bored indifference to a great
work of art.

It is because of this disharmony that we try to persuade other
people to change their attitudes when we witness their wrong
approach, or indifferent response to a personality or a work of
art. We try to persuade them, not because we want to impose
our opinion on them,[1] but because we have a clear consciousness

---

[1] This does not mean that a dictatorial tendency to dominate other persons
does not sometimes find similar expression. Certain people cannot tolerate any

of the objective interest involved in a true appreciation and adequate response to the value.

In order to elaborate the specific nature of this "due relation" and of the metaphysical value which is embodied in the fulfillment of it, we must eliminate several other related factors which could easily be confused with it. Let us consider what happens when we see someone scorning a pious man as a bigot. We may worry about this contemptuous response for many reasons and try to show the scorner his error. First, we may be concerned with the wrong inflicted upon the pious man, or with the suffering which may come to him because of this wrong. Second, we may be concerned with the moral disvalue of the wrong response as such and with the disrespectful bias against religion which it reveals. Here the stress is laid not on what this attitude means in terms of the person who suffers under it, but rather on what the attitude of the scorner is in itself, on its moral disvalue. In either case, we are not yet concerned with the objective disharmony which is embodied in the fact that an inadequate response has been given.

Now this disharmony plainly differs from the objective evil for the person to whom a wrong response is addressed, and also from the moral disvalue which the wrong response may convey to the person who gives this response. This difference is marked by the following characteristics. First, the disharmony embodied in a wrong response is not restricted only to responses addressed to living human persons. If a person were to say that Plato is superficial or lacking in intellectual power, or were even to despise him, we should be no less shocked than we would be if this were said of a living human being. We would try to persuade such a person of his wrong opinion and improper response, and we should have the clear consciousness that we are doing so not in order to protect a great man from being wronged but rather to insure the response which *ought* to be given.

Whenever historians attempt to evaluate the achievements of Caesar, or Alexander, or Charlemagne, their judgment is based

---

opinion other than their own. But the difference between such an outrageous and obtrusive attitude and the genuine, elementary desire that the objectively adequate response, which is rooted in a pure value response, should be given can hardly be overlooked.

on this one immanent norm: that the right response should be given, a response which is adequately proportioned to the intellectual or moral values of the person. Every dispute of historians about a person, every contrast in their responses of admiration for, or condemnation of, the figure is fought under the flag of this same immanent norm. If someone should consider St. Francis of Assisi to be merely a lovely religious troubadour, and respond to him with benevolent and smiling condescension, here again and in the most acute manner we would experience the objective disharmony of this response. Needless to say, in all these cases where the person in question is no longer living, the point of view of an objective evil inflicted on him is no longer in question.

Secondly, the disharmony embodied in an inadequate response is not restricted to the responses addressed to human persons, whereas the infliction of an objective wrong obviously presupposes a human person, or at least a being capable of suffering. If we hear someone say that the Ninth Symphony of Beethoven is trash, or if we see someone listening to it in bored indifference, we experience the same disharmony as if this inadequate response referred to a human person. This cannot be interpreted as wrong done to the artist as a person, since with respect to this objective disharmony it makes no difference whether the artist is living or dead. Or if someone, instead of responding to the sublime beauty of Toscana's scenes with deep admiration and joy, ignores their beauty, finds them just "nice," we are once more aware of the objective disharmony and are rightly scandalized at this inadequacy. We then try to open the eyes of such a man, to disclose to him the true value of these landscapes, and to prepare the way for an adequate response on his part.

After having clearly seen that the objective disharmony of an inadequate response to a good endowed with a value cannot be reduced to a wrong inflicted on a person, it remains to elaborate the difference between the moral or intellectual disvalue of the wrong response and the objective disharmony which lies in the non-fulfillment of the implied "oughtness."

The objective disharmony refers also to all cases in which the wrong response is given because of an error for which the person giving such a response is not responsible. If somebody is hood-winked by a Tartuffe and responds with deep veneration, this objective disharmony is present. We may try to open such a person's eyes, we may wish for this response to be replaced by the more appropriate one of indignation. Moral guilt, or moral disvalue on the part of the man who is the prey of a hypocrite, is obviously out of the question. It is even possible that, in being influenced by this erroneous opinion, and sincerely believing the hypocrite a saint, morally he *had* to respond with veneration. Our consciousness of a disharmony, of something objectively wrong, of the fact that the hypocrite should be despised, does not refer in these cases to the moral quality of the response. We pity the man who falls prey to the hypocrite; we endorse his response from the moral point of view, but we are eager to see it replaced by the response which is objectively due the hypocrite. The difference between the metaphysical disharmony and the moral disvalue of the response becomes manifest in this fact: that the objective disharmony remains the same whether or not the presuppositions for a moral disvalue of the inadequate response are present; that even if there is no objection to be made against the response from the moral point of view, the objective "oughtness" calls for a fulfillment.

This objective disharmony, however, differs not only from the moral disvalue which a wrong and inadequate response may actualize, but equally from any other disvalue of the wrong response. We may be shocked by the silliness of a man which manifests itself in an inadequate response or in a wrong judgment about the value of something (e.g., when somebody responds with enthusiasm to a flat and flimsy philosophy and ridicules a great genius such as Plato or Aristotle). Again we may be disgusted by the bad taste and triviality of a man who is full of enthusiasm for artistic trash. But in these cases we are focused primarily not on the objective disharmony but on *intellectual* disvalues manifesting themselves in the wrong response. The intellectual disvalues may be the reason for the absence of the adequate response. But the disvalue created by the non-fulfillment of the *oughtness* relation is in itself obviously not identical with the intellectual insufficiency as such.

Again we have to state that, in a manner similar to moral disvalues, the objective disharmony in itself is not dependent on the presence or absence of an intellectual disvalue. In the case where someone becomes prey to a hypocrite and responds to him with veneration, not only a moral but an intellectual disvalue may be absent. Nevertheless, we clearly experience that another response should be given, that in truth a negative response is due.

What matters is to see that neither the moral nor the intellectual value of the adequate response is the basis for the principle which declares that an adequate response is due to every object endowed with a value. Not for the sake of the responding person, but for the sake of the value of the object to which the response is addressed, should the adequate response be given.[2] The relation between a value and the oughtness of the adequate response to it is one of those ultimate principles belonging to the very basis of the universe. It is one of those principles which have often escaped a philosophical *prise de conscience* despite the fact that they are self-evident and always presupposed by us.[3] But as soon as we focus on them in a real philosophical *prise de conscience,* we realize their ultimate character and this excludes any further "why." [4]

We saw in the preceding chapter that the due, adequate response requires a correspondence between the inner word of

---

[2] Without doubt the adequate response should also be given for the sake of the realization of the moral and intellectual value which this response may embody. But what matters here is to see that independently of this moral or intellectual value, the fact that an adequate response is given embodies a harmony and a value of its own.

[3] Nowhere in philosophy has the *oughtness* relation been grasped so clearly as in St. Anselm's work *De Veritate,* although he approaches it from a different angle: "Then when it signifies that that which is is, it signifies as it should." (*Selections from Medieval Philosophers,* trans. R. P. McKeon, Chap. II, p. 153.) "Wherefore whoever thinks that that which is is, thinks as he should, and consequently the thought is right. . . . For if he (the devil) had always wished what he should have wished, he would never have sinned. . . . For if he was in rightness and truth as long as he wished that which he should, that, namely, for which he was given will, and if he abandoned rightness and truth when he wished that which he should not have, then truth cannot here be understood to be other than rightness, for truth or rightness was nothing other in his will than to wish that which he should." (Chap. II, p. 157.) "For if anything ought to be, it rightly and justly is; nor is anything rightly and justly, except what ought to be." (Chap. XII, p. 173.)

[4] Cf. Part One, I, "Value and Motivation."

the response and the rank of the value to which it responds. We also saw that a "more" in the inner word of the response is due to the higher value. Now we have to add that the impact and urgency of the call to give an adequate response increases in proportion to the rank of the value, i.e., that the oughtness itself of an adequate response increases according to the rank of the value. We clearly see that a false or inadequate response given to a good possessing a high value constitutes a greater disharmony than the one created by an inadequate response given to a good possessing a lower value.

Hence, the oughtness relation as such increases according to the rank of a being. The disharmony created by a disregard of the principle of oughtness is obviously incomparably greater when, for example, a saint is ignored or despised—instead of being venerated—than when an honorable man is ignored instead of being esteemed. We shall see later on that as soon as the response to the infinite goodness of the absolute person is in question—the praise and adoration of God—this principle assumes an infinitely greater impact. Furthermore the very existence and validity of this principle becomes more obvious as the rank of the value increases. But before we turn to this oughtness which pervades the entire liturgy, we must first make the following distinctions for this principle manifests itself in a multifold manner.

It is to be found, first of all, in the cognitional sphere as well as in the sphere of theoretical responses. Truth obviously has a value. By truth we here mean the adequation of propositions, which has been termed (none too fortunately) logical truth. The great dignity and the sublime pathos which truth embodies clearly testify to the fact that being should be grasped adequately, and that a positive theoretical response is due reality. We are not dealing here with the intellectual values of the person, which may reveal themselves in the adequate knowledge and the adequate theoretical response; nor are we dealing with the tremendous importance which the adequate knowledge has for the person and for the attainment of his end. We are thinking here of the fact that an adequate knowledge and an adequate theoretical response is *due* being. Error is an evil, not only insofar as the intellectual deficiency of a person is concerned; nor only insofar as the error may have disastrous effects for him; but rather insofar as the discrepancy between a statement and the real nature of the object is in itself a disharmony.

Plainly enough the above-mentioned gradation of the oughtness which is determined by the rank of the object plays a specific role in the sphere of knowledge and theoretical responses. So long as the only thing at stake is a mere contingent fact which lacks any deeper interest, the disharmony of inadequate knowledge is reduced to a minimum; but the disharmony involved assumes an undeniable gravity when the error refers to a *veritas aeterna* or to an object endowed with a high value. It assumes a still greater impact when the *veritas aeterna* in question has a metaphysical content of decisive importance, such as the spirituality of the soul, the freedom of will, the immortality of the soul, and, above all, the existence of God. But the summit of this oughtness in the sphere of theoretical responses is reached when revealed truth is at stake and the due response is faith.

It is impossible in this context to insist further on the many differentiations which should be made in the sphere of knowledge with respect to this fundamental principle, viz., that an adequate response is due to every being. We must content ourselves by simply stating that being should be grasped such as it is, and that an adequate theoretical response is due being.

Again, this principle refers to the sphere of evaluation or appreciation which embraces the knowledge of a being's value as well as the theoretical response to its possessing a value. At first sight this may seem to be a mere subdivision of the sphere of knowledge. If being *ought* to be grasped such as it is, the value of a being should also be grasped. Thus it would appear that appreciation in its oughtness character, insofar as it is adequate knowledge of the value of a being, insofar as it is the theoretical response to a being's value, has already been covered by what we mentioned above.

But in fact we are here confronted with a new manifestation of the general principle of this oughtness. As we saw in the preceding chapter in the sphere of knowledge and theoretical responses, the theme is *truth*. The immanent question about being is, "What is a thing's nature?" and the answer toward which everything points is, "Such is its nature." This answer is given by the object and is repeated as it were in our theoretical act. Thus the theme of truth dominates the fact that our knowledge should be adequate.

Now when we are concerned with the adequate *appreciation* of a being, the theme is not exclusively truth and existence. An axiological element is present which refers to the nature of value, not only insofar as it is existent, but also insofar as it is important-in-itself. Thus we may say that the general principle calling for an adequate response displays itself in a new direction as soon as a value is at stake, as soon as the immanent question is not only, "What is a thing's nature?" "Does it exist?" but, "Has it a value?" or, "What value does it have?" Despite the fact that values are disclosed to us in an authentic act of knowledge, and that we can speak of a value perception and of an intellectual intuition of values, the very nature of values is such that in perceiving them a specific object-communion already takes place which has no analogy in any other kind of knowledge. In understanding a value, we surpass the mere ontological and enter into the axiological rhythm. We cannot understand value if we try to grasp it from without, or try to see it neutrally as something merely existent. The very nature of value insures that in our grasp of value, we simultaneously surpass the theme of a mere knowledge of being.[5]

In adequately recognizing the true value of something, or in admitting its true value, we fulfill not only the call of being for an adequate noetic grasp, but also the call issuing from the value and its rank. Or, in other words, a twofold disharmony arises when a saint is misunderstood: when as the Book of Wisdom says, "We fools esteemed their life madness." There is first the disharmony which results from inadequate knowledge, implied in error as such, and which includes here the gravity of error in proportion to the rank of the object; and there is secondly the disharmony which results from the absence of appreciation and from the denial of the object's value.

There is a most important and third unfolding of this fundamental principle that an adequate response is due to every value; it refers to the sphere of being affected and of the affective as well as the volitional responses. It declares that we ought not

[5] The problems here touched upon will be treated in detail in a later work.

remain indifferent to and untouched by the value of an object, and more evidently as the value ranks higher. If someone remains untouched in witnessing a noble moral attitude, e.g., a heroic sacrifice, we clearly grasp the disharmony. Such a sight *ought* to affect the soul: that the soul should be touched is due the value. The liturgy is pervaded by the awareness that we ought to be affected by Christ's infinite love and moved to tears by the divine sacrifice of the God-Man on the Cross, as, for instance, in the *Popule meus quid feci tibi* of Good Friday.[6]

In our own life too we realize that certain things call for tears: *sunt lacrimae rerum,* and we experience an objective disharmony when someone remains indifferent to, or is even affected inadequately by, something tragic or something sublime. But the climax of this principle is obviously to be found in the realm of the value response.

Not only the text of the entire liturgy but also the very meaning of the liturgy itself testifies to the existence of this principle. The words, *te decet hymnus, te decet laus,* clearly express the main intention of the liturgical prayers of the breviary. Praise is due to God *because* He is God, *because* of His infinite goodness and sanctity.

The modern utilitarian and pragmatic mentality often fails to understand the very meaning of the divine praise; and one can hear, even among Catholics, voices claiming that contemplative monasteries are outdated, that the religious would be more pleasing to God in accomplishing some social or charitable work rather than in filling their day with Gregorian chant and the recital of the Divine Office.

Against the background of such a complete misjudgment the role of this fundamental principle in the liturgy is thrown into relief in a special way. The meaning and *raison d'être* of the liturgical praise of God is not primarily the moral and religious value which the act of praising embodies, but the fact that infinite praise is due God, *quoniam tu solus sanctus, tu solus altissi-*

---

[6] Although the main stress is laid on the subsequent fruits of being affected, i.e., on our transformation in Christ, yet when we pray in the liturgy that our hearts may be pierced and our entire being may be affected by Christ, there is implied nevertheless the fact as such that we *ought* to be touched to the very depths of our soul by Christ.

mus—". . . for Thou alone art Holy. Thou alone art the most High."

In every true value response an awareness of this ultimate due relation is implied. Whether it is an act of veneration, of love, of admiration, of esteem, or of enthusiasm, it is always accomplished in the knowledge that the response does not derive from our arbitrary mood, or from the appeal which the object has for us, but that this response is due the object. From this consciousness stems the note of humility and of objectivity which is proper to every true value response.

We have stated that an adequate response is objectively important in proportion to the rank of the value involved. Now in addition we may say that a person becomes more explicitly aware of the response obligation in proportion to the value rank considered. Yet in saying that the awareness of what is objectively due the good is an essential part of every true value response, we do not thereby imply that there must always exist a consciousness of *moral* obligation to respond adequately to a value. We have already mentioned that a moral obligation to respond to a value is not in all cases implied by the general principle that to every value an adequate response is due.

We shall discuss the moral obligation later on. Here it may suffice to state that in order to constitute a moral obligation, there are several other presuppositions than those required for the "dueness." Analogously there exists a definite difference between being aware that a response is objectively due and being aware of a *moral* obligation to give this response. It would be a complete error to believe that the awareness of a due relation would reduce all value responses to acts of obedience. In rejoicing about the conversion of a sinner, we are aware that joy is due the event, and this awareness in no way makes of this joy a mere volitional response fulfilling a duty in the Kantian sense.

Enthusiasm about a great work of art (which certainly entails an attraction in delight and a spontaneous movement of our mind and heart) is necessarily pervaded by the consciousness that such a response is due. St. Peter's contrition after his denial of Christ is a classical example of an affective plenitude and a spontaneous voice in man's heart, although it cannot be separated from the consciousness that this contrition is *due* as a response to the sin committed.

Hence we have to stress emphatically that the awareness that a response is due entails no antithesis whatsoever to the spontaneous movement of our heart: "The enlarging of the heart is the delight we take in justice. This is the gift of God, that we are not straitened in His commandments, through the fear of punishment, but enlarged through love, and the delight we have in justice." [7]

Finally we must state that although in every value response lives the consciousness that our response is due the object, the person is aware, nevertheless, that when he fails to give an adequate response, it is at his own cost and not at the cost of the object. Saying that an adequate response is *due* every object possessing a value clearly differs from saying that the object *needs* a response.

This becomes especially clear if we think of the supreme value response, the one directed to God: adoring love and adoring praise. They are due God, but it would be nonsensical to say that God needs them. The consciousness of owing this response in no way implies that the object *needs* it, as would be the case, for example, if a person in danger required our help.

Every value response is itself endowed with a value. Fulfilling the due relation; conforming to the objective demand; abandoning ourselves to the value; participating in the value in a unique way: this bestows on the act itself a value. But this value must be clearly distinguished from the one to which the response is given. It is obviously always a personal value, a value which by its very nature can be realized only in a person. In the next chapter we shall analyze the fundamental fact that the response itself embodies a qualitatively new type of value.

It is clear that an adequate response of enthusiasm over a great work of art has not an aesthetic value; but rather that this enthusiasm is endowed with an intellectual value (i.e., depth and sensitivity toward beauty) and in addition, with a spiritual *élan*. This double value is consequently distinct from the beauty value of the work of art. This fact is evident, too, in the value response to a great genius. Without any doubt such a response is

[7] St. Augustine, *In Ps.*, CXVIII.

not something neutral, like the tendency to speak quickly or slowly, but is endowed with a personal value. Our hearts are won over to the person who gives such an adequate value response.

But if we can state that every adequate value response is itself endowed with a personal value, this does not mean that every value response is already endowed with a *moral* value. We do not praise a man as morally good because he gives an adequat response to the genius of Plato or Shakespeare. We may say he is intelligent or that his personality interests us because, having the understanding and enthusiasm for such great men of genius, he therein reveals a certain intellectual excellence as well as the general values of breadth and depth of mind. But we cannot say therefore that this enthusiasm is endowed with a moral value.[8] It suffices merely to compare this enthusiasm with the joy over a sinner's conversion in order to understand that enthusiasm about Plato or Beethoven, praiseworthy though it is and itself possessing a value, is not yet morally good.

We saw before that every morally good attitude is, or at least implies, a value response. But this relation is not reversible. We cannot say that every value response is as such morally good, in the sense that it embodies a specific *moral* value.

Thus we must inquire into the additional conditions fulfilled in the case of a *morally* good value response. Our inquiry will be concerned first with an analysis of those values on the object side which motivate the morally good response. We shall ask whether the presence of moral values in the response does not therefore require a specific type of value in the object-good to which our response is directed. This question will be answered in the next chapter. Furthermore, since there plainly exists a deep connection between morality and freedom, our inquiry will next be concerned with the problem of the freedom of the person. We have already seen [9] that one of the chief distinguish-

---

[8] Certainly this enthusiasm may be a symptom of the presence of certain general moral attitudes, such as, for instance, reverence. Whether or not this is the case depends upon the specific nature and quality of the enthusiasm. But even when this enthusiasm manifests the presence of those general moral attitudes, it never conveys, as such, a moral value to the person, and clearly differs from those value responses which are endowed with a moral value.

[9] Chapter 15, "The Nature of Moral Values."

ing marks of moral values and disvalues is the factor of personal responsibility for their presence or absence. Responsibility clearly presupposes the freedom of the person. Although it is easy to see that the volitional value response is free, it is yet problematic in which sense an affective value response (such as a sublime joy, charity, contrition, or a deep veneration) can be called free. It would be necessary, were they really to be endowed with moral values, that they should be free.

The nature of the freedom of the person, its different dimensions, and the different zones accessible to our free influence will thus be examined in detail in Section II which follows in this Part of our work. Only after these analyses shall we be able to answer our main question. What are the sources of moral goodness in man?

CHAPTER 19

MORAL CONSCIOUSNESS

IN ANALYZING a value response which is endowed with a moral value in the strict sense of the term, we can state that in addition to the response to the value on the object side, it implies a general response to moral goodness as such. The man who resists a pressure and endures sufferings rather than betray someone, responds, not only to the value of a human being and against this background to the objective good of this person, but also to the moral goodness of this attitude of loyalty or to the moral evil of a betrayal. The moral significance of responding to the value on the object side is present to his mind and plays a decisive role in the motivation of his act. We could say every morally good value response implies in some way the *general will to be morally good,* to act and behave in a morally right manner.

The will to be morally good is itself a pure value response. In no way must it be confused with the unconscious striving for self-perfection which, according to the traditional philosophy, is found in every being, and therefore also in man. This will to be good is not something which every man necessarily possesses independently of his free decision. This will to be morally good is absent not only in all those persons who in their basic attitude are immoral, being the prey either of concupiscence or pride; it is also absent in the morally unconscious type of man who may be good-natured and thus in many cases may respond in the right way, but in a somewhat accidental manner and without the sanction of his free personal center.[1] Hence the will to be morally good is in no way an immanent gesture of our nature

[1] This most decisive factor of sanctioning as the core of man's freedom will be expounded in detail in Chapter 25, "Cooperative Freedom."

as is our self-affirmation and our natural desire for happiness, but a pure, free value response.[2]

It would however also be a radical misunderstanding to see in this will a mere response to our own objective good. To be morally good is indeed a fundamental objective good for the person, intimately connected with his ultimate good. But the objective good of moral perfection is such that we never can understand its character of a supreme objective good for us, if we have not grasped the importance in itself of the moral values. It is imperative to understand that any desire to possess this good which is not rooted in a pure value response, in a will to be good for the sake of goodness, is intrinsically impossible. There exist fully legitimate interests in our objective good which are not the fruit of a value response. Our natural interest in our life, not only the instinctive self-preservation but also the conscious will of self-defense, or the defense of our property, the attitude in defending a fundamental right of ours: they are all fully legitimate, typical responses to our own objective good. But they are not value responses; the motivating importance of these goods is their character of objective good for us, or, in other words, our own legitimate interest.

The general will to be morally good, which as we saw is to be found only in the morally good and morally conscious person, clearly differs from any such response to our own objective good: it is a pure value response to the world of moral values, in the last analysis, to God, and only as a secondary element does it also imply the consciousness that it is in our ultimate interest to tread the paths of the Lord. We do not require a preceding value perception to be aware that to live is an objective good for us, that it is in our interest that our rights should be respected. But in order to understand that moral goodness is in our ultimate interest, we have to grasp the intrinsic importance in itself of

---

[2] As we saw before in Chapter 17, "Value Response," this does not mean that man is not destined to give this free response. He is, on the contrary, in his very nature ordered toward moral goodness. This direction is part of his being directed toward God, as St. Augustine expressed it in saying: *Fecisti nos ad te, Domine*—"Lord, Thou hast made us for Thyself" (*Confessions*, I, 1). But, as we saw before, being objectively ordered toward moral goodness and called to this free response to moral goodness in general, willing to be morally good, clearly differs from an unconscious teleological striving for self-perfection.

moral goodness; we must in a pure value-response attitude abandon ourselves to it. Then only can we understand that it is in our ultimate interest. In other words, this general will to be good, of which we are speaking here, is not a manifestation of self-love, of this natural inevitable solidarity with himself which man necessarily possesses and which the evil man shares with the good one. It is the manifestation of our love of God, which is the indispensable presupposition for true self-love. St. Augustine saw this clearly in saying:

I know not, forsooth, in what inexplicable way he who loveth himself, and doth not love God, loveth not himself; and he who loveth God and doth not love himself, loveth himself. For he, indeed, who cannot live of himself doth verily die in loving himself: wherefore he doth not love himself, who loveth himself not to live; when that one is loved of whom he liveth, he loveth the more in that he loveth not himself, who for this reason loveth not himself, that he may love him of whom he liveth.[3]

Here it is clearly seen that the value response to God is the indispensable presupposition for true self-love, which is to be found only in the good man.

Summarizing we can say: The general will to be good (general, not because it is proper to every man, which as we saw is not the case, but because it is a basic response that is not restricted to a single concrete good or situation) is a pure value response, and in its fully mature form the response of loving obedience to God. Secondarily, it is also imbued with an awareness that this way is the real good for us, but this awareness presupposes the value perception and value response, and loses every sense if we try to interpret it as something similar to our legitimate self-defense or self-preservation.

In order to grasp the nature and character of this value response which is concerned with the moral significance of our responding to the value of a concrete good that confronts us, we must above all understand the relation between the moral significance and the value on the object side.

[3] *Nescio quo enim inexplicabili modo, quisquis seipsum, non Deum amat, non se amat; et quisquis Deum, non seipsum amat, ipsum se amat. Qui enim non potest vivere de se, moritur utique amando se: non ergo se amat, qui ne vivat se amat; cum vero ille diligitur de quo vivitur, non se diligendo magis diligit, qui propter ea non se diligit, ut eum diligat de quo vivit.* Tractatus 5 in Joannem.

Someone's life is endangered; we realize that we are able to save him. The value of the life of a human person is drastically presented to our mind, and we understand the call which it implies that we interest ourselves in the preservation of this man's life. Our will to save this man is motivated by the value of the life of a man; nevertheless the moral impact of our intervention is also present to our mind, and our will to save him likewise implies a response to this moral significance.

The fundamental error to avoid is that which sees the relation between the concrete value and the moral significance in the light of means and end. We need only compare a moral action or any morally good value response with an ascetic practice. Fasting, for instance, has the character of a means for our moral and religious growth. Fasting in itself has no value. It is a typical means assuming an indirect importance which depends in its nature upon the kind of importance of the end for the sake of which this means has been chosen. As long as somebody fasts for the sake of keeping the slenderness of his figure, fasting is morally indifferent. If, on the contrary, as in the case of religious ascetic practice, it is chosen as a means to free ourselves from the fetters of concupiscence, i.e., to remove the obstacles for an unfolding of charity in our soul, fasting assumes a high indirect value.[4] Yet what matters here is that in this case the value response is directed toward the value of our inner freedom, and the fasting has the character of a mere means. The fundamental difference between the cases which form the object of our present analysis is obvious.

We see a poor man in great need. The need of this man, his sufferings and troubles, are a disvalue. We grasp the call to do away with this disvalue. Our value response of love for this suffering man is at the basis of the negative response to his sufferings. Our will to help him is really motivated by the value of a human person, and the disvalue of his sufferings. A real interest in the alleviation of his suffering is included. And yet the moral significance of helping the other person is also present to our mind;

---

4 Equally, fasting may possess a moral value if it is done as an act of obedience toward the commandment of Holy Church. In this case fasting, as such morally neutral, has acquired the superimposed importance which a command of Holy Church bestows on everything which forms the content of her commandments.

the desire to do what is right, what is good, is implied in our action. It is not difficult to see that the role of the good which is here the object of our action differs thoroughly from a mere means. We help the poor man for his own sake. In no way do we look at his misery as simply an occasion for accomplishing something which is a mere means for our moral perfection. There is on the contrary a deep interpenetration of the value of the good and its moral significance; both are on the object side. We cannot detach a person's awareness of the moral goodness of protecting someone's freedom from his grasping of the value of the human person and his freedom.

In order to grasp clearly the nature of this interpenetration which is unmistakably different from a means-end relation, we have to keep the following points in mind. First, we must realize that the moral significance of an action or an attitude does not present itself as the value of the person's own action or attitude, but as something which is as much on the object side as the good is which calls for that action or attitude. It presents itself as the moral goodness of the action or attitude as such, as a task which we want to fulfill. It clearly differs from any reflective focusing on our own personality and the positive or negative qualities there. To look at the moral significance, i.e., at the objective goodness, of an action or attitude which we are about to accomplish is radically opposed to the attitude of the pharisee who squints at himself whenever he acts and relishes the moral goodness of his act.

We have to realize that the moral values of our attitudes are not experienced as such in the accomplishment of our attitudes. They appear, as Max Scheler says, "on the back of our attitude or action." We are unable to look at them lest we distort the normal and genuine accomplishment of our attitude. Such a distortion need not, however, always have the character of pharisaism. It is often a sign of a neurotic egocentrism or a hysterical ungenuineness. There are unfortunate people who never succeed in having a genuine contact with the object because they continually remain spectators of themselves, and look at their acts as it were from without. They feel themselves virtuous and good in acting in a certain way, just as in other cases they feel and relish feeling important, intelligent, and brilliant. This general and rather sickly self-complacency when accidentally extended to the moral sphere makes of every act a sham and of life a stage play, and is certainly bad enough. But incomparably more serious is the self-glorification of the pharisee; here the perversion assumes a much more vicious character. The pharisee anticipates the moral goodness of an act and relishes it, not because he wants to give a value response, but because this goodness serves as satisfaction to his pride.[5]

Whatever may be the character of any squinting at the moral goodness of our act, of this reflective turning during the very accomplishment of this act to what the act is from without, it is radically opposed to the awareness of the moral significance of the call from a value on the object side. Everyone knows the danger of squinting at his objective moral goodness in doing good; it is a temptation of pride which we must reject and fight as a poison corroding the real moral value of our attitude. We know it and distinguish this temptation from the awareness of the moral significance of a certain action or attitude, of the moral impact at stake in the call of a value on the object side. We clearly realize that the concern with the moral significance of an action is even radically opposed to this temptation. We are aware that in the temptation, concern with the moral value of our act is rooted in pride and lacks any character of value response. Concern with the moral significance, on the contrary, is inseparable from understanding the call of the values to conform to them. The general will to be morally good has the definite character of a value response.

But if the way in which this moral significance presents itself to our mind is radically opposed to any squinting at the value of our own act in the accomplishment of it, it also differs from all morally necessary and legitimate forms of reflective consideration of our own attitudes. Our own moral values are not only normally not experienced as such, they are not destined to form the object of reflexive contemplation. Humility places a veil over them. Our own moral disvalues, on the contrary, should be made into an object in an examination of conscience or in contrition. In these cases of a legitimate and even morally obligatory reflexive self-contemplation, our own attitude forms the very

[5] Cf. *Transformation in Christ,* chap. 7, p. 138ff.

object of our consideration, and in looking at its disvalue we must precisely consider it from without; we must look at the disvalue on the "back" of our attitude. In the awareness of the moral significance of our action, on the contrary, we look at the value of the object and the call issuing from it; it is from the understanding of the value and its call that the moral impact of this call presents itself to our mind without a reflexive turning to our future act itself and its value.

The difference between these two attitudes is clear. In the one case we are focused on the good, its value, the call issuing from it. And, remaining in this objective direction, we become aware of the moral impact of this situation. Our general will to be morally good, which is better and more authentically expressed in the words, "We want to tread in the path of moral righteousness," our will to share in moral goodness, definitely has the character of an unreflexive attitude. In the examination of conscience or in contrition, however, we are focused on the disvalue of our own attitude.

But before we go on with our study of the awareness of moral significance we must stress from the very beginning the difference that results if this awareness refers to a moral disvalue which we want to avoid or if it refers to a moral value which we want to share. We have already faced this fact in grasping the decisive difference between a reflexive consideration of our own values and a reflexive consideration of our own disvalues.

We shall see time and again in our analysis of morality that values and disvalues, apart from their contrast, differ in many additional respects and the negative situation is often in no way analogous to the positive one. Thus we must now analyze separately the awareness of the moral good and of the moral evil.

Certainly the general will to be good implicitly includes the general will to reject anything which is morally evil. But not in every case in which we do something morally good is the simple omission of it morally evil. This would only be the case when a good imposes a strict obligation on us. Then the failure to conform to the obligation is necessarily morally bad. Thus the awareness of the moral impact of an obligation includes both the awareness of the potential positive moral value of conforming to the obligation and awareness of the potential moral disvalue of failing to conform. But in the many cases wherein a strict moral obligation is not at stake, the potential moral disvalue is not in question. Here the awareness of the moral impact refers only to a positive moral value.

Although later on we shall have to discuss separately the awareness of both the positive and the negative moral value, as mentioned above, it must here be said that whenever an awareness of both the negative and positive value is to be found, as happens in every moral obligation, the awareness of the disvalue is much more in the foreground. This is so because our conscience, which clearly plays a predominant role in the awareness of the moral impact of our acting and behaving, refers above all to the moral disvalues. In the first line, it warns us to avoid anything which is morally evil.[6]

We have sufficiently ascertained the character of the awareness of moral significance and have distinguished it from any illegitimate squinting at the moral value of our own act, and also from the legitimate posterior consideration of our own act. We now have to insist on the relation between the value of the good and its moral significance. We have already mentioned the disastrous error of interpreting this relation as one of means and ends. We saw the radical difference between this relation and the one involved in the field of ascetic practices. Ascetic practices really are means for our self-perfection.

In the last chapter we saw that every value response is pervaded by the consciousness that the object deserves this response, that the response is due to the object. We also saw that this awareness does not yet necessarily imply the consciousness of a moral obligation to respond. The due relation may imply a moral obligation, but it need not do so.

We now have to go a step further. We have to add that moral significance is not identical with the fact that a response is due. The awareness that an adequate response is due to a good endowed with a value definitely differs from the awareness of the moral significance of a value response.

---

[6] The fact that the avoidance of moral evil has precedence over the performance of morally good actions is also stressed by St. Augustine: "The order whereof is, first, to do no man hurt, and secondly, to help all that he can." *De Civitate Dei,* XIX, 14. (J. Healey, *op. cit.,* Vol. II, p. 252.)

Thus we have to distinguish the following three things: First, the moral obligation to respond to a good, for instance, to respect the property of my neighbor; secondly, the moral significance of a value response without moral obligation, for example, risking one's own life to help a person in danger; thirdly, the fact that an adequate response is due to a good endowed with a value, for instance, admiration for a great work of art.

The adequate response is due to all values; the moral significance, on the contrary, is restricted to goods endowed with certain values. Finally, the moral obligation presupposes not only the type of goods which are required for moral significance but, in addition to them, specific new factors.[7]

We shall term all those values in which a moral significance is found, and to which a right response is morally good in the full sense of the word, "morally relevant values."

Before discussing the difference between morally relevant and morally irrelevant values, we still have to concentrate on the following problem. There exists a difference between morally conscious and morally unconscious persons. In saying morally unconscious persons, we do not think of evil people who, being a prey of concupiscence or pride, are indifferent or even hostile toward values in general and toward moral values in particular. We are not thinking of the man who knows only one category of importance, the subjectively satisfying, who never asks nor cares whether something is important in-itself, and *a fortiori* never bothers about whether something is morally relevant or not. We are thinking of the type who lives in an indisputed solidarity with himself, and takes it for granted that one need only follow the trend of one's own nature. He may be goodhearted and grasp many values; he may be disposed to respond to them. He may for instance have a deep artistic sense and grasp the beauty and sublimity of great works of art and of nature. He may be deeply moved by this beauty. He may also grasp the moral goodness of a great sacrifice or of a faithful love. But nevertheless this man has not the superactual will to be morally good, he has not taken a conscious definitive position toward the basic moral problem. In him there is not present this fundamental decision to tread in the paths of rightness, to abstain from moral evil, to remain

[7] Cf. Chapter 28, "Moral 'Rigorism.' "

in harmony with moral goodness. Whether a person super-actually wills to be morally good, or whether this superactual conscious will is absent, is a question of decisive importance. It is here that the difference between a morally conscious or unconscious man is to be found.

The morally unconscious man has never grasped the ultimate seriousness of the moral question, this drama is not known to him. His individual disposition is for him the undisputed norm; whatever his "nature" inspires him to do, wherever it leads him, there he will go. Not that he need make his nature explicitly a venerable norm, which he expressly decides to follow. This is a special kind of moral unconsciousness which might perhaps be called a "conscious" moral unconsciousness and which we find, for instance, to a certain extent in Goethe.

We are here concerned with the much more common type of moral unconsciousness which is to be found in all those people who respond to values only when and if their nature grants them an understanding of them and a disposition to respond to them. They understand the important-in-itself, they are occasionally able to conform to it to a certain extent, they may even understand occasionally that an adequate response is due to a great work of art or to a great intellectual value. They may even grasp that we should have an interest in helping someone in need, that a great kindness deserves admiration, and so on. But what they definitely lack is awareness of the moral significance of certain situations, of certain values and of their call. And, above all, they lack the superactual will to conform to the moral challenge, to act and behave with moral rightness. This remains true notwithstanding the fact that in the morally unconscious man there are certain analogies to this general will to be good.

First, there exists a certain, naïve general tendency to be good. It is not the free attitude of the morally conscious. It is more a general antipathy to immorality, a half-conscious desire to abstain from moral evil. There is without any doubt also an element of value response in this attitude, but with a stain of the accidental. It is not the response to the ultimate seriousness of the moral sphere, to the majesty of moral values, but a natural antipathy against immorality. When asked why he acted in this way on a certain occasion, this morally unconscious type will answer, "Because I dislike being mean or bad."

The very characteristic of this kind of naïve general direction toward moral goodness is to be found in the fact that what is considered to be immoral is more or less arbitrary. His natural disposition determines the frame of what is considered morally evil. There is nothing of this unconditioned readiness and eagerness to conform to what is objectively moral or to avoid what is objectively immoral, a readiness characteristic of the morally conscious man.

This general tendency, although including a value response and differing definitely from any mere teleological tendency, is ultimately rooted in the character of that man, such as it happens to be; it shares with the single responses of this type, given in a certain situation at a certain moment, the character of something accidental, determined by the specific personality, such as it happens to be. The difference between the free conscious, superactual will to be morally good and this naïve tendency is clear.

Secondly, sometimes we find in morally unconscious persons a general intention to remain in conformity with the implicit ideal of the community or society in which they live. There are many people in whom exists an intention to be a decent man or a respectable man, or to behave like a gentleman. They shrink from seeing themselves as disrespectable, so that it does not matter much whether they want to stand the test before their self-esteem or before the esteem of other people. This general direction may be a powerful deterrent against criminal acts. Some elements of respect for the moral order may even be invested in this attitude. Yet this preoccupation of the loyal bourgeois to be decent clearly differs from the superactual will to be good of the morally conscious man. First, the conventional taint and, above all, the element of pride which is present in this attitude forbid us to speak of a real value response.

It is thus still more remote from the superactual will to be good of the morally conscious man than the above-mentioned naïve direction toward the good. It is not only an accidental value response, but also a qualitatively impure one. This attitude, even if it has a very conscious character, is thus in no way incompatible with *moral* unconsciousness. But in both cases the consciousness of something objectively due is absent; in both cases the response to the call of the moral values, to the ultimate seriousness and intrinsic impact of morality, is lacking.

Hence the fact that the morally unconscious man may also have a certain "general will to be good" in no way affects the fundamental difference between the morally conscious and the morally unconscious type. On the contrary, the difference between the genuine, general will to be good and those embryonic analogics distinguishes all the more clearly the morally conscious from the morally unconscious man.

The morally unconscious man moves through life following the inspirations of his nature; he is perhaps tense and awakened in his relation to many values, but blunt to the *religio*, the fundamental bond to God in which lived the "just man" of the Old Testament and also, to some extent, such a man as Socrates. The morally unconscious man does not live under the sword of moral good and evil: to be in harmony with the moral law is not a fundamental concern for him. True, he does not consciously and expressly refuse to submit to the moral challenge; but he ignores it. He is caught up in a deep insouciance in a most central direction, and this is certainly something that is not outside the range of man's responsibility. Since it is not yet the moment to discuss the reasons for moral unconsciousness, let it suffice here to state the fact of the difference between moral consciousness and moral unconsciousness.

The morally unconscious man, therefore, may in a certain situation accomplish a value response, he may even act objectively according to the moral call but not because he has grasped the moral significance or because of his will to act morally right. The morality of his act has, as it were, an accidental character.[8] This does not mean however that when he helps another person, or perhaps even risks his life to save another's, or when he rejoices sincerely about the recovery of another person, he does this for

[8] In his work *De Veritate*, St. Anselm stresses the importance of moral consciousness in stating: "You understand clearly that these two are necessary to the will for justice, namely, that it will *what* it should, and because it should." (R. P. McKeon, *op. cit.*, p. 176.)

some foreign motive without accomplishing a genuine value response. We are not thinking of the man who would save the life of a person simply because he wants to show off his physical strength; nor of the man who rejoices about the recovery of someone because he has some egoistic interest in it. The response we are thinking of is not accidentally moral in this sense.

No, it is a response which is motivated by a value, even by a value which is objectively morally relevant. But this response is accomplished without understanding its moral relevance, without understanding the call issuing from it, without an awareness of the moral significance of the response, and, above all, without the underlying superactual will to act morally. The difference between morally relevant and morally irrelevant values is not grasped, they are all approached in the same way. And this gives to the responses an accidental character, insofar as they lack the consciousness of the *religio,* and also the express interest to conform to the call of the values, whether or not their requirements correspond to our nature.

The difference between an awareness of moral significance and the absence of it discloses itself in a specific way when we think of certain persons who are even ashamed of showing any concern for the moral question. They may help other persons, may even make sacrifices in doing so. They certainly grasp the value at stake. Their attitude is in fact a value response, but perverted by a wrong objectivism. They say: I do not care whether it is morally good or bad to act so, I do not even care whether it is obligatory, the important thing is the other man, that he does not suffer, and so forth.

This may sound very noble and may seem to be completely centered on the object and free of any egocentrism. But in reality it is a pseudo-objectivity which implies, first, a deplorable indifference toward the moral question and the world of moral values; and, secondly, a limited understanding of the morally relevant value; and paradoxically enough, this attitude has even a slightly anti-personal character. It would be a fundamental mistake to confuse this type with the touching humility of a saintly person who refuses to accept any moral praise, and in order to avoid it declares that he helped another person or made a sacrifice to serve him only because he found joy in doing so.

This is obviously only a screen which humility wants to place before the moral value of one's own attitude, for others and even for oneself, insofar as the accomplished attitude is concerned. But before acting the same person will fully grasp the moral significance of the task with which he is confronted, and in his motivation his will to act in the spirit of moral goodness plays a decisive role.

The saintly man wants neither to be admired nor to glorify himself in his moral value; indeed, he is aware of the insufficiency of his response or action. But he burns to obey God and to glorify God, and this even has primacy with respect to the realization of any other value. This glorification of God is accomplished through the moral value alone, by his conforming to the moral commandment or the moral invitation, by conforming to that which is pleasing to God. Thus he is on the one hand fully concerned with the moral significance of the call of the morally relevant value, and on the other hand eager to hide the moral value and merit of his person or action. The type of morally unconscious man who manifests pseudo-objectivism, far from being motivated by humility, shuns submission to the moral order. He may be a prey of human respect and thus shun appearing as someone aspiring to be morally good. He is indifferent toward the moral question, even slightly hostile to it, seeing it in a wrong and distorting light. He looks at the moral question as if as such it already had a tint of pharisaism, or at least of a moralist acidity. The moral sphere appears to him in the guise of an inopportune moralistic zeal. He therefore wants to neutralize his value response by making it simply an instrument for the realization of a physical good, for instance, the life of another person or the alleviation of his sufferings.

We thus see that, despite the apparent resemblance, the two cases are strictly opposed. In the saintly man, the left hand does not know what the right is doing, notwithstanding his seeking first the kingdom of God and his willing above all to glorify God and never to offend Him. In the unconscious "neutral" man there is a complete indifference toward the moral question, toward glorifying God and not offending Him, and there is a shame of betraying any submission to, or even concern for, the moral impact.

Within the frame of the morally conscious type we still find decisive differences concerning the nature of the awareness of moral significance and of the will to be morally good. There are several different types of this awareness and consequently of this will.

In all these cases, however, the "being good" has the character of something which we want to share. Thus it presents itself on the object side and therefore differs from any objectivation of ourselves such as, for example, being concerned with the development of our faculties.

The first type of a morally conscious man is exemplified in the great figure of Socrates. Here we find a general basic will to be in harmony with the world of moral values, an always present general concern for the moral question, and the resulting attitude of approaching every situation and every value of concrete goods in the light of their possible moral significance.

The value response of the will to be good is here directed to the world of moral values. And in any concrete case in which a good endowed with a morally relevant value calls for a response, whether morally obligatory or morally good though not obligatory, the moral question is present to his mind, or in other words, the world of moral values in some way incarnates itself in this concrete situation.

We saw earlier that any attempt to break up the unity between the morally relevant value of the good at stake and its moral significance would be a disastrous misinterpretation leading to far-reaching errors. It is in grasping the need of someone, in having a real concern for his suffering, in accomplishing a true value response to the preciousness and nobility of a human person, it is in all this that the moral significance of a situation presents itself to our mind. The moral significance of our compassion and of our helpful intervention issues organically from the morally relevant value and its call. But, as we have already seen, it is in no way a reflexive turning to the moral value of our own attitude, but rather to the moral impact of the task before us. The response to the morally relevant value on the object side and the response to the moral significance of the action or attitude for which the morally relevant value calls are one and the same act. We must never forget that it is the moral significance of the response to the morally relevant value which cannot be detached from the perception of a morally relevant value and our interest in it. The general will to be good, the general response to moral goodness, is not something superimposed upon, or in any way detached from, the concrete response to the morally relevant good. On the contrary, this general will predisposes our grasping the morally relevant values, our deeper relation to them and more genuine interest in them.

The specific nature of the general will to be good, of moral significance, and of the awareness of the latter, reveals itself more clearly, however, when we turn to the second type of morally conscious man. It is the man who wants above all to obey God and never to offend Him, to walk in the paths of the Lord. Here the general will to be morally good assumes a still more definite character, since it is the outspoken response to God, the infinite goodness itself.

The moral significance is obviously the one decisive point in which our direct relation to God flashes up. The suffering of our neighbor is an evil; it calls for our interest; the value of this human person calls for our concern for his suffering. Nevertheless the moral value of our intervention alone glorifies God and, in the case of a moral obligation, our moral failure alone offends God.[9] The consciousness of the moral significance is here a clear expression of our confrontation with God, of our value response to God, the absolute Lord and absolute moral goodness. The call of God issues from the morally relevant value, and is definitely not something superimposed as in the case of a purely positive divine commandment. The very nature of the morally relevant value, its importance in itself, which it possesses independently of moral significance, is the basis of its moral significance.

The misery of a man in distress is an evil whether or not I know of it, whether it invites anyone to a moral action or not. The life and the well-being of a man has its value independently of any moral significance, and if it is saved by exterior circumstances, it remains a high good. The morally relevant good is important in itself, it has a value even if we abstract from any possible consideration of a moral significance. And if in a concrete situation such a morally relevant good or evil addresses

[9] *Liturgy and Personality*, p. 11ff.

itself to a person, either imposing an obligation or inviting him to a morally good attitude, the moral significance is rooted in this morally relevant value and the situation, and not vice versa. Though this second type of morally conscious person will be preoccupied with the morally relevant good or evil, by the desire to do away with the suffering of his neighbor or to save his life or to save him from a moral danger, and though the call of God issues from this value, nevertheless the moral significance of his attitude implies a direct, new relation to God. And to obey God, to walk *in viis Domini*—"in the paths of the Lord"—to be in harmony with God, has a primacy with respect to the existence or non-existence of the concrete good or evil. This must in no way be misunderstood in the sense of religious egocentrism. The religious egocentric looks at the entire world surrounding him and at all other men more or less as occasions or means enabling him to accomplish something morally good and to grow in moral perfection. If, for instance, these people see a man whose life is in great danger, yet without being able to help him, the fate as such of this man will not affect them. Their exclusive concern is centered on whether or not they have a duty to intervene, or on the possibility of accomplishing a meritorious act. But even when they are able to intervene and to accomplish a morally good act, they do it without any real interest in the life of the man whom they help. These people are also more or less indifferent toward the moral perfection and the eternal welfare of their neighbors, so long as they have no responsibility in this matter.

The interest that these people have in their moral perfection clearly differs from the general will to walk in the paths of the Lord. The attitude of the egocentric is not a pure value response. Although they may say that their only concern is to do something pleasing to God, in reality their indifference toward the glorification of God through other persons, as well as their lack of any real love of neighbor, clearly testifies that they look at their own moral perfection primarily as their *own* good and not *propter Deum* (for the sake of God). They have no real abandonment to God; they do not hunger and thirst for justice; they do not seek first the Kingdom of God, but their own good. Certainly it is not a distinct and clear position in one or another direction. It is a mixed attitude in which elements of value response are intermingled with an egocentric pursuit of their own good.[10]

The following decisive marks distinguish the general will to be good from this pious moral egocentrism: A general attitude of value response toward all morally relevant values is to be found in the man who wants to walk in the paths of the Lord. Genuine interest in the morally relevant values on the object side goes hand in hand with the general will to be good. He will have a deep concern for the objective good of other persons independently of the question of whether or not a duty to intervene, or even any possibility of intervention, is given. Furthermore, the morally conscious man will never look at the morally relevant goods as mere occasions or means for his moral perfection. He will, on the contrary, grasp the organic and intrinsic link between the morally relevant value on the object side and its moral significance.

The general will to be good of the morally conscious man is a pure value response free of any egocentric taint. The primacy which the moral significance of one's own actions has with respect to the moral perfection of other people is in no way rooted in a primacy of one's own person, but exclusively in the fact that moral values or disvalues are the only points in our actions and attitudes *in which we refer directly to God*. This primacy does not imply that we consider ourselves as more important than any other person, that our moral goodness is more important than their moral perfection. But it *does* mean that not to offend God and to glorify Him is indeed more important than any created good, such as the happiness, the moral perfection and the eternal welfare of our brothers. This is not so because we are more important than any other man, but because our moral conduct alone implies a direct relation to God, and this direct relation to Him gives it an undisputed primacy for us, with respect to anything else. *Our* primary concern has to be not to offend God, and to glorify Him.[11] Yet for all that, this direct relation to God in

---

[10] The fundamental problem of moral egocentrism will be analyzed in detail in a later work.

[11] This primacy is revealed in the fact that we are not allowed to commit a sin in order to bring a good into existence, whatever its rank may be. Even if in sinning we could obtain the eternal welfare of another person, we would not be allowed to do so. As soon as we understand this absolute primacy of moral significance we clearly grasp the intrinsic error contained in the thesis that we are

the moral significance of our attitude implies our response to the morally relevant value and our full interest in it, for it is not something which replaces the interest in morally relevant values. On the contrary, in the light of God everything morally relevant reveals itself in a much more luminous way, with a greater significance, and our interest in it becomes deeper and more intense.

In the third type, for instance the saint, it is in the imitation of Christ that the will to be morally good reaches its highest and most sublime expression. Complete loving abandonment to Christ, one great preoccupation to act in the spirit of Christ, to avoid anything which cannot stand the test of Christ, to follow Him in everything—this lives in every value response to a morally relevant good and is thematic in every morally relevant situation which calls for a response in one way or another. Whether it is the health or the life of our neighbor which is at stake, or the rights of a man, or his moral integrity, whether it is the protection of an innocent person, the response is never made to this value exclusively, but always to Christ as well. The will to follow Christ is always present. Here it becomes clearer than ever that concern for moral significance is not a reflexive turning of the saint upon his own act but a being focused on Christ. Awareness of moral significance then becomes inseparable from his looking at Christ.

But on the other hand it also becomes clearer than ever that we do not turn away from the concrete morally relevant good, but rather that we find Christ and His voice *in* this good, in the suffering neighbor, in the morally endangered man, in every good possessing a morally relevant value. What shows me the

---

permitted to transgress the moral law in order to conform to a so-called hierarchy of values. This thesis is a basic tenet of the "new morality" condemned by His Holiness Pope Pius XII (cf. Preface). It completely overlooks the fact that a conflict between the moral law and the hierarchy of values is essentially impossible. It is precisely the moral law that is concerned with the moral significance of our actions and attitudes and that clearly delineates the difference between morally relevant obligatory values and all other values. Thus the moral law is always and necessarily in conformity with the hierarchy of values. For moral values, because of their direct relation to God, hold the highest rank in the hierarchy of values, and should always be given primacy over all other things. In a later work the nature of the moral law, its being rooted in moral values as well as its immutable, eternal character, will be further expounded.

direction in which I have to go in order to follow Christ if not the morally relevant value and the call issuing from it? Any attempt to interpret the relation between the morally relevant good and Christ as a means-end relation is evidently nonsensical. Even the formula: they are doing or responding in this way for the sake of Christ, is misleading. The action or attitude which is in the spirit of Christ, and in which we want to follow Christ, is not a mere exterior behaving *as if* we would love our neighbor, but a real interest in him. Our love of neighbor is a participation in Christ's love for him, and thus—far from implying any indifference toward one's neighbor—it is an incomparably greater love than any natural love could be. Our genuine value response to a morally relevant value is precisely the real following of Christ.

Here indeed we face the most radical antithesis to the neutral unconscious type who is ashamed of showing any concern for the moral question, the type embodying a pseudo-objectivity. However inseparable the moral significance is from the morally relevant value, however deeply each interpenetrates the other, nevertheless the will to follow Christ, the will never to betray or deny Him by any immorality, has primacy with respect to any concrete morally relevant good, primacy above all in the sense of being our first and absolute task. We easily realize that the value response to Christ is as such more essential than any other, and that the absence of this motive would deprive these attitudes of their most sublime moral value without, however, depriving them of a moral value as such. Analogously, the absence of the role of the moral significance would frustrate the moral value itself.

We may conclude this analysis concerning moral significance by stressing again that any morally good attitude implies both the awareness of the moral significance and the will to be morally good. If we saw that a value response need not be necessarily morally good, even though it is always praiseworthy and noble, we must now add that in order to be morally good it necessarily implies an awareness of the moral significance and a will to be good. But this presupposes that a morally relevant value is at stake, since the grasping of moral significance depends both on the condition of the subject (i.e., whether or not he is morally conscious) and on the nature of the value on the object side (i.e., whether or not it is a morally relevant value).

We mentioned before that the awareness of the moral significance differs according to whether the avoiding of a moral guilt is at stake or the accomplishment of something morally positive. Certainly the positive and the negative moral value are mostly so connected that it seems artificial to deal with them separately. Without any doubt, to abstain in a concrete situation from something evil in which the evil-doing presents itself as a concrete temptation, is also morally good. In being aware of the negative moral significance of this tempting action, we inevitably also grasp the positive moral character of abstaining from the evil. The will to avoid moral evil can obviously not be separated from the will to be morally good.

On the other hand, to abstain from doing good is in many cases something morally evil. The attitude of the priest and the Levite in the parable of the Good Samaritan is undoubtedly a morally negative one. Certainly doing good is not restricted to abstaining from doing evil and doing evil is not synonymous with omitting to do good. But in all cases of abstaining from moral evil, there is not only the absence of moral evil but also the presence of something morally positive, because the abstaining is not only the objective absence of a moral evil, but a real positive attitude, a will to avoid that which is morally evil.

To abstain from something morally good, however, is not always morally evil. This is the case only when the situation implies a moral obligation. Whereas in the case of the Good Samaritan it was morally obligatory to do something for the wounded man, it would not be obligatory to save a man whose life was in danger at the risk of one's own life. Thus there exist cases in which abstaining from a morally good action or attitude is not yet morally negative.

In summarizing we can therefore say: In all cases wherein something having a morally relevant disvalue is at stake, the call is to avoid the moral evil. In these cases awareness of the moral evil obviously prevails; in the foreground is the horror of the moral badness, the warning of our conscience. Nevertheless this horror of moral evil, which in the case of the higher moral consciousness presents itself in the light of offending God, is rooted in the positive will to be morally good, to conform to God, His infinite goodness and His will. The main stress in our consciousness is certainly on avoiding any offense against God, but objectively in a certain way the direction of the will toward positive moral goodness is presupposed. The love of God implies primarily the will to be morally good, and secondarily the will not to offend God. Thus we can say: On the one hand, the will to be morally good is the basis for the will to avoid any moral evil; on the other hand, this will displays itself primarily in the eagerness to avoid moral evil.

In the case in which a moral obligation is absent, the awareness of the moral significance assumes a different character. The warning of conscience, the horror of offending God, is absent; present is the will to be good. It is certainly a response of a unique character. For in all other value responses we speak an inner word to the object, we conform to it, we are interested in it, but in the will to be morally good the response is a desire to participate in the value, to be endowed with it. It is not only the obedience to the moral commandment as in the case of an obligation. As a matter of fact, such a commandment is absent. Nevertheless, in this case also, the will to be good is not motivated by *our* objective good. It is a pure value response. Though concerned with our conduct, the will to be good finds its authentic expression in the love of God. It is for the sake of God or to use a more adequate expression, the Augustinian *propter Deum* (because of God), and not *propter me* (because of myself). The stress in this will to be good is on the *propter Deum*, flowing out of the love of God, though also organically implying the desire of union with God and the desire for our own beatitude.[12]

Thus we see that every morally good attitude is a value response, not only to the value of the good on the object side, but also to its moral significance,[13] which pertains either to the

[12] We shall see later on the organic convergence of the *propter Deum* and *propter meipsum*. According to St. Augustine, only the one who loves God *more* than himself really loves himself. *Nam si non diligit Deum, non diligit seipsum, Tractatus 135 in Joannem.* Cf. St. Augustine, *De Moribus Ecclesiae,* 26, 48c, 1331; and 26, 49, 1331.

[13] In his work *De Veritate,* St. Anselm mentions the importance of this consciousness: "Therefore that will is to be called just which preserves its rightness because of the rightness itself." (R. P. McKeon, *op. cit.,* p. 177.)

world of moral values or to God or to Christ. But, as we saw, this also implies that the value of the good is a morally relevant value. To be sure, obedience to a positive commandment of God may likewise be the basis of a morally good action. But this type of morally good attitude will be discussed later. Here we are interested in attitudes whose moral goodness is rooted in their nature and which are therefore imposed on us by the natural moral law. We thus prescind here from attitudes which are as such morally neutral and only become morally relevant because of a positive commandment.

The difficult question arises: Which element makes a value morally relevant? Or in other words, can we indicate any factor the presence or absence of which clearly separates the realm of the morally relevant values from that of the morally non-relevant ones?

It is easy to see that this difference between morally relevant and morally irrelevant values exists. Enthusiasm for a great work of art is a praiseworthy value response, but still it is not morally good in the strict sense of the term. It is not endowed with a specifically moral value, nor does anyone have the consciousness of a moral significance in his response when confronted with a great work of art. Whereas he has the consciousness that this response is due to the work of art, he has not the consciousness that the moral question is at stake. The same applies to the devotion of a scientist to his research work: the value response to the value of knowledge for its own sake. But almsgiving to a poor man or enthusiasm for the moral goodness of another person or the refusal of anything impure—these are definitely morally good and they imply a consciousness of the moral significance of the situation.

There undoubtedly exists a difference in the nature of the values themselves which permits us to distinguish between morally relevant and morally irrelevant values. Morally relevant values are those values of which we can predicate that to be interested in them, to conform to them, to let ourselves be motivated by them, is something morally good in the full positive sense of the term. Morally relevant values are also characterized by the fact that the morally conscious man in grasping their call also grasps the moral significance of an adequate response to them. They evoke in the morally conscious man, as soon as they address a call to him, a consciousness of moral significance and an actualization of the general will to be good.

The term "morally relevant value" is obviously much more inclusive than the term "moral values." Many ontological values, such as the life of man or his rights, are morally relevant values, though they are clearly not moral values. The ontological value of man's life and his dignity, though not moral values, are definitely morally relevant values, because to give an adequate response to them is undoubtedly morally good. It must be said that all moral values are morally relevant, but not all morally relevant values are moral values. The term "morally relevant" indicates exclusively that the positive response motivated by it is necessarily morally good, and that the grasp of this value is for the morally conscious man necessarily connected with the grasp of the moral significance.

We saw before [14] that there exist very different types of values, such as ontological values on the one hand and qualitative values on the other, and that among the qualitative values different value domains exist; now the distinction between morally relevant and morally non-relevant values goes in a completely different direction. The morally relevant values neither form a specific value domain nor are they centered around the ontological value of one being. The mark of moral relevance is not such that it would suffice to form one value domain. Values of many different types are to be found among the morally relevant values. The element conditioning their moral relevance cuts across the different domains.

It is not possible in the frame of this work to analyze the distinctive mark which separates morally relevant values from morally irrelevant ones, i.e., to analyze the reason upon which depends this difference. An unprejudiced contemplation of reality evidently discloses that such a difference exists. Insofar as obligatory morally relevant values are concerned, the moral law clearly circumscribes their realm and implicitly stresses that they differ from morally irrelevant ones. It can be intuitively grasped with absolute certitude. The distinction between morally relevant and morally irrelevant values must thus be made—even

[14] Confer Chapter 10, "Ontological and Qualitative Values."

before being able to discover the reasons for this difference. Though it is not our intention to enter into a detailed discussion of this problem, this much may be said for the clarification of the question as such.

In inquiring into the marks of moral relevance, one might be tempted to limit the field of moral relevance to things which directly or indirectly are related to personal beings. Yet this limitation would not be correct. Although the overwhelming majority of morally relevant goods are related to a person, there exist also morally relevant goods beyond the personal sphere. For example, to torture an animal, to make him suffer without any necessity, is undoubtedly immoral. Thus the suffering of an animal is also morally relevant, though it is assuredly not connected with a person. And on the other hand, many values presupposing a person are not morally relevant; for example, an adequate response to the intellectual qualities of a genius is not as such morally good.

Here we are confronted with one of those situations, mentioned in the Prolegomena, in which a univocally given difference must not be denied simply because we are not yet able to explain why it is so. For our context it suffices to state that we must distinguish in the vast realm of values between the morally relevant and the morally irrelevant values; and that a human act in order to be morally good in the strict sense must be, not a value response as such, but rather a value response to morally relevant goods, and this implies an awareness of their moral significance and an actualization of the general will to be morally good. But even this is not sufficient. Every morally good act must also be free or related to our freedom in such a way that we are responsible for it. This fundamental problem will be the topic of the next section.

II. Freedom

CHAPTER 20

INTRODUCTORY REMARKS

WE HAVE seen, in dealing with the nature of moral values, that there exists a deep essential link between morality and responsibility. While we can possess an intellectual disvalue (e.g., a poor intelligence) without being responsible for it, we are always *responsible* for moral disvalues, as, for example, dishonesty or impurity. Morality extends as far as does responsibility.

But, as we saw before,[1] in saying responsibility we imply freedom. A man is responsible only for something which he can freely choose or refuse, something which in one way or another is within the range of his power. The necessary link between responsibility and freedom is as evident as that between responsibility and morality. The relation of responsibility to morality as well as that of freedom to responsibility are classic examples of essentially necessary facts, typical *veritates aeternae* in the sense in which St. Augustine used the term.

Thus we can say that morality cannot be detached from freedom; that man's freedom is an indispensable presupposition of his being morally good or bad. As a matter of fact, in saying that moral values presuppose a person, we already include that they presuppose a free being, since freedom is an essential feature of the person. Hence a person who is not free would be an intrinsic impossibility. A person may *de facto* be *deprived* of freedom (e.g., an infant or an idiot), yet being unable to actualize freedom or being frustrated in the actualization of freedom, as in the case of an idiot, does not confute the fact that, potentially, freedom belongs to the essence of the person. In considering the

---

[1] Chapter 15, "The Nature of Moral Values."

child *as* a person, we include consideration of his freedom, for we expect that it will become operative with the use of his reason. Not only for the human person, but also for every other personal being, freedom of will is as essential as the capacity for knowledge. Freedom is one of the greatest of man's privileges; it is one of the essential features constituting his character as an image of God.[2]

It is impossible in this book to offer an analysis of the entire metaphysical problem of freedom. We shall therefore restrict ourselves to a discussion of those features of human freedom indispensable to an understanding of morality.

[2] *Transformation in Christ,* p. 174.

CHAPTER 21

THE TWO PERFECTIONS OF THE WILL

THE VOLITIONAL response, the act of willing in the strict sense of the term, possesses two outstanding perfections. It is first of all free, insofar as the spiritual center of the person can engender a free response to an object endowed with one or another kind of importance; secondly, it is capable of starting a new causal chain by freely initiating certain activities of our body and mind and by having the power to command them freely.[1] A brief analysis of these two perfections will clearly show the dual necessity of distinguishing between them and of grasping their relationship.

The first perfection of the will displays itself in the relation of the will to the motivating object. It refers to the will as a volitional *response*, to the will's decision with respect to the object. This perfection includes the capacity man has of conforming himself freely to an important object and of actualizing a volitional response, whereby it depends on him alone whether or not he gives this response. The volitional act, in which the person takes a specific position in relation to an object, can neither be interpreted as being determined by anything exterior to him, nor by his dispositions, his character, or any unfolding of his entelechy. The act is indeed motivated by the object, but

---

[1] St. Thomas points to the difference between the two perfections of will in the context of another problem: "I answer that, the act of the will is twofold: one is its immediate act, as it were, elicited by it, namely, *to will;* the other is an act of the will commanded by it, and put into execution by means of some other power: e.g., *to walk* and *to speak,* which are commanded by the will to be executed by means of the power of locomotion." *Summa Theologica,* 1a–2ae, vi, 4. Quoted from *The Basic Writings of St. Thomas Aquinas,* trans. Anton C. Pegis (New York: Random House, 1945), Vol. II, p. 231.

it rests exclusively with the freedom of the person to allow himself to be motivated, to yield to the motivating power of the object: to say "yes" or "no" to it. This first perfection, which also includes the capacity to choose between different objects possessing a motivating power, is the more decisive and deeper dimension of freedom.

The second perfection of the will refers to its role as master of all actions. It is concerned not with the will's intentional response character or its decision with respect to the object but rather with its power to command certain activities. Man is able, through his will, to command different activities: to move his arms or legs, to speak or to remain silent.

The first dimension of freedom refers to the engendering of an act of will itself and of the ultimate "yes" or "no" to an object. It concerns our attitude toward the object, our turning to one or another good, our conforming to a moral obligation or our ignoring it: it concerns our morally relevant *decision*.

The second dimension of freedom concerns the capacity of the will spontaneously to command certain activities, to become the free cause in a new chain of causality. It concerns our relation, not so much to the motivating object, as to those activities through which we realize the as yet unrealized state of facts. It concerns the influence of our will on the bringing of something into existence; it concerns our capacity freely to intervene in the course of events and to alter or change a thing.

It is one of the great and outstanding privileges of man that he is able freely to intervene in the events of the world around him and also in events of his own physical and mental life. The capacity to be a cause for many processes belongs to all creatures, to pure matter as well as to living beings, to plants and animals as well as to personal beings. St. Thomas stresses the reality of this capacity granted to all secondary causes: "Consequently to detract from the creature's perfection is to detract from the perfection of the divine power." [2]

Man shares this causal capacity with all things, but in addition he is able freely to intervene in events and purposely to change things, to build up and to destroy, to shape freely and consciously

[2] *Detrahere actiones proprias rebus est divinae bonitati derogare. Summa Contra Gentiles*, III, 69.

many things in the world around him and in his own soul. Man has the capacity not only to be a link in a chain of causality, but also, after having grasped the importance of a good, to start a new and freely chosen chain which he can meaningfully and consciously direct toward an end.

Someone may object: The capacity of the will to command certain activities, such as certain movements of our body, is nothing but a specific type of causality. As a fit of anger has the power to make our heart beat or our face redden, so too our will has the power to move our hands.

In answer, it must be said: Certainly the link between our will and the activities commanded by it is a causal relation. But in comparing this with psychophysical causality it becomes precisely evident why we speak here of a completely new kind of causality, of one which by its nature includes a dimension of our freedom. Causality in other cases takes place without the intervention of our freedom; for when we are angry we in no way command our heart to beat faster or our face to redden. These are pedestrian cases of causality, whereas in the case of the will there is a capacity to *command* certain movements, to use them for the realization of the state of facts which we have decided to realize. They are within the range of our power. The causality linking the will with these activities is such that they are dominated by our will; and it depends completely upon our free power to command them in one or another direction, or else to abstain from initiating them.

It is not enough, however, merely to distinguish the two dimensions of freedom or the two perfections of will. We must also show the intrinsic relation between them. The two perfections as such, despite their differences, are nevertheless deeply interrelated from the point of view of the specific "inner word" of willing. The second perfection, the capacity of intervention in the world around us, is deeply related to the specific inner word of the volitional response. We saw before that only states of facts which are as yet unrealized (though realizable) can become the object of our will. We have to add now that the object, in order that we may will it, must be realizable not only in principle but must even present itself as something accessible to our own power. What precisely distinguishes the inner word of willing from any wishing or ardent interest in the becoming of something is that we not only say to the object, "Thou shouldst be," but add, "Thou shalt be *through myself*." This inner word of willing, the specific content of the volitional response, would be impossible if the will did not possess the marvelous capacity to command, spontaneously and freely, activities through which the goal of the will can be attained.

Whereas the free value-response to the existence of something as such (i.e., the inner word "Thou shouldst be") does not presuppose man's capacity to start a new causal chain, willing in the strict sense *does* presuppose it, and even presupposes an awareness of this capacity. The inner word "Thou shouldst be" as it may also be found in wishing does not constitute willing in its proper sense. Even if to the "shouldst be" a "thou wilt be" is added, we do not yet reach the specific inner word of willing. This would rather be the inner word of hope. But the response which implies the inner word "Thou shouldst be and thou shalt become real *through* me"—the distinguishing mark of willing— necessarily presupposes awareness that the coming into existence of this good is at least to a certain extent in our power, i.e., the awareness of the second perfection of willing.

Thus we see that on the one hand we must distinguish clearly between the two perfections of the will or the two dimensions of freedom, and on the other hand we must understand that the second perfection is also presupposed in what concerns the specific inner word of willing.

After having examined the two perfections of freedom, we still have to add a few remarks concerning freedom as such. The freedom of the person refers to that unique, marvelous capacity to posit an act which by no means can be considered merely the effect of a former chain of causes. To be sure, if we are confronted with any change, any becoming, or any perishing in the sphere of matter, of life, or even of the psychical, we must ask for a cause and we must consider the changes as effects determined by certain causes. But a similar inquiry into the cause of an act of willing would be pointless; moreover, the assumption that this act of willing is an effect determined by certain causes would be a completely wrong and thoroughly unfounded assumption.

The will to act in a certain way is not strictly determined by the character of a man, his education, his milieu, his former experiences, nor even by the importance the object may have. The will to act is not a resultant of a parallelogram of these forces, but something which issues from the marvelous creative capacity of man, and which, notwithstanding all the influence of these factors, is never strictly determined by them. An act of willing can by no means be considered a link in a chain of causality whereby the person would merely be the *causa proxima*, and education, milieu, dispositions, and so forth the *causae remotae:* so that the person would be, as it were, the "transformer" of all these causes. Although these factors make it understandable that a man wills and acts in a certain way and not otherwise, we are nonetheless aware that they never necessitate him to act so, that they never determine his will in the sense of a strict causality. Notwithstanding the influence of all these factors, a man *could* will and act otherwise, and in many cases he does so.

Every man, independently of any philosophical conception, presupposes this fundamental fact. As soon as he makes a moral judgment about another person or about himself, as soon as he has a bad conscience or becomes indignant at any action of another man, as soon as he is filled with admiration at someone's action or with esteem for another person, he thereby presupposes man's responsibility; and this again implies the capacity for free decision.

In addressing a question to someone we likewise assume his freedom; we clearly realize that we are confronted by a situation different from that in which we try to obtain a result from a calculating machine. We presume not only that this person is able to understand us but also that he has the freedom of answering if he so chooses. We realize that his answer is not the effect of our questioning him as his leaping up could be the effect of our screaming. We are aware that this person is free either to answer or to decline to answer.

In every social act we presuppose and refer to the freedom of man. In exhorting another person, we presuppose that he is able freely to decide whether he will or will not follow our exhortation. In no way do we believe that his response is necessitated by our exhortation; that we press a button which will effect the desired result in the other person. We clearly distinguish the exhortation which appeals to his freedom as opposed to any psychical effect which we may create in his soul in giving him a drug, and even from the sorrow which bad news will create in his soul.

In every exhortation, in every rule, in every law imposed, freedom of will is essentially presupposed.[3] We are constantly aware of this reality and we always count on it; it is as self-evident as the stability of being or the principle of causality. We must realize that if we seriously denied the freedom of will all morality would immediately collapse, and the notions of moral good and bad would lose all sense.[4] This argumentation should not be confused with the introduction of freedom of will as a mere postulate in the Kantian fashion. Again, we have to emphasize what we already said with respect to values.[5] In stressing the inevitability of presupposing freedom of will, we intend only to lead the reader to a deeper stratum in which he becomes aware of the freedom of will, in which it is univocally given as an essential feature of a personal being. In leading the reader to a deeper stratum, we want him to discover the fact that he clearly and firmly knows about his freedom.

Yet the creative power of freely engendering an act of will does not imply that we could engender it without any motive. We have already seen that willing presupposes not only an object (that is to say, a state of facts which is as yet unrealized, although as such realizable) but also that this object is endowed with an importance—the importance may be a value, an objective good for the person, or something subjectively satisfying. The object, in order to have the potentiality of moving our will, must be important either as an end or as a means toward an end. Something completely neutral cannot become the object of our will. Thus in every act of willing there is presupposed an object which

[3] "Man has free choice, otherwise counsels, exhortations, precepts, prohibitions, rewards, and punishments would all be pointless." St. Thomas, *Summa Theologica*, 1a, lxxxiii, 1.

[4] Even the most obdurate "determinist" admits in practice the freedom of will, by presupposing responsibility. He certainly presupposes it when he is in a rage about the nondeterminists, angrily accusing them and holding them responsible for spreading errors.

[5] Cf. Chapter 6, "The Role of Value in Man's Life."

has a motivating power. But the motivating importance by itself does not engender the will. Our freedom displays itself in the capacity to say "yes" or "no" with our will to the invitation of a situation; or, in other words, displays itself in the capacity to conform in our will to the invitation or call of this importance, or else to refuse for a specific reason to initiate an activity.

Willing cannot be brought into existence simply by our free center without any motive supporting it from the object side. In this sense St. Anselm says: "Every will, inasmuch as it wills something, wills as it does because of something . . . Wherefore every will has a *what* and a *why*, for we will absolutely nothing unless there be a reason why we will." [6]

A conception ascribing to the person the capacity of willing without any motive would be a complete misunderstanding: it would make of the willing something purely arbitrary, thereby depriving it of its meaningful, spiritual character. In trying to stress the free character of willing, such a conception actually destroys the dignity and rationality of willing and even places it below merely blind urges. To confuse freedom with the arbitrary would imply a total misunderstanding of the very nature of willing, its intentional, meaningful character as a response rooted in an act of knowledge. Freedom and the arbitrary are essentially incompatible. For the arbitrary deletes the will from the great dialogue between person and universe. It separates the will from the logos of being, and above all from the world of values. Willing would thus no longer be a position taken by man toward something, becoming a merely blind movement.

No, the true sense of freedom of will does not imply the capacity to engender an act of willing without the presence of any motivating object. Willing necessarily presupposes not only an object to which it is directed, but also the importance this object possesses, and in addition our awareness of this importance capable of motivating the movement of our will and of forming a meaningful basis for our willing. The freedom which so deeply distinguishes willing from all other motivated responses consists in this: that it is entirely within our power either to conform to the invitation of the object or to decline to conform to it; or in many cases to choose freely between different

[6] *De Veritate.* (R. P. McKeon, *op. cit.*, p. 176.)

possibilities and even to decide in a direction contrary to our pleasure or the promptings of our heart. The really pertinent and decisive difference between willing and all affective responses is that willing never comes by itself as a gift. It always implies a free decision which we can accomplish with our free spiritual center, though never independently of some motive and always supported by the importance of the object, and furthermore it always consists in a turning to an object because of its importance. In a case mentioned before we observed that we may sometimes be confronted by a situation in which we understand that we should be full of joy, that the object deserves joy, yet we realize that it is beyond our power to engender this joy. Now such a frustration is not possible with respect to willing; it is always in our power to engender an act of willing when we understand that the object deserves a positive decision.

Someone might object: Is it not a self-evident metaphysical principle that every change presupposes a cause? How can the willing of man and the subsequent action issuing therefrom and directed by it (since both willing and acting involve a becoming of something) take place without being caused or at least without having a sufficient reason for their becoming? Must it not be that the experience of this freedom in one's own person and the presupposition of it in other persons is a mere illusion, since the principle of sufficient reason forbids us to accept such a thing as freedom of will?

In answer it must be said: Certainly every becoming (or even every contingent being) requires a cause for its coming into existence. But this fact in no way means that every becoming (or every contingent being) is necessarily the result of a long chain of causes, or that it must have the character of a link in this chain.

Freedom of will is in contradiction neither with the principle of causality nor with the principle of sufficient reason. The act of willing which arises freely, inasmuch as it cannot be considered a link in a chain of causality, has its sufficient reason in the nature of the person; this nature is endowed with the mysterious capacity of engendering an act of will and of starting a new chain of causality.

In its nature as well as in its existence, the freedom of any created person certainly demands a *causa prima*, inasmuch as the created person himself demands it.[7] Freedom is a privilege granted to man by his character as a person. Now just as the soul of man cannot be caused by any *causa secunda* but rather issues directly from God, so too the freedom of man does not depend upon any secondary cause; this capacity in man presupposes only the *Causa Prima*, God.

There exist analogies in impersonal nature for this aspect of freedom. The laws of nature cannot be considered as links in an uninterrupted chain of causes. When we ask what their cause is, we have to quit the sphere of secondary causes and turn to the extramundane cause, to God. No one will claim that the admission of such natural laws contradicts the principles of causality or of sufficient reason.

In the case of freedom, however, we have to grasp that it is by its very nature a capacity for starting a new chain of causality which, as a capacity rooted essentially in man's personal nature, presupposes God for its existence and actuation, but does not thereby make of our free decision something necessitated by God. The capacity freely to engender an act of willing and to start a new chain of causality is created by God and is actuated independently of Him. The spiritual center of the person, however, is really the free cause of a concrete act of willing.[8]

The freedom of the person undoubtedly belongs among those data which have the character of natural mysteries of being and which call for a special wondering about them. It certainly differs in its intelligibility from causality. The fact that every contingent being needs a cause for its existence is, in another way, "transparent" to our reason; it is something which we can more fully penetrate than we can the fact that man is able with his will to start a new chain of causality.

But this does not mean that freedom of will is therefore less certain. It is evidently given as an essential feature of the person, with the difference only that the person is that kind of being

[7] "It is not of the essence of liberty that what is free should be its own first cause, any more than that a thing's cause has to be its first cause." St. Thomas, *Summa Theologica*, 1a, lxxxiii, 1, ad 3.

[8] In this context it is not possible to dwell at length on this fundamental metaphysical problem. In a later work, it will be analyzed in detail.

which, because of its higher rank, possesses a richness and mysterious depth that, in spite of its objective, luminous intelligibility, does not have for our minds the kind of transparent intelligibility which a mathematical truth possesses.

In distinguishing the two perfections of will which we can also term the two dimensions of freedom, we mentioned those activities which are under the immediate command of the will. We still have to examine briefly the nature of these activities as well as their relation to our freedom.

We saw before that all cognitive acts and all responses, theoretical as well as affective, include a meaningful conscious relation of the person to an object, whereas mere states, for example, lack this intentional character. Furthermore, all responses are motivated, whereas many states are merely *caused*. Activities such as eating, walking, running, or any voluntary movement of our limbs form from this point of view a separate class. They differ on the one hand from the responses, inasmuch as they include no meaningful, conscious relation to an object. They are thus not intentional in the strict sense. But they differ also from mere states, inasmuch as they are guided by a will, which itself has a clear intentional character, and are pervaded by a certain finality. They are certainly caused and not motivated; but they are caused by our will, they are voluntarily actualized. When we say that those activities are free or that they are in our power, we mean that they are accessible to our free will. They themselves are caused by our will, but since our will can command them and since they depend upon our will, which itself is free, they partake of its freedom. Inasmuch as they happen not *in* us or *on* us, but rather *through* us they belong to the zone of our free power; we consider them free and hence hold everyone responsible for them. In fine, they are free insofar as they are accessible to the command of our free will. The freedom of these activities, however, clearly differs from the freedom of willing itself. Whereas the person can be impeded in the freedom displayed in the command of activities by the will (e.g., by sickness such as paralysis, or by exterior compulsion), the first dimension of freedom can never be frustrated as long as the person is in possession of his reason. No force whatsoever can ever compel man to speak a "yes" or a "no" with his will.[9] Calderón admirably expresses this peerless privilege of man: "Though my fancy it will gain, it will never my consent. . . . Then the will no more were free if a force could it compel." [10]

Thus the freedom of willing has its own unique character, which is not shared by the freedom of these activities insofar as willing is not so much something which we command as something which we engender. Being so much nearer to the free spiritual center of the person, it is an actualization of this center itself; it is a position of the very core of ourselves and not something which is somehow distant from ourselves and which we dominate and command in the strict sense of this term. We experience the different activities in the zone of our power, as submitted to us, as below ourselves, whereas willing presents itself as an immediate actualization of ourselves.

[9] "As regards the commanded acts of the will, then, the will can suffer violence, insofar as violence can prevent the exterior members from executing the will's command. But as to the will's own proper act, violence cannot be done to the will." St. Thomas, *Summa Theologica*, 1a–2ae, vi, 4. (A. C. Pegis, *op. cit.*, Vol. II, p. 231.)

[10] *El Magico Prodigioso*, Act III, Scene 6.

CHAPTER 22

FREEDOM AND ANIMAL VOLUNTARINESS

BEFORE WE proceed in the analysis of the freedom of the human person, we have to distinguish free will from the mere spontaneity which we find likewise in the animal sphere. Physiology distinguishes between voluntary and involuntary muscles. Certain muscles are inaccessible to any voluntary influence, and they are activated by the autonomic or visceral nervous system. Others, on the contrary, are accessible to a voluntary innervation.

Now the voluntariness here in question is patently not identical with freedom. This is the spontaneity which distinguishes animals from plants, and which clearly expresses itself in the capacity of spontaneous movement; it is distinct not only from those beings moved by extraneous causes such as we indeed find in the mechanical sphere, but also from those moved by the teleological process of growth and other vegetative physiological functions. As mysterious as this animal spontaneity is, as much as it differs from the autonomic vegetative processes which we find in plants, animals, and even in men, it is yet separated from the freedom of the human person by a great abyss.

In the first place this voluntariness does not in the strict sense start a new chain of causality. It is itself necessitated by certain internal and external stimuli; although it represents a quite special type of causality which differs very much from any mechanical causality, it nevertheless remains in the general frame of causality. A special role is entrusted to this spontaneous capacity in the entire teleological process, in which autonomic and voluntary activities cooperate, so that an end necessary to the life of an animal organism may be attained. In the animal sphere life displays itself in the two streams of voluntary and involuntary processes; the two streams sometimes develop in a parallel direction and sometimes converge in a cooperative effort.

Freedom of will, on the contrary, is precisely characterized by the fact that the will can never be considered a link in a causal chain. It is, as we saw before, never strictly determined by any causes in or outside of the person. It is engendered by the free, conscious center of the person.

Secondly, willing, because it is a conscious response, presupposes the knowledge of a state of facts which although as yet unrealized is realizable, and in addition the understanding of the subjective or objective importance of this state of facts. Voluntary innervation does not imply such an intervention of intelligence or reason. Certainly animal voluntariness may also be based on the perception of an object. If a lion sees an antelope and jumps at it in order to devour it, the sight of this animal causes the activity of the lion. The fact that a sense perception is presupposed for the displaying of an animal voluntariness in the lion's attack in no way diminishes the decisive difference between animal voluntariness and freedom, or between the spontaneity of an animal's acting and freedom of will. Perception cannot be interpreted here as a knowledge implying reason. St. Thomas states this in distinguishing between *cognitio finis perfecta* and *imperfecta* (perfect and imperfect knowledge of the end).[1] The difference between an intentional act of response and an evoked reaction is, if possible, still greater than the one to be found between perfect and imperfect knowledge. Moreover, meaningful, authentic motivation, which is a mark of the spirituality of an experience, does not yet guarantee freedom. Neither theoretical responses (such as conviction and doubt) nor affective value responses (such as admiration, enthusiasm, and love) are free as the will in the strict sense of the term is free, although they are typically intentional and meaningfully motivated. Hence the fact that a quasi knowledge may also interfere in the

---

[1] "Now knowledge of the end is twofold, perfect and imperfect. Perfect knowledge of the end consists in not only apprehending the thing which is the end, but also in knowing it under the aspect of end, and the relationship of the means to that end." St. Thomas, *Summa Theologica*, 1a–2ae, vi, 2.

realm of animal voluntariness in no way lessens the essential difference between animal voluntariness and freedom of will.

Thirdly, the difference between animal voluntariness and freedom of will also discloses itself in the fact that our will is able to counteract a desire; we can decide to do something not only *à contre cœur*, but to a certain extent even against some vital tendencies of our nature. Animal voluntariness can only follow the direction prescribed by instincts and natural tendencies. Though by frightening an animal we can induce it to abstain from the satisfaction of an urge, such as hunger, the voluntariness involved in those cases does not display itself in a free counteraction against the instinct, but in yielding to the stronger instinct of fright, which turns the scale on the instinct to satisfy hunger.

Man is able freely to decide to abstain from satisfying an urge; thus a man may refuse to drink, not because of another instinct which counteracts the invitation of his thirst (a powerful disgust, for example) but because of motives which his *intellect* offers him and which are completely beyond the whole realm of instincts. The will can freely choose between different possibilities whereas in animal voluntariness no such choice is to be found.[2]

Someone could object: Animal voluntariness too seems to imply free choice, because, in contradistinction to mechanical processes, the reactions of animals cannot be forecast. Yet the inaccuracy of precalculations concerning such reactions in no way suffices to guarantee the presence of freedom of choice. Any result of a process of causality in the organic world as such is already so complex that it cannot be foreseen with the same certainty as the result of mere mechanical forces. The same bacilli cause a disease in one organism and yet do not affect another, although all known circumstances are the same in both cases. We explain this by saying that the "disposition" was lacking in one organism. By this, we introduce a factor which escapes strict calculation. Now the causal process at stake in the sphere of animals, so far as voluntariness is concerned, is still more mysterious and incomparably more complicated than the vegetative causal process. Therefore the fact that the reactions of an

[2] St. Thomas calls will *appetitus rationalis* or *voluntas,* and animal voluntariness *voluntarium.* Cf. *Summa Theologica,* 1a–2ae, Q. vi, art. 2. (A. C. Pegis, *op. cit.,* Vol. II, p. 229.)

animal cannot be calculated in advance does not prove the presence of free choice.

Finally there exists here no conscious assumption of a position in relation to an object. The voluntary activity has in no way the character of a response. Though it is a conscious process, insofar as we can speak of consciousness in the sphere of mere animals, and though it has a final character, in no way does it possess the character of a response.

The will displays itself in the great dialogue between person and object; this includes that luminous rational consciousness of the subject confronted with the meaning of the object and especially with its subjective or objective importance. In the animal voluntariness on the other hand no confrontation of this kind is to be found.

The difference between freedom and animal voluntariness is not difficult to grasp so long as we compare the free will in the sphere of action of the person with the voluntariness in animals. But the question next arises: How does the voluntary innervation of striated muscles differ in man from freedom? The innervation of the muscles which mediate the breathing process is voluntary but does not imply an intervention of our free will. On the other hand, there is no doubt that we can with our will command a temporary withholding of breath: when we plunge under water, for example; or when we fear that someone will notice our presence though we wish to conceal it; [3] or when we want to learn a new method of breathing and therefore command the respective muscles with our will. In these cases our intelligence obviously intervenes; the understanding of a certain situation is involved; our will is motivated by the importance of an object. Here it is clearly the will which commands our breathing. The difference is obvious between the normal cases of breathing and such cases in which our free will intervenes. Hence we must say that not only in mere animals do we find this voluntariness which must be clearly distinguished from free will, but also in man. But a decisive difference from animals

[3] The fact that our will can influence a bodily process is, however, not a mark distinguishing animal voluntariness from autonomic processes. Psychosomatic medicine tells us that conscious processes and even the will may influence autonomic processes such as the circulation of the blood and others.

remains even in those cases where the will does not actually intervene, since man in possessing a free will could also command this innervation by his free will, whereas the animal cannot do so since it does not possess free will.

With respect to the difference between mere animal voluntariness and freedom of will in the realm of the human person, we must distinguish the following main cases. There is first of all the case in which activities are involved which can be commanded exclusively by the will, which by their very nature involve an intervention of intelligence and a decision of will based on the understanding of an object's importance. Such are, for instance, all actions in the strict sense of the term; but also many other activities, like the construction of a machine, the manufacturing of a tool, the undertaking of a journey, and so on.

In all these activities, a person is presupposed; no mere animal could perform them. By their very nature they cannot be initiated by mere animal voluntariness (even as it is to be found in persons), but essentially presuppose free will. Hence, the way in which they are commanded forms the most obvious antithesis to mere voluntariness.

Secondly, there are those cases in which activities are at stake (for instance the appeasement of certain urges) which can be initiated by mere animal voluntariness and do not presuppose the intervention of our intelligence and of our will. In such cases the only thing needed is a voluntary yielding to the urge, or cooperation with our animal voluntariness. But it is also true that our will is able to command this cooperation and likewise to refuse it. The will in man even has the task of controlling and regulating the appeasement of these urges. Normally man controls them with his will and does not permit himself to be ruled simply by animal voluntariness. Education aims expressly at such control, which in small children is not yet installed in its function.

Activities ruled by habit and accomplished subconsciously form a third case. For instance, we return a book to its place on the shelf without intending to do so with our will and without even having a clear consciousness that we are doing so. We are distracted and being always accustomed to do so we accomplish an activity which we could not originally do without the intervention of our intelligence and our will, but which we now do out of habit and mere routine. Afterward we do not know whether we did it or not. Here things which, as such, originally require an intervention of our intelligence and will, and which can be commanded only by our will and never by mere voluntariness sink, as a result of long habit, into the sphere of those activities which can be directed by mere animal voluntariness. Indeed, for many things it is better and even necessary to sink into the sphere of mere animal voluntariness in order to make room for the higher activities of the soul.[4] This third type has in common with the second that in both cases the activities in question can be initiated either by mere voluntariness or by the will. But whereas in the former case the activities are originally guided by mere voluntariness and later on (as a result of education) are controlled by the will, in the latter case these activities must at the beginning be directed by the will and only by habit can they become accessible to mere voluntariness.

Fourthly, there is the case in which activities are at stake which are normally regulated by mere animal voluntariness, and even as a result of the teleology of life function without an intervention of our intelligence and will. Such is true of breathing. It is normal that we should activate our breathing without an intervention of our will. As a rule we do it instinctively. The urge of breathing itself is beyond any kind of voluntariness, but the movement of our muscles, which are necessary in order to satisfy this urge, implies voluntariness. Such is true also of much more complicated activities which first must be learned but which, when once known, should function without any intervention of our will; thus after a child has learned how to walk, he does so "instinctively" and by routine for the rest of his life. The same is true of many other activities. But even here our will can intervene in extraordinary cases, as, for instance, in the above-mentioned case of holding our breath for a certain period.

After having stated these four main types of cases concerning the role of the will and the role of mere animal voluntariness in man, the difference between them becomes still more apparent.

---

[4] Actions in the strict sense of the term, however, can never be done purely out of routine habit. By their very nature, they can never sink into the sphere of instinctive accomplishments.

Our will alone is free. Animal voluntariness, on the contrary (as mysterious as it is in many respects and as different as it is from many other types of causality), is not a real "beginning from the beginning."

In trying to explore the nature of human freedom, we thus have to oppose it not only to being determined by an extraneous cause (as when we are pushed by someone in a crowd with the result that we unwillingly knock down another person), but also to any mere animal voluntariness which, because of its spontaneity, has sometimes not been sharply distinguished from free will.[5]

[5] Aristotle, *Nicomachean Ethics*, Bk. III, 1111a–1111b.

CHAPTER 23

THE RANGE OF THE FIRST DIMENSION
OF FREEDOM

ARISTOTLE SAYS that our freedom of choice is restricted to means and does not concern the end, since the end of the will necessarily is happiness.[1] Yet the inaccuracy of this statement becomes manifest so soon as we recall the case of a choice between something merely subjectively satisfying (such as playing a game of bridge) and something endowed with a value (such as succoring a sick friend). This choice is certainly not one between means nor is our decision based on the question: Which of the two possibilities will procure the greater happiness for us? This situation differs completely from the one in which we have to decide whether to accept a position which flatters our ambition (although it is financially disadvantageous) or another position which is better paid but is less appealing to our pride. In this instance of choice, we are indeed concerned with the question of which of the two possibilities procures more happiness for us; whereas in the former choice the question of a greater or lesser happiness does not turn the scale, since the game of bridge attracts us precisely from the point of view of self-centered happiness, but succoring the sick friend appeals to our conscience as something important for its own sake.

Thus it seems pertinent and necessary to reexamine whether our free choice is really restricted to means. Is the end really always the same? Is the nature of the end an inalterable datum?

No, it is not true that in every case our will aims at our own

[1] *Ibid.*, Bk. III, 1113b.

happiness [2] as the end, and that everything else is merely considered as a means to this end. In deciding to submit to the call of a moral obligation we are concerned not with our happiness but with the moral value to which we conform for its own sake. In striving for justice we are not necessarily motivated by the happiness which may result for us in doing so; rather we can seek justice for its own sake. What is more, it is precisely in this case that our striving for justice has a *full* moral significance. This does not mean that man as such does not necessarily seek happiness. But certainly in the case we have cited, happiness is *not* the end and the bringing about of justice a mere *means* for it. The relation between them is in no way a final one. The end is really justice, justice for its own sake. The indistinct awareness that the interest in justice is also the path leading us to true happiness, or the perhaps more distinct awareness that an unjust action is also the path leading to true unhappiness, has the character of an accompanying phenomenon; it is not the decisive motive of our will. In conforming to the call of justice for its own sake (even if it involves us in many troubles and sufferings), we merely have the vague awareness that we nevertheless move in a direction which will be conducive to true happiness. The fact that true happiness cannot function here as an end and justice only as a means to it will become obvious later on when we shall see that in order to understand true happiness, we must precisely be able to interest ourselves in a good endowed with a value *for its own sake.*

Moreover, the choice which really matters from a moral point of view is essentially concerned with the question whether we conform to the merely subjectively satisfying or to morally

---

[2] In truth, the concept of happiness is not a univocal one, as we shall see later on, but an analogous one. We saw before (Chapter 3) that we use the term for completely different things, having in common only their character of being something positive. The decisive moment from the moral point of view precisely concerns the question of which kind of happiness is at stake, a difference which is not only important for the moral value of our will, but which also touches the role it can play in the process of motivation.

St. Augustine was clearly aware of this when he said: "For they who are happy . . . are not therefore happy because they willed to live happily, for that the wicked also willed; but they are happy because they willed to live rightly, which the wicked did not will." *De Libero Arbitrio*, Bk. I. (F. E. Tourscher, *op. cit.,* p. 77.)

relevant values. It is the old distinction between *commodum* and *justum*,[3] between the expedient and the just; or the distinction of St. Augustine between a life according to the flesh (in the Biblical sense of the term) and a life according to God.[4] This decision between the subjectively satisfying and the morally relevant value, which we must make in innumerable situations of life, is free.

In concrete situations it is within our power whether we conform to the appeal of the merely subjectively satisfying, or whether we turn instead to the implacable but never necessitating challenge of the morally relevant values. And the deepest moral difference between men precisely consists in this: that either their superactual will is directed toward the important-in-itself and makes of the important-in-itself the general denominator of all their concrete decisions, or their superactual will is directed toward the merely subjectively satisfying and makes the agreeable the general denominator of all their decisions.

The freedom of man thus extends itself to the decision, whether we follow the appeal of the merely subjectively satisfying or the call of the morally relevant values; whether we choose, in general as well as in a concrete situation, the *justum* or the *commodum* as the measure for our willing or acting. This applies to ends as well as to means. To save someone from a fatal danger is certainly an end for our will and in no way a means, or at least the life of the other person is an end and not a means. When, on the contrary, we direct our will to the purchase of a medicine in order to help an ill person, the medicine functions as a pure means. In deciding to obtain this medicine, we are motivated by the value which the medicine possesses as a means to restore the health of the sick person; and hence this person's health is the end in this case.

Aristotle's tendency to press everything into the scheme of means and ends partly accounts for his assertion that free choice is restricted to means. In fact, the principle of finality is but one among many others that play a prominent role in the cosmos.

---

[3] St. Anselm, *De Concordia*, Bk. III, chap. 11–13, *Patrologia Latina*, Vol. 158, c.534 A; and Bk. III, 13, c.540 A.
[4] *De Civitate Dei*, XIV, 3.

For example, the relation between morally relevant values in general and their concrete actualization in a real good is not a relation of finality, but a completely different one. Living for God, willing to conform to Him in every single situation, doing what is pleasing to Him: this direction of life (expressed in Augustinian terms) does not at all imply that we consider a concrete moral value in a concrete situation to be related to God as a means to an end. On the contrary, every morally relevant value, in its relation to God (the Source of all goodness, the Infinite Goodness Itself), may be compared to a ray of the sun in its relation to the sun itself; it is a special reflection of God's infinite goodness. In willing what is good by its very nature (i.e., justice, purity, humility, veracity, and charity) we find in these values a reflection of the infinite justice, purity, and charity of God. In responding to their value, we do not consider them as means for attaining God. Rather, we conform to them for their own sake and thereby conform ultimately to God Himself, the Source of these values. This becomes more patent when we consider the sphere of action, for example, when our will aims at the rescue of our neighbor's life, or at his moral integrity, or at his conversion. In all these cases we do not consider these ends as means for God, but we find Christ in our neighbor; we are really interested in him for his own sake. The connection with the absolute good is here not one of means and end. These things are precious in God's sight because of their authentic morally relevant value, and these values reflect God in a specific way. The connection of these values with God, which clearly differs from finality (as we saw time and again), can also be expressed in saying that in being interested in these goods, we implicitly follow God.

Furthermore, the great principle which pervades the moral sphere of abandonment to God and to the authentic value of a good for its own sake (embodied in the words of our Lord: "He that shall lose his life . . . shall save it") cannot be interpreted in the light of finality. Beatitude is a gift bestowed on us when we abandon ourselves to God for His own sake. The words of Christ: "Seek ye first the kingdom of God and his justice, and all these things shall be added unto you" clearly point to this relation. It would be a complete misinterpretation to make of the "seek ye the kingdom of God" a means for the attainment of all the rest.

Again, Aristotle fails to distinguish clearly the important-in-itself from the merely subjectively satisfying. Though he hints at this difference several times in speaking of honorable or noble things, opposing them to the merely pleasurable ones, and in stressing that the good man not only wills the good, but also rejoices over the good,[5] this distinction remains purely implicit; it never finds its place in his conclusions, especially when he discusses the character of man's ultimate end. Consequently he never explicitly distinguishes between self-centered happiness and authentic happiness which only goods having an authentic value can bestow on us. In failing to see that there are essentially different types of positive importance, Aristotle thus treats the positively important or the *bonum* (as well as happiness) as a univocal concept.

We saw before that our positive will necessarily presupposes an object endowed with a positive importance. Neither something neutral nor something negatively important as such could ever motivate our will. We can never will something exclusively because of its being an evil or because of its negative importance. In failing to see that the term *bonum* has essentially different meanings and in interpreting every relation here in question as one of finality, Aristotle came to the conclusion that our freedom of choice is concerned only with means and that the end, happiness (or as we would put it, the positively important), is always the same, and is given as an unalterable presupposition for any willing. But as soon as we distinguish between *bonum* in the sense of the merely subjectively satisfying, *bonum* in the sense of value, and *bonum* in the sense of the objective good for the person, we also understand that the main task of man's freedom precisely refers to the choice between the merely subjectively satisfying and the value.

This decisive free choice obviously does not refer only to means. So soon as we see that finality is not the only relation to be

[5] "Now virtuous actions are noble and done for the sake of the noble." *Nicomachean Ethics*, Bk. IV, 1120a, 23. (*The Basic Works of Aristotle*, trans. R. P. McKeon, p. 985.)

found in the realm of will, that our abandonment to a good endowed with a morally relevant value does not imply that we consider this good as a means, but rather as something sought for its own sake and linked with God (the source and sum of all goodness) but not by a final relation in the strict sense, then we must admit that our freedom extends to ends as well as to means. It embraces the ultimate decision between the value and the merely subjectively satisfying, both in general, as the norm of our life, and in particular, when in concrete situations we have to choose the invitation of the agreeable or the call of a morally relevant value. This conflict may occur between two ends (for instance, attending an amusing social affair and succoring a sick friend); it may also arise concerning the question whether a means is morally objectionable for a certain end which is, as such, either morally good or at least neutral.

To sum up, we can say that the conflict between the value and the subjectively satisfying may be found between two or more possible concrete ends, as well as between certain means and their end. In both cases it lies in our freedom to conform to the value or to the subjectively satisfying. It is pertinent to stress that the moral character of our choice of means is not related to the aptitude of the means to bring about an end. This is rather the concern of man's intelligence. Our decisive choice from a moral point of view, on the contrary, refers to the question whether a means is morally objectionable or not, whether it is endowed with a morally relevant disvalue, whether it is neutral from the point of view of the morally relevant values, or whether it is even endowed with a positive morally relevant value.

To substantiate his own thesis, Aristotle quotes the example of a doctor for whom the end, viz., the health of the patient, is beyond being an object of choice, and who consequently has his choice limited to the means which will enable him to attain this end.[6] But, evidently, this example does not express the typical situation concerning the moral choice of our will. The difference between a good doctor and a poor one is not primarily a moral matter. The aptitude of the good one to find the efficient

6 "We deliberate not about ends but about means. For a doctor does not deliberate whether he shall heal. . . . They assume the end and consider how and by what means it is to be attained . . ." *Ibid.*, Bk. III, 1112b, 13ff.

means to heal his patient depends primarily upon his intelligence, his intellectual medical formation, and only secondarily upon his moral attitude: his spirit of responsibility, his readiness to make sacrifices, and so on. In the realm of our professional activity the end is more or less undisputed, and the stress lies on the means we use in order to attain this end. But as soon as we examine the doctor from the moral point of view we have to go beyond the realm of mere means. First, we must consider whether the doctor really seeks to restore the patient's health for its own sake, or whether his chief intention is to make money, so that he views the patient's cure more or less exclusively as a means of making money. This question precisely concerns the end chosen and not mere means conducive to this end.

Secondly, we must ascertain whether a doctor has a real spirit of responsibility and uses medical means with the necessary caution—always conscious of the high good which has been entrusted to him in his patient, always guided in his acting by a value-response attitude.

Finally we must ask to what extent, if any, he is disposed to make personal sacrifices for his patient's cure, whether he will yield to any immoral temptations, such as euthanasia or even a brutal killing of the patient—situations in which, unfortunately, many doctors have been placed in our time. In these cases the patient's life and health become not only the means for another end (e.g., making money), but the preservation or protection of the patient's health is replaced by its destruction. In other words, the normally pre-given end has been contradicted.

Thus we see that even in the example taken from professional life the thesis that our free choice is concerned only with means and not with ends no longer applies so soon as we examine it from the moral point of view, and not merely from the point of view of the immanent professional perfection. *A fortiori,* this thesis does not apply to the whole of our moral life, where the great task for man's freedom and the great moral drama of man's life consist precisely in whether he conforms to morally relevant values and their call, or whether he conforms to the merely subjectively satisfying.

This last statement in no way contradicts the fact that in the soul of every man lives a "vague" desire for happiness. Nobody will consciously seek unhappiness as an ultimate end nor can he do so. More than that: man is objectively ordered toward happiness; it belongs to the very nature and meaning of man as a person that he should be happy. Whereas the objective destination for happiness univocally refers to *true* happiness, happiness as the object of our longing is so vague that the statement that every man seeks happiness gives us no sort of information as to the kind of happiness which is sought. The decisive question from the moral point of view is precisely whether a man primarily desires authentic happiness or self-centered happiness. Thus, although it is true that "every man by nature seeks happiness," it is erroneous to assume that every man subjectively desires the same happiness.

Again, self-centered happiness alone can be directly intended. Authentic happiness, on the contrary, by its very nature cannot be the end of our actions, but it is definitely a gift bestowed on us when we abandon ourselves to a good endowed with a genuine value. Ultimate authentic happiness can only be the object of a general longing, but not the primary motive of our actions and desires. It presupposes precisely that we abandon ourselves to a good possessing a genuine value *for its own sake*. Furthermore, it is impossible to view all the objects of our will and of our affective responses as united with man's ultimate end by a relation of finality. We have already shown that the relation between the concrete single goods possessing an authentic value and the Absolute Good, God, has not the character of finality, but of another much deeper connection.

Thus we see that, notwithstanding the truth of the statement that every man desires happiness, it would be erroneous to pretend that our freedom does not refer to the choice of ends, but only to means. Furthermore, we must state that the very essence of freedom is not exclusively and even not primarily to be found in the capacity of free choice. For in those cases too which offer no multiplicity of goods among which my will could choose, the possibility of free volition remains unaltered. It need not always be that in a concrete situation two or more different goods force me to choose among them. Neither an alternative between different goods endowed with a value, nor an alternative between different objective goods for me, nor an alternative between different subjectively satisfying goods needs to be implied in every concrete situation. Indeed, even a choice between the different categories of importance (i.e., value, objective good for the person, agreeable) need not always be present. At least subjectively this alternative is often absent, even though we might say that objectively every decision implies the rejection of innumerable possibilities. But this would be just as artificial as if we were to claim that in every positive judgment we include innumerable negative judgments, because objectively all these innumerable judgments are potentially included.

I feel thirsty and decide to drink water without thinking either of the possibility of drinking something else or of the possibility of eating instead. I see someone whose life is in danger and freely decide to help him, without considering all the other things which I could have done instead.

But someone could object: In all these cases the alternative between doing something and abstaining from doing it always remains present. Even if subjectively there are no different goods to choose from, the choice between acting and not acting is still given. This indicates that even here, though less apparently, there are at least two goods able to motivate my will: the one which calls for action, the other for abstention. Abstention also must be motivated by a good, either a subjectively satisfying good or an objective good for the person or a good endowed with a value.

In reply we must state that even this kind of choice need not always be present. The general intention of the will may be directed so univocally to the world of morally relevant values that as soon as a morally relevant value is at stake the person freely conforms to this good, without considering in any way the possibility of not doing so. The person does not choose, as in other cases, between different possibilities. For there is no struggle in his soul; there is not even the slightest inclination to abstain from acting in this way and no consideration whatsoever of failing to act. Although objectively there exist always at least two possibilities (that of conforming with our will to the good and that of not conforming), a real choice does not take place in these cases. Nevertheless, the "yes" of the will is not less free than in the case where a choice is to be made.

Our analysis has clearly shown that the first dimension of freedom is not restricted to means, but extends equally to ends. We have seen that the morally decisive choice is concerned with the question of whether we let ourselves be motivated by the important-in-itself or by the merely subjectively satisfying. Now we have to turn to an analysis of the range of the second dimension of freedom. We have to ask: How far does man's free influence reach? Which things can be commanded or at least influenced by our free will and which things are completely withdrawn from our free influence? This will be the topic of our next chapter.

CHAPTER 24

DIRECT AND INDIRECT FREEDOM

INQUIRY INTO the range of responsibility is one of the classical problems of ethics. It is closely connected with the problem concerning the extension of man's freedom because, as we stressed several times, without freedom there is no responsibility.

Yet it does not seem possible to restrict responsibility to our will and that which can be commanded by our will. It is certainly not in our direct power to possess a virtue. We cannot give meekness and justice to ourselves with a free decision of our will, as we can command an action of almsgiving. But while no one would deem us responsible for the weather or for an earthquake, he would nevertheless deem us responsible for not attaining a virtue and even for not responding with joy when it is called for by the value of the object.

In some way we are responsible for such failings, even though we can neither freely engender a virtue or an affective response as we can engender willing itself, nor command them by our free will as we can our actions; that is to say, though they are not directly in the range of our power. But if there are things for which we are responsible and which are not in the range of our direct free influence, these things are nevertheless not completely beyond our freedom. We can indirectly do something for their existence or non-existence. From the viewpoint of our responsibility, the fundamental classification which imposes itself is this: on the one hand, there are those things for which we are somehow responsible, and which embrace zones of both our direct and our indirect influence; on the other hand, there are all those things for which we are in no way responsible, which are

312

beyond any possible influence on our part. If we read the *Confessions* of St. Augustine, the range of all those things for which we are in one or another way responsible presents itself in all its amplitude and depth. The objects of St. Augustine's contrition are not restricted to those things which are in the zone of man's direct power, but also extend to all those belonging to the zone of man's indirect influence. It would be erroneous, however, to consider that the decisive mark distinguishing the direct and indirect zone of our free influence is simply the degree to which a thing is within our power.

In the zone of our direct influence many important distinctions have yet to be made concerning the completeness of the role which is granted to our influence in bringing into existence this or that state of affairs. It is impossible to analyze all these differences in this work: we have again to refer to a later work in which these things will be treated. But it may suffice for our purpose here just to mention them. First, there exist differences in the nature of commanding, from the immediate innervating of the movements of our limbs through the will, to the achievement through a long normal chain of causality started by our activity.

Secondly, we must distinguish whether our power of free intervention refers to a positive or a mere negative influence. There are things which we can freely bring into existence but which we are not equally free to destroy. The bond of obligation to another person can be brought into existence, for example, by promising something to him. It is in our freedom whether we promise it or not. But once this bond is real, we no longer have the power to dissolve it.

Again with regard to other things, we are able to destroy them, but it is not in our power to restore the *status ante quo,* for example if we kill someone. Finally, there are things over which our power extends both in bringing them into existence and in restoring the *status ante quo,* for instance, in putting on a light and in extinguishing it.

All these and many other differences concerning the nature and range of our direct influence must be distinguished from the fundamental difference between direct and indirect freedom. This difference between the direct and indirect zone of man's free influence goes in another direction. It refers to whether or not the coming into existence or the destruction of something is in one way or another within the realm of our power. Characterizing this difference is the way in which we aim at the coming into existence or the disappearance of an object. In the case in which it lies in the direct zone of influence, we realize that we ourselves can at least bring it into existence either through a long causal chain, or else partially, through cooperating with other factors. We thus make it a goal not only of our volitional response but also of the command by our will.

In the case in which an object lies in the zone of our indirect influence, we realize from the very beginning either that we can only prepare the path for its coming into existence or else that we are in a situation where we could say: I must at least do everything which is in my power toward its realization. We then hope that in one way or another our contribution may be used by God's providence as an element for bringing the desired end actually into existence. This zone of our indirect influence includes our own affective responses as well as our virtues and even the responses and virtues of other persons. It reaches from our sanctification to the coming of the Kingdom of God on earth.

But our indirect influence refers especially to those things which by their value or disvalue call for a zealous interest in their existence or their destruction, but which are withdrawn from our command, and whose realization cannot therefore become our aim, in the strict sense. Nevertheless we can do our share. There is a large scale as to the nature of this share. It may consist either in a removal of obstacles (e.g., this is the purpose of ascetic practices) or in creating favorable circumstances. Insofar as our own perfection is at stake it may consist in exposing ourselves to the right and salutary influence of the irradiation of good examples. It may also consist in a word which might, if spoken at the right moment, bear fruit in the souls of others; or in many cases it may consist only in the prayers or sacrifices which we can offer to God for the coming into existence of a certain good.

Our share is free in the sense of being in the direct zone of our power; it is something which we can freely command. But the end to which this free intervention aspires is not accessible to our direct power. There are many degrees, as we have seen, concerning the extent of our share, and the degree of our responsibility will be proportionate to this extent. Yet if we have not exhausted all possibilities in our direct power, we cannot consider ourselves as having no responsibility whatsoever. On the other hand, if we have done our share, we are entirely free of responsibility.

By the realm of our indirect freedom, we shall signify the sphere of all those activities which aim at an end for whose existence we can do something, although its realization lies beyond our *direct* power. It can easily be grasped that this indirect role of our freedom is a decisive factor in ethics, and that our responsibility embraces more than simply the direct zone of our power. At the end of this section, we shall come back to man's indirect free influence and its paramount purport for morality. Prior to that, we have to deal with a third type of freedom which is even more decisive than our indirect influence, and is in certain cases presupposed for the displaying of this indirect influence.

CHAPTER 25

COOPERATIVE FREEDOM

IN THE preceding pages, we have been concerned with the role of our freedom in bringing something into existence, in destroying it, or else in hindering its coming into existence. All the different distinctions had their bearing on this direction of our freedom. We distinguished between a free engendering of our will on the one hand and the commanding of our activities on the other; between the immediate innervation of our limbs and the influence exercised through a normal causal chain; between positive and negative influence; between direct and indirect influence.

There also exists a fundamentally different way in which man's freedom displays itself: the free attitude toward experiences already existing in our soul. We have the freedom of taking a position toward experiences which have come into existence without our free intervention, and which also cannot be dissipated by our free influence. The way in which we endure bodily pains which are imposed on us is an example of cooperative freedom. But we want to restrict ourselves here to two main cases in which this cooperative freedom acquires its most typical form and its greatest moral significance: the realm of being affected and especially the realm of affective responses. As we have seen, being affected as well as affective responses arise spontaneously. They cannot be freely engendered as the will can, nor commanded by the will as actions can. Yet we can take a position toward them which greatly modifies the character of the experience, and which can also be of great moral significance in itself. Let us first consider the cooperative role of man's free-

dom with respect to being affected. We can abandon ourselves
to this experience, we can open our soul in its very depth, we
can expose our soul to the action of the value; or we can close
ourselves, we can abstain from accepting it freely, from letting
ourselves be pervaded by it: we can counteract it.

We can freely engender several different attitudes toward our
being affected. Above all, with our free center we can say "yes"
or "no" to our being affected. Furthermore there is in us the
capacity of consciously "drinking" into our soul, as it were, the
contents of the object. We can expose our soul to it; we can
freely surrender to it; we can let ourselves be permeated by it.
These free attitudes deeply modify the experience itself: only
in them does it become fully our own.

This new way of displaying our freedom, which concerns the
manner in which we accept something bestowed on us, is to be
found not only with respect to being affected by *values*. It also
extends to every kind of being affected, and even to every experience in our soul which is inaccessible to our influence, both
in its becoming and in its dissipation. It is thus a vast realm in
which we find this way of displaying our freedom. Not only are
we able to make use of our freedom in this direction, but we are
also morally obliged to do so. A great part of morality is concerned with this type of freedom; man is called not only to
accomplish moral actions in which something is brought into
existence through his will or is destroyed by it, but also to take
a free position toward those experiences which exist in him and
which he can neither create nor destroy by his will.

Before examining the role of cooperative freedom with respect
to affective responses, it is still pertinent to indicate the following. Apart from our free position toward a concrete experience
of being affected, there remains a vast realm for our free intervention with respect to the *fruits* which this being affected should
bring about in us. Being affected by values and especially being
affected by morally relevant values—as so many other gifts bestowed on us—implies a call addressed to our free center. It
implies the task of harvesting lasting fruits from it, of making
proper use of the gift. Certain persons, especially those morally
unconscious and lacking continuity, remain unchanged even
though they often receive the gift of being deeply affected. They

are deeply moved by the charity of another person, but so soon as their normal life continues its course, no trace of this experience can be found in their attitude. It washes away without changing them, like water from a body smeared with oil. Yet there are others who start a new life after such an experience. Making the right use of such an experience is certainly not unrelated to the way in which we accept it. But the right use of an experience is still distinct from the manner of its acceptance. The former is concerned with what happens after the experience of being affected has vanished, whereas the way of accepting this experience concerns our attitude at the moment of being affected. Above all, the former surpasses the frame of our cooperative freedom and includes our conforming to the experience by our actions and voluntary attitudes; whereas the way of accepting the experience is an exclusive manifestation of our cooperative freedom.

One of the great areas of our inner growth and especially of our sanctification centers around the right use of the gifts bestowed on us; we have dealt with this in another work.[1] There is a threefold role of our free influence in this area. First, there is the indirect influence in preparing the ground in our soul for being affected by values. Secondly, there is the free cooperation with this experience when it is granted to us. Thirdly, there is the role of our freedom in harvesting fruits of this experience. Thus apart from the cooperative acceptance of our being affected, there still exist a prologue and an epilogue to man's freedom.

The Spheres of Affective Responses

We saw before that the affective responses such as joy, sorrow, enthusiasm, indignation, love, and hatred cannot be freely engendered like willing, nor innervated like bodily activities. They are definitely not in the zone of our direct, immediate power.

We must realize that not only is it impossible to command an affective response in the same way as we command certain bodily and mental activities, but beyond that such a possibility would be in contradiction to the essential nature and rank of affective responses. For in order to respond with joy or sorrow, we must have before us an object endowed with a positive or

[1] *Transformation in Christ.*

negative importance; and it is this object which must enkindle our response.

The idea of being able to command affective responses by our will, to innervate them as we innervate a movement of our limbs, would by implication deprive them of their meaningful relation to the importance of the object. It would deprive them of their essential perfection, which is that of a response motivated by the importance of the object, and in addition place them on the level of certain activities without even giving them the specific (although much lower) perfection which these activities possess. No one who realizes the nature and meaning of joy, love, or veneration could even desire that his affective responses should be accessible to the command of his will. For he can see that this would be incompatible with the dignity of these responses.

We mentioned before the cases wherein we face an object endowed with a high value and are aware that it deserves a value-responding joy or sorrow, love or veneration, but nevertheless find ourselves unable to give the adequate response; we then experience as a trial our incapacity to freely engender these responses. What is really our wish in those moments is to be able simply to *engender* the responses freely; never could we seriously wish to be able to *command* them by our will. We may regret that insofar as the affective responses are concerned we do not possess the first dimension of freedom, or that they are not free in the same sense as is willing itself. But never—so long as we understand the nature of affective responses—could we regret that they cannot be commanded in the same way as any action or movement of our limbs or an act of attention.

Here we touch a deep problem closely connected with man's creaturehood. The things which can be commanded by our will, which we can bring into existence, are limited in their ontological rank. The higher something is, the more it possesses the character of a gift, which we cannot simply give to ourselves. We may by scientific discoveries widen the range of our influence in an unheard-of manner. We may accomplish things in the realm of physical and physiological processes which would have been considered as magic in former times. This extention of our influence, this enlargement of the field of things which we can dominate by our free command, is indeed something great.

But the idea of ever being able to command an affective response is nonsensical, and such a possibility is anything but desirable. These things are not only *de facto* beyond our command, but by their very nature exclude such a way of coming into existence. Their intrinsic depth and nobility surpass the sphere for which a command by our will is adequate.

It would thus be considered only as a privilege if we were actually able to engender an affective response in the same way as we are able to engender an act of willing, i.e., freely, but motivated by the object and in strict correspondence with its value.

But this precisely is not granted to man, at least in his condition as a wayfarer. In comparing the volitional and the affective responses, we can easily grasp the superiority which the former possess over the latter: freedom. But we can also see that affective responses possess a plenitude in which willing is deficient. In affective responses the *heart* and the plenitude of a human personality are actualized. It is not granted to man to possess this affective plenitude and freedom in one and the same act. He is free in his volitional responses, which lack the affective plenitude. In affective responses he is able to give himself with his heart, with the plenitude of his personality, but without being capable of engendering them freely as he can in the case of volitional responses.

Can it then be inferred that affective responses are completely withdrawn from the domain proper to man's freedom? No. When joy arises in our soul (although its becoming is a gift and not something which we can freely engender), our free spiritual center has nonetheless a decisive function to fulfill, namely, the free sanction or disavowal of this joy or this love. We can freely identify ourselves with our joy, or we can emancipate ourselves from it. Here we touch upon the deepest point of man's freedom, i.e., the ultimate "yes" or "no" which our free spiritual center can utter. This freedom is not actualized in morally unconscious people.

We saw in a preceding chapter the abyss that separates morally conscious and morally unconscious men.[2] Now we come

[2] The morally unconscious man is patently not identical with the morally evil man. We shall deal with the morally evil man on page 328.

to a new fundamental mark of the morally conscious man. It consists in making use of the very core of human freedom: the capacity of sanctioning and of disavowing our own spontaneous attitudes.

Someone feels joy because another person recovers from an illness. This man is by nature goodhearted, and thus responds with joy to this recovery. But his free spiritual center still remains asleep. Unaware of the necessity and possibility of a free position toward the object, he lives in an undisputed solidarity with his responses, which are consequently deprived of the *signum* of freedom. He takes this position of joy because his nature invites him to do so, but not because the object deserves it and calls for it. Thus if he should happen to dislike this person, he would remain indifferent or even respond with regret. His response has, therefore, an accidental character since the full understanding of the value is not given, and since his response is not fully nourished and supported by the intrinsic value but merely conditioned by an accidental coincidence between his nature and the call of values. When his response contradicts the call of values, this fact will create no uneasiness in him. He will remain in undisputed solidarity with it in this case just as in the former one which entailed a coincidence between his response and the call of values.

There exist many men who simply follow the trend of their nature, having not even discovered the possibility of taking a free conscious position toward their own affective responses. They ignore the possibility of sanctioning and disavowing their affective responses with their free spiritual center. They are tacitly in solidarity with everything which arises in them spontaneously. When angry at other persons, these unconscious men consider the role of their freedom to be limited to taming their ire in suppressing actions to which anger is conducive, and in controlling any expression of their feelings. They do not emancipate themselves from it by saying "no" to it with their spiritual center. Again, joy arises in their soul over the misfortune of an enemy and they deliver themselves completely to this joy, they yield to the tendency of their nature. With their free center they are always tacitly and implicitly wherever their nature draws them, not in a conscious, outspoken way, but rather insofar as they make no use of their capacity to sanction and disavow. A great and decisive difference between a morally conscious and a morally unconscious man consists in the fact that the one has discovered and made use of the capacity of this free sanction and disavowal, whereas the other has neglected to do so and, indeed, has often never even discovered it.

This essential mark of the morally conscious man is deeply connected with another fundamental mark possessed by him which we analyzed in a preceding chapter: the superactual general will to be morally good. While the morally unconscious man makes use of his free will and dominates thereby his affective responses at best only from "without" (i.e., with respect only to these actions which are inspired by the responses, or with respect to the expression of these responses) the morally conscious man knows his capacity to sanction or to disavow affective responses from "within," with his free spiritual center.

Again we must stress that this sanction or disavowal does not refer to the coming into being or the disappearance of affective responses as such. Neither is the sanction an engendering of an affective response nor is the disavowal a dissolving of a response. The sanction presupposes the existence of an affective response; but it modifies this response from the moral point of view in a very decisive manner. Analogously, disavowal does not effect a dissolution of the response, but deeply modifies it. Let us suppose that a morally conscious man feels joy because of the misfortune of his neighbor for whom he feels a strong aversion. Being aware of the morally negative character of this joy, he disavows it with his free spiritual center. This "no" is not a condemnation of his malicious joy in the sense in which we make a judgment condemning the attitude of another person. It is, on the contrary, something which he can accomplish only toward his own affective responses. In this disavowal the person emancipates himself expressly from this affective response and counteracts it with his free spiritual center; he withdraws from it in such a way that he desubstantializes the response, "decapitates" it, so to speak. In this disavowal the free "no" affects the response from within and takes from it its character of a valid position toward the object.

Certainly disavowal of a response does not yet eradicate it.

After having been disavowed, it may remain in our soul, but not without having undergone a deep modification. Moreover in disavowing it we necessarily also aspire to its dissolution. But whereas the invalidation of the response is completely in our power (since the disavowal which effects this invalidation is an ultimate actualization of our deepest freedom), the dissolution of the response is not in the zone of our direct power. It can be influenced by our freedom merely in an indirect way. By a long process we can work toward uprooting this response, or rather toward uprooting the presuppositions of its becoming. This is the process of a moral transformation of our nature, and such transformation is the purpose of all ascetic practices. Later on we shall deal with the forementioned kind of indirect influence. At present our topic is limited to the direct role of our freedom in disavowal as such.

Just as disavowal "decapitates" our affective response, sanction endows it with a new, decisive character. Our free spiritual center expressly identifies itself with the response. This identification makes our response to be *our own* in a new sense, and in this way only does it become our full, conscious position toward the object.

So long as we respond to a value without this cooperation of our free spiritual center, our response still has the character of something accidental; it is bereft of a fully conscious conformity to the value, conformity demanded by the good. Our free spiritual center does not cooperate with the value. But this cooperation alone can fully make the response a real "concerting" with the value, and this alone renders justice to the majesty of the value, for it calls for an adequate response independently of our natural inclination to give this response or to fail to do so.

We saw in the previous chapter that a value response acquires the character of a fully valid moral response only when it implies the awareness of the moral significance of a morally relevant good, the response to this moral significance, and the super-actual will to be good. Now we have to add a new indispensable requirement: the cooperation of our free spiritual center, which in the case of affective responses consists in their sanction or disavowal.

It is essential to grasp that this sanction and, analogously, the disavowal, are not positions toward our response taken from "without." It is not a "let it be," such as we can give to the fulfillment of our instincts, and still less an affirmation, such as we can give to an attitude of another person. In sanctioning an affective response, we join it with our free spiritual center, we place ourselves in this response, forming it from "within." And here the difference shows up between the sanction and the role of our freedom with respect to being affected. Though the cooperation of our free spiritual center in the case of being affected acts likewise from "within," and is by no means a mere indorsement from "without," still, in opening our soul to being affected, this free cooperation does not become an integral element of the being affected itself in the same way as the sanction does with respect to the value response. The affective response is in itself the position which we take toward an object; thus the sanction, which is the most outspoken conscious position, can join it as its very soul, can go in the same direction as the affective response, can, in melting with it, become one single attitude.[3]

Being affected, inasmuch as it has a receptive character, is not our response to the object, but rather something which is bestowed on us, and our free cooperation is something which encounters, so to speak, the being affected; sanction and affective responses are, on the other hand, both spontaneous. Thus our free cooperation and our being affected remain two different sides of one attitude, notwithstanding their deep and organic interpenetration; whereas our sanction and our affective response interpenetrate each other in such a way that we can no longer speak of two different realities. They merge into one attitude.

Only the sanctioned response can be considered as a fully awakened response; it is the only fully conscious, *free* response. As we have seen before, affective responses have much in common with willing, and they both claim to be positions which man takes toward something; this is not in the same way the case with being affected. Through sanction, they acquire really, what they pretend to be. They become free positions of ourselves, not-

---

[3] The distinction between the free cooperation with being affected and the sanction does not imply, however, that this free cooperation is a less deep actualization of our freedom.

withstanding the fact that their affective plenitude is not something which we can give to ourselves, but which is granted to us.

Let us compare the sanctioned affective response with the unsanctioned one. The morally unconscious man identifies himself, as we said before, implicitly or tacitly with the affective response that arises spontaneously in him. He loves and hates, rejoices and sorrows, esteems and despises, because his nature inspires him to do so—but not so the man who has taken possession of his power of sanctioning and disavowing.

The disavowed response stands in unmistakable contrast with the tacitly sanctioned response, insofar as the person expressly withdraws from it, emancipates himself from it, destroys his implicit solidarity with it. The sanctioned response, however, does not differ in a like manner from the response without sanction.

Affective responses arising in our soul without the direct intervention of our freedom have, nevertheless, the character of a position we take toward an object. So long as our free spiritual center does not disavow them, the person implicitly identifies himself with them. This is not the case with mere states. When we feel a pain in our finger or a great weariness, no position toward an object is to be found, since these states are simply caused and lack any intentional relation to an object. Desire, fear, love, and hatred, on the contrary, have the character of positions toward objects; thus, so long as there is no counter-action by the spiritual center, they involve in a certain sense our whole person, and pretend at least to be our valid position toward something. Thus the affective response without any sanction is not something standing between sanction and disavowal, not something which is as far removed from sanction as from disavowal, but is definitely more opposed to the disavowed response. The person who makes no use of his power to sanction and disavow lives in an undisputed solidarity with his own affective responses. But this fact must not make us overlook the decisive difference between the tacit, undisputed solidarity and the real, positive and explicit sanction. The morally unconscious man does not even envisage any role that his freedom might play in the realm of his responses. In any action, however, he is forced to actualize his freedom. Even if he followed without hesitation the promptings of his instincts, the action would inevitably impose on him the necessity to actualize his free will, i.e., in order for him to initiate the action in question. But when the realization of something through the will is not at stake (as in the case of affective responses since they can be neither engendered nor dissolved by our free intervention), the morally unconscious man simply ignores the possibility of an intervention of his freedom. Much more is required for a man to be aware of this role of freedom than is necessary for him to be aware of the role of freedom in the sphere of actions. This brings us to a point of the greatest interest: the difference between the freedom embodied in the sanction and disavowal and the freedom embodied in willing.

Our sanction and disavowal are possible only when our approach is rooted in a *general* attitude of value response, especially in the disposition to conform to morally relevant values and their moral significance. So long as no such value is at stake, any actualization of this ultimate freedom is out of the question with respect to our affective responses.

In order to understand that the sanction is only possible toward affective attitudes having the character of a value response, and disavowal only possible toward attitudes which are endowed with a disvalue and especially with a moral disvalue, we must clearly distinguish the sanction and disavowal from several other types of outspoken solidarity or dissolidarity with affective responses in one's own person. A morally unconscious person may throw himself expressly and consciously into his affective responses in rejoicing about the misfortunes of his enemy. If he were to be blamed because of his malicious joy over his enemy's trial, he would say: "I *want* to rejoice, for I dislike that man and I am glad now that he suffers an affliction." In such a case the undisputed and tacit solidarity becomes an explicit one.

Although this outspoken solidarity certainly implies a formal actualization of freedom, it is in no way the deep ultimate stratum of man's free spiritual center which is actualized in the sanction. It is in no way an overcoming of moral unconsciousness, a breaking through to this deepest sovereign freedom which is in the sanction, but, on the contrary, it has the character of an obstinate spasm. Though the position taken in these cases is within the power of the person and no longer something arising by itself (such as affective responses themselves), it is in outspoken antithesis to the freedom proper to the sanction for it has the character of voluntary self-imprisonment. This identification, far from being a manifestation of sovereign independence from our nature, is in reality a complete yielding to the trends of our nature, a throwing ourselves into our affective responses and especially into our passions. It is one of the typical cases of actualization of our "physical" freedom which entails simultaneously the complete absence of "moral" freedom.[4]

This also applies to cases in which this explicit identification with an affective response reaches a climax; we are thinking of a case such as when the Flying Dutchman [5] expressly and freely flings himself away. Here passionate impatience receives, as it were, a pseudo-sanction, which is antithetical to every true sanction and, moreover, a caricature of it. Characteristically enough, a person does not even give up his moral unconsciousness by thus expressly and freely flinging himself away.

The antithetical character existing between this type of making one's implicit solidarity into an explicit one, on the one hand, and the sanction, on the other, manifests itself also in the fact that this obstinate identification is only possible with respect to morally negative or morally indifferent responses, but never toward morally positive attitudes; the sanction, on the contrary, is only possible toward a value response and especially toward a morally positive attitude.

The sanction is only possible as a "concerting" with the world of values, in the last analysis with God. This supreme actualization of our ontological freedom (which is always simultaneously a moral freedom) can only take place when sustained by the logos of the world of values.[6] Thus we see the decisive difference

---

[4] C. N. Cochrane points to this fact in saying of St. Augustine: "And, if he asserts a right to freedom, it is not the freedom to say what you think, and think what you like, but the freedom which consists in subjection to truth." *Op. cit.*, p. 510.

[5] The legendary figure in Wagner's opera.

[6] "This is our liberty when we are subordinate to the truth. And our God Himself it is who frees us from death, that is from the condition of sin." St. Augustine, *De Libero Arbitrio*, Bk. II. (F. E. Tourscher, *op. cit.*, p. 189.)

existing between this outspoken and explicit identification of the morally unconscious type and the true sanction.

Yet we have also to distinguish the sanction from another form of outspoken identification which is to be found in the man who can neither be called morally unconscious nor morally conscious. In certain immoral personalities (such as Cain or Iago in Shakespeare's *Othello* or Rakitin in Dostoevski's *Brothers Karamazov*) there exists a general superactual rebellion against the world of values and ultimately against God, rebellion which has the character of a conscious and free position of one's person. This general attitude does not arise by itself, but is an attitude which is immediately in man's power. Now this general will directed toward the satisfaction of pride is in a certain way antithetical to the morally unconscious type. Here we are not confronted with the absence of a general conscious position toward the world of values, as in the morally unconscious man who follows naïvely the changing aspirations and bents of his nature. Yet this type is still more remote from the morally conscious man (in the sense we have given this term).

We have stressed several times that there exists (even from a merely formal point of view) no strict analogy between morally positive and morally negative attitudes. Real moral consciousness implies both the general will to be *morally good* and moral freedom which only the value response can possess; that is to say, which presupposes that we are not complete slaves of our pride and concupiscence. But above all we have to understand that explicit, free identification with morally negative responses (for instance, with one's hatred, envy, malicious joy) also forms an outspoken antithesis to true sanction, although it differs from the accidental, implicit solidarity which an unconscious man has toward his affective responses.

This type of conscious enemy of God will not fail to take a position toward affective responses which spontaneously arise in his soul. He will explicitly identify himself with his hatred, his envy, and he will also in some way emancipate himself from noble affective responses which may actually arise in his soul, such as, for instance, compassion or friendship. This identification has not the character of an obstinate spasm; it is not flinging oneself into the stream of passion, as we found in the morally unconscious type. It is in no way a yielding to the dynamism of the affective response and has not an accidental character (as it does in the morally unconscious man). The enemy of God does not possess a tacit solidarity with his affective responses whether morally good or morally bad, but he has a free general position toward God which implies an outspoken identification with morally evil affective responses, an identification *by principle*.

But, on the other hand, the difference between the position of God's enemy and sanction or disavowal is not a lesser one than in the case of the unconscious man. The attitude of God's enemy is even to a greater degree opposed to sanction and disavowal. It has the character of a diabolical caricature of the sanction. If from a purely formal point of view the antithesis is still more manifest in the above-mentioned "free" flinging oneself away, from a qualitative point of view the contrast between the explicit identification of the enemy of God and the sanction proper to the morally conscious man is still greater. This pseudo-sanction is, first, only possible toward morally negative attitudes, and not even to morally indifferent ones, as was the case in the morally unconscious man. Secondly, it is the most radical absence of moral freedom, as here the enslavement by pride has reached an incomparably greater depth than in the unconscious man.[7]

Instead of the spasm of obstinacy of the morally unconscious man—often possessing the character of a reaction against the blame of others—we find in the enemy of God a habitual spasm, not of obstinacy, but of a much deeper and most vicious pride. As the prototype of moral enslavement it thus forms an outspoken antithesis to moral freedom which displays itself in sanction and disavowal.

We saw that true sanction and disavowal are inner gestures which are only possible as participations in the objective intrinsic rhythm of values. Only in being supported and nourished by the very logos of the values are we able to actualize this deepest "word" of our freedom. Again we find here the most radical opposition between true sanction and the explicit solidarity with evil affective responses proper to an enemy of God.

---

[7] St. Augustine stresses this moral enslavement in saying of the members of the *civitas diaboli* that they wish to dominate others, while being enslaved by their own vices. *De Civitate Dei*, XV, 4.

The general free attitude of this type is the outspoken refusal to conform to the call of values. We shall analyze the attitude of the morally unconscious type and of the enemy of God in more detail when penetrating into the roots of moral evil.[8]

After having distinguished sanction and disavowal from other forms of explicit solidarity of the person with his affective responses, we understand why sanction is only possible with respect to affective value-responses, and not with respect to responses motivated by the merely subjectively satisfying so long as these responses are morally unobjectionable. Analogously, disavowal is only possible with respect to an attitude which has a disvalue.

Yet another possible misunderstanding has to be eliminated. Someone could object: Should we not test everything which occurs in our soul and take a position toward it with our free spiritual center? It is obvious that everything which we do, i.e., every activity or action, even if in itself it is morally indifferent, has to be endorsed by our free spiritual center. Just as every doing presupposes an act of willing, it is obvious that this willing should not take place without a confrontation of those activities with the call of the values, or better, with God's will.

In order to be endorsed, every action or activity, even if it belongs to the realm of permissible or morally unobjectionable things, requires, first the ascertainment of its moral neutrality; secondly, the recognition of any positive or negative moral connotation which it receives through circumstances; then only should the decision of our will take place.

Should not something similar take place with respect to morally neutral affective responses? Should not, for instance, the joy which we feel in playing a game, or in eating a good meal, or in going to an amusing social affair also be endorsed after ascertaining their morally unobjectionable character? Thus it seems that the sanction should also be extended to morally unobjectionable responses which are not value responses.

It must be said: Such an argumentation confuses sanction with a mere endorsement from "without." We already distinguished the sanction from any mere "let it be," which endorses something in giving free rein to its development, analogously to the "let it be" granted to the satisfaction of bodily instincts

[8] Cf. Part Two, IV, "Roots of Moral Evil."

or urges. But such an endorsement of joy at winning a game of chess or a tennis match is in no way a solemn identification of our free spiritual center with this joy, is in no way a forming of this joy from "within" which grants to it a new significance.

The distinction between sanction and disavowal on the one hand, and the pseudo-sanction (as well as moral endorsements from without) on the other, has thrown into relief the specific nature of sanction and disavowal. Now we are in a position to understand why sanction is only possible toward a value response. But, above all, the unique type of actualization of freedom displaying itself in the sanction and disavowal clearly discloses itself now. In no other explicit position toward an affective response, in no other explicit identification with it, is this deepest stratum of freedom actualized. A completely different stage of being morally awake is required for an actualization of our freedom in sanction and disavowal from what is necessary in willing.

The preceding analysis, however, has also thrown a new light on another problem mentioned above: the difference between value response without sanction and a sanctioned value response.

An example of an unsanctioned affective response is, for instance, the above-discussed case where a naturally goodhearted man rejoices in the recovery of another person whom he likes, but remains indifferent or even responds with regret when he dislikes the man whose health is restored. This morally unconscious person remains solidary with his response in the former case as well as in the latter.

The fact that his solidarity with the response is unaltered, whether it is a value response or one which contradicts the call of values, reveals clearly that even his value response is not free from an accidental character. It lacks the real conscious conforming to the value which is precisely demanded by values. Thus the response (though it may be intense and thoroughly sincere) is nevertheless in some way blind. Its relation to the person's freedom is merely a potential one. In failing to actualize the cooperation of his free spiritual center (which is objectively in the power of the person), he remains undisputedly solidary with his affective response. In itself this affective response does not imply a positive actualization of freedom. It arises by itself, and one's free spiritual center remains silent. But since man could objectively actualize his free center in sanction or disavowal of his response, he is responsible for not doing so.

Not only is man in some way responsible for his affective responses because of his implicit solidarity with them, but there exists also another link between affective responses and our freedom and responsibility. Though affective responses arise spontaneously and without the intervention of our free spiritual center, we are indirectly responsible for their coming into existence. Man's general superactual free direction of will has the capacity of influencing indirectly the status of our affective responses. There exist various indirect ways of influencing our character, upon which again the nature of our responses depends. We shall deal with this indirect role of our freedom in the next chapter. Thus there exists also an indirect responsibility for affective responses, apart from the one which is rooted in the failure of making use of our freedom in sanctioning or disavowing them.

As we saw before, a completely different stage of being morally awake is presupposed in order to discover this role of our freedom in sanction and disavowal than in order to be aware of the possibility of a free intervention in cases where our will in the strict sense is in question. Affective responses of the morally unconscious man are thus connected with freedom only in a negative and potential sense.

But this loose connection suffices to render a man responsible for his affective responses, at least to a certain extent. It must be said that an affective response which contradicts the call of morally relevant values (such as, for instance, envy or joy over the misfortune of an enemy) is definitely morally evil, and we are not without responsibility for it. It goes without saying that the moral responsibility is here much less than in the case of an immoral action. But it constitutes, to say the least, a moral imperfection so long as it is not disavowed.[9] However, the affective response which coincides with the call of morally relevant values

[9] It is clear that the responsibility increases and with it the moral guilt, if the implicit tacit solidarity is replaced by an explicit one, as in the forementioned attitude which we termed a caricature of sanction. Again, the responsibility and the moral guilt become incomparably greater if an evil affective response receives the diabolical pseudo-sanction, as in the case of the enemy of God.

is not in the same way something morally positive so long as it is not sanctioned, although it is incomparably better than the one which contradicts the call of the morally relevant values.

It even renders a person lovable, but it is not the positive counterpart to the moral fault which the non-disavowed morally evil affective response represents. It is not a moral merit or perfection to the same extent as the other is a moral fault or imperfection. Not to actualize our freedom by disavowing a morally negative response suffices to make us to a certain extent responsible for its moral ugliness. In other words the undisputed solidarity with this response suffices to stain us morally, though much less so than an immoral *action*. On the other hand the undisputed solidarity with a morally *good* affective response does not suffice to endow us with a full moral value. The failure to actualize our free center by disavowing the morally negative response is enough to make us responsible for this negative response, for it is in our power to do so. The unsanctioned morally positive response, however, since it lacks the cooperation of our free spiritual center in being unsanctioned is not sufficiently connected with our freedom to constitute a morally good attitude in the full sense.[10] It shares with the morally negative attitude the imperfection of failing to actualize our free spiritual center, despite the fact that the value on the object side calls for it; hence it is incapable of granting full moral merit.[11]

A higher cooperation of freedom is required for the morally virtuous attitude than for the morally bad one in the sphere of affective responses. The decisive difference between a good affective response without sanction and the sanctioned morally good attitude now becomes clear. Its being sanctioned makes it free in a completely new sense. As we saw before, what is at stake here is not merely the difference between an undisputed implicit solidarity and an expressly conscious solidarity, but the actualization of man's deepest freedom, which is indissolubly connected with full moral consciousness.

[10] "An action is not good, simply speaking, unless it is sound by all these tests. As Dionysius says, the good is from an integral cause, while evil results from any single defect whatsoever." St. Thomas, *Summa Theologica*, 1a–2ae, xviii, 4, ad 3.

[11] It goes without saying that in speaking of "full moral merit" we in no way pretend that any attitude of man who is stained by original sin could without grace have a merit in the eyes of God.

In the sanction the person places himself on a completely different level, the objective level of the free confrontation with the call of the morally relevant values and their moral significance. On this level, which is illuminated by the logos of moral values, man is able to accomplish this ultimate, genuine confirmation with his free spiritual center. This unique actualization of his freedom endows his affective responses, though they arise by themselves, with an element of genuine freedom.

Our analysis has disclosed the great role of our freedom in the affective sphere, but it has also led us to the discovery of the deepest stratum of freedom, i.e., the sanction. Above all, it has shown to us the way in which affective responses can embody moral values. By being sanctioned, they share in freedom, and this share is an indispensable presupposition for both responsibility and morality.

The role of freedom in the affective sphere can be summarized as follows:

(1) Affective responses arise in our soul without the direct intervention of our freedom. We can neither freely engender them as we can the will, nor dissolve them freely once they have arisen. From this point of view, they are similar to "being affected," despite other essential differences.

(2) Despite the fact that they are not free in their becoming, affective responses have, by their very nature, the character of a position we take toward an object, and they can possess a morally positive or negative character.

(3) Our freedom has a great role to play with respect to affective responses. This role is not related to their coming into being, but to the way in which our spiritual center cooperates with them when they have arisen.

(4) So long as man makes no use of this capacity, he identifies himself implicitly with his affective responses, and is solidary with them. The fact that one could objectively sanction and disavow them connects every affective response with freedom, at least potentially, and makes one in some way responsible for these affective responses.

(5) This undisputed solidarity suffices to stain us morally in the case of morally negative affective responses. But it does not suffice to endow us in the same sense with a full, moral positive

value, a moral merit, in the case of a morally positive affective response. The accidental character of such responses is an imperfection frustrating a fully positive moral attitude of our own.

(6) The freedom which is actualized in sanction or disavowal originates in the deepest stratum of our free spiritual center and surpasses (as far as it concerns the degree of being morally awake which it presupposes) the actualization of freedom which is required for a decision of our will in the sphere of actions.

(7) Sanction and disavowal are not mere endorsements of our attitudes "from without," by our free spiritual center, such as when we endorse attitudes of other persons. They are also different from the endorsement we give to the fulfillment of instincts. They are, on the contrary, a unique organic cooperating with or withdrawing from our affective responses, modifying them from within. They even surpass the organic cooperation or withdrawal which is to be found in the sphere of being affected, insofar as the sanction joins the affective response and becomes an integral element of it, and disavowal affects it in its very core and deprives it of its soul.

(8) This supreme actualization of our freedom present in the sanction (which elevates the spontaneous affective response to the level of a free position) is only possible toward value responses, and especially toward responses directed to morally relevant values. It must clearly be distinguished from any outspoken and express solidarity of the morally unconscious man with his affective responses, as well as from the diabolical pseudo-sanction proper to the enemy of God. True sanction and disavowal are only possible when we cooperate with the logos of the world of values.

(9) The disavowal does not effect a dissolution of the morally negative response, but it "decapitates" it, so to speak, it deprives it of its validity. The desubstantialization of the affective response by its disavowal disrupts the undisputed solidarity which the person has with his affective response, and counteracts in a decisive way the moral contamination which this response contains. Moreover, it is the first step toward a real dissolution of this response which as such can fully be attained only in an indirect way. The sanction, far from only changing the implicit

undisputed solidarity into an explicit one, endows the positive affective response with an element of freedom and conscious conformity to the values. Only through the sanction does the good response become our own to such an extent that its accomplishment fully endows us with a moral value and crowns us with moral merit.

Sanction and disavowal, however, do not exhaust the role of our immediate freedom in the affective sphere. We can also cooperate with our affective responses by means of several other free attitudes. When affective responses arise in us, we have the possibility of abandoning ourselves to them, or of refusing to do so. We can turn away from them, we can struggle against them with our will, we can try not to think of the object which has motivated them, and so on. Someone feels a deep love arising in his soul, but he refuses to let this love take hold of his soul, because he shuns being drawn by an experience which is to effect deep changes in his life. Because he dreads the force of love which would overthrow the commodious routine of his existence, he tries to destroy it at its roots, to think no more of the person concerned, to concentrate on other things. This kind of voluntary refusal to cooperate with an affective response is different from the sanction or disavowal. It does not necessarily require a moral motivation, nor does it presuppose the state of being fully awake proper to the morally conscious man.[12] Nevertheless we find here a vast field open to our free intervention with respect to our affective responses. This free intervention has an influence not only with respect to actions which the affective response can inspire us to perform, but also with regard to the final disappearance of our affective response itself. Our will plays a great role in the development of our affective responses. And those free interventions assume a still greater and higher significance when they are inspired by sanction and disavowal, that is to say, when they have the character of a normal prolongation

---

[12] The refusal to cooperate in this sense with an affective response, the "running away from it," as it were, may even be the outgrowth of a subconscious resistance. Far from being a position of our free center toward it, it then has the character of a mere inhibition. It is even opposed to an actualization of our freedom. We disregard, however, these cases in our context, and are concerned with a cooperation or a refusal to cooperate which has the character of a conscious decision, though not yet necessarily of a sanction or disavowal.

of the process which takes place in both sanction or disavowal. It is clear that in sanctioning an affective response the morally conscious man does not restrict himself to this ultimate inner cooperation, but places himself, as it were, consciously into this response, gives free way to its dynamism, favors it voluntarily by focusing his spiritual eyes on the object which motivates his response, voluntarily avoids everything which disturbs the full flow of his response, and so on. Analogously, the morally conscious man, in disavowing an affective response, will not restrict himself to this invalidation of this response but, eager to dissolve it, he will close himself, turn away, in short, he will accomplish all these other forms of free intervention. When those different types of intervention of our freedom toward an affective response flow out of sanction or disavowal, they are equally elevated to a higher level; they assume the character of a cooperation or counteraction issuing from the point of deepest freedom, and arise from an ultimate "concerting" with the logos of the world of values.

The preceding analysis was concerned with the role of our freedom toward affective responses which have spontaneously arisen in us. Our inner cooperation with or withdrawal from these responses was the topic. We have seen in the course of this analysis that sanction implies the sincere desire and aspiration that the response "should" exist. In this deep actualization of our freedom we affirm its existence. The very act of disavowing implies that we wish the response to vanish. This leads us again to the question which we have already previously treated in another context: What is the role of our freedom with respect to the coming into being and disappearance of affective responses? Now that we have clarified the new dimension of freedom which we possess in the power of sanction and disavowal, this problem presents itself in a new light.

CHAPTER 26

INDIRECT INFLUENCE OF MAN'S FREEDOM

THE INDIRECT influence which we have over our affective responses consists in preparing in our soul the ground from which the right responses, rather than the wrong responses, will arise spontaneously—an intervention which presupposes moral consciousness and the actualization of the deep freedom which is present in sanction and disavowal.

In order to understand the nature of this indirect influence, we must first examine the obstacles preventing right responses from arising, and the sources in man which are favorable to the growth of wrong responses. Affective responses, as well as being affected, depend above all upon that which we call the character of a man, his heart, his sensitivity to good, and especially his superactual attitude, his general inner direction.

Here we touch a problem which surpasses by far the realm of affective responses, and being affected: it is related to the question of the role which man's freedom plays with respect to his character, to the lasting qualities of his nature. It encompasses the role of man's freedom in acquiring virtues, in overcoming vices, in the moral perfecting of his personality. It is in the molding of our personality that our indirect freedom displays its paramount importance. Affective responses, however, and being affected depend themselves upon our character, upon our sensitivity for values, upon our habitual state of being awake, upon our superactual attitudes and responses. Thus our free influence on the coming into being and vanishing of affective responses, as well as being affected or not affected by some good, is only possible through the change of our character.

The elements which condition the character of an individual person are very complex. We shall mention only the main ones. First, there is a person's natural disposition, such as the potentiality of a person to perceive values and to respond to them, his temperament, his specific affinity to certain spheres of goods such as artistic sensitivity, his special talents and gifts. We can sum up these elements as the "dowry" which a man possesses by nature and which he cannot give himself. It embraces as well mere temperamental tendencies, the nature of his instincts, his spiritual gifts and talents, his psychical tendencies as well as the general potentiality of his capacities, i.e., the size of the vessel he represents as a personality.

This first group of elements is beyond our freedom; neither can we give ourselves an affinity which we do not possess, nor can we endow ourselves with a potentiality we do not have by nature. With respect to this natural "dowry" the words of our Lord that we cannot add a cubit to our stature are pertinent.

A second group of elements playing a role in the formation of a person's character consists of the influences which he undergoes from outside. These include his education, the milieu in which he lives, the love he receives or the oppression he suffers from, the persons who influence him, the books that he reads, the world in which he moves, and so forth.

These elements are partly beyond our power, partly accessible to our free influence. A child can freely choose neither his education nor the milieu in which he lives. But it is often in the power of an adult person to choose the milieu in which he wants to live, the things with which he feeds his mind, the persons with whom he enters in contact, and so on.

Third, there are single decisive experiences that a person undergoes, which develop certain trends in him or deform others; which stamp his nature in a specific way by creating, for instance, a general attitude of anxiety or mistrust (which often follows bitter disillusions), or by melting his self-centeredness through the experience of a great charity poured on him. Patently, this third group of factors is completely withdrawn from our free influence.

A fourth group of decisive factors playing a role in the formation of a person's character is the way in which a man "digests" all his different experiences; his free attitude toward them; whether or not he repents after having fallen prey to sin; whether or not he represses a humiliation or accepts it consciously and patiently; whether he closes himself in when he endures a disillusion, or realizes its accidental character and remains open-minded; whether he generalizes single experiences and fills his mind with prejudices or instead restricts the conclusion of this experience to its legitimate scope and significance.

This fourth group of determining elements, on the contrary, is completely within the realm of our freedom, at least potentially. Though the way in which we "digest" the milieu which surrounds us and the different experiences which we undergo may often imply that we make no use of our freedom, but rather let ourselves be drawn by our subconscious reactions or our spontaneous responses, we nevertheless objectively have the power to intervene with our freedom; hence we are not at all forced to yield to our spontaneous responses.

Finally we must refer to a person's general superactual attitudes. General superactual responses toward an entire realm of goods and values are a most decisive factor in a man's character. These responses, as we shall see later on, are the very core of man's virtues and vices.

The role of freedom in the general superactual attitudes is obviously of the utmost interest, as it is synonymous with the role of freedom in acquiring virtues. The changing of our superactual position toward a realm of goods, bodily comfort for instance, is not in our direct power as is a concrete act of willing or, in a deeper stratum, the sanction and disavowal. But we can indirectly contribute to a removal of the obstacles preventing the morally good, general superactual responses from reigning in our soul. These general superactual responses are the backbone of man's moral personality. Their presence is the spiritually decisive factor.

It is here that the all-important role of our indirect freedom manifests itself. The greatest moral tasks are within the realm of man's indirect influence and in that of his cooperative freedom. We understand now why it is possible that moral perfection, the possession of moral virtues, and even the affective response of love toward God and our neighbor can be imposed on us as moral obligations. Now we see why we are responsible for our moral imperfection and the absence of the full response of love. It becomes understandable as soon as we take into account the existence of cooperative freedom and indirect influence, and the responsibility connected with them.

It must, however, be said that in extraordinary cases a widening of the range of our direct influence is granted to man. Without discussing whether such an extraordinary opportunity is granted once to every man, we have to state that to certain personalities, in certain moments, such a gift is definitely granted. I think of situations in which a man stands at a crossroad, and in which his decision reaches, as it were, into deeper strata which are in general withdrawn from our direct influence. In these moments a man is able to pierce through, to give a decisive turning to his superactual attitudes. Such was the kissing of the leper by St. Francis, a deed in which he not only overcame his momentary disgust, but in which he cut the fetters, so to speak, which linked him to a certain sphere of goods and freed himself from his habitual imprisonment in a certain sphere of sensitivity. But this freedom must in a certain sense also be called a cooperative one, since it presupposes an extraordinary gift which we cannot grant to ourselves. Certainly the actualization of our freedom in these extraordinary situations has not the character of sanction or disavowal, but of a definite intervention. It is, as it were, a prolongation of the direct power of our free will. But this prolongation itself is a gift which is in no way in our power.

Thus we see that our freedom has a definite role in preparing the ground from which our affective responses arise, and also in forming the way of our being affected. As we have already mentioned, we cannot consider the preparation of this ground simply from the point of view of the role which it plays for affective response and the being affected. In itself it definitely has the greatest moral significance. The great moral task of transforming our nature—to which, for instance, all our ascetic practices aspire, the task of improving morally to attain a higher moral standard —refers to the changing of the very ground of our personality. It is a part of the fulfillment of Christ's command: "Be ye therefore perfect, as also your heavenly Father is perfect."

III. The Sources of Moral Goodness

CHAPTER 27

THE THREE SPHERES OF MORALITY

OUR FOREGOING analysis has furnished us the different elements which are required for the moral value of a human act. It must first of all be a value response. As long as we are motivated only by something subjectively satisfying, our attitude will not be endowed with a moral value in the full sense of the term. This attitude as such will not bestow a moral value on anyone.

But, secondly, it must be more than simply any value response: the value motivating our response must be a morally relevant value. Thirdly, the value response must be based on an awareness of the moral significance of the situation, and imply a general will to be morally good. Fourthly, the value response must be free. This fourth condition is *a fortiori* fulfilled in every volitional value response, because the will is by its very nature free. But affective responses must be sanctioned in order to have a share in man's freedom and therefore in order to be endowed with moral values.

There are three fundamental spheres in which moral goodness is to be found. The first is the sphere of actions. Every ethics has taken it into account. Some philosophers have even restricted moral goodness to that sphere. This sphere is, as we saw before, dominated by the will. Every action necessarily issues from an act of willing and is guided by it. The will commands the action; it is the master of all actions. Though the will is not restricted to actions but has also a tremendous function to perform in the sphere of our indirect power, the sphere of action is nonetheless

342

the specific kingdom of the will and it is here that the will attains its most immediate, full moral significance.[1]

The second is the sphere of concrete responses; this includes both the volitional responses, which do not result in actions but remain immanent activities, and above all the affective responses: contrition, love, hope, veneration, joy, or acts such as forgiving, thanking and so on. This sphere of concrete responses and acts has, in general, been much less stressed and sometimes even neglected. It is not difficult to see, however, that it is precisely in this sphere of concrete responses, volitional and affective, that we are confronted with an immense realm of moral goodness and evil. Many of our moral judgments refer to such acts. We admire a morally noble enthusiasm, the nobility of an act of gratitude, we are touched by the moral beauty of a deep contrition, we praise the depth and ardor of a love, we exalt the firm will to acquire greater moral perfection, and so on.

We must therefore distinguish this sphere of single concrete responses from the sphere of action, as an independent field of morality. It would be a grave error to look at the concrete responses merely from the point of view of what they might mean for eventual action. The joy of St. Simeon, the contrition of David, the reverence of St. Joseph before the mystery of the Incarnation, the longing love of St. Paul for Christ which he expresses in saying, *Cupio dissolvi, et esse cum Christo*—". . . having a desire to be dissolved and to be with Christ" (Phil. 1:23) are all attitudes endowed with sublime moral values, even with supernatural moral values. They glorify God, not in their indirect importance for eventual actions, but directly in themselves. In themselves they are as much endowed with moral values as any action could be.

The third fundamental sphere of morality is the lasting qualities of a person's character, i.e., the sphere of virtues and vices. This sphere is the very core of morality. It is here that we find moral values such as generosity, purity, veracity, justice, humility; as a matter of fact, ancient as well as medieval philosophies have always seen in this sphere the center and summit of all morality.

[1] Cf. D. von Hildebrand, *Sittlichkeit und ethische Werterkenntniss;* and *Die Idee der sittlichen Handlung* (Halle: M. Niemeyer, 1916).

Each of these three spheres has a full moral significance of its own, and we must not look at one of these spheres merely as a precondition or a favorable disposition for any of the others. A morally good action enriches the world, as it were: it is a moral good as such which comes into existence just as a morally bad action is a moral evil as such. This much will readily be acknowledged. No one would consider an action to be exclusively a mere symptom of a man's character, although this might be its main significance under certain circumstances. For example, someone's trust in, or love for, another person might be shattered or weakened because a certain action of the other justifies the inference that his character is different from what it was believed to be. A lie may be looked upon not only as a single deplorable action but also as a symptom of the person's unreliability. But no one will reduce the entire sphere of action to a mere symptomatic expression of the virtues or vices of a man. Everyone will admit the meaningfulness of a statement such as: "What a pity that this noble man fell and acted immorally." When Lodovico in speaking of Othello's act of murder, says at the end:

> O thou, Othello! that wert once so good,
> Fall'n in the practice of a dammed slave,
> What shall be said to thee? [2]

the moral significance of an action as such is clearly disclosed.

But often the sphere of single volitional or affective responses has not been grasped in its autonomous moral significance. It has either been neglected as a whole, or conceived only as a favorable or unfavorable source of actions, or else as a mere accompanying element of actions; or affective responses have been interpreted as volitional responses. Love has been considered as morally good because it may be a motor for many morally good actions, and because it may be a facilitating element for good actions. Others have equated love with a mere act of willing. The moral value of affective responses, independently of any possible actions resulting from them, has often been overlooked. Likewise the specific moral value which is indissolubly connected with their affective character has been disregarded. This is the case in Kant's ethics, in which a moral significance is

---

[2] Shakespeare, *Othello*, Act 5, Scene 2.

attributed to the will only.[3] It is true that Kant does not restrict morality to actions, since willing can be morally good, according to him, not only when leading to actions, but in itself. Even if an action is frustrated because of some chance impediment, the will retains its full moral significance for Kant. But nevertheless a restriction of morality to the sphere of action is in some way to be found here, since the good will for Kant is always concerned with an action even if at times it does not lead to it.[4] In any case, affective responses have no moral significance for Kant, as his distinction between pathological and moral love shows.[5]

Aristotle's position toward this problem is more complex. On the one hand, he admits that joy can embody a moral value in saying that the good man not only wills the good but rejoices in it.[6] On the other, he identifies the moral sphere to such an extent with the sphere of action that there is no place left for contemplation or a contemplative attitude in the sphere of morality. Everything belonging to the moral sphere has to be a transient activity, according to Aristotle. Since love, joy, veneration, enthusiasm, and hope are as such typically contemplative, independently of the question what actions they may inspire, it clearly results that, for Aristotle at least, the entire stress of moral goodness and moral badness is laid on the sphere of actions.

It is of the utmost importance to see that these single affective responses are endowed with a moral value of their own, and that the accomplishment of a real act of charity or contrition or a holy joy over the conversion of a sinner is in itself a moral good, an enrichment of the world as such, a full moral reality, and in no way merely a favorable disposition for a morally good action. Moreover, we must beware of interpreting affective responses as mere symptoms of virtues, or, at best, as means for the acquisition of virtues.

The sphere of virtues has also been fully ignored by Kant,[7] and

[3] Immanuel Kant, *Grundlegung zur Metaphysik der Sitten* (Munich: Bremer Presse, 1925), p. 1.

[4] It will not be discussed here whether Kant included in his statement the will to acquire a virtue, the will to change morally.

[5] Immanuel Kant, *Kritik der praktischen Vernuft* (Leipzig: Felix Meiner, 1920), p. 105ff.

[6] *Nicomachean Ethics*, Bk. I, 1099a, 17.

[7] *Grundlegung zur Metaphysik der Sitten*, p. 2.

most of the ethicians since Kant have stepped into the same path. In contradistinction to this consideration of virtues, the ethics of antiquity, as well as the ethics of St. Augustine and St. Thomas, have attributed to virtues a great moral significance.[8]

It has to be stressed that virtues are an actualization of moral values of their own, independently of single responses and actions. We have to understand that virtues are not at all mere dispositions for acting with moral rightness, that they cannot be interpreted as a mere potency with respect to single responses and actions. They are in themselves a full and definitive moral good and moral reality. We shall have to come back to this point later on.

The Sphere of Actions

In order to throw more into relief the difference between the first and the second sphere of morality, we have still briefly to circumscribe the nature of action.

In using the term "action," we are thinking of the activity in which a state of facts is purposely realized. To rescue a man in danger of drowning by drawing him out of the water is an action; so is the giving of an alms. Again, to intervene in order to protect the rights of another person is an action.

The characteristic marks of actions are the following: A state of facts is realized through us. An objective change in the world is brought about through our intervention. The state of fact in question must always be extraneous to our action, i.e., it must be a change beyond the mere accomplishment of our act. In order for us to perform an action, we must not only be instrumental in this change, but we must intend its realization. As long as we are only a link in a causal chain bringing this fact into existence (for instance, in tripping over another person because we have been pushed by someone else), no action is in question. Only when the activity through which the change is effected is intended by our will can we speak of an action.

Thus an action implies the following elements: First, a knowl-

8 Many dialogues of Plato are concerned with the nature of virtues. In Aristotle's ethics the analysis of virtues occupies a predominant place. Virtues play a still greater role in the Augustinian ethics. The *secunda secundae* of St. Thomas is dedicated to them.

edge of the not-yet-real state of facts and of its value; secondly, an act of willing motivated by the value of the state of fact and intending its realization; thirdly, activities of our limbs commanded by our willing, activities which initiate a more or less complicated causal chain which will bring about the coming into existence of the state of fact in question. This third factor is the *differentia specifica* between actions and responses, because it is here that the intervention into the world surrounding us is accomplished. It embraces the conscious, intelligent use of all the means we need for the realization of the intended goal, whether they have the function of a mere instrumental cause or of a *causa proxima.*

Yet actions must not only be distinguished from acts and responses in our soul which have been termed "immanent" activities in contradistinction to the transient ones. They must also be distinguished from other transient activities. Not every transient activity is an action in the full sense. Eating, walking, reading, smoking, winding our watch, swimming, and so on are not actions in the full sense. They have in common with actions that they are not immanent [9] activities such as responses of joy or sorrow, an act of inference or a conviction. But they differ from real actions because the role of willing in these cases is different from the one it plays in actions; secondly, in the case of an action in the true sense the state of fact realized is much more autonomous, much more independent of our activity as such.[10]

In all actions, the activities performed have exclusively the character of means; the entire stress is laid on the coming into existence of a state of fact. Moreover the state of fact must have a certain weight of significance. To brush one's teeth, to wash one's hands, though these activities also bring a fact into existence (namely that one's hands and teeth are clean), can obviously not be called actions in the full sense of the word. The habitual character of something which has to be repeated time and again in a certain rhythm forbids calling it an action in the full sense.

[9] Obviously this "immanence" of the affective response in no way contradicts the above-mentioned transcendence. It only gainsays the transient character of actions.

[10] Cf. Aristotle, *Nicomachean Ethics,* Bk. I, 1.

We want to restrict the term "action" to a full and typical intervention in which a state of fact of a certain importance, distinctly separated from our activity, having a certain character of uniqueness, is purposively realized through certain means.

Hence action in the full sense not only differs from such repeated activities, but also from any kind of activity which has the character of a work. Neither the creation of a work of art, nor writing a philosophical book, nor the work of an artisan (such as making shoes), nor driving a car can be considered as an action in the full sense. To drive a car, however, can certainly be a part of an action, for instance, if someone in driving a car escapes from his persecutors.[11] An activity such as chatting with another person is not an action, but if we denounce someone to the police, it is undoubtedly an action. Eating is not an action, but feeding another person who is hungry is. Hence, it is not the kind of activity as such which determines the character of an action, as one and the same activity may in one case be part of an action and in another case give rise to no action at all.[12]

After having briefly sketched the nature of action in the full sense, we can easily see how morality displays itself in that sphere. In every morally good action the will commanding this action must be a value response, and the object (i.e., the state of fact which is brought into existence by the action) must be a good endowed with a morally relevant value. This morally relevant value may be a direct or indirect one. But as soon as our will is motivated only by something subjectively satisfying and has no reference whatsoever to something important-in-itself, the action has no positive moral value. If I enter into the affairs of another in order to insure a profitable financial gain for myself, or if I make a business contract with someone, my action as such is morally neutral. And even if the state of fact which I bring into existence through my action were endowed with a morally relevant value, my action would still have no moral value so long as it was not motivated by this value, at least so long as this value played no role in my motivation. If someone helps another per-

[11] It might seem that we identify action with an intervention possessing a moral significance. This is, however, not our intention. To escape from people persecuting us can also be morally neutral. Buying or selling a house is another example of a morally neutral action.

[12] Cf. *Die Idee der sittlichen Handlung.*

son exclusively with the expectation of some profit to himself, the moral value of the action of helping another would be frustrated, without necessarily making it in any way morally evil.

Hence we see that in order to be morally good an action must bring into existence a state of fact endowed with a morally relevant value. Moreover, the will commanding this action must be motivated by this morally relevant value, including also a response to its *moral* significance and the general will to be morally good.

Yet in stating the requirements which guarantee the moral value of an action, we have only answered the most elementary question among many others which impose themselves in this realm.[13] In a future work which we mentioned several times, an analysis of the sphere of actions will be presented, and the problems mentioned above will be treated in detail.

The Sphere of Responses

The sphere of single concrete responses (both actual and superactual), which we must distinguish from actions, offers a great and rich field of ethical exploration. It is here that the incredible wealth and manifold character of moral values disclose themselves. This sphere embraces an act of sublime renunciation as well as an act of forgiveness, the holy joy over the conversion of a sinner as well as the meek acceptance of a great humiliation. It is in this sphere that one encounters the moral value of an

[13] We only cite the following main problems: What elements are responsible for the difference in rank among morally good actions? The moral value of every morally good action has not necessarily the same rank. On the contrary, we are confronted with great differences of rank in the frame of morally good actions. Martyrdom patently ranks incomparably higher in moral value than almsgiving. What factors determine this difference? A second great problem concerns the factors determining a morally bad action. It is clear that the absence of the factors determining the moral value of an action does not necessarily render an action morally bad. The roots of the moral disvalue of an action is thus a new problem. Here again the question arises as to the elements determining the difference in rank of moral disvalues in the realm of action. Another set of problems centers around the omission of good actions. Under what conditions is the omission of morally good actions morally bad? In many cases it may only be the absence of a moral value, but in all cases in which the action is morally obligatory its omission embodies a moral disvalue. And this again leads to the great classical problem: Upon what factors does the morally obligatory character of an action depend? What elements have to intervene in order for an action to be not only morally good, but even obligatory from the moral point of view?

unshakeable confidence and of a noble compassion, the moving humility and freedom proper to a deep contrition. Here we find the most sublime of all human acts, the adoring love of God and charity toward one's neighbor. It is here that are manifested all the different types and nuances of moral badness and wickedness—the meanness of envy or malicious joy, the horror of poisonous hatred, the moral badness of supercilious contempt for other persons, the ugliness of anger.

The sources of the moral goodness of *volitional* responses which do not lead to actions or manifest themselves in actions are the same as those of actions. Yet in order for *affective* responses to embody moral values in the full sense of the term, they must be sanctioned and through this sanction they share in man's freedom. Our former analyses of the nature of value responses and especially of cooperative and indirect freedom have removed the obstacles preventing us from doing justice to the moral value of affective responses. They have unmasked the wrongness of the view that love, joy, contrition, must either be interpreted as volitional responses or else lose the possibility of embodying moral values. Having seen that it is the character of a free response to morally relevant values which is the source of moral goodness in volitional responses, we are now in a position to see that sanctioned affective responses also possess the requirements for embodying moral values. But, as we shall see immediately, we find even in this sphere specific moral perfections which the volitional response does not possess.

We have to keep in mind that the great variety which we find in the field of action is exclusively determined by the nature of the fact which is brought into existence and by the difference between the means needed to achieve this end. There exists indeed a great difference between saving a man's life and the giving of an alms; or between the declaration of war by a king and the punishment of a naughty child by his parents. These differences are exclusively determined by the end and the means used to attain this end. However, the soul of actions is always one and the same, namely the volitional response. But in the sphere of single responses a great variety of attitudes is to be found. We already stressed that will, enthusiasm, joy, hope, veneration, and love, even when they are all motivated by a value, differ from each other by their "inner word." And this difference between the inner words of responses, which determines their specific nature, has a bearing on the type of union established with the good and its value on the object side.

We saw before that there exists a deep, meaningful relation between the inner word of a value response and the value-endowed good on the object side. Now we have to stress that each inner word entails a specific way of entering into the spirit of the value. In the inner word of each type of value response a new aspect of communion with the value-endowed good is displayed. Hence, even in the case that two different affective responses are directed to one and the same object, these responses differ in their approach to the value. Sometimes the difference between inner words also corresponds to a different aspect of one and the same value, i.e., of the value as such. The difference concerning the aspects of union with the value-endowed good is particularly striking if we compare the inner word of willing with an affective response such as joy.

Our willing to bring something of high value into existence has a unique perfection: the interest embodied in the inner word of willing is incomparable with other responses, because through willing we become instrumental in the coming into being of the good. Moreover in willing we commit ourselves in a unique way, sometimes against the tendencies of our nature and even against the wishes of our heart. We give ourselves in a decisive, valid, definitive way. But the joy over the existence of a value-endowed good embodies a conforming of our heart to the good, a much more intimate and qualitative union with the value, making the good and its existence our innermost, personal affair; all of which represents a perfection not possessed by the will. Again, veneration implies an element of submission and reverence which in a particular way does justice to the fact that values come from above.

In considering love, we easily detect that its inner word has a unique perfection. The element of self-donation in love is incomparable with any other value response. We only need to think of the difference between our being esteemed and our being loved; certainly an abyss separates the two. What we receive in being loved surpasses incomparably what we receive in being admired, esteemed, and even venerated. The inner word of love embodies the greatest possible interest in the beloved, the most radical and intimate concerting with the object's value, the closest union with the good to which it is imparted.[14] Love is the most total, central, and intimate of all value responses.

Thus we see that every value response has its specific perfection from the point of view of its concerting with the value on the object side, its entering into the spirit of this value, its participation in it. Hence the specific union established with the value-endowed morally relevant good grants to each affective response a moral value of its own, as we saw in comparing joy with will, and especially in considering love. This does not mean, however, that one affective response ranks necessarily higher than another, being granted that in both all the general requirements for moral values are fulfilled.[15] Many affective responses may as such have the same moral value. Yet there is also a hierarchy among the specific moral values of the different affective responses. Its degree of participation and its degree of self-donation may give one affective response a higher moral value than another. It is in this context that the superiority of love over all other value responses again discloses itself.

In analyzing the specific nature of each value response, we shall soon discover that some of them, such as joy, love and above all adoration, have an outspoken contemplative character. It is of the utmost importance to understand that it is impossible to go along with Aristotle in considering morality and contemplative attitudes as excluding each other. Aristotle takes for granted that morality and moral virtues are concerned with the practical sphere alone, and thus that the contemplative element and morality seem to exclude each other. The contemplative element is reserved for the cognitional virtues, such as philosophic wisdom, which he considers as ranking higher than the moral virtues precisely because of their contemplative character.[16] As right as Aristotle is in giving the contemplative attitude precedence over the active, he yet commits a grave error in

---

[14] Cf. *Metaphysik der Gemeinschaft,* Pt. I, chap. 4.
[15] Joy is, *ceteris paribus,* on the same moral level as enthusiasm.
[16] Cf. *Nicomachean Ethics,* Bk. X, 1177a ff.

restricting morality to the practical sphere, an error which implies also a wrong conception of contemplation:

Antiquity itself discerned the pre-eminence of the contemplative as against the active attitude. The magnificent words of Aristotle regarding the dianoetic (cognitional) virtues in the conclusion of his *Nicomachean Ethics* sufficiently testify to this. But ancient thought erroneously limited contemplation to the cognitional sphere. This identification contains a two-fold error. First, not every search for knowledge implies contemplation. The scientist who is tensely working for definite results, who strides from fact to fact in order to solve a given problem, is not doing his researches with a contemplative intent. Only the intuitive penetration of the essence of a thing, and the conscious "dwelling" in a truth already established, are truly contemplative attitudes. Secondly, contemplation embraces not only *cognition* but also the conscious state of *being affected* by a value; dwelling in the bliss derived from the light of beauty and goodness. The *frui,* the "enjoyment" of value, the "absorption" in beauty—these are attitudes purely contemplative in nature. Responses of joy, love, and adoration are typical embodiments of contemplation. Thus, Mary Magdalen not only listened to the words of Our Lord but in loving adoration "immersed herself" in the beatific presence of Jesus.[17]

The great value which is proper to the contemplative element is in no way the exclusive privilege of the sphere of knowledge or of the intellect. The line separating contemplative and non-contemplative (i.e., active) attitudes goes through the sphere of knowledge and the sphere of responses, dividing each of them into two different realms. It is only when we have freed ourselves from this wrong conception of contemplation and contemplative attitudes that we can do justice to the role granted to love by St. Paul when he said: *Caritas numquam excidit*—"Charity never fails."

In comparing the inner word of the different value responses, we are struck by another fact of fundamental importance. Certain value responses, for instance the love and the gratitude of a saint, possess a moral value which is not exclusively due to the communion with the value on the object side or to the interest in it.[18] Charity which has the character of outpouring goodness,

---

[17] *Transformation in Christ,* chap. 6, p. 93.
[18] In referring to the charity and love of saints, we are not concerned with the

and which is the actualization of intrinsic moral goodness, is morally good, but not exclusively because it responds to the value on the object side. This fact becomes clear when we compare willing with love. The will evidently possesses a high *ontological* value of its own, being in its very freedom one of the most essential marks of the human person as an *imago Dei*. But it is obvious that the *moral* value of an act of willing is due to its being a response to a good having a morally relevant value. All its moral goodness accrues to it from the interest in the value-endowed good, an interest which is embodied in the specific inner word of willing.

As soon as we prescind from the value of the object and from the participation of the will in it, willing offers only ontological values and not moral ones. In charity, on the contrary, even if we prescind from the value-endowed good and our participation in it, moral beauty and preciousness remains. If we think of St. Francis of Assisi's loving attitude toward animals, we easily grasp that the sublime goodness embodied in this love does not depend only upon participation in the value-endowed good. This statement must not be interpreted in the sense that the moral value of love could exist independently of a value response. We do not pretend that moral goodness can be actualized elsewhere than in a value response, but we say that the moral goodness of charity, though presupposing that a response to value is given, does not spring from its character of response alone. Certainly every love is distinguished from willing also by the fact that it is essentially a value response. An act of willing may be a value response, but it may also be motivated by the merely

---

character of charity as theological virtue and with the fact that it is infused. We prescind in this philosophical context from what theology tells us about charity. We are here concerned with the love of saints which, as an undeniable and manifest reality, is in its specific unique quality accessible to a philosophical analysis. It is this undeniable reality which Bergson declares to be the higher source of morality in his work *Les deux sources de la morale et de la religion*. We shall see that this love presupposes the Christian Revelation as intentional object. It is only possible as a response to the God revealed in Christ and to our neighbor seen in the light of Christ. We mentioned already that the morality of the saints is the most important topic for an ethics, for, apart from the fact that it is something completely new, it is also the fulfillment of all mere natural morality.

subjectively satisfying. The concept of willing, as such, gives us no clue as to the category of importance which has motivated us. The notion of love, on the contrary, implies the character of a value response. The beloved person must present himself to our mind as precious, lovable, noble, beautiful. We have already mentioned this difference.[19]

However, the fact that love is always a value response does not yet suffice to explain the moral value of its own which the love of a saint embodies, that is to say, independently of its relation to the value-endowed good. We need only compare love with other affective responses, which are also essentially value responses, in order to see that the moral goodness proper to it cannot simply depend upon the fact that it necessarily embodies a value response. Esteem, for instance, is always a value response. We can never esteem a person if we do not believe that he is endowed with values. But, nevertheless, esteem does not possess this intrinsic moral goodness apart from its interest in the value on the object side. Esteem is morally good as response to morally relevant values. Esteem for a morally noble person is certainly something morally good, but all its goodness accrues to it from its interest in the value-endowed good. It does not, as such, display this intrinsic goodness, this actualization of a treasure entrusted to us, which is a typical mark of charity. Since esteem, though essentially a value response, does not possess a moral value of its own, charity must possess it from some other source than being essentially a value response.

In comparing charity to esteem, we are struck by a difference concerning the plenitude and originality of their inner words. In esteem the inner word is, so to speak, absorbed by the appreciation of the object; it has a rather thin, affectively poor character. Certainly it is a real affective response, and not a mere judgment attributing certain values to someone. But compared with other value responses, with joy, enthusiasm, or love, esteem is closest to a pure judgment about the values of a person. We need only compare veneration with esteem in order to see how much richer the former's inner word is, how much more personal is its content. Esteem has the coolest and most formal character, and

[19] Chapter 17, "Value Response."

this is probably the reason why Kant conceded to it alone a moral significance apart from willing.[20] Charity is the other pole in this sphere. Here the inner word attains an incomparable qualitative plenitude and significance.

The qualitative plenitude and originality of the inner word of a value response is indeed connected with its having a moral value "of its own," i.e., apart from its participation in the value of the object. Yet this does not mean that the moral value "of its own" and the qualitative plenitude are identical. Nor does it mean that the qualitative plenitude is the root of this moral value "of its own."

There is a mysterious spontaneity in charity; it is as if something were opened in this value response which superabundantly flows in its goodness, overflows, and surpasses the frame of a value response. It is this element which is expressed admirably by the traditional term: *bonum diffusivum sui*. The saint whose love flows without limit—love which may also manifest itself in his attitude toward animals—reveals clearly this element of charity which, apart from being *the* fundamental response to God, is also a unique partaking of the Divine Love Itself.

But this spontaneity of love (which Max Scheler saw and stressed time and again), must not be interpreted as a kind of exuberance, comparable to an overflowing of spiritual energy or vitality—a confusion which Scheler did not quite succeed in avoiding in his book *Das Ressentiment im Aufbau der Moralen*.[21]

The spontaneous overflowing generosity of love evidently manifests itself above all in the love of God for creatures, a love inconceivable for antiquity, inconceivable for any human mind without revelation. In every charity which partakes in some way of divine love, this spontaneity has not the character of mere dynamism, of an overflowing of life and energy, whereby the object assumes the role of a mere occasion for the unfolding of this exuberance; rather love implies the ultimate interest in

---

[20] Cf. Kant, *Grundlegung zur Metaphysik der Sitten*.

[21] *Vom Umsturz der Werte* (Leipzig: Der Neue Geist, 1919), Vol. I. Scheler was no doubt tempted to fall prey to this confusion because in his refutation of Nietzsche he wanted to show that Christian charity, far from being an outgrowth of the vitally poor and incapable, was the most exuberant manifestation of inner plenitude.

the object, and thus is more focused on the beloved than is any other value response on its object.

The elaboration of this source of moral goodness in charity, which we termed an actualization of the innermost center of all moral goodness,[22] and of this treasure of goodness entrusted to man which can be actualized only in a value response is however deeply linked with the fundamental problem of the relation existing between natural moral goodness and the morality of a saint, the fruits of the Holy Ghost as St. Paul calls them, the love which is to be found only as a response to God through Christ and as a partaking of the love of Christ Himself.

This problem, in its application to the sphere of single value responses, refers to the great difference between all those value responses which are possible without divine revelation and those which presuppose it as their intentional object, such as the love of Christ, the Christian love of neighbor, holy joy, true humility, and many others.

The Sphere of Virtues

We have already mentioned that virtues must not be confused with mere dispositions for acting or responding rightly. In calling someone pure, just, or generous, we do not indicate a mere power to act with moral rightness. This would make of the moral value of virtues something merely potential. We mean a quality of a person's character, a quality which is fully actualized in his person and which may manifest itself in his facial expression, his demeanor; whereas a mere potency to act has neither a qualitative character nor can it manifest itself in a person's deportment.

Virtue must further be distinguished from a mere ability, such as the ability to play the piano, which has also definitely the character of something potential; it assumes its fulfillment in the exercise of this ability, i.e., in our example, in playing the piano. This is not the case with moral virtues. They are full realities in themselves, and do not merely achieve their meaning in single actions or responses.

The reason underlying this fact will become apparent if we

[22] This will be one of our main topics in our next ethical work.

realize that the backbone of every virtue is a superactual value response. We have already distinguished superactual attitudes from actual experiences; we also saw the great role which those superactual responses play in man's life.[23] Whereas certain states and attitudes are restricted in their existence to actually being consciously experienced, others are by their very nature able to subsist in the depth of our soul, even when we are focused on something else. A love does not cease to exist because in a given moment the performance of some work calls for our concentration, and prevents us from thinking of the beloved at that particular moment. We saw that it remains alive and colors all our actual preoccupations, and profoundly influences our entire approach to life and the universe.[24]

We have seen the decisive difference which exists between attitudes which are "experience-immanent" and those which are "experience-transcendent." It is clear that our personal life is not restricted only to "actual" experiences, but that it also contains superactual attitudes, such as our love, our convictions, our faith, our hope in a future life. Now we must go a step further and add the following distinction. Some attitudes are not only superactual but also *general* insofar as they respond, not to a single good, but to an entire sphere of goods or to a certain type of value in general.

We say of someone that he has no interest for art. By this, we do not refer to his attitude to one or another work of art, but to his general position toward artistic beauty. Again when we say that someone is a misanthrope, we once more refer to a general attitude, i.e., this person's attitude toward men as such. In speaking of such a general attitude we do not forsake the sphere of concrete reality to turn to something merely abstract. We do not mean general in the sense of universal; no, we refer to a real attitude of a person. But it is a basic and fundamental one, underlying, as it were, the concrete actualized attitudes and having as its object something generic, insofar as a type of value is concerned, and not merely one concrete individual good. These general attitudes respond to an entire sphere of goods, and to

___

[23] Chapter 17, "Value Response."
[24] Needless to say, this is in no way the sphere of the subconscious which is the concern of psychoanalysis.

one type of ontological value or to one domain of qualitative values. As "general attitudes," in this sense, they are situated in a deeper stratum of the person.[25]

These general superactual attitudes can have a very different character. First, they can be responses motivated by the merely subjectively satisfying or they can be value responses. Secondly, their character of position toward objects may be very different. General value responses may have the character of a fully conscious position toward objects, or they may have an accidental character. The response motivated by the merely subjectively satisfying may have the character of an implicit inclination, or of an explicit, outspoken position as in the case of a hedonist.

These general superactual attitudes range from a natural inclination to consciously sanctioned positions. Important as these differences are, we merely want at present to stress the character which the term "general" should indicate and which is often covered by the term "habitual." We have selected the term "general" because it lays more stress on the position toward a realm of goods, whereas the word "habitual" only stresses the lasting character of this position. Furthermore the term "habitual" connotes habit (in the sense of "the customary") which may give birth to many confusions, as we shall see in a moment. We constantly refer to these general positions in characterizing a personality. We say of a man that he is interested in art or in sport, and of another that he has no sense of sport; we call one man an intellectual person, and mean thereby that scientific or philosophical problems attract him, whereas we characterize another person as a nonintellectual type, meaning that he is not interested in intellectual problems.

Again, we say that a man has no sense for human relations, for other persons play a secondary role in his life, all his interest being absorbed by research or by political activity. In all these cases we refer to a man's general position toward a realm of goods. We also include thereby a general sensitiveness to an entire realm of goods, either for the pleasure which this good may procure to us, or for its value. This sensitiveness to a realm of goods is the very basis for this general position toward it.

[25] If we are speaking here of deeper, we are not thinking of the qualitative depth, but of depth in a purely structural sense. Cf. Chapter 17, "Value Response."

The larger the realm which is the object of such an attitude, the more general will the attitude be. One's attitude toward the entire realm of artistic beauty is patently more general than one's attitude toward beauty in the realm of music. A man who lacks any artistic sensitivity will also be unable to grasp the artistic beauty proper to music; but a man who is unable to grasp the artistic beauty in music may possess a sensitivity for artistic beauty in general. A general sensitivity to artistic beauty is presupposed for grasping beauty in music, but not vice versa.

This does not mean that certain persons cannot be found who are able to grasp artistic beauty only in one field of art, either in music or fine arts or literature. It only means that sensitivity to beauty in one artistic domain necessarily implies sensitivity to artistic beauty as such, independently of the question of whether the capacity to grasp beauty in one specific realm of art may be frustrated by other special reasons.

But the point that matters in this context is that among the general superactual attitudes we have mentioned, one can find more or less general ones, and that in certain cases—as far as the same sphere of goods is concerned—the one broader in scope is presupposed for the narrower one. The depth of this attitude goes hand in hand with the character of being more general, in the structural sense of this term.[26] In delving deeper and deeper in this direction we may reach a man's fundamental attitude toward God and the universe, as the most general superactual attitude, underlying all his less general and all his single attitudes.

We have already touched the central and decisive role of man's ultimate fundamental response to the world of moral values as such. In quoting St. Augustine's distinction between the two fundamental directions of life,[27] we had reference to this one basic decision upon which our approach to every single good depends. This most general ultimate position can be more or less implicit or explicit. In the "enemy of God" we find an explicit, hostile general attitude toward God and the world of values. A carnal, brutelike type who does not believe in God and is blind to the world of values cannot take a conscious, explicit position

[26] Confer Chapter 17, "Value Response."
[27] De Civitate Dei, XIV, 1

toward God and the world of values. Yet his concupiscent, basic attitude implicitly includes an indifference toward God and the world of values. This implicit indifference is the very basis of his value blindness and of his ignoring God.

Evidently this ultimate response is in a structurally deeper stratum than any other response, and it lies at the deepest basis of all our other attitudes. If we said before that the general attitudes respond to something generic and not individual (for instance, to moral goodness as such) this characteristic is not contradicted when our response is directed toward God. For notwithstanding the fact that God is the absolute being, concrete and real, possessing supereminently all the perfections of individuals, nevertheless He also embraces all plenitude of being, and thus our response to God is the most general one in this sense.

Later we shall come back to this ultimate position and response of man, which is the very basis of everything else. It is here that we touch the core of morality in man. But in our present context our interest lies in general attitudes which are already ramifications and differentiations of the ultimate basic attitude: the general superactual responses to a basic type of value or even to one basic aspect of the world of moral and morally relevant values. Such a general response is the very backbone of each virtue. In purity, we have a general superactual response to the mystery of the sphere of sex in the light of God.[28] In reverence, we find the superactual response to the dignity of being as such; [29] and in justice, the superactual response to the metaphysical *due* relation, that to every good the adequate response should be given.

However, although we find a general superactual value response as the backbone of each virtue, many other essential features must still be added. There are undoubtedly many persons who possess the general will to be good and who also respond with their free center to the generic value of a certain sphere of goods, yet do not possess the virtue which corresponds to this free response. The morally conscious man will see the value of a human person and his dignity, and he will understand that this value calls for respect, reverence, and gentleness. He will thus strive for these virtues, but this striving, as such,

[28] Cf. *In Defense of Purity.*
[29] Cf. *Fundamental Moral Attitudes* (New York: Longmans, Green & Co., 1950).

clearly differs from their possession. A general good intention is plainly not identical with the possession of a virtue. This lasting superactual character is common to both virtues and to the general good intention directed toward one realm of goods. This general superactual value response is, as such, an important feature of the moral standard of a person, a lasting, habitual character of his personality. But in order for this attitude to become a virtue, this general superactual value response must have victoriously pervaded the entire personality; it must form the very nature of this person.

When we call someone just or generous or pure, and thus attribute these virtues to him, we include thereby the following elements apart from the general superactual intention which we find in the morally conscious man striving for those virtues, but not yet possessing them. First, we expect that the generous man will always act generously, and especially that the performance of these acts will cost him no effort. We expect that in order to share with others what he possesses he has no inner obstacles to overcome; we expect him to give joyfully. Secondly, we expect that, in the virtuous man, affective responses which are in conformity with this general superactual intention will arise spontaneously. The generous man will precisely rejoice about the fact that he can be instrumental in the welfare of his brethren; he will suffer from being unable to help poor people; the pure man will suffer if he witnesses something impure. Finally, in attributing a virtue to someone, we expect that this moral quality will manifest itself in his demeanor; we speak of the purity expressed in a person's face, of the charity revealed in his smile, in the way in which he greets other persons. . . . In his twelve degrees of humility, St. Benedict enumerates last the way in which a person moves, behaves, and deports himself.[30]

Thus we see that a virtue requires not only the presence of general superactual attitudes toward a realm of goods and their generic value, but also that this intention has victoriously pervaded the entire personality of the virtuous person. It requires that the obstacles of pride and concupiscence have been done away with, and that the general superactual attitude has formed the person's character to such an extent that it has become his

[30] Rule of St. Benedict, chap. 7.

second nature. It is *this* aspect of virtues that the term "habitual" or "habit" tends to indicate.

In order to understand the nature of virtues, however, we must not only distinguish them from concrete, single responses, but also from other habitual elements in the person. We mentioned already that virtues must not be confused with capacities such as the capacity of willing, the capacity of knowing, the capacity of feeling, and so on. We also saw that virtues must not be confused with mere abilities, such as the ability to play an instrument or to play tennis. Apart from the above-mentioned differences, the outspoken qualitative character of virtues clearly distinguishes them from both capacities and abilities.

Now we have to distinguish virtues and vices from mere temperamental dispositions such as a phlegmatic or sanguine temperament, loquacity or taciturnity. These features are also habitual and lasting elements, and, moreover, they have an outspoken qualitative character. They can thus be the more easily confused with virtues. But in reality they differ fundamentally from virtues. Neither knowledge of a certain sphere of goods, nor a response to this sphere, is to be found in these mere temperamental dispositions. Like mere urges, they possess no genuine intentionality. To be vivacious implies patently no knowledge of a good and no attitude toward it, whereas every virtue presupposes the knowledge of a realm of goods and implies a general superactual response toward it. Here we may quote a passage taken from our book *In Defense of Purity*, which deals with the difference between virtues and temperamental dispositions.

In the strict sense a temperament, or subordinately a particular temperamental quality, is a personal idiosyncrasy which in no way depends upon a freely chosen general outlook or particular attitude, and involves nothing in the nature of an apprehension, affirmation, or rejection of values, but, like physical characteristics, is simply "given," and which, if capable of any alteration, can be altered essentially only by means in whose mode of operation the will plays no part. No doubt the part played by temperament can also be influenced by the person's freely chosen attitude—a temperamental sensibility can remain undeveloped or become starved—but the existence of that temperament is not thereby destroyed. Nor is the distinction between temperament and virtue in the very least affected by the fact that a temperament is not acquired. There is no lack of cases in which a man possesses a particular virtue from the very beginning of his moral life and has never acquired it. There are those who have been gentle from the nursery, others who have only become gentle by dint of long struggles. But in both cases alike, the gentleness is not temperamental in the true sense—in contrast to sham gentleness, lack of spirit, which is a genuine temperament, but also in contrast to the mild temperament due to weak passions, which, though it presents a favourable environment for the virtue of gentleness, has no claim to be regarded itself as gentleness. True gentleness is never a temperament, because it is always bound up with the fundamental orientation of the spirit, and because it is always accompanied by a loving attitude and by what that implies— a perception of the value of others as persons and a corresponding response: indeed, it also involves the will to be gentle and a characteristically delicate perception of the unloveliness, hardness, restlessness and malice inherent in anger and violence.

True gentleness, therefore, implies, and this is the most important point, a distinctive *apprehension of values* and a surrender to them which is more or less conscious according to the measure in which the gentleness is due to the soul's deliberate choices or to a natural disposition. But whether this surrender is difficult or easy, in either case there is here a genuine virtue, a section of morality, something grounded in the general moral attitude, not something which is simply "given."

We must guard against introducing into the concept of virtue the notion of achievement, and therefore admitting a virtue only where a particular moral attitude has been acquired by previous struggle. Otherwise we should be involved in the most ridiculous consequences, and the virtue of a St. John as compared with that of a St. Paul would not count as genuine virtue; indeed, the exemplar of all virtues, our Blessed Lady, could not be regarded as in the true sense virtuous, for she came from God's hand all beautiful (*tota pulchra*).* Therefore, in distinguishing between a natural disposition or temperament and virtue, we must, once for all, put aside

* In contrast to acquired virtue stands not only the virtue which attaches to a man from the outset, but also that which is bestowed upon him at one stroke in some moment of crisis. An instance of the latter is the conversion of St. Paul, when there came instantaneously to birth in his soul new ethical attitudes which it would be quite impossible to regard as acquired, and which, nevertheless, were undoubtedly genuine virtues and not mere temperamental dispositions.

Nor can the virtue which slowly matures in us without conscious action on our part, but which at the same time is our reward for moral purpose and striving in other fields, be termed "acquired."

as irrelevant the question whether the characteristic in question was only acquired in course of time and after a struggle, or by the grace of God belonged to the person from the outset, or was bestowed at a particular moment of his life. The distinction must rather be decided by the relation between the quality in question and the subject's fundamental moral position, by the degree to which it involves a perception of values and responses to them, and is grounded in and upheld by the general attitude its possessor has freely adopted. Naturally, the distinction is also closely connected with the quality of the characteristic. Virtues are always of an entirely different quality from temperamental dispositions. A characteristic identical in quality cannot be sometimes a virtue, sometimes a temperament. No doubt there are temperaments which favour the development of particular virtues. For example, natures in which the instinctive life is weak are adapted by their temperament for spirituality, gentleness, patience, modesty, etc. For natures whose instincts are stronger and more primitive these virtues are more difficult of attainment. Courage, fidelity to truth once perceived, unreserved devotion of the entire person to what has been recognised as good, are, on the contrary, the virtues which have affinity with this temperament. But these temperamental affinities do no more than render the corresponding virtue easier to attain and invite to its attainment, and though they may present a certain counterpart of the virtue on a far lower plane, they are not even its germ, for powerfully developed instincts are equally to be met with in the bestial debauchee who is the slave of his passions and possesses none of the above-mentioned virtues. Such temperamental dispositions in no way predetermine the virtue or otherwise of their possessor, whether a man's fundamental attitude is good or bad; they simply represent special paths already made which are equally at the disposal of a good or a bad moral attitude. They merely decide which vices and virtues are affine to the person concerned. But this affinity is not a decisive factor. For there are men, for example, who in spite of strong passions are markedly spiritual, gentle and patient, as was very often the case with the saints.

All this is but further proof that a quality of temperament can in no case be regarded as a virtue, any more than a genuine virtue, though it has not been acquired, can be explained as a mere temperament. Truthfulness, justice, purity, patience, gentleness, kindliness, humility, may be "natural" virtues in contrast to fully conscious virtues, which are in the strict sense products of the spirit—a distinction obviously accompanied by a profound difference of quality, which we must discuss in greater detail later (pp. 50–4).

Thus we see how virtues clearly differ from other lasting, habitual elements in the human person. They must not only be clearly distinguished from capacities and abilities, but also from temperamental dispositions.

Yet in order to grasp the nature of virtues, a fundamental difference in the frame of what may be called virtue in a larger sense of the word must still be elucidated. Morally unconscious men can be called generous, or pure, or gentle, just as they can also be called stingy, impure, or violent. Though we do not find in them a general superactual value response in the full sense of the word, though they do not have the real general will to be good, though they have not discovered their capacity of sanctioning or disavowing, they can still possess virtues in a broader sense of this term. Their virtues certainly differ thoroughly from the virtues of the morally conscious type. They differ by their unconscious, accidental character, as well as by their quality. We could term them "dispositional virtues," in contradistinction to the true, spiritual virtues which are, as it were, born out of the spirit.

Dispositional virtues must also be clearly distinguished from temperamental dispositions. We saw that temperamental dispositions, such as a choleric or phlegmatic temperament, great vitality or poor vitality, quickness or slowness, imply neither a knowledge of a specific realm of goods nor a general superactual response to it. The dispositional virtues (such as the justice or the veracity of the morally unconscious man) definitely imply a knowledge of a realm of goods and of the type of value which is proper to these goods, as well as a response to this value. A morally unconscious man such as Tom Jones in Fielding's novel, or the Ingénu of Voltaire's work,[31] sees the value of honesty and the disvalue of dishonesty; he is aware that it is mean to betray another person.

But the essential difference lies in the fact that in this dispositional virtue, the kind of value perception is on a completely different level than is found in the morally conscious man.[32]

---

[31] Hero of one of Voltaire's novels, bearing the same title.

[32] With respect to vices, this difference only exists in an analogous sense, and, above all, it does not have the same bearing on the moral significance of a vice. We saw before that there are also many levels of consciousness in the morally evil

Morally relevant values which have been grasped are not understood in their majestic character, nor is the call issuing from them fully understood. Their moral significance is not fully comprehended. The difference between morally relevant and morally irrelevant values is not clearly grasped. But above all, the general will to be morally good is not present. Hence dispositional virtues also have the character of something accidental. They are lovable adornments of a personality and we therefore consider the possessors of these virtues as fortunate. These dispositional virtues are full qualities which share with true spiritual virtues all the above-mentioned characteristics. They also manifest themselves in the ease with which certain good actions are accomplished, as well as in the fact that they lead to spontaneous affective responses. They also find expression in the face and demeanor of a person. They are real, lasting qualities of a personality. But notwithstanding these features, which justify our calling them virtues, dispositional virtues fundamentally differ from the authentic moral virtues, which are, as we said, born out of the spirit.[33]

We have already mentioned the danger of misinterpretation present in the terms "habit" and "habitual." We also call things "habitual" which are accomplished by custom, such as winding

---

man. There are men enslaved by vices, such as drunkenness or lechery, whose indifference toward the world of morally relevant values has a more implicit character. We shall deal with this problem in the next section, "Roots of Moral Evil."

[33] "There are, indeed, men who have about them something undefiled, which reminds us of nature in her virgin state. They avoid sex isolated as its own end with its tainted and oppressive atmosphere; they can breathe only in the clear, open air. But they lack that spiritualisation of the entire man, 'the spiritual riches,' which characterizes perfect purity. Their purity seems rather the manifestation of a splendid untarnished vitality, though this natural purity is, of course, never something *merely* vital, but extends also to the moral sphere. Nevertheless, the atmosphere which invests it, and which we breathe in the presence of a naturally pure man in contrast to the potent spirituality of the purity which is begotten of the spirit, is the nobility of life unsullied and uncorrupted, as it were, fresh from the hand of God.

"Nature's pure men have about them something of the purity of the mountain torrent, something of the clear, fresh air of early morning, but nothing which substantially transcends this world and moves in a higher region. Unlike those whose purity is born of the spirit, their being is not redolent of something 'not of this world.' Obviously a gulf divides this natural purity from the virtue just described, a product of the spirit in the strict sense, which alone has, strictly speaking, the right to the name of purity. Nevertheless, this natural purity is something wholly positive, beautiful and attractive." *In Defense of Purity*, p. 71.

our watch, closing the door, putting our shoes back in place. Many other things are habitual because we are used to doing them, and they take place, as it were, by themselves, without effort, even without our focusing our attention on them. Again, we may speak of the habit of getting up early, or of taking a nap after lunch, or of reading the newspaper after dinner, and so on. Once again the notion of habitual connotes that the performance of these things costs us no effort or even that we have a natural inclination to do them because we are used to doing them.

It would be a calamitous error to confuse the ease which is indeed a true feature of virtue, with the ease which is a result of our being used to something. The meaning of the term "habitual," as applied to virtues, differs radically from the term "habitual" used in the sense of being accustomed to something. As this point is of paramount importance for a true understanding of virtues, we shall briefly examine the different types of habits (in the sense of being accustomed to something), and their relation to morality and especially to virtues.

We have mentioned above [34] that certain activities which are originally commanded by our will may, after a certain time, be initiated by mere animal voluntariness. Such are the activities which we just mentioned as one type of habit (closing a door, winding our watch, and so on). "Habitual" means here that these activities are performed without full consciousness, automatically, as it were, and that they have sunk into the sphere of animal voluntariness due to the fact that we have gotten used to them through repeated performances. We saw before that actions in the strict sense of this term can never be accomplished in this way. Actions are necessarily commanded by the will, and can never be ruled by mere animal voluntariness. This meaning of "habitual" can never be applied to actions, and virtues are patently not habits, in the sense of the habit of winding one's watch. The ease with which a generous man distributes alms obviously differs from the automatic character of those activities which are performed without actualization of our will and without even a conscious realization that they are being performed. As a matter of fact, this semiconscious way of performing activi-

[34] Chapter 21, "The Two Perfections of the Will."

ties which are initiated by mere animal voluntariness is incompatible with the very nature of an action.

The same applies to the ease proper to the accomplishment of activities which we have practiced for so long that we can fully handle them. The pianist acquires a great technique through continuous practice. This ease and facility are out of the question with respect to virtues. The idea that a generous man accomplishes the action of giving alms without effort, because through constant practice he has acquired a great technique, is obviously nonsensical. There are many things which can be accomplished with great efficiency because one has learned them through practice, such as typing, lacemaking, driving a car, learning by heart, learning a language, and many others. The facility in these cases always refers to something technical. Insofar as the above-mentioned activities surpass the merely technical sphere, this ease proper to skill is no longer to be found. Actions in the strict sense are never a question of skill or technique, and the ease of accomplishing a morally good action without effort patently differs from one which is a result of skill. Actions in the full sense of the term exclude the notion of skill, as we see if we think not only of the technical, subordinate aspects of actions, but of their value-responding core. To view an action (for instance, the saving of a man's life) as if it were something merely technical would prevent it from being the bearer of moral values or disvalues.

Adaptation is another type of effect which habit can bring about. It refers especially to things related to the body. Through habit we may obtain that things which are disagreeable and difficult for us become easy and can be done without effort. Such is the case, for instance, with the habit of getting up early in the morning, or of being able to sleep in spite of noise, or of taking medicine which has a bitter taste, and so on. The role of habit, which is paramount for our bodily life, has here the character of an adaptation which makes possible certain things which were impossible before, or at least which required a great effort on our part in order to be performed.

This adaptation presupposes that we get used to something; it presupposes its continuous repetition. This capacity of adaptation through habit is indeed a precious gift granted to men in the sphere which has, more or less, a biological character. In doing away with obstacles which exterior circumstances and our body may impose on us, it makes man free for the real life of his soul. The strident voice of a person with whom we have to work may in the beginning be unbearable and irritating to our nerves, but after a while we adapt ourselves to it and it no longer hinders us in our work. Noisy surroundings may be an obstacle for concentration and recollection. We may be unable at first to make a mental prayer elsewhere than in church. Later on we may be able through adaptation to recollect ourselves and to make our mental prayer in our home, or even in the subway. We could quote innumerable other examples.

It is not difficult to see the radical difference between the "ease" brought about by adaptation, and the "ease" proper to virtue. The virtue of patience makes it easy to bear the shrill voice of another person, not because through adaptation his voice no longer makes an impression, but because the humble, loving basic attitude is so predominant in the patient man and so present at every moment that the disagreeable impression of the unmusical voice is no longer able to alter his charitable and gentle attitude toward this person. The effect of adaptation presupposes no special moral attitude. The ease which is a mark of virtue is a fruit of the superabundance of love. Hence we see that the ease which is a result of adaptation also clearly differs from the ease which is proper to virtues. Adaptation does not apply to our moral life.

Habit and "the customary" play a great role, not only in a sphere which is more or less related to our body, but also in man's psychical life. The intrusive role of habit in our life is a great trial to man, a trial which is a result of the tragic insufficiency of man's fallen nature. On the other hand, it may also be considered as something beneficial. Habit will display its positive or negative aspect according to the type of experiences which are affected by habit.

It is a tragic human weakness that in getting accustomed to a high good one is in danger of appreciating it less. If it is a great objective good for the person, man takes it for granted after a while; he no longer fully realizes the gift which he has received, and is no longer filled with gratitude for its possession.

His sensitivity for its value may diminish; his joy over its possession may become weaker. We should consciously fight against this blunting effect of the customary and of the habitual. To be spiritually awake is a great and fundamental virtue, and in being accustomed to something we run the risk of losing it more and more.[35] This effect of the customary is obviously a definite danger for our moral life.

Yet the same circumstances which may blunt us to the value of a good through habit may also be a source of specific appreciation of the good in question. There are conservative persons who shun the unknown and the new, and like only that which is familiar to them. Hence to be accustomed to a good, far from neutralizing their relation to it, is rather a condition for a full appreciation and sometimes even the source of an attachment as such. Habit can have two different kinds of positive effects.

First, there are people for whom habit is a source of attachment; they like something solely because they are accustomed to it. Familiarity renders something dear to them. The new and unfamiliar frightens them and they approach it with suspicion. This mentality entails a lack of objectivity, just as the *cupiditas rerum novarum* (the craving for new things) of the sensation-loving man is also unobjective. The man craving for sensational experiences despises all things which are familiar to him and longs for new things for the very reason that they are new and unknown. As soon as something becomes familiar, it is "used" and has no longer the capacity to affect him. The conservative type, on the contrary, is closed and hostile to everything new, and adheres to things which are familiar because they are familiar. Both types are determined by an illegitimate factor and are unable to do justice to a good.

The second kind of positive effect which habit can have is that familiarity with an object is not the source of our attachment, but is an indispensable condition for a true relation to the object. The true value of a good discloses itself only after a longer acquaintance with this good has been granted. So long as something is new and unfamiliar, these persons are not able to penetrate it; some sort of shyness closes them up; they feel them-

[35] Cf. *Liturgy and Personality,* chap. 7.

selves as outsiders, and this feeling bars them from a full appreciation of the good at stake. It is only when something is known to them, is inserted into their life, as it were, that they open themselves and that their love is no longer hindered. Patently there is no danger of confusing this aspect of habit with the ease of virtue. Neither the negative blunting effect nor the positive familiarizing effect of habit offers any possibility of such a confusion.

Finally custom and habit may play an important role in our motivation; we do certain things for no other reason than that we are accustomed to doing them. We saw before that the customary may create in us certain bodily desires, for instance, the urge to sleep at a certain hour or to smoke. Something analogous exists in the psychical sphere. We have formed the habit of playing a game, and it has become a need for us. We do not choose it, as we did before we formed the habit, only because it amuses us, but also because it has become a need through habit. But even things which are in no way agreeable as such, but neutral, may acquire through habit a motivating power for us. Just as associations are formed by our imagination through habit, custom can also create a tendency which becomes a motive for our will. We yield with our will to this tendency. A kind of psychical law of gravity pulls us in the direction of the habitual, and gives to something neutral (which as such cannot motivate our will) a power to attract our will. The more primitive a man is, the greater will be the role which habits play in his life—the more he treads in certain paths simply because he is accustomed to do so, the more will he let himself be enslaved by the habitual.

With respect to motivation we can say this: First, habit may increase the attractive power of an agreeable thing and make the desire for it an uncontrollable urge and need. This applies not only to alcoholic beverages, to smoking, and to the use of narcotics of all kinds—cases in which the bodily sphere plays a predominant role—but also to playing games, paying social calls, going to the movies, and so on.

Secondly, habit may even give a motivating power to something which is neutral as such (e.g., the routine followed in the performance of daily activities). It is then less the object which attracts me than a kind of *vis a tergo* which pushes me to follow in the tracks formed by a habit. In this case, as in those just mentioned, we can obviously no longer speak of a mere "ease" in acting in the direction of habit. We are rather pushed or drawn in this direction; we follow not only without effort, but it would cost us a great effort not to obey this "law of gravity."

It is of the utmost importance to understand that to act objectively in conformity with the call of the morally relevant values because we have formed the habit of doing so radically differs from actions which are the fruits of virtue. When our will is not motivated by the morally relevant values but only pushed by the neutral force of habit, an action has no moral value. If someone should give to the poor, and upon being asked why should say, "Because it is an old habit of mine," the correspondence with the moral law would here be completely accidental. Such a person has no participation in the morally relevant values. It is by mere chance that his habits push him in the direction of the moral law. To be a prey to habit, instead of responding to the value or disvalue of an object, is, as such, even something morally negative. Certainly we may consider it as preferable to acting immorally. The fact that a sin is not committed is always a good, even if someone should refrain from sinning in postponing it for a better occasion. But an action in which the will, instead of being a value response, is motivated by mere habit has patently no positive moral value. It is mainly this connotation of the terms "habitual" and "habit" which leads to confusion. The character of a virtue, for instance generosity, designated by the term *habitus* in no way implies that we act generously out of habit, in the sense of the customary, instead of being motivated by love of neighbor. The "habit" of generosity not only excludes our being motivated by mere habit, but radically opposes this motivation. A man who would always act generously because of mere habit (a difficult fiction) would in no way be endowed with the virtue of generosity.

A completely different question is whether habit may not have a beneficial function as a secondary factor, for instance, after one has chosen something in a genuine value response. A person who is genuinely religious may, under the wholesome influence of a friend, decide to go daily to holy Mass and Communion. After a while he may form the habit of doing so, and though he does it primarily for the sake of God, his habit supports his good intention and makes it easier for him to do so.

There is no doubt that a good habit can be a valuable help in the performance of many morally good things, especially those which should be accomplished every day, and which do not depend upon a special situation and the call of a morally relevant good which invites us to intervene. It may be an invaluable ally, for instance, in being faithful in our daily prayers, or in having a certain regard for other persons with whom we live, or in abstaining from speaking too much, and so on. But habit must never replace the value response, for were this to happen, the genuine, positive moral value would be frustrated. But as a secondary support, in making it easier for us to act, it is without any doubt, of great avail. From a pedagogical point of view, this function of habit may legitimately play an important role.

Yet it is precisely in comparing the ease which habit may procure us in the performance of things which are sought because of their value with the ease which is a mark of virtue that their difference appears most clearly. The virtuous man, for instance the veracious man, will without any effort never lie, because the value-responding superactual attitude of truthfulness has victoriously pervaded his nature, because he has such horror of the disvalue of a lie, such a fundamental reverence for reality and truth, that all temptations to tell lies, temptations which may arise because of fear, concupiscence, or pride, have lost their power over him. The saint will without effort make sacrifices for his brethren; he will easily renounce a pleasurable good in order to give it to his neighbor; he will remain patient without effort. But he will do so because of the superabundant love for God and his neighbor, because this love has victoriously pervaded his nature, because it has become the principle of his life and being.

In all these cases, habit or custom plays no role. The ease which is a mark of virtue is a fruit of love and is in no way the result of a neutral psychical law of gravity. It is not a wholesome support of a natural neutral tendency which luckily coincides with our value-responding will, but it is a pure fruit of the value response, of the "loving, reverent value-responding center" in us. Thus we see that the ease which habit may bring about differs radically from the ease which is a mark of virtue. Even in cases in which a good habit may favor, support, and facilitate our walking in the path of moral righteousness, it differs radically from the ease in acting rightly which is a fruit of virtue. For the man who has not yet acquired a virtue, the support of an extramoral factor, as an ally, may be desirable. Once he has acquired the virtue in question, no extramoral factor intervenes. It is precisely the general superactual value response which has penetrated man's entire being, and the ease is here exclusively a victory of the value-responding center over pride and concupiscence. This ease is not a welcome facilitation, as analogously certain temperamental dispositions may be, but is itself something morally precious. It is a symptom of the moral standard of a personality, of the victory of the value response in this person, and something possessing a high moral value of its own. "God loveth a cheerful giver" (II Cor. 9:7). The ease resulting from habit or custom, far from being a symptom of the victory of the value-responding center as such and still more from being morally good in itself, is at best a valuable ally in the good fight, a facilitating circumstance.

Thus we see that in calling a virtue "habit," we have to distinguish clearly this meaning of habit from the habit or custom which plays a great role in our extramoral life. We must, above all, clearly distinguish the ease present in both virtue and custom: it is only after having dispelled confusions in this respect that the nature of virtue (and especially of the authentic, spiritual virtues, born out of the spirit) reveals itself clearly.

Someone could object: Granted that habit in the sense of custom has no affinity with virtue, is it not true that in the process of acquiring a virtue the repetition of good actions plays a decisive role? Is Aristotle not right in saying that we cannot acquire a virtue in merely learning what its nature is, i.e., in perfecting our knowledge, but in practicing it time and again? And does this not show that, at least concerning the acquisition of a virtue, an element which is very similar to custom or to skill plays a decisive role?

There is no doubt that time and repeated practice in responding to a value plays a great role in the acquisition of virtues. But this effect is definitely not identical with the effect of habit.

Time has an irreplaceable importance in man's life. Many great and important things require their own time in order to unfold themselves. Thus the acquisition of a virtue also requires time. The influence of a good environment upon a person does not display itself in a very short time. It is only when someone is exposed for a longer period of time to the irradiation of a great and morally noble personality that he may undergo a process of moral change or growth, that a new world is disclosed to him. He has to breathe this atmosphere for a while, to move and live in it, in order to undergo its beneficial organic influence. Analogously, time has its irreplaceable function in human relations. The sharing of great experiences in common is of deep importance in these relations.

But all this has nothing to do with habit or getting accustomed to something. It concerns the role of time for taking root in the good, for permitting values to fecundate our soul, to penetrate every fiber of our personality. It is a process of assimilation which, in its meaningful organic character, clearly differs from the mechanical effect of habit. This role of time manifests itself also in the religious sphere. The process of transformation in Christ also unfolds itself in time, and implies that we strike deeper and deeper roots in Christ, *radicati et fundati* . . . ("that we may become rooted and grounded in love"). In order to be transformed in Christ, our mind needs to contemplate divine truth time and again, our spirit must always be nourished anew with the *panis angelicus* (the bread of angels), our heart must always be exposed anew to the irradiation of Christ.

In order to acquire a virtue we must set our course again and again in the *viis Domini* (the ways of the Lord) by repeatedly acting in the morally right way, in order to be more and more incorporated into the good. But between this repetition of right action, this taking root ever anew in the realm of the morally good, and habit there exists a wide abyss. To confuse these would be equivalent to claiming that eating is a mere habit as though the necessity of feeding our body time and again in order to live and grow were nothing but the effect of habit.

We have seen that the backbone of every virtue is a general superactual value response to a sphere of morally relevant values. With this in mind, the shortcomings of the Aristotelian "mesotes theory" come to the fore. The difference between virtue and vice cannot be reduced to a matter of proportion whereby vice is either a defect or an excess and virtue the mean between the two. Avariciousness and prodigality are not opposites from the moral point of view: they are both superactual attitudes, motivated by the merely subjectively satisfying—both ramifications of concupiscence—both implying indifference toward values and especially moral values, and both are thus strictly antithetical to generosity, which is a general superactual value response. Were we to take it for granted that an avaricious person could become less and less avaricious until he became prodigal, this person would not become generous halfway between these two extremes. The road leading from avariciousness to prodigality never crosses generosity or liberality.

In many extramoral domains, the good thing is really the mean between two evils. Great cold as well as great heat are evils (at least for our body). The mean is an agreeable and healthy temperature. Meat should neither be too salty nor have too little salt. Especially in the sphere of health, this principle is time and again confirmed—men should neither eat too much nor too little. This principle applies also to many other spheres, insofar as their immanent logic is concerned. Thus it would be correct to state that the reasonable balance between income and expenses lies halfway between avariciousness and prodigality.

But as soon as we come to moral values, this principle no longer applies. The reasonable balance between income and expenses is an extramoral affair; it is related only to the reasonable observance of a neutral, immanent logic of the economic sphere. Economic reasonability does not disclose a person's moral standards; the most refined egoist or criminal can possess this reasonability. There exists a wide separation between this type of reasonability and the moral virtue of generosity. As we have already seen, generosity as a moral virtue is in no way the mean between avariciousness and prodigality. It presupposes a general superactual value-response, and as such is incomparably more remote from avariciousness and prodigality than each is from the other.

The real antithesis between virtue and vice is determined by whether a person is superactually directed toward morally relevant values or whether he is absorbed by his interest in the

merely subjectively satisfying.[36] Whether prodigality or avariciousness satisfies his concupiscence is a relatively secondary
question, for it concerns an antithesis from the point of view of
temperamental disposition, and not from the moral one.

All vices are outgrowths of either pride or concupiscence, or of
both together; [37] they are ramifications of an ultimate fundamental attitude which, implicitly or explicitly, is either indifferent
or even hostile to God and the world of morally relevant values.

Before turning to the roots of moral evil, one more problem
pertaining to the sphere of virtues remains to be stressed. The
hierarchy among virtues is one of the most central and fundamental problems of ethics: not only the rank of the value-endowed
good must be minutely studied, but also the specific nature of the
inner word of the superactual response. It is here that the question
of the "value of its own" of the response arises again with respect
to the very quality of the virtue and its intrinsic moral sublimity:
How are the virtues ordered according to rank? Which is the
highest? But this question cannot be answered without including
another of a still more fundamental importance. It is the problem, mentioned before, of the relation between natural virtues
and the virtues which are so resplendent in a saint, in the "new
creature in Christ." The transformation of man's nature in
Christ is not only an object of our faith, such as the Holy Trinity,
or the presence of Christ in the Eucharist. It also manifests itself
in a way which is accessible to our mind, at least insofar as certain
fundamental aspects are concerned. Certainly the action of sanctifying grace which is ingrafted in our soul in baptism is something inaccessible to the eyes of our mind, something which we
can embrace only in faith. But, insofar as saintliness is concerned
—the fruits of the Holy Ghost in the person (that which forms
the basis of inquiry in the process of beatification)—we are
confronted with something which also manifests itself to the
eyes of our spirit. In the concluding chapter of this book we shall
come back to this great problem, which is at the core of Christian
ethics. At present this hint may suffice.

[36] Aristotle admitted this in Book IV of his *Nicomachean Ethics,* but unfortunately he failed to see that this admission contained an implicit refutation of
his Mesotes theory.

[37] This will become clearer in our analysis of the Roots of Moral Evil (Part
Two, IV).

CHAPTER 28

MORAL "RIGORISM" [1]

WE HAVE seen that an adequate response is due every good endowed with a value. The adequacy of the response implies that the inner word of the response corresponds in degree to the rank of the value. We have seen that in the case of a full value perception and a pure value response, this correspondence will necessarily take place. But not only is it so, it should be so. We must realize that we are here confronted, not only with a fact, but also with an "oughtness" relation.

The adequacy of a response thus also implies that we give preference to the good endowed with a higher value as against the one possessing a lower value.[2] We should have greater veneration for a saint than for a noble figure such as Socrates; we should admire Mozart's opera *Don Giovanni* more than Rossini's *Barber of Seville*, and so on. The validity of this general principle has to be admitted, despite the fact that with regard to certain value responses many other factors interfere. Insofar as an adequate value response implies an appreciation, insofar as the

---

[1] The term "rigorism" is used here in a wider sense, and is thus not equivalent to the official term used in moral theology.

[2] The term "prefer" or "give the preference to" can have different meanings; we use it in the sense of a choice between two alternative possibilities, and this is certainly the more authentic sense of the term. Preference in this sense is to be found in the sphere of action. Again we use it in the sense of indicating the "more" of love, of veneration, of esteem, of joy, of which we spoke in Chapter 17 on "Value Response." This "preference" has no character of choice; it does not entail a turning away from one thing in order to select the other. This sense of "preferring" applies to the sphere of affective responses. Finally, we sometimes use the term "prefer" in a sense which merely indicates that we like something more. In this case neither a value nor a value response is in question, but merely a subjective inclination.

inner word of our response refers exclusively to the value and its rank, this principle is self-evident, and we presuppose it continually. It is a necessary consequence of the fundamental due relation, which we have expounded before. This hierarchical principle governs the liturgy; we find it in the display of rejoicing and splendor observed in the different ranks of feasts, in the precedence given one feast over another which conflicts with it. We find it in the enumeration of saints in the *Confiteor*. Everywhere the principle commanding a greater or lesser response is present. The role of the *ordo amoris* in St. Augustine's ethics is well known:

> Now, he lives a just and holy life who appraises things with an unprejudiced mind. He is a person who has a well-regulated love and neither loves what he ought not, nor fails to love what he should. He does not love more an object deserving only of lesser love, nor love equally what he should love either more or less, nor love either more or less what he should love equally. Every sinner, insofar as he is a sinner, should not be loved, and every man, insofar as he is a man, should be loved for the sake of God, but God is to be loved for His own sake.[3]

For St. Augustine, the very source of moral goodness is to have our love follow the objective order of love, to love more that which deserves more love. In line with his thought we might add, to love more that which has a higher value.[4] In *De Libero Arbitrio*, St. Augustine claims that the source of all moral evil is the preference of a lower good over a higher one.[5]

Max Scheler lays still greater stress on this point.[6] For him the morally significant act is always a preference of one good over another, and the source of its goodness lies in the right order of

---

[3] *De Doctrina Christiana*, I, 27, 26.

[4] It must be said that this applies to our love of God, our love of the saints, and our love of impersonal goods. But with respect to love for a friend, a spouse, a child, a brother, a mother, and so on, certain other factors legitimately intervene conditioning the order of our love and even the uniqueness of a certain love. There is a mysterious affinity, a being ordered to each other, which enables us to discover the beauty and preciousness of an individual personality. This beauty engenders a love which is not possible for persons who have not been ordered to us in the same way. But this greater love and even incomparable, unique love does not imply any inadequacy in the response to the hierarchy of values. (Cf. my work *Metaphysik der Gemeinschaft*, chaps. 5 and 6.)

[5] Bk. I. (F. E. Tourscher, *op. cit.*, pp. 47 and 89.)

[6] *Der Formalismus Kant's und die materiale Wertethik.*

this preference, that is to say, in the fact that the higher value is preferred to the lower one. Analogously, the preference of the lower one is the source of moral evil.

We have already shown in our criticism of Scheler that it is not possible to restrict moral goodness to a right preference, and moral evil to a wrong one. The real moral drama does not lie in the observance of the hierarchical order in our value response, but in the basic decision of whether to conform to the important-in-itself and morally relevant values or to the merely subjectively satisfying. It refers to the decisive difference concerning the direction of our will which St. Augustine so clearly described in distinguishing between a life directed to God and a life lived according to oneself: "In this very thing the great difference of the two cities, the godly and the ungodly . . . lies most apparent; God's love prevailing in the one, and self-love in the other." [7]

We have dealt with this problem [8] and we shall return to it in our analysis of the "Roots of Moral Evil."

If, therefore, we must insist that the right preference is not the source of all moral goodness nor the wrong one the source of all moral evil, it yet remains true that we should prefer the higher value to the lower one, and that, prescinding from all special circumstances, it is better to prefer the higher good to the lower one. In what concerns the question of whether it is morally better, however, we must realize that reference to something morally better presupposes that the preference refers to morally relevant values. If morally irrelevant goods are at stake, it still remains true that among these we should give the preference to the good having a higher value, but to do so does not guarantee that our attitude is endowed with a moral value.

In this context, ethics must examine the following problems:

First, is it morally better to prefer a good having a higher value among the morally relevant values?

Secondly, is it morally obligatory to prefer the higher ranking morally relevant good?

The first question requires no answer if we prescind from all other circumstances which may occur. For, it is clear then that

[7] *De Civitate Dei*, XIV, 13. (J. Healey, *op. cit.*, Vol. II.)
[8] Chapter 3, "The Categories of Importance."

to prefer the higher ranking morally relevant good is morally
better.

Every morally conscious person will, in a situation in which
he is forced to choose between two different morally relevant
goods, be eager to find out which of the two goods ranks higher;
for he has the self-evident intention of choosing the higher one
if there are no other circumstances involved which may induce
him to act otherwise. The principle that it is morally better to
conform to the higher morally relevant value is self-evidently
presupposed, even if due to special circumstances our final decision goes in another direction. Hence it remains true that
ceteris paribus it is morally better to conform to the higher
morally relevant value. This is as self-evident as the principle
that our actions should be morally good. Of course many differentiations must be taken into account, according to whether we
are concerned with the sphere of affective responses or with that
of actions. In the sphere of affective value responses the preference—apart from the forementioned exceptions concerning the
different categories of love directed to a specific individual—
will necessarily be in harmony with the rank of the value, granted
that no other motive interferes and that an adequate value response underlies it. Since a disharmony here is possible only if
other motives intervene, either in darkening the value perception or in corroding the value response, the question really is
whether a pure value response is morally better than a mixed
one. Now there can be no doubt that the pure value response
ranks morally higher.

But in the sphere of action the problem presents itself in a
different light because of the freedom of will. Here many elements may modify this general principle. It may be altered, first
of all, by the theme of a situation, i.e., the task which this concrete situation entails. The call of God manifests itself, not only
in a morally relevant value and its rank, but also in the specific
nature of a situation,[9] that is to say, in the *theme* which is at stake

---

[9] It would be completely erroneous to confuse the modifying role of circumstances with an invalidation of the general and inalterable character of the moral
law as is done by the *Situationethik* (ethics of circumstances)—cf. Preface. The
moral law does precisely take into account the role played by circumstances, that
is to say, it requires consideration, not only of morally relevant values, but also of
the specific circumstances involved in a concrete situation.

here and now and which addresses itself in a specific way to one's own person.[10]

It is impossible to enumerate the countless factors which may condition the theme of a situation; we must restrict ourselves to the main ones. The first factor is the theme of a situation as such. In church, for instance, the theme is to adore God, according to the words of the Holy Scriptures: *Domus mea, domus orationis*—"My house is the house of prayer." Occupations which may in themselves be good, such as the act of comforting an afflicted person, are not the theme during Mass. The same applies *mutatis mutandis* to the performance of some work, such as giving a lecture, and so on. The objective theme of a situation or an activity is a first decisive element which must be taken into account. Another is the dramatic call for immediate intervention, for example, when something is at stake which must be granted preference, not because of its value, but because of its emergency character. If, during Mass, my neighbor faints, I am called upon to take care of him. If my neighbor's house is on fire, whatever may be the good with which I am concerned, this emergency has precedence.

Equally, certain things though in themselves inferior take precedence over others if there is an urgent need for them at the present moment. Though man lives not by bread alone (though it is much more important as such to give someone decisive help on his way to Christ), there is no doubt that if a man is starving, I must above all give him food. This precedence of something in itself lower is partly rooted in its indispensability and its indirect importance for a high value, and partly in the fact that it cannot be postponed, whereas the higher good may be realized at some later date.

Another element determining the theme of a situation is revealed in the case when a specific task has been entrusted to a person; this gives precedence to one good over another in a certain situation, independently of the rank of the value. If a person has been entrusted with the care of a child, and if in a certain situation this child is one of several children who are in danger,

---

[10] "Human activity is similar: its perfection is not entirely guaranteed by what kind of action it is; additional accidents are also required, namely its due circumstances." St. Thomas, *Summa Theologica*, 1a–2ae, xviii, 3.

he must think first of the child who has been entrusted to him and for whom he has assumed a specific responsibility.

These examples may suffice to show that the theme of a situation can modify the application of the general principle that preference should be given to the higher ranking morally relevant value. It is clear that, given a choice between two goods of equal rank, circumstances may reveal which one should be chosen. The theme of a specific situation may make it even morally preferable to choose a lower good. The circumstances may be such that the call implied in that situation indicates that we should choose the lower good. This modification, however, only changes the application of the general principle mentioned above and in no way invalidates it. The question as to which value ranks higher remains always of essential importance; it remains true that *ceteris paribus* it is better to choose the higher ranking value.

We can summarize our inquiry as follows: In the realm of morally relevant values, it is, as such, morally better to choose the higher ranking value. As soon as a choice between morally relevant goods is imposed on us, the first question we should examine from the moral point of view is which is the higher ranking one. Only after having answered this question can we consider the different circumstances at stake in order to understand the specific theme of the concrete situation. The theme of the situation may be such that we are called upon to choose the value of lesser rank, that is to say, it may grant the lower good additional weight, turning the scale in its favor. Instead of contradicting the general principle that it is better to prefer the good possessing a higher morally relevant value, the eventually modifying role of circumstances testifies to the validity of this principle because it presupposes it as self-evident.

Before considering the second question, i.e., how far this principle applies to moral obligation, we still have to mention a problem concerning the relation between morally relevant and morally irrelevant values. We saw that the difference between these two types of value is not simply a difference of rank. There even exist extraordinary cases in which a morally irrelevant good, as such, ranks higher than a morally relevant one. If a great sculptor, in order to create a work of art, were to torture an animal in using it as a model for his work, we would rightly consider this to be morally wrong. The suffering of an animal is a morally relevant evil. A great work of art is not a morally relevant good; but its qualitative value ranks, as such, higher than that of the animal. The destruction of a great work of art is in itself a greater evil than the death or suffering of an animal. Hence the fact that a good has a morally relevant value does not always necessarily imply that its value ranks as such higher than that of a morally irrelevant good.

Despite this fact, we must give the preference to morally relevant values because, insofar as our actions are concerned, morally relevant goods and above all morally obligatory ones have an incomparable precedence over all morally irrelevant values on account of their moral significance. Our first task is not to offend God, and thus no striving for any good whatsoever can suspend our obligation to obey the moral law. However, this latter statement in no way contradicts our former one that higher ranking values have precedence over others. We have seen time and again that moral values rank incomparably higher than any other value. The idea that a moral disvalue could be outweighed by any morally irrelevant or even morally relevant value but not a moral one, issues from a complete misconception of the hierarchy of values (Cf. Preface).

Without entering into a detailed discussion, we wish to state that every response directed to a morally relevant value entails a response to moral goodness as such, and this fact explains that the preference given to morally relevant values is not in contradiction to the principle that it is better to prefer the higher ranking value.

We now come to the second question mentioned before: Is it not only better but even *morally obligatory* to prefer the higher ranking morally relevant value, as long as no special circumstances turn the scale? Obviously this second question is of the greatest interest. Would not the thesis that we are obliged to choose the higher morally relevant good result in a kind of rigorism, an ethical theory which has often been proved false?

In posing the question of whether it is morally obligatory to prefer the higher morally relevant good to a lower one, we have still to distinguish between two different problems. The first is concerned with the question: under what circumstances does the call of a morally relevant good assume the character of a moral obligation? The second refers to the question: under what circumstances is the preference of the *higher* morally relevant good obligatory? These two problems clearly differ and the first one has no direct connection with the *ordo amoris* or the role of the hierarchy of morally relevant values. The second, on the contrary, precisely deals with the relation between moral obligation and the general principle to give the preference to the higher ranking good.

The first is a much discussed problem playing a great role in the history of moral theology. There is no doubt that we have to distinguish between the fact that an attitude is morally good and the fact that it is morally obligatory. It is evident that in saying that an action is morally sublime we have not yet answered the question of whether or not we are obliged, in a concrete situation calling for such an action, to accomplish it. The action ascribed to St. Vincent of Paul of having served nine months in the galleys, in place of an innocently condemned young man whom he saved by this heroic sacrifice, is certainly of an extraordinary moral sublimity, but obviously in no way obligatory. The lives of the saints are filled with such extraordinary actions which, though of a great moral sublimity, are in no way obligatory.

To deny this difference and to contend that as soon as something is morally good and praiseworthy, it is morally obligatory is a fundamental error which is at the basis of moral "rigorism." Obvious as it is that the moral goodness of an attitude differs from its being morally obligatory, it is yet difficult to circumscribe the frontier which separates them. It is one of the great classical problems of ethics to explore the factors which determine this important difference. Here we must restrict ourselves to some remarks illustrating the depth and difficulty of the problem concerning the factors which make a morally good action or attitude morally obligatory.

We saw that the free response to a good endowed with a morally relevant value is itself morally good. In many cases the call issuing from the morally relevant value has the character of a moral obligation, and the failure to conform to it is stained with a moral disvalue. In other cases, on the contrary, the call of the morally relevant value does not have this character. Conformity to it is morally good; failure to conform is not morally bad, but morally permissible.

It would, however, be a great error to believe that the frontier separating obligatory and non-obligatory morally good actions is determined by a certain rank of moral goodness which would be the minimum requirement and hence would always be obligatory, whereas everything surpassing this degree would be pure merit and no longer obligatory. The most sublime action of martyrdom is obligatory if the situation imposes it on us. Now it is not obligatory to give our life in order to save the life of another person who is in danger, and yet martyrdom is obligatory although it surpasses by far in its moral goodness and sublimity the sacrifice of our life for our neighbor. To love God and our neighbor is not only the morally most sublime response, but it is obligatory.

Thus it is clear that the question of whether or not something morally good is obligatory does not depend on the sublimity of the moral value; it does not mean that the morally more modest attitudes form an obligatory minimum and that whatever surpasses it in rank is a praiseworthy merit but not obligatory. Yet it seems that the question of whether something is obligatory or not depends on the size of the sacrifice which the morally good action implies and requires.

But in speaking of sacrifice we must use this term in its true sense, namely, the giving up of an objective good for us, or at least risking the loss of it, insofar as such a renunciation is morally allowed. We must clearly distinguish sacrifices from the mere effort which is implied in a good action. If this effort is due to the fact that moral faults, vices, spiritual laziness, must be overcome, obviously it can in no way be called a sacrifice. As long as morally illegitimate obstacles make the performance of a good action more strenuous, there can be no question of sacrifices made in order to act with moral rightness. If a man, for instance, has to make very great efforts to overcome his avariciousness, or in order to help his neighbor, notwithstanding the fact that he envies him, none of these efforts can be considered as being a sacrifice.

Hence the necessity of overcoming such morally negative obstacles has no influence whatsoever on the question of whether a morally good action is obligatory or not. A person may see a man whose life is in great danger, whom he could save without any risk to his own life, and yet, because it is his enemy, he has to struggle against revengeful feelings in order to save this man. Plainly the obligation to save the man does not become less simply because it causes a great effort on the part of one who regards him as his enemy.

The presence of a true sacrifice, on the contrary, seems to have a bearing on the question of whether something is obligatory or not. We are obliged to save a man whose life is in danger provided there is no one else present who could help him, and provided also that it does not imply a risk to our own life. We are no longer obliged when it can be done only by risking our own life. Thus it is the fact that a great sacrifice is implied which outweighs our obligation to save another person.

It even seems that the proportion which exists between the sacrifice and the rank of the good on the object side calling for our intervention plays a role in our strict moral obligation. If we risk only a cold or a certain amount of money, our obligation obviously remains. On the other hand, no sacrifice is great enough to outweigh our obligation to avoid moral evil. If a man imposes on us something immoral (e.g., the murder of another person, doing something impure), we are obliged to refuse, no matter what may be threatened against us. To die rather than to do something morally evil is plainly obligatory.[11] In these cases it is no longer a great sacrifice and the preservation of a good on the object side which are in balance, but the great sacrifice is weighed against the moral evil of an action. Now it is evident that no objective evil for us, however great, can outbalance the moral evil which offends God. Here the two possibilities are: either to preserve an objective good for us and offend God, or to sacrifice this objective good and not offend God, and it is clear that not offending God should in any case have the priority.[12]

[11] Obviously this applies above all to martyrdom. Martyrdom is not only the most sublime action, but it also implies the alternative of making the greatest sacrifice or of offending God.

[12] Of course our ultimate good always coincides with the conforming to God. The fictitious claim, "I would sacrifice my eternal welfare rather than offend

These remarks, which in no way claim to solve this difficult problem, must suffice here. We must return to our specific topic which refers to the question of whether it is morally obligatory to choose the higher ranking good in the frame of morally obligatory goods.

We must hereby clearly distinguish concrete situations in which certain morally relevant goods call for an intervention from situations in which no such call is addressed to us. Not every moment of our life is filled with morally relevant goods calling for our intervention. Our daily life offers many situations which leave room for occupation with goods either having a morally irrelevant value or being merely legitimately subjectively satisfying. The attitude of the saint who makes a vow to choose in every situation what is objectively more perfect obviously refers not only to the situation in which objective morally relevant goods call for an intervention, but also to all so-called morally neutral situations.

Someone eats something which he likes very much. The question may arise in his mind as to whether abstaining from eating would be more perfect. This decision in no way refers to a morally relevant good calling for an adequate response. There exist innumerable potential sacrifices which can be made even when any realization of a morally relevant good on the object side is out of the question. In all these cases, there is no question of preferring a higher objective good to another objective good; rather, the alternative is, on the one hand, a morally allowed attitude or activity or the enjoyment of an objective good for us, and on the other hand, a laudable sacrifice.

Again, the error of rigorism is to pretend that in every concrete situation we are *obliged* to choose the more perfect attitude; this implies that we take the initiative of choosing the higher ranking good even in situations in which no morally relevant good objectively calls for an intervention on our part. This difference is of the utmost importance for our problem. Let us once again compare two different situations. In the one case, we see some person in great moral danger and we realize that an intervention on our part can save him. We clearly understand

God," is intrinsically impossible because to give up our eternal welfare precisely implies that we would definitely turn away from God and offend Him.

the call of God to respond to the high morally relevant good at stake and to act. In the other case, we read a novel and suddenly it comes to our mind that it would perhaps be more perfect if instead of reading this novel we said a prayer. In the first case, an objective morally relevant good calls for our intervention; in the second case, we take the initiative of preferring the more perfect activity to a less perfect one. The decisive difference is obvious.

In the first case, many morally relevant goods calling for our intervention may be at stake or only one. For instance, before I saw the person in moral danger, I may have promised to come to an important meeting at which my presence was badly needed; my choice, then, would be between these two morally relevant goods. Without any doubt we have to find out which has the higher value, which is more important in itself, and then we should take into account all the questions concerning more immediate urgency, etc. To claim that when facing different morally relevant and obligatory goods we are not obliged to choose the higher ranking good, *ceteris paribus*, would be plainly erroneous. And this obligation has nothing to do with rigorism. If there is only one good at stake the alternative would be either to abstain from helping the morally endangered man or to help him. We must realize that in such cases the alternative present is not one between two possibilities (one of which is morally allowed or even morally good, and the other only more perfect). The alternative is either to disregard the dramatic call of a value imposed on us from without or to conform to it: the first would be something morally negative—not something morally neutral—and the second would be morally good. It goes without saying that we are obliged to avoid evil and do good.

As we saw before, when the sacrifices entailed by my intervention surpass a certain limit, only then is my obligation outweighed. In such cases, intervention would be morally very noble, but abstention would not be morally evil. Thus it would again be rigorism if one ignored the outbalancing role of sacrifices. But the main error of rigorism is not concerned with situations in which a morally relevant good calls imperatively for an intervention. Rather, the chief error lies in the attempt to obligate one to choose the morally more sublime possibility, to accomplish the morally higher ranking attitude. Apart from any call addressed to us by a morally relevant value, this general attitude of rigorism demands that a person of his own initiative continually seek to do the thing which is morally more sublime. Hence it excludes, under a moral obligation, any merely allowed activity. It claims first that we are always obliged to do something morally good instead of something morally neutral; second, that even in seeking for the occasion of something morally good we should choose the most sublime one.

We see now why it was necessary to distinguish the choice between the moral value of attitudes from the choice between different morally relevant goods on the object side. If an attitude is morally allowed, there can be no obligation to abstain from it in favor of a morally good one, and, *a fortiori*, still less can there be (in a situation where different morally good attitudes are possible) an obligation to choose the higher one.

When, however, the choice refers to different morally obligatory goods all of which call for an intervention on our part, then the question is no longer whether a morally allowed or a morally good or even the morally best thing has to be chosen, but rather what is the moral character of conforming to the lower value and ignoring thereby the higher good. When all the circumstances are equal and when the one good does not imply a greater sacrifice, then to prefer the lower value would clearly be morally evil. As long as we approach the situation in the pure attitude of value response for which it objectively calls, there cannot even be question of a preference for the lower good. Only if other motives besides the value are at stake, is a preference for the lower good possible. If these motives refer to sacrifices, to the loss or risk of high objective goods for the person, the choice of the lower may be morally allowed. If these motives are concerned with the merely subjectively satisfying or are even outgrowths of concupiscence and pride, preference of the lower good is then a typical case of a morally evil action.

Thus we see that the general principle that we should prefer the higher ranking morally relevant good on the object side in all situations which imperatively call for our intervention, and in which the call has a morally obligatory character, applies, as such, even in the sense of an obligation. But obviously all the restrictions made before, resulting from the theme of a situation and from the proportion between the sacrifice implied in the action and the rank of the good on the object side, may alter or suspend the obligation. The thesis that we are obliged at every moment to seek that which is morally more perfect is *untenable* and pure rigorism. Though we are not only obliged to have the general will to be good, but even compelled to strive for our moral perfection, we are not obliged in all concrete situations to replace with what is most perfect those attitudes, actions, or activities which are less perfect or merely permissible. For we are now concerned with attitudes the moral character of which is already shaped and ascertained, and our choice is between the morally allowed on the one hand and the morally good on the other, or between the morally good and the morally better.

This may suffice to explain why the principle that we should give to the higher value the preference in our response and in our actions (a teaching which St. Augustine stresses in his *ordo amoris*) in no way implies rigorism if it is seen in its reference to the goods on the object side, and against the background of all modifying and restricting circumstances.

CHAPTER 29

THE ROLE OF THE OBJECTIVE GOOD
FOR THE PERSON

WE HAVE stated that no response motivated by the merely subjectively satisfying is, as such, endowed with a moral value in the
full sense of the term. Morally good acts are always value responses, though not all value responses are specifically morally
good.

Now we have to delve into the moral character of responses
motivated by the type of importance we have called the objective
good for the person. It would surpass the scope of this work to
analyze this problem in detail. Here it may suffice to outline this
very important problem. We shall concentrate first on the responses or actions referring to an objective good for our own
person, and then on the very different situation when the objective good of another person motivates our response or action.

We have seen before that there exists a great range of different
objective goods for the person, and we distinguished the following main kinds:

A first fundamental type of objective good for the person is to
be endowed with values. To be morally good, to be intelligent,
to have charm, all this is objectively in the line of our own good;
it is objectively of benefit to us; it is as such a blessing. But the
rank of these objective goods embraces a very wide range, from
the ultimate objective good for us, the *similitudo Dei,* to an attractive physical appearance. This great difference of rank is not
our problem; our interest lies in studying the formally different
categories of objective good for the person.

The second type refers to the possession of goods which are

able to bestow true happiness on us because of their value. Again we are faced with an enormous scale of objective goods for the person, culminating in the eternal union with God (i.e., beatitude) and embracing the love union with human persons, the possession of a truth, dwelling in a beautiful country, and so on.

The third category of objective goods includes things indispensable for our life: food, a roof to shelter us, etc., primarily the indispensable elementary necessities for our life, and secondarily useful goods. These goods do not bestow happiness on us, but they are mostly indispensable for our normal earthly existence, and their absence is a source not only of suffering but even of absolute misery. Insofar as the useful goods are concerned, they do not bestow happiness on us, as such, but they facilitate our life and may even serve indirectly as means for the possession of goods of the second category, for instance, a car enables us to have a wider and more intimate knowledge of a beautiful country.

It is characteristic of this third type of objective goods that their possession cannot grant us the delight proper to the possession of goods having a value. They are objective goods because of their indispensable role for our life. They have an elementary relation to our existence, not because of any value, but because they are not to be dispensed with either in their role as means for a comfortable life or indirectly in their role as means in procuring for us an undisturbed or easier possession of goods bestowing authentic happiness on us. Instead of a hierarchy of values, here the scale is arranged according to the elementary indispensability of these goods, beginning with our daily bread and things related to our bodily existence.

Fourthly, merely agreeable things (insofar as they appeal to a legitimate center in us) are objective goods for the person. The existence of agreeable things testifies to God's bounty. Every lover desires to offer his beloved every possible agreeable good, such as good food, a comfortable chair, etc. These things are objective goods for the person because of their objectively friendly character, which is rooted in their being legitimately agreeable.

The moral character of a response motivated by the objective good for the person obviously varies very much according to which of these four types of objective good for the person is at stake. But before embarking upon a discussion of the moral difference determined by the type of objective good in question, we still have to stress another point. The moral role of the objective good for the person also changes completely according to whether we are concerned with the desire or will to possess an objective good, or with our gratitude for the possession of an objective good bestowed on us.

Gratitude is one of the basic morally noble attitudes; it is always endowed with a high moral value, and ingratitude is something especially base morally. Moreover, gratitude is a typical response to an objective good for the person. Thus, we are here confronted with a response which on the one hand, is morally good and noble and on the other hand, has as its immediate and specific object an objective good for us.

The object of gratitude implies more than the necessarily presupposed value response to bounty (either that of God or that of another person). We respond to this bounty also in praising God for what he has done for another person or other persons. In witnessing the miraculous healing of a sick man at Lourdes, we can be moved by the infinite goodness of God. But gratitude implies specific reference to an objective good for *us*, either for our own person or for a beloved one with whom we have such solidarity that the favor conferred on this person presents itself as a benefit for us. We easily realize that gratitude is something obligatory, and that a bountiful gift makes us indebted to the donor and calls in a particular way for gratitude.

We must reserve for a later work any further discussion of the essence of gratitude; nevertheless we do want to stress here that all objective goods for the person, as soon as they are bestowed on us by God or by the intermediary activity of a human person, imply a morally relevant call for appreciation and a response of gratitude to the donor, not only because these goods have a value, but also because they are objective goods for *us*.

Indeed it is obvious that the value response to the bounty of the donor is an indispensable and fundamental element conditioning the moral value of gratitude; so too is the recognition of being dependent upon the donor and the element of humility which this recognition implies. But on the other hand, gratitude essentially implies a response to the objective good for us. And what matters above all in our context is that gratitude essentially implies a response to an objective good for us, and that this response is specifically morally good and even obligatory, whether or not the value of the objective good is morally relevant.

In turning now to the moral difference determined by the type of objective good at stake, we must always distinguish two questions: What is the moral character of a striving for an objective good for us, and what is the moral value of gratitude for its possession?

Insofar as the first category of objective good is concerned, we must state that the desire to possess moral values is primarily and by its very nature a value response, and only secondarily a response to an objective good for the person. We have seen (in our analysis of the awareness of moral significance and our being motivated by it) that it is always a pure value response. The same applies to the conscious will directed toward our moral perfection. It belongs to the very nature of this objective good for the person that it can never be detached from the corresponding value response, ultimately the value response to God. Even if someone looked at it as a mere means for beatitude (an impossible fiction), he could not prescind from this value response, since the very nature of beatitude as the eternal love communion with God implies both the love of God and the longing to partake of His infinite goodness. The striving for this objective good for us is not only a duty; it is endowed with the highest moral value because it is necessarily and primarily a pure value response.

The moral significance of our striving for the possession of other values, such as intellectual, vital, or aesthetic values, is very different. This striving, as such, is not endowed with moral value, though it is something praiseworthy. It may have a moral connotation if it is achieved in the light of dealing with our talents according to the will of God. We prescind here from the danger of an ambitious and proud interest in being endowed with values. Later on [1] we shall speak about looking at values on account of our pride. But here we must stress that the striving to be endowed with other values, insofar as they can be acquired by our

[1] Part Two, IV, "Roots of Moral Evil."

own efforts, is in itself morally neutral [2] so long as it does not absorb us in a way that distracts us from the value response to, and the preoccupation with, the *unum necessarium*.

Our concern with any extra-moral values must have rather the character of a task which one wants to fulfill. A person may desire to succeed in a project of scientific research, or want to be an actor or to create an important and good work of art: these are all objectivated fruits of his talents and gifts. If this interest is pure and free from ambition, it will primarily be a value response to the truth of the research and the artistic value as such; in other words, it is simply a natural interest in the work. Or again, it may be directed toward the objective good for us which success in noble professional achievements entails.

One may raise the question of whether one should pray for goods such as great intelligence, physical beauty, charm, etc. In any case it can only be allowed, but is never specifically morally good, apart from the value of prayer as such. The moral aspect changes completely, however, as soon as we are no longer concerned with our desire or will, but with gratitude for objective goods such as intelligence, vitality and charm.

Certainly our own values are not meant to be objects of our concern; the danger of pride and vanity is so great that any dwelling on the consciousness of our own perfections is morally very precarious. In the case of moral values, humility moves us to place over them a veil which should never be lifted; but in the case of other values, an admission of their presence is not morally illegitimate. A gifted person cannot be expected to feel himself absolutely ungifted. A certain experience of his possibilities makes him aware of the gifts which he has received, and he cannot be blamed for this awareness. To be sure, he should always live in the consciousness of being an unworthy servant inadequate to the greatness of his task; nevertheless, he should also respond with deep gratitude for having received these gifts, conscious of the fact that they were granted to him without his own merit. We cannot even expect someone with a beautiful physical ap-

[2] It must be emphasized again that in saying "morally neutral," we mean that it does not, as such, bestow a moral value on us. In a wider sense, every human attitude which is not morally evil partakes of the moral goodness of the basic attitude of man. We have stressed time and again that this "secondary" moral goodness cannot be our topic in the inquiry into the roots of moral goodness.

pearance to consider himself ugly. Nor can we blame him for being grateful for having received this gift. Thus the response of gratitude to God for all these objective goods received is even a morally good attitude.

In what concerns the second type of objective goods for the person and their possession, it must be said that all interest in the possession of these goods, or in the objective good which their possession represents, implies or presupposes a value response to the good in question. Interest in dwelling in a beautiful country presupposes a response to beauty; interest in the precious good for us that a friendship is, presupposes the value response of love to our friend.

Insofar as the good possesses a morally relevant value, this value response is good; otherwise it will be praiseworthy and noble, but not in a strictly moral sense. Insofar as the desire to possess these goods is in question and we aspire to a more intimate contact with them (i.e., insofar as we look at them as objective goods for us), the response is ontologically good and in no way morally negative. It even shares in the value of the underlying value response since it organically grows out of it. It would be wrong to see anything egoistic in this desire. We may rightly call egoistic the desire for a self-centered happiness but not the noble desire for a more intimate union with something possessing a value. So much are noble desires organic consequences of a value response, that a love which lacked this *intentio unionis* (desire for union), this longing for union with the beloved person (and in an analogous sense with the beloved object), would be a defective love. So long as the values involved are not morally relevant values, and so long as our value response to them is noble (but not yet good in the moral sense of the term), the desire to possess them shares in this nobility. As soon as the values of the object are morally relevant and the love for them is morally good, the desire for union and possession is also morally good.

In the case of the Absolute Good, God (in which case love is obligatory and is the center and source of all our moral goodness), also the desire for the beatific vision is endowed with the most sublime moral value and is morally obligatory. But if we prescind from this unique case, we must say that though the desire for the possession of a good organically and necessarily issues from the value response, the will to possess it is not necessarily morally good. It may even be either morally illegitimate or at least less perfect than to renounce its possession.

Whereas the possession of the absolute good is such that there is essentially no possible conflict between ourselves and other persons, in all other cases there may be conflicts between our fruition and the fruition by another person. St. Augustine admirably says that this good is so common to all that not only does fruition by one person not exclude fruition by another, but that the desire for an exclusive fruition of goodness would entail the loss of any fruition whatsoever.[3] Such a desire would exclude us from the fruition of God. We do not think only of those cases in which a good can be possessed only by one person —at least in a specific sense of possession—as in the case of a love communion or marriage. But the nature of this type of union is based on such extraordinary presuppositions—requited love— that any conflict with another person that would force us to renounce our claim in his favor is excluded. The problem of selfishness is here out of question. But there is the possibility of a moral prohibition of such a desire, e.g., if the beloved person is bound by the bond of marriage. This is always the case when I want to dispossess another who is already in possession of a good, in order to make it mine.

Hence, with respect to the will to appropriate to ourselves such a good having a value, we must state, first, that there may be an obstacle of a morally relevant nature which would make such an act of willing morally bad. Secondly, even if no other person is in possession of the desired good, we must consider whether our own fruition does not deprive another person of a possible fruition. Here, of course, the inner possibility of our renunciation of the good at stake is taken for granted. Even if the good in question is, as such, in no way exclusive, e.g., the beauty of a symphony or of a landscape, the conflict may arise that if I take the last ticket left for a concert, my friend cannot go, or if I use

---

[3] "For the possession of goodness is not lessened by being shared: nay, it is increased when it has many possessing it in one link and league of charity. Nor shall he ever have it, that will not have it in common; and he that loves a partner in it, shall have it more abundantly." St. Augustine, *De Civitate Dei*, XV, 5. (J. Healey, *op. cit.*, Vol. II, p. 64.)

the money at my disposal for a journey to a beautiful country, I can no longer provide a poor acquaintance with the opportunity to make the same journey. Is it morally better to let him go and to renounce my own delight? Certainly the best attitude morally speaking will depend upon many circumstances. The important point is to see that in such cases the problem of selfishness may arise, a problem which was irrelevant in the sphere of the pure value response.

The moral significance again radically changes when we turn from our interest in an objective good for us (insofar as it expresses itself in our desire or will to possess such a good) to the question of our gratitude for possessing it. As we saw, the striving for this type of objective good is not obligatory, apart from the case of the absolute objective good for us. Gratitude for the possession of these goods, on the contrary, is always obligatory.

It is in the realm of this second type of objective goods that gratitude unfolds its most specific significance. The more a person appreciates not only the value of a good, but also the gift which he received in its possession, and the more he responds with gratitude, the higher will he rank morally. We only need to think of the role that gratitude plays in a saint's life, for instance, in the life of St. Francis of Assisi, in order to grasp the fundamental moral role of gratitude in the sphere of these goods.

We come, thirdly, to the elementary and useful goods for the person. The interest in elementary goods, the will to eat, to sleep, and so on, the pursuit of the necessities of life, the striving for daily bread: these plainly are ontologically good, but morally neutral as such. We do not praise any one as morally good because he eats and sleeps or because he is striving to obtain the necessary money to live. It is something natural, imposed on us as a necessity and not something chosen. It belongs to those attitudes which in themselves have no moral value or disvalue. It would be as preposterous to see something selfish in the striving for these goods as to attribute to this striving a moral value in the specific sense of this term.

But neglect of these elementary goods may have a morally negative character. I am not referring to special negative motives which may interfere, as for example, the refusal because of laziness to work and provide the minimum for life or the abstention from food and sleep in a suicidal intention. I am thinking of people who neglect their health by permitting themselves to become undernourished, perhaps because they have no appetite, or who do not sleep enough because of their work. This is not even something morally neutral. Not only has man the normal tendency to appropriate to himself these necessary goods, but he has also the duty to abstain from things which endanger his health, provided that great values do not impose this duty on him as something inevitable. Since man is not his own master, since he has received as gifts from God his existence, life, and health which he is called upon to employ according to the will of God, he is not allowed to neglect these goods or to deal with them arbitrarily.

In short, so long as someone strives for these elementary goods in a self-evident conformity to something necessary and inevitable, his attitude is reasonable, but not yet morally good in itself. As soon as he neglects these elementary goods to an extent which may injure his health, his attitude is morally negative if this neglect is not the result of a value response to God's will.

In the saint, however, even the positive concern for these elementary goods assumes a morally positive character. He does not direct himself simply to these goods as something self-evident, inevitable, necessary, but considers them as gifts coming from God which he must use in the right way since they are entrusted to him as a mere administrator. He will eat because he knows that it is indispensable for the preservation of a high good which he has not the right to jeopardize. It is no longer a conscious achievement of self-preservation which is natural and good but morally neutral, but a conscious response to a good which belongs to God, a good of which the individual is not the master but the administrator responsible to God. This attitude toward these elementary goods is embodied in the words of the Our Father: "Give us this day our daily bread."

Again we are confronted with the great difference between the desire for these goods and the gratitude for their possession. Gratitude in this case, as well as in the preceding ones, is always endowed with a high moral value. And gratitude for the possession of these goods should always prevail over the interest in attaining them.

The average man does not feel any special gratitude for the possession of these elementary goods. He strives for them as being necessary and inevitable and, again, accepts their possession as something normal and natural. Only in situations of great need and misery (as during a famine or in a desert) are these elementary goods fully seen as precious gifts of God's bounty; then receiving them engenders a deep gratitude in one's soul.

The true attitude toward these elementary goods is embodied in the liturgy, e.g., in the prayers before and after meals. Nothing is accepted as self-evident, nothing is taken for granted; every good, whether we receive it without our intervention or whether we attain it by our own efforts, is accepted with deep gratitude as an unmerited gift, as an expression of God's infinite bounty.

Our interest in useful goods is morally allowed and neutral so long as it does not absorb us to such an extent that it deflects our focus from the important-in-itself. Insofar as they serve as means for something endowed with a morally relevant value, interest in their possession even acquires a moral value. We saw before that means for the attainment of morally relevant good possess a secondary morally relevant value. Hence it is morally good to take interest in them. Again, gratitude for their possession is something morally good.

Finally, in what concerns the category of things which are objective goods for the person, because of their legitimate, agreeable character we have to state the following: These goods normally present themselves to us as merely subjectively satisfying. We see a tempting dish and desire to eat it. Our will to acquire it is motivated by the pleasure which this good can bestow on us. We want to eat it because it tastes good. The gift character which these goods possess, their objective friendliness as embodiments of God's bounty, normally plays no role. The pursuit of the agreeable and the striving for it, at least in our present fallen state, is motivated by pleasure and not by its character of objective good for us.

This pursuit is morally allowed and neutral so long as this interest does not lead us to neglect a value. In order to be morally neutral it even requires an outspoken attitude of *religio*, the attitude of our reverent submission to God and the world of values.[4] But within this frame interest in the pursuit of these objective goods is morally neutral and not morally negative.

However, the saint does not pursue such goods; he makes no effort to obtain them for himself. But he will accept them with gratitude when they are bestowed on him without his endeavor, if there are no special ascetic reasons for his refusing them. He alone will see them in the pure light of objective goods for the person, and thus will respond with gratitude to the bounty of God manifesting itself in them.

This brief summary may suffice for an understanding of the role in morality of the objective goods for the person insofar as we are concerned with goods for ourselves. A completely different situation prevails when we think of the role of this kind of importance in relation to other persons.

The fundamental value response of charity, responding to the value of a human person as an *imago Dei*, obviously entails an interest in all objective goods for other persons. Love necessarily desires to bestow objective goods on the beloved person. We need not discuss again all these different categories of objective goods. The very fact that true love both implies and engenders a vivid interest in bestowing every possible objective good on the beloved reveals to us the completely new moral significance proper to the interest in objective goods for other persons. It is here, in the sphere of the objective good for the person, that the mysterious moral difference between ourselves and our neighbor manifests itself, a difference which is expressed in the terms "selfish" or "egotistic," and "unselfish."[5] In the sphere of pure value responses, there is no room for this difference. As long as moral perfection, which is primarily a value response to God, is in question, there is no difference from the point of view of the moral sublimity of this attitude between interest in our own moral perfection and interest in the moral perfection of another person. The same applies to beatitude.

But with respect to all other types of objective good, the moral significance of the interest in our own goods and of the interest in goods for other persons differs very much. The pursuit of

4 This will be discussed in detail in Part Two, IV, "Roots of Moral Evil."

5 Cf. D. von Hildebrand, *Das Objektive Gut für die Person*, Festschrift für J. Geyser, Habbel, 1930.

these objective goods for our own person has, as such, no moral value; although gratitude for their possession is always endowed with moral values. To pursue the objective good of *other* persons is, on the contrary, *always* morally good, because these attitudes are rooted in the fundamental value response of love. Thus the concern with objective goods for our neighbor plays a fundamental role in morality, and many of the morally good acts are directed toward the objective good for other persons. Equally morally negative is disinterest in these objective goods for other persons, and still more negative is the inflicting of objective evils upon them.

But we have to realize that concern in the objective good of our neighbor is deeply linked with love and is a necessary expression of the *intentio benevolentiae* which is one of the main elements of love. And not only is love the value response par excellence, but it also possesses an intrinsic goodness of its own.[6] Thus it need not surprise us that interest in objective goods for other persons is a source of high moral values.

In our relation to other persons, therefore, it is even more perfect if we regard objective goods for them not only in the light of their value, but also from the viewpoint of their beneficial character for these persons. Due to an austerely religious attitude certain persons are not concerned with whether or not something is a source of happiness or pleasure for others. The only question that seems important to them is whether another person glorifies God by his conduct or whether he lacks something indispensable for his eternal welfare. When the possession of such goods bears no tangible relation to the other's eternal welfare, they do not consider it worthwhile to bother about it. Their attitude is less perfect than that of a person interested in all objective goods for others, since this latter attitude flows out of charity, the very core and summit of all moral goodness, by which God is glorified more than by all else.

Perfect love of God leads organically to love of neighbor. It includes partaking in God's infinite love for man. Thus the true lover of God embraces his neighbor with that abundant warmth and devotion found in the Epistles of St. Paul and overwhelmingly manifested in the first miracle of our Lord at Cana.

6 Cf. Chapter 27, "The Three Spheres of Morality."

IV. Roots of Moral Evil

CHAPTER 30

THE PROBLEM OF MORAL EVIL

WE HAVE seen that in order for an action to be morally good it must be commanded and guided by a willing response to a good endowed with a morally relevant value. So long as the willing which commands this action is a value response motivated by a good endowed with a morally irrelevant value, the action has a value but not a moral one. So long as the will is motivated by something that is legitimately subjectively satisfying, the action, as such, is morally unobjectionable. But if in the pursuit of something merely subjectively satisfying a morally relevant good is ignored, shown disrespect, destroyed, contradicted, the action is morally evil.

Let us suppose a man wishes to possess a car. If he buys it without in so doing rendering himself unable to fulfill certain obligations, his action is morally neutral. But if he steals it, his action is morally evil. The desire for the car is not immoral, but it is immoral to disregard the morally relevant value of a person and his rights in order to satisfy this desire.

Or to take another example, of a man who wants to be promoted in his professional work. This is, as such, a legitimate, morally unobjectionable desire. Any action tending to attain this goal would also be unobjectionable so long as no morally relevant value is contradicted. But should this man stage an intrigue in order to oust a competitor, he would be acting immorally. It thus seems that it is the disrespect for, and ignoring of, a morally relevant value, or the destruction of a morally relevant good (destruction consented to in order to attain what one desires), which is the source of the moral disvalue of an

405

action. Yet if disrespect for, and contradiction of, the call of a morally relevant value is the immediate source of the moral disvalue of actions, the question arises as to how it is possible that one can ignore the call of the morally relevant good and override it in order to attain something subjectively satisfying. The morally unobjectionable desire for a subjectively satisfying good explains in no way indifference toward the morally relevant value.

The ordinary thief may be blind to the value of justice and to the offense against human dignity which is implied in his over-riding another's rights. But even if such value blindness is at stake, the question is only postponed, because we must inquire into the source of this value blindness. We saw before that moral value blindness is never due to a lack of natural gifts, but is determined by an attitude for which we are responsible. Hence it remains ultimately unexplained how the legitimate desire for something subjectively satisfying can lead to the ignoring or even the destruction of a morally relevant good, independently of the question as to whether or not a moral value blindness is implied in the morally bad action. Thus the great question imposes itself: What is the source of value blindness? What is the source of our ignoring morally relevant values when no value blindness is involved?

In posing this question, we do not however intend to embark on the metaphysical problem of the origin of moral evil. This problem surpasses not only the scope of our book, but is one of the great mysteries which can never be exhausted by human reason. Our question refers to the sources of moral evil in man, such as they reveal themselves in experience. This question becomes still more urgent when we realize that the basis of a morally evil action is not always an accidental overriding of morally relevant goods which hampers the acquisition of a sub-jectively satisfying good. There are also morally evil actions in which the underlying desire is already morally evil, such as in the case of impure actions,[1] and in which a morally relevant evil is expressly willed, such as in the case of a murder committed out of hatred or from a spirit of revenge. The slaying of an

[1] The isolation of the sexual desire as such is morally evil. Cf. *In Defense of Purity*.

enemy is something to which the revengeful person assents, not because he could not otherwise attain the possession of a subjectively satisfying good (as in the case of robbery with murder). In the case of the murder of an enemy, the link between the morally relevant evil (the slaying) and the good which is sought (the satisfaction of revenge) is not only one of means and end, is not only an accidental connection. In this case the subjectively satisfying object which is sought can *never* be legitimate, as opposed to the case of theft in which the desire for possession *as such* is morally neutral. The destruction of a morally relevant good is here precisely the thing which is subjectively satisfying. The desire, as such, is already evil and the morally relevant evil is not only accepted, but expressly willed. In all these actions there comes to the fore a type of moral wickedness which cannot be reduced to an ignoring and overriding of a morally relevant good as a means to which one assents because no other way to attain a morally neutral end seems to present itself. This very wickedness forces us to probe anew into the roots of moral evil in man which manifest themselves in this perverted desire, a desire in which something tainted with a disvalue becomes especially attractive and desirable. This perversion manifests itself even more patently in all morally evil affective responses, such as envy, malicious joy, hatred. The intrinsic moral disvalue embodied in these attitudes is obvious, as well as the intrinsic antithesis to charity which is implied in their very quality. The same applies to vices: impurity, avariciousness, covetousness, hardheartedness. It is here that the *mysterium iniquitatis*—the mystery of iniquity—discloses itself in all its inscrutable horror.

In our former analysis we have already mentioned that pride and concupiscence are the sources of moral evil. We also saw that they antagonize the loving, reverent, value-responding center. Now, it is necessary to explore systematically the nature of pride and concupiscence, and their role as sources of moral evil.

CHAPTER 31

CENTERS OF MORALITY AND IMMORALITY

WE HAVE analyzed [1] different types of exclusiveness which are to be found in the realm of values, exclusiveness ranging from a complementary polarity to a strict, antithetical contrariety. The sphere of human acts also offers different fundamental types of exclusiveness.

First, certain acts exclude each other in the sense that they cannot be actualized simultaneously because of the limitedness of human nature. This applies, for instance, to the impossibility of fully focusing our attention on completely different topics at once. We cannot think of two different things simultaneously; we cannot answer two questions at once. This type of exclusiveness is completely formal and is rooted in man's limitedness; it includes neither any antithesis nor even any polarity between the two acts, attitudes, or actions which exclude each other, that is to say, which cannot be accomplished at once. This limitation can be designated as a structural one.

Secondly, there are attitudes which exclude each other in a deeper sense of the term, for instance, our being in love with one person excludes our loving a second person at the same moment with the same love. The totality of self-donation proper to this type of love excludes its being simultaneously directed to a second person. The reason is here rooted in the very nature and meaning of this love. This exclusiveness would more correctly be called uniqueness.

A third type of exclusiveness is determined by the contradictory character of the inner word of two responses. It is patently

[1] Chapter 11, "Unity of Values."

impossible simultaneously to respond to one and the same object with a "yes" and a "no." Just as we cannot affirm and deny one and the same simultaneously, so is it analogously impossible to be simultaneously indignant and enthusiastic about one and the same object, or to venerate and simultaneously despise one and the same person. This kind of exclusiveness results from the relation of our response to the object. It is the exclusiveness proper to a positive and negative attitude, proper to "yes" and "no," and it could thus be called a *logical* exclusiveness, provided that we understand the term "logical" in a very wide sense of the term.

But there exists in addition a completely different exclusiveness of human acts, when these refer not to one and the same object, but to different objects. A man cannot hate someone and simultaneously accomplish an act of true charity or Christian love of neighbor toward another person. Again, a man cannot accomplish a deep act of true contrition and simultaneously be full of envy or hate for another person. Nor can a person forgive an enemy in the full sense of the word and yet remain full of revenge toward another person. The general superactual attitude which is presupposed for these responses is incompatible with the general attitude presupposed for the respective negative responses. The actualization of the center of the value response, "the charitable, reverent, humble center," excludes the simultaneous actualization of the center from which hate, envy, and revenge derive. At least for the moment we become, so to speak, "another" person when we perform an act of real charity, real contrition, or real forgiving. Hence our general attitude toward the morally relevant values, in the last analysis toward God, is such that morally negative acts are excluded. This exclusiveness does not imply, however, that we cannot afterward return to an inner mood conducive to the blossoming of evil flowers.

This exclusiveness clearly differs from the above-mentioned logical one. It is an incompatibility proper to the very quality of certain acts, and is rooted in the essentially antithetical character of the centers from which these responses derive. The contrariety which exists between such acts is a much deeper and more radical one, for they exclude each other, not only with respect to one and the same concrete object, but as such.

Someone might object: It seems that at times we *can* simultaneously actualize morally positive and negative attitudes, at least toward different persons. Do we not often find that a man forgives an enemy and joins him in his revenge against a common, more formidable enemy? Thus the act of forgiving the minor enemy can coexist simultaneously with the revengeful attitude toward a major enemy.

It is easy to see that this objection is wrong. This so-called forgiveness is not a real act of forgiving. It is merely a "technical" forgiveness, in reality a truce which is made with our minor enemy in order to be able to fight our major enemy more efficiently. This forgetting our former feud, this canceling of the moral indebtedness of our enemy, this replacement of our former, hostile attitude with a friendly one, has in no way the character of a victory over oneself; it has nothing of the breakthrough of charity which is proper to true forgiveness. This technical forgiveness has no moral value since its motive is not charity but a kind of expediency. Even if this turning away from our rancor against an enemy has the character of a brushing aside of the minor enmity by the more virulent one, it differs completely from true forgiveness which always implies a victory of charity over our hardened and hostile attitude, and hence always has a moral value. True forgiveness always implies more than a mere attitude toward an individual person whom we forgive; it is always a radical change in our own ethos and mentality as such. Thus the objection is invalid, since it does not consider a case of true forgiveness.

It is, however, possible that a man who has been wronged by different persons could say: "I forgive all my enemies except one, who has injured me too gravely. I cannot forgive him." Now this utterance may have different significations. It may be that a man has the disposition of will to forgive everyone, but that he has not yet come to a total break-through which would also dissolve his deeper rancor. In this case it is obvious that a revengeful attitude no longer exists even concerning the one enemy whose offense has been so grave. For the man disavows his rancor though he has not yet been able to eradicate it. Therefore this situation in no way contradicts our thesis that it is impossible for a true forgiveness to coexist with a revengeful attitude which lives in our soul without being disavowed by our free center.

Or it may be that a man does not forgive in the full sense of the word, i.e., that his forgiveness has a restricted character, though not a technical one. For some particular reasons he is able to dissolve his rancor toward those persons who have not wounded him to the very depth of his soul, but he adheres to it toward the one person who has injured him more deeply. His forgiveness does not flow out of the great victory of charity; it does not entail a break-through to a new inner freedom and the emergence from self-centeredness to the intuition of the repugnant and abominable moral ugliness of revenge and rancor as such. Instead, the reason is based on merely accidental grounds: the nature of the wrong inflicted by those persons whom he deigns to forgive or the actual attitude of these persons; that is to say, he looks to whatever elements can make the wrong done to him seem forgivable without forcing him to change radically the general attitude of his soul.

This forgiveness is evidently not the true act of forgiveness, though it is much closer to it than is the merely technical one. The possibility of the coexistence of this accidental forgiveness with a revengeful attitude is thus no objection to the exclusiveness of true forgiveness with respect to any revengeful attitude.

Thus we see that certain attitudes cannot simultaneously coexist because of their qualitative incompatibility, that is to say, because they derive from different centers in the person which exclude each other inasmuch as they can never be actualized simultaneously. But this qualitative incompatibility of certain attitudes is not the only symptom which reveals to us the existence of different centers in the person from which several attitudes derive. These centers find their expression also in the inner affinity or congeniality of different acts.

We saw before that every morally good act is a response to morally relevant values, and that even in the cases wherein the objective good for another person is the immediate object which motivates our response, the interest for this objective good flows out of love, which is the value response par excellence. The indispensability of the value response in morality reveals the essential unity of all morally good acts.

Yet besides this general feature of all morally good acts, there exists a deep *qualitative* affinity between love, humility, reverence, justice, generosity, and all other virtues, as well as between the act of contrition, the act of forgiving, the gratitude for benefits received, the indignation over moral evil, and every act of will which conforms to an authentic morally relevant value. This ultimate qualitative affinity reveals the existence of a homogenous center in the person, which we can call the "loving, reverent, value-responding center."

An analogous affinity manifests itself in various morally negative acts. The same attitudes which we saw to be incompatible with forgiveness, charity, and contrition, such as revengefulness, hardheartedness, and envy, are clearly characterized by a deep qualitative affinity. They also have their root in one and the same center: pride, which forms a definite antithesis to the loving, reverent, humble center. But whereas all morally good attitudes derive from one and the same moral center, we find two different centers as the source of moral evil. Covetousness, impurity, and laziness have not the same affinity with envy, hatred, revengefulness, and ambition that these attitudes have among themselves. They have their root not in pride but in concupiscence.

A fundamental fact discloses itself by the exclusiveness of morally good attitudes and morally evil ones, as well as by the inner affinity of all morally good attitudes, and the affinity between certain morally evil attitudes. For these symptoms declare that there exist different centers in the person: one of them is the source of all morally good attitudes, the other two seem to be the source of all morally evil attitudes. The positive one we called "the reverent, humble, loving center," the two negative centers are pride and concupiscence.[2]

---

[2] Recognition of the role of concupiscence as a root of evil antedated Christianity. In several dialogues (*Phaedro, Phaedrus, Timaeus*), Plato stigmatizes concupiscence as the source of many moral failures. However, apart from Revelation, pride was never fully recognized in its character as a center of moral wickedness. Only in the Old Testament was pride unmasked in its morally evil character. Yet it is in the Gospel alone that pride is *fully* shown in its character of arch-wickedness, and that the true sinfulness of concupiscence is stigmatized more profoundly than ever before. The Augustinian term *cupiditas* embraces both pride and concupiscence; the term *cupiditas* is identified with false self-love (*amor sui*). "*Sicut enim radix om-*

In speaking of three different centers in the person, we in no way intend to say that these centers are, so to speak, ontological elements of the human person, such as the faculties of the soul. Pride and concupiscence are patently outspoken perversions. The reverent, humble, loving center is not something given to man, such as his character of *imago Dei*, but something which man is destined to actualize, such as the *similitudo Dei*.

The term "center" in no way indicates any constitutive element of the person, but only the qualitative unity of a basic attitude from which many other attitudes derive. The term "center" is only meant to express a kind of fundamental approach to the universe and to God, a qualitatively unified "ego" which is always more or less actualized when the person accomplishes a morally good act. In opposing the reverent, humble, loving center to pride and concupiscence, we in no way place these three centers on the same ontological level; whereas the positive one belongs to the very meaning and *raison d'être* of man, the two others are mere *perversions*, proper to fallen man, i.e., man as he is known to us in experience. The incompatibility of the value-responding center with the centers of pride and concupiscence does not, however, dismiss the fact that in the average man all three centers are in some way to be found. Before entering into the analysis of pride and concupiscence and their role in the realm of morality we must briefly discuss the problem of the coexistence of these three centers in man.

---

nium malorum est cupiditas, ita et radix omnium bonorum est caritas" (*Sermo* 350, I, c. 1534).

". . . and what could begin this evil will but pride, that is the beginning of all sin?" *De Civitate Dei*, XIV, 13. (J. Healey, *op. cit.*, Vol. II.)

CHAPTER 32

FORMS OF COEXISTENCE OF
GOOD AND EVIL IN MAN

THE FACT that we have distinguished pride and concupiscence as two different genuine centers of moral evil does not mean that we normally find in the immoral man one of these two centers in an absolute domination. In certain immoral men pride may prevail; in others, concupiscence; in others again, pride and concupiscence may play an equal role. The case is exceptional in which one of these two centers dominates a person exclusively. At any rate, both are always to be found potentially. These two centers, notwithstanding their essential difference, are in no way incompatible. Not only can they coexist in the same person, but, further, they cooperate to such an extent that in many vices, morally negative responses, and actions we find a mixture of pride and concupiscence. Despite this cooperation, however, it remains true that pride and concupiscence clearly differ as such, that neither of them depends upon the other, and that normally we find a preponderance of one over the other.

From this *cooperation* of pride and concupiscence—each of which implies an incompatibility with the value-response attitude—we must clearly distinguish the *coexistence* of these two morally negative centers on the one hand, and the morally positive center on the other, a coexistence found in all men who are neither saints nor satanic or brutelike types. In the average man we normally find an awareness of moral good and evil, a certain readiness to conform to morally relevant values, and simultaneously a desire to satisfy pride and concupiscence. It is important to understand that this *coexistence* never has the char-

414

acter of *cooperation,* and that it completely differs from the above-mentioned cooperation of pride and concupiscence.

The fact that the value-response attitude can coexist with the centers of pride and concupiscence does not, however, contradict their incompatibility in any way. In the measure that the value-response attitude prevails, pride and concupiscence lessen.[1] The coexistence here in question has the character of a presence of contrary principles in our soul. This type of coexistence is a specific mark of the mystery of man's fallen nature.

There exist five main forms of this coexistence. In the first, the person is fundamentally willing to conform to the reign of morally relevant values and to submit to their call. But the value-response attitude has not yet penetrated the whole person to such an extent that concupiscence and pride are either completely expelled (as in the case of a saint), or at least silenced.[2] A relentless fight between the value-response attitude and pride or concupiscence takes place in the soul of this man; again and again he must struggle to dominate pride and concupiscence.[3] Sometimes he may succeed, sometimes he may fall prey to them. When he notices in his soul the presence of affective responses deriving from pride or concupiscence, he will disavow them at times, and at others he will fail to do so. At any rate, in the measure that the value-response attitude dominates in this man's soul, pride and concupiscence are tamed, and vice versa. There are innumerable degrees in which the value-response attitude is victorious over pride and concupiscence. The decisive mark of this type, however, is that in this man the value-response attitude definitely prevails over pride and concupiscence, and that he experiences these two evil centers as incompatible with the value-response attitude; the fight between them always has the character of a decision made between different worlds which exclude each other.

---

1 "Now in proportion as the dominion of lust is pulled down, in the same proportion that of charity is built up." St. Augustine, *De Doctrina Christiana,* III, X, 15–16.

2 In saying "expelled" we do not imply that the threat of pride and concupiscence ceases to exist, so long as man remains *in statu viae.*

3 "And therefore as long as we have to reign over sin, our peace is imperfect because both the affections not yet conquered are subdued by dangerous conflict." St. Augustine, *De Civitate Dei,* XIX, 27. (J. Healey, *op. cit.,* Vol. II, p. 266.)

A second type of man in whom we find a coexistence of the two antagonistic centers is the morally unconscious man we have mentioned before. In him we find a juxtaposition of the value-response attitude with pride and concupiscence. Owing to this person's unconsciousness, these two antagonistic centers never confront each other. According to his personality and the situation in question, this man will actualize morally noble or morally evil attitudes. Because this man is morally unconscious, his value responses will be stained with accidentality; but the same holds true of his yielding to pride and concupiscence. He takes no definite, conscious outspoken position toward the moral question. He has neither a fully conscious general will to be good, nor a general hostile attitude toward morality and, in the last analysis, toward God. His basic attitude is neither a cynical and perverted conscious general attitude, nor a conscious, outspoken indifference. Sometimes he will disconcert us by his generosity and again he will shock us by his impurity. We may be touched by his goodheartedness, and again we may be revolted by his indifference toward horrible sins. Plainly enough, an enormous scale of difference can be found within this type, extending from a man like Tom Jones in Fielding's novel, to Svidrigailow in Dostoevski's *Crime and Punishment*. A morally unconscious man may be lovable, due to a prevalence of the value-responding center in his nature. Yet this prevalence does not entail a conscious victory of the value-responding center in his nature. This prevalence remains in some way accidental, for no full actualization of the value-responding center can take place without moral consciousness. Another morally unconscious man may be, on the whole, intolerable. Concupiscence and pride may prevail in him and manifest themselves in his selfish attitudes, in his brutality and covetousness. Yet, surprisingly enough, he may reveal a touching love and gratitude toward a benefactor, or be known to reject an immoral yet profitable proposal.

It is important to see that the morally unconscious man has no general, conscious attitude in the direction of evil. This type of man has not, like Cain, a satanic hatred of God and of moral goodness; he does not share with Aristippus a cynical, conscious pursuit of the merely subjectively satisfying; he has not turned away from God; he has no declared indifference toward God and the moral law, but in a given situation he yields naïvely to the promptings of his nature and his accidental moods. No wonder that in such a type elements of pride and concupiscence coexist with elements of the value-response attitude. This type of man is opposed to the first type, since no open war between the value-response attitude and pride and concupiscence takes place in him. Because of his moral unconsciousness, no outspoken general attitude is to be found in him, and thus the coexistence of those intrinsically antithetic elements, having the character of a juxtaposition, is possible.[4] Yet, in the very moment in which the morally good attitude is actualized, pride and concupiscence will be at least silenced. This coexistence, in which a transition from one center to an opposite one is possible without full awareness of it, in no way contradicts the essential incompatibility of the value-responding center on the one hand, and of pride and concupiscence on the other.

In the third type we are confronted with a completely different situation. The coexistence of the antithetic centers in the person assumes the character of a compromise. It is no longer the disconnected juxtaposition proper to the naïve morally unconscious man. This type, though certainly not morally conscious, neither wants to ignore completely the call of morally relevant values, nor to renounce the satisfaction of his pride and concupiscence. But it must be said that his readiness to conform to the call of the morally relevant values is never a pure and genuine one. These values are never grasped in their full, inner preciousness and beauty, not even in their majestic ultimate importance. They are grasped rather as something which inspires a certain awe, and of which the validity is supported by convention, tradition, and public opinion. Persons in this class never want to come into open conflict with the moral commandments; they abhor considering themselves as disloyal, and *a fortiori* as criminals. They desire to be able to esteem themselves as decent, honorable men.[5] Their relation to the reign of morally relevant

---

[4] We saw before (Chapter 19, "Moral Consciousness") that all morally positive attitudes of the morally unconscious man lack the requirements of a full value response.

[5] We already mentioned this type in another context. Cf. Chapter 19, "Moral Consciousness."

values is thus far from the true and genuine readiness to conform to the values for their own sake, not to speak of a response to their inner beauty and preciousness. It is mixed with many elements of pride and concupiscence, but nevertheless morally relevant values play a role for them: these values are neither ignored nor does any hostile and rebellious attitude toward them exist.[6]

The readiness of these men to conform to the call of morally relevant values is, however, limited and conditional. They are willing to conform to the call of the morally relevant values only so long as it does not hurt their concupiscence or pride too much. They set a limit, determined by their pride and concupiscence, in which they are willing to conform to the moral commandments; they have a crippled conscience which functions only so long as too much is not demanded of their pride or concupiscence. They try to find a middle road between the call of the morally relevant values and their pride and concupiscence. Their whole life is a compromise. Within this third type of coexistence of the morally positive center and the centers of pride and concupiscence there are many degrees. The scale among those representing this type, therefore, is based on the degree of readiness to conform to the morally relevant values and to accept a dissatisfaction of pride and concupiscence for the sake of the call of the morally relevant values. Without doubt, the moral standard of an individual of this type varies very much according to this scale. Nor should it be overlooked that the purity of his value-response attitude, its qualitative genuineness, and the adequacy of his understanding of the values depend upon the degree of readiness to conform to the moral commandments or to overcome pride and concupiscence.

But notwithstanding this scale, this compromise type always clearly differs from the type first mentioned above. In the first type the coexistence has the character of a struggle, in this case it has the character of a compromise. In the first type, the in-

---

[6] This compromise type embraces many different degrees and subdivisions. In the worst, the typical embodiment of mediocrity and bourgeois self-complacency, the transition to a *ressentiment* against the world of values can certainly be found. Both Ernest Hello and Max Scheler often refer to this special type. But as a whole the compromise type is not in open warfare with the world of values, as is the man who is dominated by pride.

compatibility of pride and concupiscence with the call of the morally relevant value is clearly experienced and admitted. There is no attempt to repress this incompatibility or to span it. The value-response attitude is thus a genuine and pure one, although pride and concupiscence still exert a certain power in the soul of this man, since his morally good attitude has not yet victoriously penetrated his entire person.

In the compromise type, there exists a fundamental insincerity which tries to adjust these incompatible centers. The incompatibility is no longer experienced and the person will not admit that his attitude endeavors to reconcile two incompatible elements. The compromise type will not admit that he makes concessions to pride and concupiscence; rather he will find a name for his attitude which makes it appear before his own conscience as remaining in harmony with morality.

His value-response attitude will never be a completely genuine and pure one so long as the compromise attitude has struck roots in his soul, although there may also exist many degrees concerning the genuineness and purity of this attitude, as was seen above. The deep-rooted tendency in his soul to escape the inevitable struggle of those incompatible elements, the cowardly adherence to pride and concupiscence without risking the disagreement of a bad conscience, hinders him from giving a completely pure value response, even if the margin which he is disposed to set to pride and concupiscence is a relatively small and narrow one.

This "bourgeois" type, the so-called "loyal" and "decent" man, of whom Joseph de Maistre speaks in *Les Soirées de Saint-Pétersbourg*,[7] is also characterized by the fact that he is incapable of a true, ultimate contrition, because true contrition implies the full awareness of this incompatibility, at least the temporary collapse of any compromise and the complete surrender to the reign of the morally relevant values.

This type of compromise in no way contradicts the incompatibility of the centers of moral goodness and of moral evil. We can clearly see that their mutual exclusiveness manifests

---

7 "Si nous daignons nous abstenir de voler et de tuer, c'est que nous n'en avons nulle envie; car cela ne se fait pas. . . . Ce n'est pas le crime que nous craignons, c'est le déshonneur." *Troisième Entretien*.

itself in the fact that the perversion of the value-response attitude goes precisely as far as pride and concupiscence limit and restrict this attitude. Conversely, the influence of pride and concupiscence goes as far as the value-response attitude does not dominate. Between pride and concupiscence, there can be no question of a compromise, because they are not incompatible; hence the mixture of both assumes the character of a cooperation. Such a cooperation, whereby one center in some way supports the other, is out of the question with regard to morally antithetical centers in the person. Rather, the very fact that a compromise exists testifies to the antithesis of the two centers in question. Every concession made to one of them implies a withdrawal from the other. Though a person may try to escape from this antagonism and subjectively choose a compromise between them, in reality the objective incompatibility nonetheless subsists, and he is incapable of a true value response. He is the man who wants to serve two masters: God and mammon.

A fourth type of coexistence of the antithetical centers is to be found in the man who is subjected to idols. In him, as in the man of compromise, the two antithetical centers are not unconsciously juxtaposed as in the naïve, morally unconscious type. But in contradistinction to the compromise type, the combination of value response and pride or concupiscence is a completely different one. Instead of mediocrity and cowardice, we find here fanaticism and an impure zeal.

There exist indeed two different types of idolaters. The first makes an idol of a good endowed with a value, by making an absolute of it or at least overrating by far its importance. Such is, for instance, the man who makes an idol of the state, or the nationalist. The second type of idolater places an outspoken disvalue on the throne of a value, for example, in advocating a godless movement. He pursues something evil as if it were an ideal. We disregard at the moment this latter type of idolater, because here we no longer have a certain kind of coexistence of antithetical moral centers, but a typical case of the satanic *ressentiment* which shall be examined later on.[8]

We shall therefore concentrate here exclusively on the first type. A person of this type disconcerts us by his "idealism." He

8 Chapter 34, "Concupiscence."

is not preoccupied with merely subjectively satisfying things. He is definitely an adversary of the Aristippian *Weltanschauung*. He is filled with the desire to serve something great, having a value, and he is even ready to make sacrifices for it. But his attitude is far from being a pure value response. He responds to a good having a value, for instance, the state, and more specifically the state whose citizen he is. He grasps the value of the state, of a legitimate authority, of the juridical sphere which the state is called to defend, of the organization of community life. He grasps the value of loyalty toward the state. But he can only make of the state a supreme good surpassing the value of the individual person, his eternal welfare, and the value of the Holy Church because his approach is not a pure value response. The grandeur and power of the state to which he belongs also satisfies his pride; his fanatic submission to it satisfies his pride and even his concupiscence. Thus his attitude toward his idol is a strange mixture of a value response attitude and pride and concupiscence.

In contradistinction to the men of compromise, this mixture has not the character of serving two masters. It is not the result of a concession made on the one hand to the call of the morally relevant values, and on the other hand to pride and concupiscence. The idolater also clearly differs from the hypocrite, for he does not consciously disguise selfish interests as a value response. He does not try to deceive other persons in speaking of God when he means money.

The idolater believes in the grandeur of his ideal; he does not try to deceive others, but he deceives himself. He relishes precisely the gesture of sacrifice and abandonment; he sincerely strives for the triumph of his ideal. When asked why he strives for his ideal, he would sincerely answer, "Because this is the highest good, this is what objectively matters." But in reality this "ideal" attracts him because it satisfies his pride and concupiscence. His value response is in reality a sham one, thoroughly impure. It pretends to be a pure and heroic value response, and in reality it is an impure zeal (*zelus amaritudinis*),[9] nourished by pride and concupiscence.

[9] "As there is a harsh and evil zeal which separates from God and leadeth to hell," *The Holy Rule of St. Benedict.* (Atchison, Kansas: The Abbey Student Press, 1949.)

Very often the idolater is admired even by adversaries of his idol because one erroneously considers his so-called "idealism" to be a decisive proof of his high moral standard. One may say that after all he acted so with *bona fides:* he believes this idol to be a true, sublime good and he is ready to make sacrifices for it. The fact that he seemingly sacrifices his personal interest to the cause for which he fights is erroneously taken as a proof that he possesses a pure value-response attitude. Such a judgment is only possible as long as one remains on the surface, or as long as one has fallen prey to different confusions. It does not suffice to state that this man really considers an idol to be a supreme good. We have to ask how it is possible that he overrates this good to such an extent, and what are the roots in him that lead to this "idolatry." What are the centers in him to which this "good" appeals? If it appealed only to his value-responding, loving center, such an overrating would be impossible.

As we saw before, the blindness concerning morally relevant values always presupposes the absence of a pure value-response attitude and the interference of pride or concupiscence. Man is thus always responsible for his moral value blindness. And every "idolatry" implies a blindness concerning the good superior to the one idolized, and even concerning the true value of this good itself, because the true perception of this value is inseparable from grasping its rank in the hierarchy of values. Hence the very fact of a person's "idolatry" reveals the impurity of his value-response attitude. But apart from this fact the mere contemplation of the very quality of the idolater's zeal clearly reveals the role of pride and sometimes also of concupiscence. The fanaticism, the hardheartedness to which this "idealism" leads, the bitterness of this zeal, the intrusiveness and irreverence toward other goods endowed with morally relevant values, and many other features betray the predominant influence of pride and concupiscence.

This moral perversion is especially dangerous because this attitude is less easily detected by others and especially by the person himself. The idolater feels himself to be at least very unselfish and idealistic in the pursuit of his idol.

In this case again, it is not difficult to see that the coexistence of a value-response attitude and of pride and concupiscence in no way contradicts the intrinsic incompatibility of the morally positive and the morally negative centers. As in the case of the compromise type, the coexistence in no way implies that the antithetical centers are even simultaneously actualized. On the contrary, neither of the centers is ever actualized in its authentic form. The structure of the person's basic attitude has, in its idealism, some formal elements of the value response; the qualitative content of his attitude, on the contrary, is definitely an outgrowth of pride and sometimes of concupiscence. As a result this attitude is only a sham value response, but it is also not the typical and pure actualization of pride and concupiscence. This idolater is at many points completely opposed to the man of compromise, but from the moral point of view, they are not very different from each other, since in both cases we find this sham value response, this intrinsic falseness. The man of compromise is a static type, while the idolater is dynamic. The former is embodied in a bourgeois whose motto is *quieta non movere*, while the latter is typified in the revolutionary.

Finally, the fifth type is the person in whom the value-response attitude and pride or concupiscence dominate alternately, each in an outspoken and complete manner, and with an irrational and abrupt transition from the one to the other. Such a man is the type who lacks continuity and in whom we find alternately, so to speak, two different persons.

This type of coexistence (which Dostoevski presents marvelously in Rogoshin in *The Idiot* or in Dmitri in *Brothers Karamazov*) has certain characteristics: It offers a pure antithesis to any compromise since the response-to-value attitude is purely juxtaposed to pride and concupiscence and in no way mingles with it. But this juxtaposition radically differs from the one we found in the morally unconscious man. In the unconscious man the predominance of one center will change according to circumstances, different objects and temperamental dispositions, and it has no irrational, unintelligible character. We can understand its psychology. Here, on the contrary, the predominant feature is the unpredictable character of the transition from one center to the other. The transition is so sudden and irrational that the two incompatible attitudes never clash, and no struggle materializes between them, such as would imply a simultaneous confrontation of both. The juxtaposition has the form of an incoherent succession. There is something demoniac in this sudden change.

Certainly in the moment when the value-response attitude dominates in the soul of such a person, he will deplore his former attitude. For the discontinuity is not necessarily such that he forgets his former attitude, as might the morally unconscious type or the schizophrenic. He is able also to experience a deep contrition. But the rapidly alternating rhythm of his moral life thwarts a real fight against pride and concupiscence; it does not allow the steady, continuous struggle of his value-response attitude to dethrone pride and concupiscence, as takes place in the first type. Thus his contrition has merely the character of a deep awareness of his sinfulness, a deep sorrow over it, but it does not entail a sufficiently firm will to change. He experiences his pride and concupiscence more as a terrible, deplorable fate than as a burden which he is able and called upon to overcome by his free will.

It must be said that such a person's discontinuity also has deep consequences for the character of his value-response attitude. Although his value-response attitude is pure and genuine (insofar as it is not mixed with elements of pride or concupiscence), although it is in no way undermined by the compromise which characterizes the mediocre type, and although the reign of morally relevant values is grasped in its true importance in itself and even in its inner beauty and sublimity—inasmuch as he is really and fully interested in it for its own sake—nevertheless something essential is lacking in his value response. The discontinuity which explains the sudden and irrational changes that take place in his soul is inseparable from a deficiency in the manner in which this moral attitude is rooted in his soul. He lacks above all the full awareness of the role of freedom and also the full actualization of this freedom; there is instead an ultimate tendency to let himself depend upon the mood of his soul. In fine, there is a lack of responsibility, a refusal to initiate with his free will a durable and continuous fight against pride and concupiscence. This refusal has nothing of a compromise. It is rather to be explained by a general insufficiency. Such a man does not make enough use of his freedom; having too passive an attitude in general, he is inclined to let himself be dominated too much by his emotions. His value-response attitude has not yet struck roots in the very depth of his soul, that ultimate point which remains unshaken by the emotional oscillations of man's nature.

This formal imperfection of his value-response attitude is essentially linked to his discontinuity; continuity is an essential element of the true value-response attitude. It is the response to the immutable character of the morally relevant values and their call.[10] Such a response never restricts itself to the momentary situation, but rather demands a superactual interest in the unchangeable reign of the morally important-in-itself, and also requires a superactual direction of our will. Continuity implies that every eternal truth and every authentic value (especially every morally relevant value) which has been revealed to us should form a durable measure for our life; it requires that every new truth and value be confronted with one previously grasped. In a word, continuity is the specific response to an essential element of the important-in-itself and of the objectively valid.

If a man lacks continuity and falls prey to the momentary advantage which the present situation possesses over every past experience, his value-response attitude is formally incomplete and insufficient, although it may qualitatively be genuine. Discontinuity prevents the value-response attitude from taking root in this superactual depth of the person which is invulnerable to all the streams of actual impressions; discontinuity does not allow the value-response attitude to penetrate to a point in our soul at which it is destined by its very nature to be rooted.

As different as these five forms of coexistence are, they all manifest the essential incompatibility of the value response on the one hand, and pride and concupiscence on the other. Their coexistence always has the mark of an inner contradiction: every progress of the value-response attitude is connected with a regression of pride and concupiscence, and vice versa. Thus this coexistence never has the character of a cooperation; it could never mean that the incompatible centers might coexist without injuring each other, without an immanent hostility toward each other. This applies even to the compromise type, in which we

10 Cf. *Liturgy and Personality*, p. 171ff.

find an apparent truce between both conflicting centers. Since the compromise is paid for by a perversion of the value-response attitude the objective incompatibility of both centers is once again revealed.

We shall understand this incompatibility still more clearly in turning to an analysis of the strictly immoral man whose life is ruled by pride and concupiscence to such an extent that the value-response attitude has been more or less ousted.

CHAPTER 33

LEGITIMATE INTEREST IN THE
SUBJECTIVELY SATISFYING

WE HAVE seen that agreeable things are the lowest type of objective goods for the person, and in defining these we restricted ourselves to those things which are agreeable by virtue of their God-given, valid title. Sensitivity to agreeable goods and the desire to possess them belong to the plenitude of human nature. It is also natural to avoid disagreeable things. It is normal to have an interest in agreeable goods because of their subjectively satisfying character. Indeed the world is richer because agreeable things exist.

We have also seen that the fact a person enjoys agreeable goods is not something negative from the point of view of value, but on the contrary is definitely something having a value. It is even desirable that one should appreciate the gift of enjoying agreeable things. Yet the most perfect approach to agreeable goods is to understand them in their God-given meaning as objective goods for us.

But now another question imposes itself. We must inquire into the exact moral character of the field to which these agreeable goods appeal, and into the relation of this field to concupiscence and pride. We must examine what moral requirements have to be fulfilled in our relation to agreeable goods in order to avert the danger which undoubtedly can originate from our interest in them.

Insofar as the interest in subjectively satisfying goods that are legitimate is concerned, i.e., when we desire to appropriate such goods to ourselves, we must keep in mind that the legitimate field

427

to which these goods appeal essentially presupposes the super-actual predominance of the response-to-value attitude. There is a deep and meaningful order in man's nature, an order which is not a mere neutral fact but something which has a high value, and this also ought to be observed. We have seen that the value response, and above all the response to morally relevant values, should be granted the first place. Interest in the possession of goods having an authentic value organically issues from the value response; but as essential and important as it is, it is always secondary to the interest in values themselves.

Interest in the merely agreeable is something completely different; it issues from a field of its own, which must by its very nature play a restricted and far less central role than the appeal of goods endowed with an authentic value. Since it is not organically linked to an interest in values, its role must be greatly inferior to that played by the possession of those goods. Not only is the God-given role of this field a minor one, but, above all, because the frame of its role is determined by values, it is limited *a priori* to a sphere in which there exists no conflict with values.

This field can preserve its character in the plenitude of human existence as a legitimate, secondary element, only so long as the response-to-value attitude remains superactually the predominant element in our souls. As soon as interest in the merely subjectively satisfying becomes preponderant in the attitude of the person (and thus ceases to be restricted to this subservient role and to preserve the immanent readiness to yield to morally relevant values), pride and concupiscence make their entry and even in some ways replace this legitimate field of sensitivity. So soon as interest in the merely subjectively satisfying detaches itself from the immanent *religio* toward the reign of values and the value-response attitude, and as soon as the value-response attitude does not have in the person the predominant role which is due to it, then pride and concupiscence have penetrated interest in the merely subjectively satisfying and have substituted the legitimate field of sensitivity for the agreeable. Even the agreeable on the object side then assumes another character; it is in some way perverted or poisoned.

What matters is to understand that the field to which the agreeable or the morally neutral subjectively satisfying appeals, remains legitimate only so long as the person is superactually directed primarily toward the reign of values. It is in the very nature of this field to be restricted to a subordinate sphere, and to coexist with the value-response attitude which should be its master.

The unity of the human soul and its God-given order is such that the qualitative character of this field (though it is not directly linked to the value-response attitude) is completely changed as soon as interest in the subjectively satisfying is no longer "tamed" by the value-response attitude. This field is replaced by concupiscence or pride as soon as it no longer remains in the frame of a subservient role whereby it actualizes itself only with an immanent *placet* or *nihil obstat* (let it be) granted by the value-response attitude.

The dethronement of the value-response attitude from its primary role is inevitably linked to the actualization of pride and concupiscence; in other words, pride and concupiscence are always the causes of this dethronement. Apostasy from the reign of values is not due to the fact that the same harmless, innocuous interest in the merely subjectively satisfying becomes simply too intense. It is not a mere question of excess, but the legitimate field to which the agreeable appeals is actually replaced by the centers of pride and concupiscence. It is now either pride or concupiscence to which the same agreeable goods appeal. Interest in the agreeable goods thereby assumes a completely new and different character.

To be sure, the agreeable implies the possibility of this perversion for man's fallen nature. It is typical of this category of importance to imply the danger of an appeal to concupiscence or pride. But the difference between the legitimate field to which it appeals when the person is primarily directed to the reign of values and hence subjects the agreeable to the lordship of the values, and an untamed pursuit of the merely subjectively satisfying must be clearly seen.

The morally unobjectionable interest in merely subjectively satisfying goods and the interest in these goods which derives from concupiscence or pride, differ not only by *degree* but also in their very nature. The disorder which consists in a formal independence of interest in the merely agreeable and which immanently implies the dethronement of the value-response attitude is never only of a formal nature, but always and immediately includes a complete qualitative change, the replacement of this legitimate center by pride or concupiscence.

Chapter 34

CONCUPISCENCE

IN ORDER to understand the nature of concupiscence, we shall first study the man in whom concupiscence plays the predominant role, i.e., the man who has become a complete slave to concupiscence.

There exist certain types of men whose approach to the world and to life is dominated exclusively by the interest in drawing lust out of every situation. The way in which they superactually look at being, and in which they approach every concrete situation, is dominated by the question of how much pleasure they can get out of it. They are indifferent to the important-in-itself. The question as to whether or not something has a morally relevant value does not pose itself for them. They approach even those goods that have a morally relevant value exclusively from the viewpoint of whether or not they may bring them satisfaction directly or indirectly. They are blind to morally relevant values in general, and their indifference has blunted them for every concrete, morally relevant value. The notions of moral good and evil are for them empty concepts—which they know play a role for other persons—and they treat them as we would treat superstitions. Being completely absorbed by the merely subjectively satisfying, they are deaf to the majestic call of morally relevant values.

In the very depth of their soul, they have delivered themselves to concupiscence. This must not be understood in the sense of a decision which issues from a full use of their freedom, but rather in the sense of a failure to make use of their freedom. This decision is rather a gliding into concupiscence, a yielding to it, but they had the freedom to avoid this surrender. These persons have become slaves of concupiscence.

Concupiscence is, as we saw before, incompatible with the value-response attitude and the center which we called the reverent, humble, and loving center from which all the value responses derive. It is also incompatible with the capacity to understand the morally relevant values as well as with sensitivity to their call. The persistent craving for the subjectively satisfying, the blunt outlook toward the world which conceives it as a mere means for one's satisfaction, the brutish cramping of one's soul, the complete egocentrism: all these are ultimately opposed to reverent interest in the important-in-itself, to readiness to submit to the call of the morally relevant value, and to the response-to-value attitude. This antithetical incompatibility does not involve a consciously hostile attitude toward God and the realm of moral values on the part of the man dominated by concupiscence. His typical attitude toward God and values is one of indifference.

A man given over to concupiscence turns away from the reign of moral values, puts them aside and ignores them. He is indifferent toward them, not in the sense of a mere objective absence of the response-to-value attitude, but in the sense of positive indifference toward them. Even if concupiscence has completely blunted his conscience and blinded his capacity for grasping morally relevant values, this outspoken indifference toward the important-in-itself is immanent to the concupiscent man, in the depth of his soul. The concupiscent attitude as such necessarily implies this indifference toward the important-in-itself, toward the call of morally relevant values and the fundamental question of moral good and evil. It is inseparably linked to the gesture of doing away with the morally relevant sphere and its majestic obligation.

Not only is man objectively under the obligation of the morally relevant values, not only is he metaphysically ordered to God, but the presence of this call and the obligation to conform to the moral law is such that it simply cannot be overlooked and that an immanent position toward the world of values must in one way or another be taken. Thus, even in the person who is morally blind, in the man who seems to be ignorant of the existence of moral good and evil, there is to be found an immanent gesture of pushing this world aside. His concupiscent craving for the "emancipated" subjectively satisfying entails an immanent direction of his will to ignore the world of morality. Yet if the concupiscent man is primarily indifferent toward the world of values and ultimately toward God, every ignoring of, every positive indifference toward, the reign of values, every apostasy from their lordship necessarily leads to rebellion against the values and the voice of God implicit in them.

Since their call and obligation are by their very nature so relevant, so implacable, the apostasy can never remain a pure indifference but necessarily leads to a gesture against this obligation and against the rule of morally relevant values. Thus in order to clear the way for an illimited craving for the subjectively satisfying, the casting aside of the obstacle of the moral obligation surpasses the specific indifference which is proper to concupiscence and necessarily leads to a somewhat rebellious or hostile attitude. In this hostility the reign of values has the character of an obstacle to the illimited expansion of concupiscence. It differs from the primary rebellion against the world of values which is proper to pride. For it is not a hostility against them as such, but a secondary hostility created by their character as an obstacle to the unlimited acquirement of the subjectively satisfying.

Man cannot become a real brute; he cannot give himself exclusively to the agreeable, as an animal does. In trying to live like an animal, he necessarily falls below the animal level.

Concupiscence can never exclusively dominate man; it must always be supported by an element of pride. But this in no way erases the difference between pride and concupiscence. Those two centers are essentially different. This becomes unmistakably evident in the fact that pride can dominate a person without the cooperation of concupiscence. Satan's rebellion against God does not imply concupiscence.[1]

Both concupiscence and pride render us egoistic, close us up in ourselves, make us hard, suffocate love. They prompt us to

---

[1] ". . . yet are not all sins of an evil life to be laid upon the flesh; otherwise we shall make the devil, that has no flesh, sinless." St. Augustine, *De Civitate Dei*, XIV, 3. (J. Healey, *op. cit.*, Vol. II, p. 29.)

ignore the call of the morally relevant values and to show disrespect to these values. Yet if the suppression of the value-responding attitude is common to both centers, they differ very much in the quality of the egoism that they engender in the disregard of values proper to them. In order to grasp the very nature of concupiscence, we must consider those evil attitudes which are specific to concupiscence. Impurity in all its different forms,[2] as well as greed, drunkenness, larceny, and covetousness, are typical manifestations of concupiscence. Yet concupiscence is not restricted to these forms of passionate craving, although it is in them that concupiscence unmistakably discloses itself at first sight. The wide field of laziness in all its different shades is definitely an outgrowth of concupiscence, whether it is bodily laziness, shrinking from all type of bodily effort, even in those cases when a morally relevant good calls for these efforts; whether it is the laziness that shuns any type of work; or whether it is the deep spiritual laziness of the man who avoids every spiritual *élan*, all recollection, and shuns any gaze into the depth of his soul—concupiscence is always at the basis of these things. Again, a typical manifestation of concupiscence is the attitude which refuses the yoke of law and order, as well as the desire to be able continually to yield to our likings and moods, the pseudo freedom of the Bohemian. The general antipathy to law and order is one among the many forms of escape from the basic attitude of *religio,* an escape typical of concupiscence.[3] Many vices, many evil actions, stem from this form of concupiscence. Many dishonest and disloyal actions are rooted in a combination of laziness and this craving for a life free from the daily yoke of order and duty. In many cases, this

[2] *In Defense of Purity,* p. 35ff.

[3] The "pseudo freedom" propagated by the *Situationsethik* (ethics of circumstances)—Cf. *Acta Apostolicae Sedis,* 1952, p. 413; and K. Rahner, *"Situationsethik und Sundenmystik,"* in *Stimmen der Zeit,* February, 1950—is partly an outgrowth of this type of concupiscence. At its basis is the aversion to every precept and the interpretation of every clearly formulated moral obligation as "juridic distortion" of true morality. In this attitude one is ready to accept a dictate of one's own conscience, but everything imposed imperatively from without is considered to be a *bagage gênant* (a troublesome yoke).

It is easy to see that this ethos is a trend of concupiscence which shuns the "labor of obedience" (Cf. Prologue to the Holy Rule of St. Benedict) and which wants a morality deprived of any hardship. We say that it is partly rooted in this type of concupiscence because its other main root is pride.

attitude is the root of fraud, theft, and even of prostitution.

Again, other outgrowths of concupiscence are seen in all forms of sensationalism, such as curiosity (in the true sense of desiring to be informed about the *chronique scandaleuse* and being disturbed if anything is withheld from our knowledge, even if it is in no way our concern); the craving for movies, detective stories, the craving for things which thrill us for the sake of being thrilled. These are certainly much more innocent forms of concupiscence. Yet when we become enslaved by these tendencies, we are in danger of failing to conform to the call of many morally relevant values. Again, it is concupiscence which invites us to try to escape from confronting reality and from conforming to it, by fleeing into a world of dreams in which even the yoke of reality is absent, in which no hardship is to be found and no necessity of accepting a situation such as it is, whether or not it corresponds to our wishes.

Finally, a most typical and much meaner manifestation of concupiscence is when we relish letting ourselves go, when we oppose any self-control, when we flout all the demands of dignity, of demeanor, everything the Benedictine tradition calls *habitare secum*. In a later work, to which we have had occasion to refer several times, a thorough analysis of all the ramifications of concupiscence and pride will be offered. Here it may suffice to hint at these manifestations of concupiscence in order to illustrate its basic quality and the wide range of forms which it may assume. Yet it must be stressed that there are not only different ramifications of concupiscence, but also great differences in the rank of its moral disvalue.

The conflict between concupiscence and morality displays itself in three main forms. First, concupiscence may cause the overriding of the moral law by disrespecting morally relevant goods in order to acquire something subjectively satisfying. In all such cases, the destruction or injury of the morally relevant good is only a means for obtaining the coveted subjectively satisfying good, and these things are linked only rather "accidentally." Innumerable bad actions (ranging from the egoistic, uncharitable pushing aside of another person to crimes of all sorts) are the fruits of concupiscence. In all these cases, the rank of the moral disvalue of the action depends mainly upon the rank of the value of the good that is ignored, disrespected, or destroyed. Patently, robbery with murder is incomparably worse than robbery without murder. The higher the value of the good that is destroyed or disrespected, the worse is this disrespect or destruction and the greater is the enslavement to concupiscence which was needed to ignore this value. A great difference of scale is also to be found in the nature of the assent given to this injury of a morally relevant value, ranging from a reluctant and sorrowful "yes," typical of the weak man, to the cool, cynical assent proper to the criminal.

There are still two other ways in which morally relevant values can be contradicted and antagonized by concupiscence. Certain manifestations of concupiscence (whether in an action or in a response) inevitably and essentially contradict a morally relevant good. This is not the case in the above-mentioned destruction and contradiction of a value proper to many actions, since in these different types of concupiscence may lead to the destruction of the same value—someone may kill another person because of coveteousness, or because of a state of drunkenness, or because of a brutelike jealousy. Again, one and the same type of concupiscence may lead to the destruction of different goods—covetousness may lead to theft, bodily injury, or murder. The type of antagonism to values we now have in mind refers, on the contrary, to certain types of concupiscence in which one and the same value is in some way thematically contradicted and always inevitably desecrated by these very types of concupiscence. Such is the case of impurity. The desecration of the mystery of sex and of the value of its God-given meaning is one of the main reasons for the moral disvalue of impurity.[4] All forms of impurity have a much greater moral disvalue and more deeply, more mysteriously defile our soul than many other manifestations of concupiscence, such as gluttony, drunkenness, laziness. This is so because a high value is desecrated by impurity, whereas in drunkenness, gluttony, laziness, there is no analogous desecration.

The other way in which concupiscent attitudes essentially contradict the world of moral values does not refer to the dese-

[4] *In Defense of Purity,* p. 35ff.

cration of a good which is specifically thematic in this attitude, but to its qualitative antithesis to moral goodness in general. This latter contradiction is proper to all types of concupiscence, in impurity as well as in drunkenness and gluttony; in laziness and the desire for the sensational, as well as in covetousness. The very quality of all forms of concupiscence intrinsically contradicts and opposes moral goodness.

From the point of view of this intrinsic antithesis to the world of moral values there are again many differences in rank. The relish we take in letting ourselves go is meaner than laziness or dreaminess. It is in the frame of this very qualitative antithesis and intrinsic baseness that an important question imposes itself: What type of concupiscence is specifically antithetical to charity? What type of concupiscence is not only morally bad, low, sinful, but has also the outspoken character of "wickedness"? Later on we shall see that it is above all pride which has this character of deep wickedness, and that it is in many manifestations of pride and particularly in hatred that we find this vitriolic antithesis to charity. Although concupiscence may lead to monstrous brutality and specific wickedness in the sphere of action (for instance, in the case of robbery with murder), it is only in certain types of concupiscence that the very quality of concupiscence entails this "abyss" of wickedness. Apart from the above-mentioned grave immorality of all forms of impurity, there is a kind of demoniacal impurity which has this specifically wicked character. In covetousness, too, we find a type of concupiscence which has this deeply wicked quality. In both cases the very quality of these attitudes is filled with this dark, hellish wickedness and forms a radical antithesis to charity.

The analysis of the different qualitative ramifications of concupiscence must be left to a later publication; here we shall conclude our analysis of concupiscence by pointing to three main types of concupiscent men.

The first is the passionate type in whom the craving for the agreeable assumes a violent form and whose temperament has an impetuous character, as, for instance, in the case of the father of the Karamazov brothers in Dostoevski's novel, or the father of Eugénie Grandet in Balzac's novel. In such men concupiscence deploys itself in a passionate form, in an unquenchable thirst for the subjectively satisfying. Moreover this type is character-ized by a specific hardness and ruthlessness.

There is, secondly, the vegetative, phlegmatic type in whom concupiscence has the character of a lazy and heavy enslavement to the agreeable. Men in this category do not manifest any passionate impetus, any unquenchable thirst which holds them in a state of perpetual tension. Comfort plays a greater role in their life than the intensely agreeable. Theirs is a bovine heavi-ness characterized by the predominance of the desire not to be disturbed in the satisfaction of their animal urges. They are too lazy for any passionate craving for the agreeable. But they are nevertheless exclusively absorbed by the subjectively satisfy-ing, mostly concerned with bodily agreeable things, but they also enjoy in a "Fafnerlike" [5] manner the possession of wealth. Their carnal, blunt approach toward the world makes them com-pletely indifferent to the reign of morally relevant values and incapable of being charitable. They share hardness with the first type, but their hardness has more the character of a blunt and pachydermlike insensitivity.

Thirdly, there is the soft type of person who neither passion-ately craves the subjectively satisfying, nor is imprisoned by his laziness and dumb inclination toward the agreeable, but who is hypersensitive, yet only insofar as his own person is concerned. He is especially interested in avoiding any "rough winds"; he wants to live in a world where only gentle breezes fan him. Whereas the two former types do not care what attitude other persons have toward them, as long as they present no obstacles to their desires, the latter likes to be petted, to be surrounded by a soft atmosphere, to be caressed and cherished. He is not sensi-tive to the priceless gift of charity or love directed toward him, but is sensitive only to a soft and friendly atmosphere or a gentle touch. He does not crave passionately for bodily pleasures, but he reacts in an exaggerated, self-pitying manner to any bodily displeasure or pain. Whereas the two former types are not in-clined to weep easily, this type is tearful and easily falls into a crying mood. But for all that, he is unable to shed noble tears as the result of a true value response.

[5] Fafner, one of the giants in Wagner's *Rheingold.*

This last type differs so much from the two former ones that it seems that the three could have no root in common, and that the latter cannot be considered as another form of the concupiscent man. But a deeper analysis reveals that, notwithstanding the differences, the latter type is also dominated by concupiscence. He is not only as egocentric as the other two, but he shares with them an exclusive preoccupation with the agreeable. Furthermore, the subjectively satisfying does not appeal to his pride; it is not self-glorification that is his great theme, but the agreeable in the narrow sense of the term.[6] Again, he too is indifferent toward values. He is the man who pities himself, who feels himself to be harshly treated on every occasion, who is incapable of abandonment to the important-in-itself and of any interest in it for its own sake. He always thinks of himself and of his own feelings, and relishes every emotion, instead of focusing on the object which motivates this emotion. His tears are rooted only in his pampered softness and brought on exclusively by the slightest harsh or rough touch; sometimes he even enjoys them for their own sake.

There are certainly many different variations in this third type of man. He may respond more readily to the sensational, and enjoy being thrilled and put into an inner state of tension for its own sake. Or perhaps he is of a more sentimental mood, eager to savor a specific kind of emotion, for whom the object merely serves as a means for arousing this emotion. Again, this soft type of concupiscence may appear in an aesthete, for whom everything is merely an occasion for aesthetic enjoyment. Upon seeing a fire which destroys the home and threatens the lives of human beings, such an aesthete remains indifferent to their misfortune and is completely absorbed in the beauty of the spectacle. He is the man who says: "Throw this beggar down the steps; the aspect of his misery breaks my heart."[7]

---

[6] This does not mean that pride may not also play a great role in this type of man, but it will manifest itself in other ways.

[7] In order to avoid any misunderstanding, we must note, not only that this aesthete is unable to abandon himself to goods possessing morally relevant values, but that his attitude is perverted also toward aesthetic values. He does not grasp them in their importance in themselves, but rather he enjoys beauty in a refined, self-centered way and degrades it in approaching it as if it were something merely subjectively satisfying.

In all forms of the soft, concupiscent type indifference toward morally relevant values assumes another character than in the two former types, but it is nevertheless an analogous indifference. Whereas the two hard types are so indifferent toward the important-in-itself that it is obvious that they ignore the goods endowed with values, the soft type is seemingly directed toward many goods having an authentic value. Yet he is not really affected by their value, nor does he respond to them in a true value response; rather he uses them as means for his subjective satisfaction. He is, for instance, interested in hearing lectures on metaphysics given by a famous philosopher, not because he really thirsts for truth, but because he relishes the atmosphere created by the occasion of meeting a famous and brilliant man, and he cherishes the thrill of an intellectual event; or he goes to church because he takes pleasure in a certain religious emotion.

Persons in this category are, in general, more refined than the two former types and are less materialistic. They will not so easily commit crimes as the former types, but they are just as indifferent to the important-in-itself. They completely misunderstand values and are as egocentric as the two former types Despite their softness they are equally incapable of charity.

CHAPTER 35

PRIDE

WE SAW above that the second main root of evil is pride. Its negative role extends even further and deeper than the role played by concupiscence; above all, it is still more negative from a moral point of view. The Gospel, St. Augustine, and the whole Christian theology and philosophy consider pride to be the deepest and most fundamental root of moral evil: ". . . because the head and origin of all evil is pride which reigns without flesh in the devil." [1]

Both the proud and the concupiscent man are completely egocentric, but whereas the latter plunges into subjectively satisfying goods and throws himself away on them, the former is characterized by a reflexive gazing at himself. The relation between the subjective satisfaction and the *ego* (self) thoroughly differs in each case. Whereas the concupiscent man exclusively seeks to taste the various pleasures, and views the world under the category of the agreeable, the proud man is centered around his self-glory, the consciousness of his own importance and excellence, and around his masterly sovereignty.

Concupiscence refers to a *having;* pride to a *being.* Concupiscence is a perversion in the sphere of the possession of a good; pride is a perversion in the attitude toward one's own perfection. In concupiscence man renounces his birthright, as it were, for a mess of pottage; in pride man arrogates to himself a right that is above him; he exalts himself in an illegitimate way. St. Augustine admirably expresses the nature of pride in saying:

---

[1] St. Augustine, *De Civitate Dei*, XIV, 3. (J. Healey, *op. cit.*)

This then is the mischief: man, liking himself as if he were his own light, turned away from the true light, which, if he had pleased himself with, he might have been like. . . . But man desiring more became less, and choosing to be sufficient in himself fell from that all-sufficient God.[2]

Pride manifests itself in different main forms which correspond to different strata in the person, and which also embody different degrees of moral wickedness. We shall see that these main forms of pride thoroughly differ in their quality and nature, notwithstanding their common basic character. In order to make clearer the nature of these main different forms, we shall consider them in men who are completely dominated by pride.

The first main type is the man of satanic pride. Here pride reaches its climax and reveals itself in its most naked, radical and typical way. Satanic pride is first of all characterized by its object: metaphysical grandeur and metaphysical lordship. Mere exterior power, the opportunity to be a despot and dominate others exteriorly, the glory of being a hero—none of these can quench the insatiable thirst of this pride. Everything important-in-itself, every value, seems to this pride to entail an injury to its own glory. Thus the man dominated by this ultimate pride hates all light and the intrinsic beauty and harmony of every authentic value. The fundamental gesture of this pride is an impotent attempt to dethrone all values, to deprive them of their mysterious metaphysical power. The war which the man who is victim of this pride wages is directed against the reign of values as such, and ultimately against God Himself. The higher the rank of a value, the more will this man view it as an unbearable rival, and the more will he hate it. His hatred, therefore, is directed primarily against the moral and religious values. He not only wants to wage war against the reign of these values by bringing about the triumph of moral evil on earth, but he aspires, also, to a dethronement of moral values themselves and ultimately of God. His attempt is intrinsically futile, an impotent attempt at something essentially impossible. His attitude is metaphysically destructive and nihilistic. His pride and his thirst for metaphysical lordship, combined with the awareness of

---

[2] *De Civitate Dei*, XIV, 13. (*Ibid.*, Vol. II, p. 44.)

his own nothingness, engender in him a hatred against being, as such. The most general value of being, as such, is for him already detrimental to his desire of himself possessing the plenitude of being.

The innermost word of this satanic pride is the reversal of St. Catherine's prayer *Che tu sia e io non sia*—"That Thou be all and I, nothing." Its innermost gesture repeats to God: *Che tu non sia ed io sia*—"That I may be, and Thou shalt not be." This satanic pride is embodied in Lucifer and his rebellion against God. In man this pride exists only in an analogous form. It is found in Cain, who hated Abel because of his goodness; it is found in Rakitin of Dostoevski's *Brothers Karamazov* and in Shakespeare's Iago. The man who has fallen prey to this satanic pride is blind to the real nature of values, to their intrinsic beauty and dignity, but, unlike the concupiscent man, who in his complete bluntness ignores values, he grasps their metaphysical power. Certainly he misunderstands the nature of this metaphysical power, otherwise he could not attempt to dissociate it from values. He sees the metaphysical "throne" of values and simultaneously he misses the very nature of this "throne." He does not try to appropriate moral values to himself in order thereby to acquire their metaphysical grandeur as does the pharisee. He wants to rob them of their metaphysical grandeur and to place himself on their throne, not through possessing them but through dethroning them. Because he sees in them a rival, he wages war against them, and does so in an insidious and infamous way. He tries to replace the true order of values by a fallacious order of pseudo-values; he tries to dethrone them by placing their negative counterpart on their throne.[3] His whole personality is pervaded by a deadly hatred: hatred against all light, all goodness, hatred against God, hatred against other men; the higher their moral rank, the greater is this hatred.

This type of man is further characterized by metaphysical haughtiness. He abhors all submission, all obedience. *Non serviam* (I will not serve) is the second archword of satanic pride. The first feature of this pride is the specific hatred of the infinite goodness and divinè light of God; the second is rebellion against

[3] Cf. Max Scheler, *Das Ressentiment im Aufbau der Moralen. Op. cit.*, Vol. I, pp. 43–236.

God as Absolute Lord. Satanic pride shuns every kind of submission; the man possessed of it refuses to acknowledge any authentic authority; he refuses any submission to a God-given authority, any obedience, any admission of indebtedness to another. He shuns being helped by other persons, and, if forced by circumstances to accept help, instead of being grateful he will hate the one who helped him.

If we now proceed to a brief analysis of the other main dimensions in which pride deploys itself, we must first observe that we are no longer referring to certain types of men, but to dimensions of pride which may in part coexist in the same man, although one dimension will usually prevail and become the most specific trend of his pride. In satanic pride, as the summit of all types of pride, all the other dimensions of pride are, so to speak, surpassed and included *per eminentiam*. But the other main forms of pride, far from excluding each other, may be found in different degrees in one and the same man. They refer to different spheres of life, and their nature is characterized by their specific object. Thus, one and the same man may manifest different dimensions of pride according to the situation with which he is confronted.

The second main type of the proud man draws his consciousness of grandeur from values and perfections which he either believes he possesses or which he aspires to possess. He accepts values as the source of grandeur; he does not wage war against them nor does he attempt to dethrone them, but he desires to adorn himself with them for the sake of his self-glory. He is also blind to the true nature of values, and only grasps the metaphysical power which they embody. He is interested in them only as means for his self-glory. But their existence, as such, does not appear to him as something detrimental; he does not hate God. He accepts values as something valid and wants to use them for his self-glory; he even wants, in the worst case, to use God Himself for this purpose.

This type of pride has not the metaphysical aspiration of satanic pride; it lacks the rebellious character and the attempt to dethrone God. It aspires to grandeur in the frame of the existing metaphysical order and hence does not make its possessor a nihilist. But this type of proud man shuns every value insofar as it adorns and exalts persons other than himself; he wants all grandeur and exaltation for his own person. He is incapable of any response to value since he considers values only as means for his own grandeur. The specific objects of this type of pride are one's own values and any excellence proper to one's own activities. The possession of values as a means for self-glory is the specific end of his striving for them; in other words, self-glory through the possession of values is his specific and exclusive aim.

The specific nature of this dimension of pride will be determined greatly by the nature of the values in which the person glorifies himself or which he aspires to possess. There is, patently, a great difference between the pride of the Pharisee who seeks his glory in the possession of moral and religious values, and the pride directed to the glory resulting from intellectual values which characterizes the man who glorifies himself in believing himself to be a genius.[4]

The pride of self-glorification through the possession of values, implying, as a whole, a specific reflexive gesture toward one's own person, manifests itself in two dimensions: first, the glorification in values which one believes himself to possess; second, the craving for the acquisition of new values. We could call them the static and the dynamic dimensions of pride. Both will mostly be found in one and the same person, but it may also be that one of the two prevails, or even that one exists without the other. There is a self-satisfied type of pride in which a person relishes the possession of the wished for grandeur, and likewise a pride which craves for climbing ever higher. The prevalence of one of these two dimensions, either static or dynamic pride, will first depend upon the image which a man has of his own person, and sometimes even on the capacities and perfections he possesses in reality. Hence we must distinguish the case of a man's satisfaction in certain values of his own person which he believes he possesses, from that of a man thirsting for values which he knows he does not yet possess. Secondly, the prevalence of static or dynamic pride depends upon whether the thirst for grandeur is limited to certain values and can be satisfied by their possession,

---

[4] The fundamental importance of this factor determining the nature of the different types of pride has been elaborated in detail in Chapter 7 of *Transformation in Christ*.

or whether it is unlimited. This difference in the aspiration to grandeur is independent of the question of whether the person believes himself to possess a value or not. Not the real underlying situation, but the nature of the pride itself determines, in this case, whether this pride takes on the rhythm of a restless climbing higher, or whether there is a satisfied repose in the person's own perfection. Here the difference between static and dynamic pride reaches its full significance.

Finally, we have to distinguish three stages in the pride of self-glorification: the first consists in the conviction a man has that he possesses a value, the attribution to himself of some perfection or the feeling that he himself is endowed with it; in the second we find him relishing it, taking delight in his own beauty, intelligence, or goodness; the third consists in the specific self-glorification, the incense which he offers to his own grandeur, the outspoken antithesis to the humble attitude in which every perfection and value is considered as a pure gift from God.

These three stages constitute simultaneously three degrees of pride, the second surpassing the first and the third surpassing the second. We shall see later on that in some persons pride reaches only the first stage, in others the second, in again others the third. Each further stage presupposes the preceding one, and thus everyone who has the second also has the first, and whoever has the third necessarily has all three stages. But it may be that one has the first and not yet the second, or that in having the second one has not yet reached the third.[5]

Obviously these three stages of pride refer to the attitude concerning a value which a man believes himself to possess, and not to the attitude resulting from a consciousness of one's own insufficiency and the craving for the acquisition of values which he does not yet possess. They refer, therefore, to the static dimension of pride and not to the dynamic one.

We now come to the third type of pride: vanity. It has much in common with the pride of self-glorification, but it also differs from it in many respects. It, too, refers to values of one's own person and to the excellency of one's activities, as does self-glorification. But vanity is essentially static, and not dynamic. It is not the craving for new perfections, but relishing the possession

5 *Ibid.*, chap. 7.

of real or imaginary perfections. A second difference is that vanity does not imply a general blindness for values as such, and still less a general approach to them as mere means for one's own grandeur. The vain man may have a certain understanding of values and a readiness to conform to their call. Vanity, notwithstanding all the degrees of vanity, does not imply the poisonous, hard, and tense ethos which the pride of self-glorification always possesses in one way or another. It has the pseudo-harmony of self-satisfaction. The vain man is, above all, characterized by his naïve and ridiculous self-centeredness. Though he may have a certain understanding of values, they never play an important role in his life, since he is absorbed by his own perfection and has the tendency to refer everything to his own person. Moreover, the second stage of pride prevails in vanity, in the relishing of one's own superiority and excellence.

Finally, vanity may restrict itself to a certain sphere of values, for instance, the beauty of one's face, the elegance or grace of one's exterior appearance. Vanity may be satisfied with these perfections and be indifferent to other perfections such as intelligence or moral perfection.

Vanity has some affinity to concupiscence; it is, so to speak, the representative of concupiscence in the realm of pride. It results from a certain combination of pride and concupiscence. The ethos of vanity is soft and not hard, as are all other dimensions of pride. Vanity also displays itself in the enjoyment of admiration received from other persons. Yet it does not so much crave this admiration as take it for granted. The vain man thinks that admiration is due the perfections which he believes himself to possess, and he considers any man who refuses to offer him this admiration as stupid and inferior.

But it must be said that vanity alone is never able to cut us off completely from the reign of values. Either it is an addition to other dimensions of pride, as in the case of the man who is predominantly motivated by pride, or it is a residuum of pride coexisting with a value-response attitude, perhaps taking the form of a struggle between them.

Pride displays itself not only with respect to the grandeur issuing from the possession of values, but also with respect to the grandeur connected with might, exterior glory, and influence over other persons. The proud man of this type is not content simply with the admiration of others, which acts as a confirmation of the glory issuing from the possession of perfections, but he seeks and reposes in the grandeur which is connected with exterior glory: an outstanding position, might as such, the exterior domination of other persons, an exterior lordship.

He seeks the consciousness of "exalted being," of superiority, not in the possession of values, but in the exterior superiority which a leading position, the possibility of commanding others, or an exterior domination of a group or society conveys to him. The object of this pride is a grandeur which is not derived from the possession of values; but which originates in the exterior position which the person holds in relation to other men. Lordship, as such, manifesting itself in a dominating position in the world, is the specific aim of this pride.

This pride is clearly distinguished from satanic pride since, first, its aspiration toward lordship does not extend to the metaphysical sphere, and hence does not see moral and morally relevant values as enemies and rivals of its own grandeur. Secondly, this pride does not blind its owner in the same way to moral and morally relevant values. This pride does not even recognize the metaphysical power essentially connected with values, especially moral values. It regards them as the naïve concern of lowly and weak-minded people; in its fascination for exterior lordship, it bluntly overlooks them. It may lead to a denial of their objective validity in principle, and to a complete indifference *de facto*. The value blindness of this pride is more akin to the value blindness resulting from concupiscence. The call of values is unheeded, being regarded as an unimportant obstacle for attaining exterior lordship. Only things which present themselves as tangible forces in the exterior world, or ideas embodied in a movement, are considered as rivals and thus approached with hostility and the tendency to bring them under domination. No war is waged against God and the morally relevant values, but every moral and religious *force* which can be evaluated by that category which alone counts for this pride, i.e., exterior might, is considered as a rival. The typical rival for this pride is, not the saint, the man of genius, the great philosopher, the great musician, the great poet, and so on, but the man who either possesses great influence or a powerful position, or whose gifts may lead him to such influence or position.

Though this dimension of pride may vary according to the degree of exterior power to which it aspires, this difference does not affect its moral character, since it is essentially dynamic. Even the man who aspires only to become the chief of some subordinate group has, in his pride, the potential ambition to climb still higher. The frame for possible power which is imposed on him and which he may take for granted is rather an accidental limit; it does not essentially alter the character of this dimension of pride, which manifests itself typically in ambition.

We come now to the fourth main dimension of pride, which we may term "haughtiness." We have already mentioned it in relation to satanic pride. It displays itself in the refusal to submit to any other human person. The haughty man does not crave for a great position, for might or exterior lordship. But he idolizes his own individual position of mastery or his independence; he shuns the admission of any weakness or any dependence. This haughtiness makes a man incapable of admitting any fault on his part. He will never place himself in the weak position of asking someone to pardon him. He will look at contrition as a despicable weakness. He will make an idol of his dignity, his virility, his honor, and his rights. He lives on the *qui vive* concerning any offense against his honor and his rights. He possesses a hard and irascible ethos; he walks through life with head held high, conscious of his imperturbable strength and independence, shunning any help from other persons. He refuses to be grateful to anyone because this would be an admission of dependence. He wants to be undisturbed in the consciousness of his autonomy and autarchy.

This man does not necessarily refuse to submit to the moral law. He may be disposed to perform his duty and even to submit to the legitimate authorities. But he will never admit a fault even to himself, and certainly never to other persons. Obeying the moral law to a certain extent does not seem to him a weakness or a diminution of his autarchy and virile independence. But the admission of a fault, as well as indebtedness to another person, are regarded by him as incompatible with his honor and virile strength. Haughtiness is centered around the idol of independence and virile strength. The haughty man avoids above all bowing before other people. Anything like compassion or being moved, which implies an element capable of softening his hard and imperturbable virility, is considered by him as a weakness. Shakespeare's Coriolanus is such a haughty man; thus he regards yielding to the prayers of his mother, his being moved by her, as an unpardonable moral defeat.

The contrast between haughtiness and the other dimensions of pride is obvious. In this pride, as such, there is no tendency to dethrone the values, as there is in satanic pride. Furthermore, it conditions no complete value blindness, but it frustrates the full understanding of values. It allows an understanding of the important-in-itself and of the category of duty, especially insofar as it assumes a legal character. But it frustrates the understanding of the intrinsic beauty and goodness of moral values and excludes especially the understanding of every value which presupposes a humble, unpresumptuous mind. Every value which seems to the haughty man incompatible with his virile strength and self-affirmation—for instance, charity, compassion, contrition, and gratitude—is not understood. This pride acts more as a narrowing and falsification of value perception than as a radical frustration of it.

Finally, this pride is not concerned with the acquisition of values in order to exalt its own grandeur or to relish them or glorify in them; rather, only one value matters: strength, independence, autarchy. It considers only the possession of this value as indispensable for the desired grandeur. And it does not strive to acquire this strength, but instead starts from the consciousness of possessing it, and takes it for granted as an indisputable basis. It is concerned only with a refusal of anything which could injure the possessor's independence and virile strength. Pride imprisons its victim in a cramp of self-affirmation, a continual defense position against any offense to his honor, his rights, his independence. This pride knows only one fundamental evil: weakness. To give up the fortress of the hard, cramped, self-affirmation, to surrender the grandeur which virile strength and autarchy conveys to him: this alone is evil.

Haughtiness has a static character. It is not a craving for more and more independence, a direction toward a higher and higher exaltation. It does not imply the gesture of ascension, but the refusal to descend from the height which one presumes to possess, the resistance against anything which would imply a humiliation. The man who is obsessed with this pride does not want to be exalted, he is not filled with the unrest and tension for a grandeur which he believes himself not yet to have attained. But he defends continually the grandeur which he takes for granted that he possesses, and shuns every attitude or situation which he considers incompatible with his grandeur. This is the pride of the Stoic who speaks: *Si fractus illabatur orbis, impavidum ferient ruinae* (If the world should collapse in ruins about him, struck by its fragments he would remain fearless).[6] To this pride, fear appears as the incarnation of weakness, the very antithesis to its idol of virile strength and dignity.

The brief analysis to which we have to restrict ourselves in this book suffices to disclose pride as the very core of moral evil. Innumerable are the evil actions rooted in pride, as is seen, for example, in the murder committed by Richard III, by Macbeth, and above all by Cain; in calumny; oppression of the weak; in the humiliation of other persons. Yet it is easy to grasp that the connection between the morally relevant good and the real goal of this action (the satisfaction of pride) is much closer and thus less accidental. If in the case of Macbeth and Richard III the link is still accidental, in the case of Cain the problem is different, for the very death of Abel is a source of satisfaction to the murderer. The same applies to all actions determined by envy or hatred. The rank of the moral disvalue of actions rooted in pride depends, as in the case of actions rooted in concupiscence, upon the rank of the destroyed or disrespected morally relevant good. But it also depends upon the nature of the link between the subjectively satisfying and the destroyed good, that is to say, upon whether the destruction is accepted or sought for its own sake. According to the type of pride underlying an action, the link between them differs greatly. In the case of satanic pride, every evil action is done for the sake of the evil, i.e., because of the hatred of God; whereas in the evil deed that results from ambitious craving for might and earthly lordship (as in the case of Macbeth) this link is more accidental. Multifold are the morally

6 Horace, *Ode*, III, 3, 7.

evil responses rooted in pride—envy as well as evil joy over the humiliation of other persons, hatred as well as pharisaical self-glorification, hardhearted indifference as well as the desire for revenge. Here again, as in concupiscence, there is a scale of moral disvalue apart from the link with the destruction of a morally relevant good in the sphere of action. The different types of pride vary in their quality and the kind of antithesis to moral goodness which they constitute. And the nature of this quality also determines the rank of the moral disvalue which they embody. We have seen that the pharisaical pride which glorifies itself in the possession of virtue is worse than the self-glorification found in intellectual values. We have seen that the dynamic pride is, in general, worse than the static. Again, haughtiness is worse than vanity.

But, above all, we have seen that metaphysical, satanic pride is incomparably worse than any other pride. It is here that we find the full mystery of iniquity, that we find the radical antithesis to the saint. In the saint's love of God we find the most sublime embodiment of all moral goodness in man; in the hatred of God, the most terrible embodiment of moral wickedness.

V. Conclusion

CHAPTER 36

CHRISTIAN ETHICS

THE TITLE of this book implies a thesis: the existence of Christian ethics. Does this mean that there are several ethics—a pagan, a Mohammedan, a Buddhist ethics—and that Christian ethics is one among others? Obviously not. The entire analysis of ethical problems which we have offered points to the fact that in saying "Christian" ethics, we mean the one, true, valid ethics. If true ethics and Christian ethics are synonymous, why then speak of Christian ethics? Would it not be more correct to say simply "ethics," even if in its content this ethics is Christian?

In order to answer this question we must first make the following remarks: For a pagan also, the notions of moral good and moral evil exist; he too may admire moral goodness in another person and become indignant over moral wickedness. We have seen that a person does not need to know of God's existence in order to grasp the difference between moral good and evil in general, and between certain moral values and disvalues in particular.[1] *A fortiori* we must admit that a distinction between moral good and evil can be made and that certain moral values and disvalues can be grasped without Revelation. It is impossible to deny that a pagan can also be honest or dishonest, loyal or disloyal, selfish or unselfish. There exists a morality if we prescind from Revelation and a true natural ethics is concerned with the exploration of this morality.[2] An ethics deprived of the

---

[1] We shall come back to this point on page 455.

[2] Theology tells us that man, separated from God by Adam's fall, cannot by his own effort span the abyss separating him from God. The good will, the natural moral goodness of Socrates, could never do away with this stain. Only through Christ's death on the cross can this abyss be bridged: only the one reborn in bap-

epithet "Christian" is the philosophical exploration of the morality which is embodied in a morally noble pagan, for instance in Socrates, or, more correctly, of all the moral values which can be embodied in a human person without Revelation.[3]

Christian ethics in our terminology is, on the contrary, the philosophical exploration of the totality of morality, including the natural moral law and all moral and morally relevant values accessible to a noble pagan, as well as the morality embodied in the sacred humanity of Christ and in those men and women who have been transformed into Christ—the saints. We have stressed several times that this latter morality embodies not only a new world of moral values, unknown and inaccessible without Christ, but it also gives a new character to the entire field of natural morality. It is thus not only an incomparably higher morality, but a completely new one. Yet this morality is simultaneously

---

tism can glorify God by the morality of the "new creature" in Christ. In our philosophical analysis, we prescind from this fact which is inaccessible to our reason. We only include the given, fundamental difference between the morality of Socrates and the morality of a saint. We also include the mysterious disrupture in man which manifests itself in experience as well as the evident limitations of morality in a noble pagan. Thus in distinguishing between good and evil in a pagan, we in no way pretend that the moral goodness of Socrates, without grace, is able to glorify God, or that it could in any way alter the separation from God which is due to original sin.

Whether or not the grace of God might be necessary for the moral goodness of a pagan is not a question which philosophy can answer. In any case, this natural morality is possible without any consciousness of grace on the part of the agent, and *a fortiori* without knowledge of Christian Revelation.

[3] In opposing here Christian morality to a mere natural morality, we do not mean by natural morality, the morality of a possible man who, although without supernatural union with God, would have an uncorrupted nature. Faith tells us that such a man never actually existed. The man whom we know by experience and who is accessible to a philosophical analysis manifests a mysterious rupture in his nature; in him pride and concupiscence are undeniable realities. What the morality of a man with an uncorrupted nature would be is not a problem we can discuss in philosophy, at least not a philosophy which has its starting point in the given.

Thus in distinguishing Christian morality from natural morality we consider the morality of a saint on the one hand, and the morality of a noble pagan such as Socrates on the other. Both are data to be found in experience and thus accessible to philosophical analysis. It must however be emphasized that the morality of Socrates is before Christ and the Christian era, and thus it has the character of a prelude. Such a morality can no longer exist in the Christian era, and in a world penetrated by Christian ideas. There is an abyss separating an apostate from a pagan of the pre-Christian era.

the fulfillment of all natural morality. Once Christian morality has been disclosed to our minds, we understand that all natural morality is a prelude to Christian morality, and that everything which is to be found in natural morality is found on a higher level and in its ultimate meaning only in the light of Christian morality.

Christian ethics is, however, in no way synonymous with moral theology. It is a pure philosophical exploration introducing no arguments which are not accessible through our *lumen naturale* (light of reason), whereas in moral theology faith is presupposed, and revealed truth which surpasses our reason is included in the argumentation. Christian ethics is a strict *philosophical* analysis, starting from the data accessible to our mind through experience. It in no way ignores the essential distinction between faith and reason, revealed knowledge and natural knowledge. But it implies a relation to Revelation insofar as it includes the morality which is only possible through Christian Revelation. It is purely philosophical in its approach and method, but its object is the undeniable reality of Christian morality which is a full datum for our experience as well.

Before turning to the features of Christian morality, we still have to stress one fundamental fact: morality as such essentially presupposes God's existence. This does not mean, however, that we must have a knowledge of God's existence, either by Revelation or by rational demonstration. If we think of the Socratic statement: "It is better to suffer injustice than to commit it," we find an extraordinary awareness of moral goodness and of the obligation to conform to morality, though the notion of God is, to say the least, very vague in Socrates. The natural moral law, morally relevant values as well as moral values, is "given," and in order to grasp these values together with their call and obligation, no knowledge of God's existence, and therefore no explicit reference to God, is required. The Socratic statement necessarily implies the notion of some absolute reality, the notion of a world above us. Time and again we have stressed this intrinsic relation of the moral values to an absolute above us.[4] The experience of moral obligations, the voice of our conscience, cannot be separated from the awareness of some absolute. But the

4 Cf. Chapter 15, "The Nature of Moral Values."

notion of a *personal* God is not indissolubly connected with the *experience* of moral values, nor does the voice of conscience presuppose the knowledge of a personal God.

But as soon as one philosophically contemplates and analyzes the message embodied in moral values, in their unique gravity, in the categorical character of the obligation which can be grasped by us, we discover that only the existence of a personal God who is the Infinite Goodness can fulfill the message of moral values or can ultimately justify the validity of this obligation. We do not mean thereby that this obligation needs other reasons, for instance, the Infinite Lordship of God, or His right as Creator to impose moral obligations upon us. We do not want to reduce all moral obligations to positive divine commandments. But we want to say that moral values only possess the ultimate reality which justifies the gravity of the moral order, of its majestic obligation, if they are ultimately rooted and embodied in the Absolute Person of God.[5]

The drastic reality of the moral law and its unchangeable character would lack their indispensable foundation if, e.g., the ultimate metaphysical basis were merely the Platonic idea of Goodness. As person, man possesses an incomparably higher being than any impersonal entity. Hence it is impossible that any impersonal goodness could impose on him absolute obligations from above. Only an absolute goodness possessing personal reality can do this. In this sense we must say that if there were no God, all moral values, the moral law itself, would be deprived of their indispensable metaphysical basis.

The existence of contingent beings is accessible to our knowledge without any reference to God. But we also grasp that contingent beings necessarily presuppose a *causa prima,* i.e., an absolute Being. Thus we say *quoad se* (in itself) contingent beings presuppose God; *quoad nos* (for our knowledge) contingent beings are grasped first, and lead us by inference to God's

[5] It must be emphasized that in no way do we thereby introduce God's existence as a postulate, as Kant did. A postulate is typically something *quoad nos;* it is something *we* have to assume, or else we would have to give up the moral order. A postulate is something which we must assume because of its practical indispensability, though it is inaccessible to our reason. Our thesis, on the contrary, stresses that *quoad se* the moral values presuppose God and that God manifests Himself in them. Morally relevant values are an objective hint at God's existence and support our knowledge of God.

existence. The same thing applies analogously to our problem. For our knowledge of moral values, of the moral obligation, of the natural moral law, the knowledge of God is not required. But objectively these data presuppose God. We do not pretend that the type of demonstration leading to God in both cases is the same. But without any doubt God manifests Himself in moral values; He speaks to us in moral obligation. The moral values, the moral law, the moral order, the moral obligation, the voice of our conscience, objectively presuppose God, and are thus for our minds and knowledge hints at God's existence. The undeniable world of values, and especially of moral values, testifies to the existence of God for the one who has "eyes to see, and ears that may hear." *Dicit insipiens in corde suo: non est Deus*—"The fool hath said in his heart: there is no God" (Ps. 13:1). Thus St. Bonaventure says:

He, therefore, who is not enlightened by all these splendors of created things is blind; he who is not waked by such callings is deaf; he who from all these effects does not praise God is dumb; he who after such intimation does not observe the first principle is foolish.[6]

This fact has a paramount bearing on natural morality. Every value response, but above all every response to a morally relevant value, is an implicit, indirect response to God. Morally relevant values, and above all moral values, are linked to God in such a way that in affirming them and in giving a positive response to a value-endowed good we implicitly conform to God and respond to God. Analogously, in our disrespect for a morally relevant value we implicitly show disrespect toward God.[7] If this immanent objective relation of every morally relevant value to God, source and sum of all values, did not exist, the value response to this morally relevant value would be deprived of moral value. So long as a man does not know God, this implicit submission and conforming to God will be found in every true, morally good value response which he accomplishes. But as soon as someone, in doing something that objectively is in conformity with

---

6 *Itinerarium mentis in Deum,* quoted from *The Soul's Progress in God;* Selections from the World's Devotional Classics, Vol. III (New York and London: Funk and Wagnall Co.), Chap. I, p. 18.

7 In this sense St. Thomas says: "To disparage the dictate of reason is equivalent to contemning the command of God." *Summa Theologica,* 1a–2ae, xix, 5 ad.

the moral law expressly denies any reference to God and subjectively severs from God the morally relevant value to which he conforms, then his response is perverted and deprived of all true moral value.

We shall conclude this book with a brief glance at the nature of Christian morality. We have stressed time and again that many responses and virtues are only possible in the frame of Christian Revelation.[8] Theology tells us that these virtues are "fruits of the Holy Ghost" and only possible in the "new creature." The mysterious relation between sanctifying grace and these virtues is inaccessible to our reason and to philosophical analysis. Yet, as we have seen, these virtues also presuppose the Revelation of Christ insofar as they are only possible as responses to the God of Christian Revelation as well as to man seen in the light of Christian Revelation. And this relation to Revelation is accessible to the eyes of our mind and can be the subject of philosophical analysis.

In my work *Transformation in Christ* I have tried to elaborate many features of the "new creature," the one reborn in Christ. The unlimited readiness to be changed, true contrition, true self-knowledge, true simplicity, humility, true freedom, patience, meekness, peacefulness, mercifulness, these are only possible as responses to the God of Christian Revelation and to a universe seen in the light of Christ.[9] The same can be said of the love of neighbor. Charity, in contradistinction to a humanitarian sympathy with other persons, responds to the beauty of a human being created after the image of God, destined for eternal communion with God, loved and redeemed by Christ. Patently there can be no love of neighbor, ardent love in the full sense, such as it shines forth in St. Paul's words, *amor Christi urget nos*, which is not rooted in the love of God. Whereas justice, veracity, honesty, temperance, can also be found in Socrates, that is, with-

---

[8] Cf. Chapter 15, "The Nature of Moral Values"; and "The Sphere of Virtues," p. 357.

[9] Christian Revelation is here understood in its entirety including also all the elements already present in the Old Testament, elements which find their fulfillment and completion in the Gospel. By Christian morality, we mean the ethos of the saints of the new covenant, reflecting the sacred humanity of Christ, without raising the question what elements in their ethos can already be found in the old covenant.

out Christian Revelation; whereas these virtues can constitute themselves as responses in the frame of the world known to us without Revelation, there are many virtues which presuppose as their object the notion of God as revealed in Christ, the sacred humanity of Christ, the Christian vision of man.

It is precisely in these virtues that is to be found a moral goodness completely new and beyond compare, a transfigured, holy goodness, reflection of the sacred humanity of Christ. These virtues are the core of Christian morality. But notwithstanding their absolutely new quality, they are also fulfillments of all natural moral goodness. While surpassing it so completely, they yet contain *per eminentiam* every moral value found in a merely natural morality. Whatever is a real moral value is, as we have seen, a special reflection of God and finds its crowning in the *similitudo Dei* of the saint.

This relation of natural morality to Christian morality will become still clearer if we concentrate on the transfiguration within a saint of virtues which, as such, can be acquired by a pagan. Let us think of the difference between the justice of Socrates and that of St. Ambrose, of the difference between the veracity of Plato and that of St. Paul. The justice and veracity of the saints are filled with a new splendor, a completely new depth and inner freedom. They exhale a new fragrance, they are transfigured by the *lumen Christi*. The same can be said of the reverence, the temperance, the fortitude, the faithfulness, the reliability of the saint.

As to virtue leading us to a happy life, I hold virtue to be nothing else than perfect love of God. For the fourfold division of virtue, I regard as taken from four forms of love. For these four virtues (would that all felt their influence in their minds as they have their names in their mouths) I should have no hesitation in defining them; that temperance is love giving itself entirely to that which is loved; fortitude is love readily bearing all things for the sake of the loved object; justice is love serving only the loved object, and therefore ruling rightly; prudence is love distinguishing with sagacity between what hinders it and what helps it. The object of this love is not anything, but only God, the chief good, the highest wisdom, the perfect harmony. So we may express the definition thus: that temperance is love keeping itself entire and incorrupt for God; fortitude is love bearing everything readily for the sake of God; justice is love serving God only, and therefore ruling well all else, as subject to man; prudence is love making a right distinction between what helps it towards God and what might hinder it.[10]

All morally relevant values assume a completely new significance against the background of Christian Revelation. A new seriousness, a new realistic character, a breath of eternity pervades the moral order in which the great drama of human existence displays itself *coram Deo,* in the confrontation with God. The voice of the living God is heard in the Decalogue, it is the law of the living God and not a mere abstract law; it is the infinite Holy Lord whom immorality offends and whom moral goodness glorifies. The entire morality of the saints, whether of St. Mary Magdalen, St. Paul, St. John, St. Francis of Assisi, St. Catherine of Siena, St. Ignatius of Loyola, St. John Bosco, reveal a completely new ethos.

The first decisive mark of the Christian ethos is the indispensable and all-important role of humility. No greater revolution in the field of morality could be imagined than the parable of the Pharisee and the Publican. The ridiculousness and ugliness of vanity would certainly be grasped by Socrates. But the mysterious beauty of the man "who humbles himself," who places himself beneath the level on which he actually stands, who desires to throw away all honors and to accept joyfully all humiliations, which moves St. Teresa of Avila to say on her deathbed that she is one of the greatest sinners that ever lived, is a scandal and foolishness for natural morality. The importance of humility is such that it changes the whole of morality. It pervades every other virtue and gives to each a new and matchless value. It is only on the basis of humility that all other moral values unfold in their full beauty. Humility conveys to the entire ethos of the person a completely new note. It exalts him mysteriously, endows him with a sublime inner freedom and razes the walls in which man has imprisoned himself:

In humility therefore there is this to be wondered at, that it elevates the heart; and in pride this, that it dejects it. This seems strangely contrary, that elevation should be below, and dejection

[10] St. Augustine, *The Morals of the Catholic Church,* quoted from *Basic Writings of St. Augustine,* trans. R. Stothert (New York: Random House), Chap. XV, pp. 331–2.

aloft. But godly humility subjects one to his superior, and God is above all; therefore humility exalts one, in making him God's subject.[11]

A second fundamental aspect of Christian morality is the interpenetration of attitudes which seem to exclude each other on the level of mere natural morality.[12] In a good pagan a great zeal for justice, for moral ideals, does not coexist with gentleness and kindness. A great and powerful personality, a leader possessing an unshakeable courage, will not be modest and meek. It is only in a saint that we find holy courage, hunger and thirst for justice, interpenetrated with humility and meekness. Here we find this *coincidentia oppositorum*,[13] which is embodied in a saint and is possible in Christian morality alone. It is indeed only *holy* zeal which can be interpenetrated with *holy* meekness. It is not simply a synthesis of the same perfections and virtues which exclude each other in a pagan. The two different virtues which interpenetrate each other in the saint are themselves already something completely new and incomparably higher, but they also contain all moral values present in the two perfections which can be found separately in the pagan.

Christian morality is characterized by a holy inner freedom, an elevation above ourselves, a standing in the full light of truth, an unlimitedness which manifests itself in this boundless, irresistible charity, at the sight of which have been heard the words, *qui sunt isti et illi*, throughout the centuries since the advent of Christ, and which was the fundamental datum at which Henri Bergson "wondered," and which is according to him the source of a higher morality.

A third mark of Christian morality is the fact that here this specific goodness of charity is its very core, whereas in natural morality rectitude, uprightness, and justice are its very core. For instance, Socrates' personality emanates a spirit of veracity, sobriety, rectitude, justice. But St. Stephen's prayer for his murderers exhales the superabundant goodness of charity. And in St. Francis of Assisi's embrace of the leper there shines forth the

---

11 St. Augustine, *De Civitate Dei*, XIV, 13. (J. Healey, *op. cit.*, Vol. II.)

12 The exclusiveness in question implies no antithesis, but belongs to the type of friendly polarity mentioned in Chapter 11, "Unity of Values."

13 Cf. *Transformation in Christ*.

same luminous, irresistible charity. But above all this holy goodness of charity is embodied in the words of our Lord: "Love your enemies: do good to them that hate you" (Matt. 5:44). In this morality everything is pervaded by the spirit of mercy. The saint knows that he lives from God's mercy, that all his hope is based on this mercy; the words of the Our Father, "Forgive us our trespasses as we forgive those who trespass against us," are present to his mind. He hears the voice of Christ: *Misericordiam volo et non sacrificium*—"I will have mercy and not sacrifice." Christian morality is imbued with the spirit embodied in the parable of the prodigal son and with the message of the parable of the unmerciful servant.

Finally, the radically new character of Christian morality is disclosed in the fact that all virtues and moral attitudes, whatever their object may be, originate in a response to God; the backbone of all moral attitudes is the love of God, through Christ, with Christ, and in Christ. The most sublime of all value responses is here the basis of all value responses; every response to a morally relevant good is rooted in this love and has the character of organically issuing from this love.

Love, and do what thou wilt; whether thou hold thy peace, of love hold thy peace; whether thou cry out, of love cry out; whether thou correct, of love correct; whether thou spare, through love do thou spare; let the root of love be within, of this root can nothing spring but what is good.[14]

It is easy to realize the sublimity of a morality in which the ultimate basic response is not only directed to morally relevant values, but to the Absolute Person who is infinite Goodness Itself —a morality in which the love of God and God's love in us pervades and forms every act of will and is the first and last word in man.

A detailed philosophical analysis of the specific features of Christian morality will be presented in a later work which we have found it necessary to mention several times. In the present work we have been concerned mainly with the general philosophical features of morality. The same kinds of human acts which are an expression of natural morality are also in evidence

14 St. Augustine, *In Epist. Joannis ad Parthos*, Tr. vii, 8.

in the display of "supernatural" morality. The nature of the value response, of the freedom of the person, of value in general and of moral values in particular, had to be elaborated in order to understand the specific nature of Christian morality. It is true that at times we had to anticipate the analysis of several features of Christian morality for reasons which can now readily be understood. This applies especially to the analysis of the "reverent, humble, loving center" and its incompatibility with pride and concupiscence. This center is indeed only to be found in its full domination in the saint. And not only is the complete victory of this center to be found exclusively in the saint, but only in Christian morality does it have, in its quality, the character of a loving, humble center. Thus in the pagan the morally good center can only be termed the value-responding center, and this in an analogous sense.

We want to conclude this work with the words of St. Augustine, Father of Christian ethics, in which the spirit of Christian morality shines forth in breathtaking simplicity:

Though of himself man fell, of himself he cannot rise. But outstretched to us from above is God's right hand, our Lord Jesus Christ. Let us therefore hold to Him in firm faith, wait for Him in sure hope, desire Him in ardent love.[15]

[15] *De Libero Arbitrio*, Bk. II.

INDEX

Abandonment: to values, 39; to God, 305; to affective responses, 336

Acta Apostolicae Sedis, v, 434

Actions: sphere of, 342-4, 346-9, 382ff; and morality, 348-9; marks of, 346; elements of, 346-7; exclusiveness in, 408ff

Acts of the person, objectivity of, 28-30

Actus humanus, 180

Adaptation and habit, 369-70

Adequate response: 240-1, 250. *See also* "Due relation," Responses

Admiration, 96-7

Adoration, 161

Aesthete, 439

"Aesthetical essence," 7

Aesthetic values, 130ff, 141-2, 163-5, 170, 237, 253

Affections, in St. Augustine, 204n. *See also* Affective responses, Feelings

Affective responses: 202ff; freedom of, 203; and values, 211; sphere of, 318; cannot be commanded, 318-19; plenitude of, 320

Affirmation of the object in the value response, 238ff

Agreeable, the: 34ff; invitation of, 42; as objective good for the person: 81-4, 91, 227n, 394-402; as subjectively satisfying, 427-30

Ambition, 449

Anger, 211-12

Animal voluntariness, 295-301, 368

Anselm, St., 170n, 248n, 268n, 278n, 290, 304

Antithesis in the qualitative values, 140ff. *See also* Exclusiveness

Appearance, significance of, 6

Appetite, *see* Urge

Appreciation, 250ff

A priori, 9, 32, 47n

Aptitude of means, 64-5

Aristippus, 36, 41-2n, 47-8, 55

Aristotle. 10, 12; and philosophical analysis, 2; on error and morality, 45, 46n; notion of good, 58n, 64, 133-4; and affective responses, 204; on free choice and happiness, 302, 304; on the contemplative attitude, 345, 352-3; "mesotes" theory, 376-8

Ascent of the Soul to God (St. Anselm), 162n, 457n

Association, 203n

Augustine, St.: 36n, 45; on continence, 38n; and the objective evil for the person, 53n; on the two directions of life, 61, 304, 360, 381n; *"si fallor sum,"* 107; *ordo amoris*, 241, 380; on value and being, 145n; on God's bringing good from evil, 154; on the will, 200, 205; and affective responses, 210n; on delight in justice, 219; on appetite and the value response, 220; and the dynamism of the value response, 223; on pain, 224; on love for Christ, 226; and value blindness, 230; on knowledge and love, 233; on delight in morality, 254; on love of God and self-love, 259, 278; on happiness, 303n; on responsibility, 313; on freedom, 327n; on the sources of moral evil, 380; on participating in goodness, 399n; on charity and concupiscence, 415n; on the struggle between sin and charity, 415; on pride, 433n, 441, 442; on virtue, 346, 459-60; on love, 462; on the spirit of Christian morality, 463

Authority, value presupposed in, 128

Ayer, A. J., 122

Bacon, Francis, 112

Beauty: 163-5; objectivity of, 35; fruition of, 84; response to, 237-8. *See also* Aesthetic values

"Beauty and the Christian," 164n

464